Plato and Platonism

Issues in Ancient Philosophy

General Editor: *Jonathan Barnes*

Plato and Platonism

Plato's Conception of
Appearance and Reality in
Ontology, Epistemology, and
Ethics, and its Modern Echoes

◆

JULIUS MORAVCSIK

BLACKWELL
Oxford UK & Cambridge USA

First published 1992

Blackwell Publishers
238 Main Street, Suite 501
Cambridge, Massachusetts 02142
USA

108 Cowley Road
Oxford OX4 1JF
UK

Library of Congress Cataloging-in-Publication Data
A CIP catalog record for this book is available from the Library of Congress.

ISBN 1–557–86202–8

British Library Cataloguing in Publication Data

A CIP catalogue record for this book is available from the British Library.

Typeset in 11 on 13 pt Garamond 3 by Best-set Typesetter Ltd, Hong Kong
Printed in Great Britain by T.J. Press (Padstow) Ltd, Padstow, Cornwall.

This book is printed on acid-free paper

Contents

◆

To
Professor Dr Gyula Moravcsik
in memoriam

Preface

◆

This book is about Plato's philosophizing and Platonism. Platonism is not a rigid creed. It is a cluster of themes and claims, cutting across the boundaries of ontology, epistemology, and ethics. The varieties of Platonistic characterizations of reality converge on a conception broadly defined as taking an abstract realm outside space and time to be the most fundamental aspect of what there is and construing whatever order and harmony there is as deriving from the interrelations within that abstract realm. Humans at their best understand this cosmic order and try to mirror it in individual and communal life.

The chapters of this book do not aim at an overall interpretation of all of Plato's thought. Yet, the portraits contained in the chapters are painted with broad strokes. The interpretations focus on those aspects of Plato's philosophy that became historically influential in shaping subsequent Platonism. Thus it is hardly surprising that the main emphasis is on the various conceptions of appearance and reality that emerge in various dialogues and have an impact on epistemological and ethical theses. One finding of this investigation is that Plato's key concepts in each of the three major fields do not correspond to key concepts in modern analytic philosophy, or for that matter to key concepts in other twentieth-century philosophies either. This does not prevent us, however, from subjecting the texts to as careful and rigorous analysis as the topics allow.

The interpretation to be presented revolves around three key claims. First, The key elements of the fundamental realm are the Forms. The conception of these undergoes change in the dialogues, but they remain the basic explanatory entities. Their order is mirrored by whatever else in the world is in some way orderly, and their nature never corresponds to such modern ontological categories as properties or universals. Second, the key Platonic epistemological notions are those of insight and understanding, rather than propositional knowledge. Third, Platonic ethics revolves around the choice of an adequate ideal for individual and communal life. This ideal consists of a worthwhile overall aim for life and a character structure that fits the aim selected.

A book containing such an interpretation makes heavy demands on the philosophic reader. First, it asks that the reader rethink Platonic material in ways rarely encountered. For notions of reorienting our lives, embodying the right ideal, and finding an adequate understanding of reality and meaning for our lives are not at the center of modern philosophic thought. Thus it is tempting to think of the ontology as similar to the realism of Moore and Russell, the epistemology as an early version of the rationalism of the seventeenth to eighteenth centuries, and the ethics as either Kantian or utilitarian, with a special stress on virtues. This book asks the reader to resist that temptation.

This book asks the reader not only to rethink Plato in unfamiliar terms, but to be open to the suggestion that maybe these unfamiliar terms might be of great utility in doing philosophy today. As we build our bridge to Plato, we also need to rebuild to some extent what is on our side of the bridge. The reward is not only increased historical understanding, but the possibility of Platonistic philosophizing today, thus adding a new chapter to what is here called Platonism.

One can see from these brief introductory remarks that the book has a broad scope. Broadening it further would not be feasible. Thus many topics of standard Plato interpretation have been left out. These include the interesting speculations about the nature of language in the *Cratylus*, the philosophical psychology and proposal regarding cognition of the *Theaetetus*, not to mention the moral psychologies of the *Phaedrus* and the *Laws*, among others.

As for methodology, this book is based on the assumption that the interpretation of classical texts is an empirical enterprise and as such is subject to the same general epistemological conditions as other empirical investigations. One such condition is that of underdetermination. This is to say that, given any text and related empirical information, there can be more than one hypothesis that accounts for all the data. This is particularly important when considering ancient texts, for in this domain the empirical data are exceedingly scarce. If we take underdetermination as a fact, we cannot then look at any one interpretation as the only right reading, except on a temporary basis. There are, however, better and worse interpretative hypotheses in view of their more or less adequate fit with the available evidence. We cut down on underdetermination to some extent by adopting the principle that among several equally viable readings, we will adopt those that fit into a coherent conception of what Plato is saying in other texts as well. The whole corpus should make philosophical sense. This allows philosophical arguments to play roles in interpretation. Adopting such a stance does not entail thinking that Plato must always have been consistent or that his solutions must always have been the most viable ones philosophically. Still, one would like to present interpretations that would show why and how what we take to be Platonic claims and arguments might have seemed viable to him.

Having sketched the aim and scope of this book and a couple of its methodological assumptions, I must now make some acknowledgements. Plato's philosophy spells out a human ideal for us to try to approximate. The person who, to my mind, exemplified this ideal better than anyone I ever met, was my father. His work on Byzantinology, his wisdom, and his dedication to intellectual pursuits in general have inspired me throughout my life. I was told that when he became a prisoner in World War I, he used to exchange his meager food rations for candles so that he could pursue his studies even under those harsh conditions. I always have in mind an image of him as he sat, during and after World War II, in his unheated study, dressed in heavy clothing and his winter coat, not allowing the external conditions to interfere with his work. He could not tolerate what he perceived as intellectual sloth or laziness, but was always helpful to those in whom he detected a genuine thirst for learning. I dedicate this volume respectfully to his memory.

Many foundations, institutions, and individuals have helped me in my work on Plato and Platonism. Though any list that I might construct is bound to be incomplete, I shall acknowledge as many debts as can. The Guggenheim Foundation, the American Council of Learned Societies, the National Endowment for the Humanities, the University of Michigan, Stanford University, and the Alexander von Humboldt Foundation have all supported my research.

Over the years I have discussed material presented in this book with many people. My teachers Rogers Albritton, Raphael Demos, Eric Havelock, John Ackrill, G. E. L. Owen, and Gilbert Ryle taught me much about Plato. Among my colleagues first at the University of Michigan and then at Stanford, the following discussed with me aspects of Platonism in particular: William Alston, Arthur Burks, Richard Cartwright, William Frankena, Paul Henle, Irving Copi, Stephen Tigner, and John Woods; and later Dagfinn Føllesdal, Jaakko Hintikka, Georg Kreisel, David Nivison, John Perry, Patrick Suppes, J. O. Urmson, Stuart Hampshire, and Jean Roberts. Among visitors at Stanford, I wish to acknowledge John Cooper, Nicholas Denyer, Frank Lewis, Alexander Nehamas, Martha Nussbaum, and Gerasimos Santas.

In the course of visiting American campuses I have benefited from contacts with Reginal Allen, Robert Turnbull, Paul Woodruff, Marc Cohen, Alexander Mourelatos, and Charles Kahn.

During my European travels I have received advice from Professor Röd and Dr Thurnherr of Innsbruck University, Günther Patzig, Dorothea Frede, Michael Frede, Gisela Striker, and Jürgen Sprute of Göttingen University, Gerhard Scheibe of Heidelberg, G. Lloyd, Miles Burnyeat, and Malcolm Schofield of Cambridge University.

Gregory Vlastos and Noam Chomsky have been of special help to me during the past decades in discussions about Platonism, and so has the West Coast Aristotelian Society over the past 21 years. James Bogen, John Malcolm, and Richard McKirahan have been members more or less from the start, but I want to thank all members, past and present for stimulation and fellowship. Special thanks go to Alan Code who read the entire manuscript and made many helpful suggestions.

My students over the past 33 years have contributed greatly to my understanding of Plato. Among them, George Bowles, James Kostman, Nicholas Smith, Mohan Matthen, Dan Kolkovitz, Henry Mendell, David O'Connor, Susan Hollander, and Susan Levin deserve special thanks; Susan Levin also made many constructive suggestions about the manuscript.

I also wish to express my gratitude to Jonathan Barnes, Stephan Chambers, Jean van Altena, and Teal Lake for doing so much to help bring this book into existence.

This list is incomplete. Over the years I have encountered widespread interest in Plato, positive and negative, among philosophers with a variety of special interests and skills. Whitehead may have exaggerated when he said that all subsequent philosophy consisted of footnotes to Plato. Still, even the material that cannot be placed in the category of footnotes contains much that is either a defense or an attempted refutation of some aspect of Platonism. I hope that this book will help to place the target, be it of praise or denunciation, in proper perspective.

Introduction

◆

Language enables us to name and describe things. These activities are necessarily selective. We could not name every speck of dust or momentary event that we encounter, and we could not form predicates to single out every similarity among elements of our experience. The selectivity is not random. There are some criteria – consciously or unconsciously entertained – such as reasonably long periods of persistence or being the source of significant power, that pervade naming and describing practices across languages. Names pick out entities that are in some ways significant units, and descriptions pick out respects in which the things named are similar in some interesting or important way. We are used to the basic descriptive vocabulary and stock of names provided by our language, so we rarely notice the selectivity entailed.

Our vocabulary of names and descriptions enables us to gather information. But for the human mind this is not enough. We rank entities named and properties introduced according to various criteria of what is more or less important and more or less fundamental. We then connect some members of this partially ranked and ordered collection so as to yield explanations. Some of these are designed to account for what a certain kind of thing is, or what its nature is. "Nature" as used here can cover many things: why something can do what it does, why it has the structure it has, why it can change in certain ways. We tend to think of entities – both abstract and concrete – as having a collection of more or less permanent salient characteristics. These constitute what we just called the "nature" of a kind of thing, and it is with reference to this nature that we try to account for persistence, power, ability to change, and so forth. Thus certain "why" questions call for explanations in terms of natures of kinds.

If this rough sketch is correct, then *Homo sapiens* is also *Homo explanans*, interested not only in amassing descriptions and information. Furthermore, determining what the natures of various things are and explaining effects with reference to these natures is one of the key components of the explanatory enterprise.

Typical questions of modern ontology, by contrast, suggest not a search for explanations but a search for an adequate inventory. Sample questions are: Are there universals, events, minds, modalities, and so on? As I shall show briefly, the key questions for classical Greek ontology were: What explains the natures of things? and how do natures explain further characteristics? Questions about whether there are certain types of entities typically arise only after a certain explanatory pattern concerning natures has been challenged.

There are some tendencies that pervade all Greek explanatory ontological speculations. One of these is to regard what is observable as mere appearances and to explain these in terms of something unobservable, underlying them, something that at times is interpreted as the "real." Thus we explain the observable properties of matter by positing unobservable underlying elements and properties. Another tendency is to regard the unobservable underlying element as the *explanans* and the observable as the *explanandum*. Thus, within such patterns it is natural to think of the unobservable as the real or more fundamental. Within all such explanatory proposals there also has to be something that we take for granted: space and time, perhaps, or certain processes like condensation and rarification.

The general framework for this book is the hypothesis that the history of classical Greek philosophy up to Aristotle consists of a series of nature-explaining hypotheses, with different explanatory patterns and hence different explanatory entities evolving at different times. Below I will distinguish three main stages in this development: explanation in terms of origin, explanation in terms of constituency, and explanation in terms of a separate abstract structure governing or pervading the elements scattered in space and time.

The following is the general pattern of explanation within the first stage: "x is the way it is (does what it does, etc.) because it comes from or is produced by y." Explanation of this sort probably emerged from plain narrative. Narrative presents sequences of events. In giving explanations by origin, we single out certain special events, seeing these as linked in a causal or generally explanatory way. Theogony, cosmogony, and the explanation of the valor or might of a hero by reference to his allegedly divine origin are some examples of this type of explanation. In such explanations some power or quality is taken for granted, and its presence in an entity is accounted for by linking that presence to a certain kind of originator. Not all qualities and powers are so explained, but only those that are significant in some way and are thus part of the nature of an entity in a loose sense.

To the modern philosophic eye the limitations of such explanations are obvious. For example, if we explain A by linking it to a progenitor B, how will we explain the nature of the progenitor? Are we started on an infinite regress? Further, such explanations are basically in the form of singular propositions. Achilles' valor is explained by assigning to him a divine origin, but no one would be willing to say that everyone with that kind of origin must end up with Achilles' warrior virtues.

This kind of early explanatory model must be distinguished from modern uses of explanations involving origin, such as evolutionary theories in biology. For within these modern explanations we are already given an ontology of qualities, and the factor of origin is invoked to account for relationships between qualities. But even within this much more sophisticated explanatory framework there is a serious question as to how well individual evolutionary accounts admit of generalizability.

It is easy to see how explanations by origin change into or lead into explanations of the second main kind: namely, explanation in terms of constituency. Sooner or later someone will ask of explanations of origin why they should be taken as explaining anything. Why does reference to a divine parent help to explain the nature of the offspring? One plausible answer is that there is some element, power, spark, or whatever that is transmitted from originator to entity to be explained, so that it becomes a constituent common to the two. The alternative would be to think of what is transmitted as leaving the originator and migrating as a whole to the new entity; but in most cases this is not the path taken by the inquirer among the early Greeks.

The gradual shift from the first stage to the second may not even be conscious. The same substance can shift easily and in subtle ways from an originating to a constitutive role. It is not always clear whether "Things have moisture in them" is being construed as pointing to something that is a fundamental common denominator or as accounted for by "Things come from water." The shift to constitutive explanations, however, does bring with it important conceptual changes. It directs us to new types of investigations and admits of general lawlike statements.

The basic pattern for these explanations is: "x is what it is (functions as it does, and so on) because it has constituency a, b, c." Within this pattern there are many varieties. For one thing, the "constituent" admits of many interpretations. It can be stuff like water or air; it can be a collection of separate units, such as atoms; or it can be a group of forces like hot and cold, fire or wind. The explanation can be monolithic, positing one basic common element in everything such as water or air; or it can be pluralistic, positing a plurality of basic constituents. The earliest accounts are monolithic and explain the surface phenomenon of many distinct individuals being as they are by positing a common single underlying stuff. This pattern becomes more complex when several underlying stuffs are posited. But Democritus's genius was to suggest that instead of seeing what is covered under count-nouns (distinct individuals) as the explanandum and the stuffs that are covered by "mass terms" (not admitting of pluralization but of quantitative modifiers) as explanans, we should posit countables – of a very special sort – to account for stuffs and materials.

It is anachronistic to ask of various proposals within this pattern whether any of the explanations are materialist. Materialism is a metaphysical position that can be articulated only when one has a clear concept of matter and something – mind? the spiritual? – with which matter can be contrasted. This is not the case within any of the pre-Platonic metaphysical theories. Furthermore, common sense, as seen in early Greek documents or today, does not have a materialist or anti-materialist ontology. The sky or emotions like fear are acknowledged as existing in Homer as they are by the average person today. But one cannot saddle ancient or modern common sense with a view regarding whether these entities are material or not.

Whether the underlying constituents are monolithic or constitute a plurality, this kind of explanation faces the problem of explaining diversity either on the level of appearances or on the underlying level or on both. If the underlying entity is monolithic, then one needs to posit processes like rarification or condensation to account for the observable diversity. If the underlying stuff consists of different kinds, then some principle of blending or mixture is needed to account for the appearances. Furthermore, these principles, be they of condensation or mixing, must account for the regularity and order of diverse elements at the observable level.

A second problem surfaces when confronted with diversity. The diversity is both qualitative and numerical. Even if one either took numerical diversity for granted or assumed that it was solely a function of qualitative difference, the question arises: What makes qualitatively different things different? The third type of explanatory pattern that emerged in Greek thought attempted to answer this question by developing an ontology of abstract, independent entities that are like the properties or qualities of modern ontologies except that they correspond only to those qualities that are constituents in orderly configurations and are specified only for idealized conditions, so that whatever instantiates these in space and time does so only incompletely or imperfectly.

Thus the third type of explanation posited a realm of abstract entities outside space and time that included both the abstract elements that are necessary for measure and proportion to exist and the idealized quality-like entities that explained those qualitative differences that were responsible for the different natures of different kinds. Thus the explanations consisted of two stages: first, laws or order, proportion, and harmony in the independent abstract realm, and then derivative laws and explanations governing the elements of the realm of appearances to the extent that the structure and functioning of these elements was orderly and permanent.

Heraclitus was somewhere between the second and third stages. His account of fire and proportion governing the workings of nature does not formulate an explicit ontology of an order outside nature. On the other hand, it takes steps in that direction and is not content to give only constitutive explanations. We arrive at the third stage with Plato's ontology. As we shall see, the theory of Forms was an attempt to articulate the separate realm of abstract elements within which laws of order and harmony hold without qualification and can endow the appearances with a derivative nature guaranteeing some stability and regularity among entities in space and time as well.

This mode of explanation was hard to achieve. One reason is that while the key relationships between appearance and reality in the other two models are analogous to some observable phenomena, this is not true of the key relationship in the third model of explanation: namely, that between the Forms and the elements of the world of appearances which the Forms endow with some order and stability. Births and other processes involved in generation can be observed. So can certain types of constituency and the processes of mixing or condensing. By contrast, there is nothing observable that corresponds to many specifics partaking with various qualifications in a Form. This is why the move from the second stage to the third requires a quantum jump, and forces Plato to try repeatedly to explicate the relationship between appearance and reality within his scheme. Part of the difficulty also lies in the fact that only within this scheme do we reach a conception of reality that places that realm outside the temporal and spatial.

In this book we will look at Plato's way of achieving this "quantum jump." The story of forging explanatory patterns goes further. Aristotle, at what we might call the fourth stage, attempted a unification. Stage-two explanations involve roughly what he came to view as the constitutive factor (material cause); stage one was refined to be the agential factor (efficient cause); and stage three was reworked to become the structural and functional factors (formal and final causes) in his analysis of the natures of kinds.

Earlier it was suggested that the explanations under consideration primarily concern kinds and their natures. At stage three this focus undergoes considerable change. We are concerned with qualitative sameness and difference in relation to whatever mathematical, geometrical, and other order-producing structures Plato thought to have discovered. Thus what matters is the extent to which proportion and equality have roles in specifying the structures of relatively stable elements in nature, regardless of whether they belong to specific biological kinds or not. Thus the notion of a natural kind, while central to Aristotle, does not play a key role in the Platonic explanatory mold.

Explanations need an explanans; hence if we view these explanatory chains within a metaphysical system, either we face an infinite regress or some elements need to be viewed as self-explanatory. For Plato these self-explanatory elements turn out to be the Forms. Thus we need to try to understand what it is about the Forms that led Plato to view them in this way.

So far we have discussed only metaphysics. But Plato's forging of the new explanatory mold in his metaphysics affected also dramatically his epistemology and ethics. Given the third explanatory structure, with its two stages, the epistemology must focus on the insight and understanding that are involved in our attaining adequate representations of systems of abstract entities such as those we encounter in mathematical or geometrical proofs or the abstract models of a science like physics. Plato wants us to project onto the large canvas of metaphysics the exhilaration we all feel when we finally understand what is possibly just a simple mathematical proof and to strive to attain the same sense of discovery when eventually we understand what the Forms are and how they are interrelated. As we shall see, explicating this is the primary task of Platonic epistemology, rather than sketching the structure of propositional knowledge and information processing.

The ethics, too, reflects the Platonic division between reality and appearances. It centers on finding an adequate ideal for life. This involves an appropriate overall aim, a character that goes with pursuing such an aim or goal, and the resulting happy discovery that in being that kind of a human one can find meaning in life. The appropriate aims and goals, as well as the appropriate character structures as Plato sees these, are described — as we shall see — in terms of our relations to what for Plato is the real and fundamental and our disdain for that which for Plato belongs merely to the world of appearances.

My ultimate aim in this book is to sketch this Platonic explanatory scheme, which, with its impacts on epistemology and ethics, was revolutionary for its time, both in its historical context and so as to bring out its implications for the problems and conceptual arsenal of today.

Part I

How does Reality Account for Appearances? Plato's Notions of the Fundamental, the Good, and the Intelligible

◆

1

Insight and Activity

◆

The human mind is a many-splendored thing. It is capable of such intellectual activities as representing truths and falsehoods, understanding complex abstract structures, explaining aspects of nature, and encoding information. Its functioning is also a component in a variety of activities through which humans relate to each other, to other parts of nature, and to still other elements of reality that exist or are at least thought to exist. Some of these activities form units that are recognized as branches of knowledge, sciences, arts, crafts, and skills. There are also other such activities, less easily classifiable, that involve purpose and planning.

Theories of knowledge and cognition attempt to capture the manifold nature of our life of reason by concentrating on a few cognitive states and processes and taking these to be fundamental and then trying to account for all else as derivative. Different philosophers take different states and activities to be problematic and different ones to be fundamental. Every account has to start with some conceptual building blocks. No one scheme can force itself on all who wish to explore the mysteries of human reason.

The following are two approaches to reason, both of which have been influential in Western philosophy. I shall sketch both briefly and then see which gives the better fit to Plato's epistemological explorations.

One approach focuses on a variety of activities typically recognized by societies as legitimate, for which modern English has no single label but which in classical Greek came under the general umbrella of *technē*. It includes science, arts, crafts, navigation, commerce, and activities involved in legal procedures. The list is open-ended. Thus a philosopher might approach the analysis of reason by concentrating on technē and asking the following four questions: What do these activities have in common so as to merit a single label? What are the criteria for doing these things better or worse? Are there criteria for the legitimacy of a purported technē, and if so what are these? Are there priorities among the various technai?

There are many different ways of answering these questions. The differences are partly a function of what a philosopher finds problematic about these activities. Nobody can question everything at once; some conditions have to be taken for granted. I shall sketch approaches to technē in which the following two features are taken for granted: first, there are legitimate technai, but not anything goes; not all arts and sciences are illusory, but not everything that anyone calls a technē deserves this label. Secondly, in a technē, thought and action are necessarily interwoven; it would not make sense to think of navigation or commerce as either pure activity or mere theorizing.

In the *Gorgias*, Plato has a severely restricted notion of technē in mind. In other places he uses the word to cover other disciplines acknowledged as technai by common sense but not meeting all the criteria of the *Gorgias*. But even this notion does not include every organized activity.

Some thinkers might define success and appropriateness for a technē solely in terms of social acceptance and resulting satisfaction. Others might base their conception of technē on the notions of objective truth, value, and genuine insight.

Suppose one were to make the following remarks about technai in a modern society. The most important technē is publicity and advertisement. After all, no matter how inspired a theory of physics, no matter how deep a new mathematical discovery, unless it becomes accepted either in the community of relevant experts or in society as a whole, it will not be of any use. We need to persuade people to accept what we have to say or propose; thus the technē dealing with persuasion should be given top priority.

This story is hardly unfamiliar. Implicit agreement with it is manifested by contemporary practices such as giving very high salaries to people in these professions and stressing in professional training the skills of persuasion. Still, many of us feel that there is something wrong with this view. Underlying the above conception of advertisement as the chief technē are two assumptions: one of these is the view that technai should be assessed solely in terms of causal effects and consequences; the second is that the consequences are to be assessed solely in terms of satisfaction and utility. According to this view, there are no guidelines as to what people should enjoy and find useful; any enjoyment has merit by virtue of its being an enjoyment.

Our dissatisfaction can be captured partly by the intuition that a technē that discovers truths about reality has intrinsic value, regardless of its popularity. Following up on this thought, one can arrive at another view of technē, which bases the legitimacy of a technē on the kinds of discoveries and explanations it can provide and on how it can discover what has value in an objective sense.

These contrasting views are mirrored in the clash between what Plato took to be the prevailing view of technē in his society and his own account. The clash can be seen in how one views rhetoric; within the first approach it is given high marks, whereas within the second it is relegated to a secondary role.

We begin to understand the Platonic approach when we reflect on what he took for granted, what he saw as problematic, and what he used as explanatory tools in his analysis. He took for granted that there are some legitimate technai that explore reality, and within these thought and action are inextricably interwoven. He also took for granted that there are human beliefs that deal with the trivial and only seemingly useful. What was for him problematic was the distinction between activities that deserve to be regarded as legitimate technai and those activities that may result in pleasure but do not lead either to genuine understanding or to other aspects of what is objectively good. His explanatory framework included laying down conditions for legitimacy, and in the course of this developing a conception of human reasoning.

The approach to knowledge and cognition via a critique of what a technē is could not be the only approach to epistemology. Another approach has dominated the theories of knowledge, briefly in the Hellenistic period and again in modern times since Descartes. This approach takes the notion of believing something to be true or false as fundamental and examines this apart from any interaction with activities. It considers the legitimacy, evidential justification, and priorities of beliefs. It also erects a conception of knowledge based on justifiable evidence, be it empirical or purely logical. Finally, it views all knowledge claims skeptically, seeking to delimit a core that a single individual can accept at a given moment of time without any doubt. It also seeks to classify types of knowledge in terms of the kinds of evidence that is appropriate: hence the emergence of the distinction between *a priori* and empirical knowledge.[1]

The main interests and concerns of a technē-oriented epistemology and a purely intellectual, evidence-based epistemology are different. But we need to look carefully at Plato's account and see if it can be restated in terms of the concepts of post-Cartesian epistemology. If not, what are the basic notions of Plato's account of the life of reason?[2]

Plato's Theory of Technē

"All technai come to humans from Prometheus." So ends a beautiful passage in Aeschylus's *Prometheus Bound* (lines 440–505) in which the simple simile of "stealing fire for humans from heaven" is unpacked as the revolutionary move enabling humans to develop different crafts and disciplines and thus to become partly self-sufficient. These include house building, astronomy, the study of numbers, writing, the domestication of animals, the construction and use of ships, medicine, prophecy, and the use of bronze, iron, silver, and gold. From the modern point of view, this list of technai derived from Prometheus is heterogeneous. It does not distinguish between the theoretical and the practical, the pure and the applied. No priorities are given on this list with one notable exception: the art of dealing with numbers, which is described as the most important among the technai. One must not read Platonic meaning into this. It is not an ontological claim. Still, it shows recognition of the importance of applying arithmetic and counting to commerce, architecture, the various arts of construction, and items on the list such as medicine and astronomy.

Aeschylus's mode of presentation suggests that this list would not be controversial among his contemporaries. But it is hardly surprising that with the passing of time and the trend towards urbanization, new activities presented themselves as candidates for the list. By Plato's time, rhetoric was regarded by many as an important technē.

We find most of Plato's theory of technē in the *Gorgias*. The dramatic structure of this dialogue is woven around the rejection of rhetoric as a genuine technē. The consequences of this for private and public life involve not only a different conception of communal decision making, but also a profound intellectual reorientation away from efforts merely to be persuasive towards a search for objective truth and genuine insight. Within this dramatic structure, as a justification for the negative verdict on rhetoric, a theory of technē is developed. Plato elicits from his interlocutors five conditions as necessary and sufficient for something to be a technē. These are:

1   It must be a power and activity to produce or acquire something and, through the acquisition, to transform an agent in some way. (In the

later dialogues, Plato divides technai into those that are productive and those that are acquisitive.)

2   It must be teachable (and by implication, learnable).
3   It must be "about something" (that is, about genuine constituents of reality).
4   Genuine understanding of the appropriate objects must underlie the activity; this is typically manifested by giving an account of the objects *logon didonai*.
5   The activity or its objects – or both – must be good or lead to what is good.

We shall look shortly at evidence supporting this reconstruction of the Platonic technē conditions, but first a few general remarks. Plato does not present arguments for this set of conditions. He takes them as implicit in the concept of a technē entertained by his Athenian contemporaries. Given an ordinary commonsense understanding of the five conditions, it is easy to see how one could think of rhetoric as a genuine technē. It is an activity, and it enables its practitioner to gain power and thereby prevail in court or the political arena. It is about something that we regard ordinarily as real: namely, persuasion and human psychology. Finally, there is understanding underlying the activity: namely, an understanding of human desires, emotions, and the ways in which one can play on these when arguing for a claim. Rhetoric also leads to something that is good given an ordinary interpretation of this notion. For it gives the practitioner power to win in debate and to defend himself.

Let us now review the evidence for attributing the five conditions to Plato. It is shown in 447c2–4 that rhetoric, in order to qualify as a technē, must be a power of some sort and must be teachable. Thus the primary emphasis is on an activity, rather than on a mere state of mind entertaining beliefs or attaining some knowledge. This can be extended to all the items on Prometheus's list. On this point Athenian and modern common sense are in agreement. None of the items can be interpreted as mere passive observation and knowledge. How could one be a mathematician without partaking of the activities of producing proofs and calculating? Could one be an astronomer without drawing celestial charts, or a student of medicine without dealing with illness and health?

Teachability is acknowledged as a condition in 449b. There are, however, different ways of teaching and learning. One can learn by mere acquisition of information, by trial and error, by imitation, or by any combination of these. Learning other skills like producing mathematical proofs might include other ways of learning as well. Plato does not deny that we can learn rhetoric in one of the ways that ordinarily counts as learning. He will, however, propose much higher standards for what is really a part of reality, and thus what is understanding, than the standards of everyday conventional discourse and thus will eventually redefine also the concepts of "real" learning and teaching. Condition 3 is presented at 449d1–2. In various other places, items satisfying this condition are said to be mathematics (451b2–c4) as well as the just, the good, and what is healthy (459d1–5). These examples hardly amount to an articulated ontology, but they suggest a more selective conception of reality than that embraced by conventional wisdom. This condition of proper objects would be strange if Plato were engaged primarily in the task of singling out genuine propositional knowledge.

For genuine propositional knowledge does not seem to have unique objects. We can have trivial knowledge about mathematical objects too. The difference lies, rather, in the kind of evidence we have for the different kinds of propositional knowledge: a priori evidence of a complex sort regarding important proofs and simple empirical evidence with regard to trivial knowledge concerning mathematics – for example, that certain features were known by certain people at a certain time. If we assume, however, that Plato is not engaged primarily in evidential epistemology, the difficulty disappears. He is delineating legitimate arts and sciences in terms of subject matter, just as we do today. In academic debates today we often hear statements like "Yes, there are people who want to start a new committee or department, but do they really have a genuine subject matter?"

Condition 4 is brought out at 449e. The practitioner must have an understanding of what he does. As the dialogue continues, we see that this is so not only in the trivial sense that the practitioner must understand words of instruction, but also in the deeper sense of understanding the appropriate objects.[3] What is said at 449e needs to be combined with the elaboration at 501a, where the practitioner is said to have to give explanations of what he is doing (*logon didonai*).

Why call this a condition of understanding? Why not just one of having knowledge and being able to give definitions and deductive arguments? The full answer to this challenge will evolve in the course of this chapter. But herewith a few preliminary remarks. Understanding contrasts not only with ignorance but also with merely having information. Someone can be well informed but lack understanding of the deeper issues. Furthermore, the range of things we can understand is limited. For example, we can understand concepts, proofs, explanations, but not simple concrete objects, though we may know a lot about these. What is understood is something abstract and complex. In this way it differs from simple intuition or "knowledge by acquaintance" as introduced by Moore and Russell.[4]

We shall have to see whether this kind of understanding, or the notion of propositional knowledge, is central to Plato's epistemology and in particular to his theory of technē. But as a preparation for this task, we should keep in mind that understanding has a phenomenological and a conceptual aspect. The phenomenological deals with experiences and activities involved in the learning of mathematics, physical theory, and so forth, and the conceptual discoveries in such fields. The conceptual aspect would have to be presented in terms of a logic of understanding, similar in aim to what today is called epistemic logic, or the logic of propositional belief and knowledge. It would be anachronistic to expect of Plato an awareness of this distinction or much work in the semantic domain. Thus my aim is to show that Plato's key epistemic notion in his account of technē and recollection is understanding in this phenomenological sense and that it does not seem to be reducible to propositional knowledge.

Understanding

As we saw earlier, having understanding or insight into something is different from being knowledgeable or well informed. This contrast applies across fields such as studies of nature, politics, mathematics, or questions of value. To be well informed is to know many truths. To know something to be true cannot be a matter of degrees; whereas understanding does allow degrees. Plato's key epistemic notion does admit of degrees; this is already an indication that it is more likely to be understanding than propositional knowledge.

"Understand" can occur in a number of constructions. There is "understand that," "understand why," and so on. Our concern is with the direct object construction. We can be said to understand theories, concepts, persons, and the like. In general, the object is a complex of many parts and aspects. It may be abstract or something living or some other entity with teleological features (for example, a car engine).

Understanding, then, cannot be equated with the philosophical notion of intuition. Intuition can have simple elements as its objects and is not linked to explanations.

Understanding seems to be a basic notion that does not allow further breaking down. In general, we can say that to understand something is to see how a complex is more than the mere sum of its parts and to see how the parts or aspects fit together. This semi-metaphorical characterization would have to be unpacked in different ways in different contexts. The holistic comprehension that we are getting at here also has the characteristic that the whole may be articulated into parts in a number of different ways and with different applications. We can see this in cases of understanding a work of art or a mathematical theorem. Depending on how we break down the whole into parts, our understanding will be more or less deep, more or less insightful. In this way too, it differs from propositional knowledge.

Two features of the phenomenology of understanding are especially striking. One is the experience of exhilaration and discovery when an abstract complex that has resisted analysis or understanding suddenly "makes sense." Such experiences of sudden insight are common in the classroom and in our studies. But they cannot be taken at face value. Not all such experiences are veridical. What seemed like an experience of understanding can turn out later to have been an illusion. There is no introspective guarantee for understanding.

The other feature is that we can go over and over the same complex many times, and then, without anything new being added, we are suddenly able to see it in a new light, or see a new articulation of parts into wholes. This experience occurs often in connection with our links to works of art, but it can also surface in our study of mathematical proofs or reflections on what is valuable in social structures. The significant point here is that the new understanding is not a result of new information. No new facts or beliefs are added; we simply keep going over the same structure repeatedly, as the *Meno* suggests, until "it all makes sense."

How is understanding manifested? Depending on the field in question, different activities can be linked to understanding. But running through all the examples, we find the phenomenon of being able to offer explanations.

There are many different types of explanations. The type closest to the kind of understanding we have been investigating is explaining what (or who) something (somebody) is. There is no one logical structure that all such explanations must have. Some are inductive, some deductive, and some are neither of these. We can think of statements explaining other statements or entities – like a draught – explaining other entities – like many deaths – or theories explaining facts, and so on. An explanation makes something intelligible and hence has all the interesting characteristics such as being deep or superficial, more or less adequate, more or less insightful, or whatever. A good explanation leads to intelligibility, but not necessarily the other way around. One might understand something without being able to articulate this understanding in terms of an adequate explanation. Also, merely being able to give an explanation, even if it is a good one, is not a sufficient indicator of having real understanding. Plato wants a technē, and human life in general, to include the kind of understanding that is accompanied by the ability to give explanations. But the ability to give an explanation is merely a necessary condition for having understanding. In this respect, Plato and modern notions of understanding coincide.

Explanation, like understanding, contains an extra-logical component. "X explains Y" cannot be defined in terms of relationships between the truth-values of the two components. There is no mechanical or formal measure for depth, elegance, or adequacy of insight, and thus for understanding or explanation. As was pointed out, understanding involves fitting pieces together into a whole; and in different contexts, different articulations of composition strike us as deep or superficial.

There are at least three ways in which one can attempt to account for understanding. The first can be called the creativity theory of understanding. According to this view, the human mind is faced with various complex structures and can come up with different articulations of these. We can assess the created articulation as deep or superficial, or whatever.

Another theory is the pragmatic theory of understanding. According to this, all we really have is propositional knowledge and logical relations between propositions. All else, including what we call understanding and explanation, is a matter of pragmatics – that is, judgments having to do with psychological propensities of the human mind that change from time to time and context to context. According to both these views, there is no "fact of the matter," regardless of whether an explanation is in fact deep or adequate.

The third view is the realist view of understanding. According to this account, understanding is a series of discoveries, rather than constructions or creations or pragmatic dispositions. As we come to understand something more and more, we discover more of its parts or aspects. What makes an explanation deep or insightful and what makes an understanding adequate is that it corresponds to complex abstract structures whose existence is as independent of the human mind as the existence of anything else that is external to us.

There is a great deal more that could be said about understanding.[5] But these remarks should be sufficient to indicate the rough outlines of this difficult concept. It should also be clear that Plato holds the realist view of understanding, even if he would not have described if this way. This, in turn, requires an elaborate ontology within which the objects of understanding can be described. The ontological theory known as the theory of Forms has this as one of its functions.

The Five Conditions, with Illustrations

The goodness condition, already implicit in the Prometheus legend, crops up at various places in various contexts in the dialogue (e.g. 462d11−e1, 465a−d, and 466e−467a). This condition can be interpreted in more than one way. Does the technē benefit only the practitioner, or does it also benefit the community? Is the goodness required subjective or objective? Plato opts for the second of each of these alternatives.

Plato's five conditions must have existed already in public consciousness, since he doesn't argue for the general framework. We see, here, Plato accepting condition 1 and then presenting a reconstruction of the other four. He has an aristocratic conception of reality and a correspondingly aristocratic conception of understanding, as well as an objective notion of good. This eventually requires a revision of our notion of genuine teaching and learning.

Plato insists — for example, at 460b — that the activity must be based on what meets conditions 3, 4, and 5. Condition 3, the "aboutness" condition, has "teeth" in it, but without committing us as yet to an explicit ontology, such as the theory of Forms. We see, for example, that astronomy, being about celestial bodies and their movements is "in" (451c7−9), whereas rhetoric, being about persuasion in courts and politics, fails the test (452e). Plato does not elaborate the criterion for genuineness in this dialogue, but from the treatment of rhetoric and the way it contrasts with mathematics and medicine, one gathers that genuine objects must have permanent and stable natures and must embody such characteristics as order and harmony.

There is evidence that we cannot translate condition 4 as merely knowing a body of analytic propositions. For on that account, rhetoric too would qualify, since this practice presupposes analytic truths. Plato defines it as the art of persuasion (452e−453a); thus rhetoricians must know what persuasion is. But even though rhetoric is definable and the knowledge and know-how of the practitioner includes knowledge of some analytic propositions, it does not qualify as having genuine objects and containing genuine insights in Plato's view.

Apparently, genuine understanding is possible only in connection with the study of certain domains. Understanding can be manifested in a variety of ways. Giving arguments, representations, and so forth are some of these ways. Plato does not say that any one articulation will be complete nor that giving such is sufficient for being said to have understanding. Thus we should interpret *logon didonai* as a necessary but not sufficient condition for having understanding. For example, our grasp of a proof is never exhausted by the actual formulations available at any given time.

As to condition 5, the interpretation that Plato is after, objective value, is supported by his contrast of what is really good for the body, such as health, with what gives us pleasure. Plato and modern medicine converge on this. No physician will define a healthy bodily state in terms of experiencing the maximum pleasure possible.

The stress on the interwovenness of theory and activity in a technē should not be confused with modern "pragmatic" accounts of epistemology. Plato is not saying that insight, understanding, and explanation can be defined operationally. He maintains both that having genuine understanding will be manifested partly in terms of activities and that the acquisition of this understanding requires partaking of activities, not merely having passive knowledge of them. For example, mathematical activity such as producing proofs, constructions, or calculations helps us to attain insight and understanding of mathematical structures. This goes beyond the mere grasp of definitions and propositional knowledge. At the same time, these activities are also manifestations of understanding. This makes the epistemological assessment of someone very difficult. He or she may be producing the proof in the process of trying to attain understanding or producing the proof while having real understanding of what the proof is about; or someone may produce a proof and think that this is all that is required for mathematical understanding. Mere "behavioral" evidence will not distinguish between the three types of cases. We can also give explanations without seeing what is deep or insightful in some and not in others. We can give explanations backed by understanding or in a merely routine manner. According to Plato, the differences relate to what is deep inside our minds and not merely to external activity.

These reflections suggest that the following schema captures, roughly, Plato's conception of the understanding agent:

Understanding, insight $\rightleftharpoons$ activities leading to and also manifesting
$\updownarrow$ understanding.
Explanations $\rightleftharpoons$ knowing some propositions to be true.

This schema shows how for Plato understanding and insight underlie both activities and mental processes. Neither the activities nor the ability to give explanations or justifications are sufficient for having understanding, but both are necessary conditions. Understanding itself is a mental state that cannot be analyzed completely in terms of other mental states or activities.

Let us see now if we can redescribe the five conditions of technē in terms of the concepts of modern evidential epistemology that center on propositional knowledge. The power or ability of condition 1 would be interpreted in purely intellectual terms as the power to possess knowledge. Teachability (condition 2) would be the ability to come to know certain propositions to be true and to follow instructions. Condition 3, the "aboutness" condition, would be reconstrued as limiting the relevant kinds of knowledge to propositions about a restricted set of objects. In order to accommodate the point made above that Plato would also require knowing the existence of certain entities, this reinterpretation would add that among the propositions to be known are not only definitions and other analytic propositions but also necessary existential propositions. Thus condition 4 would be construed as knowledge of a restricted set of a priori analytic propositions and some a priori synthetic propositions and possibly other existential propositions. Finally, condition 5, the "goodness" condition would be interpreted as the requirement that the practitioner of a technē should know certain propositions expressing the fact that the objects or products of the technē or its activities are good.

There are several difficulties with such a reinterpretation. First, it leaves the relationship between knowledge and activity problematic. Why should the knowledge of some analytic propositions and propositions expressing the fact that certain entities exist lead to the ability to engage in a variety of activities? Secondly, Plato seems to object to the pseudo-technai on what we would regard as two distinct grounds (453–5): first, that they aim merely at conviction and not at objective truth, and secondly, that they are not about appropriate objects. If Plato had had in mind a scheme corresponding to the reconstruction just sketched, then the distinctness of the two conditions would have been quite apparent. But neither in the *Gorgias* nor – as we shall see – in the *Republic* or the *Timaeus* are these grounds distinguished. This suggests that he had in mind something more like the nonpropositional insight or understanding that is being posited in this chapter. We have to turn towards the right entities and understand these and their complex structures. This entails interest in objectivity and truth but leaves this interest as a preliminary step rather than a separate demand. Furthermore, this reconstruction leaves teaching as a heterogeneous concept. We need to be taught analytic propositions, as well as a variety of skills that will enable us to engage in activities. But it seems that Plato has only one condition of teachability in mind, indeed – as we shall see – a very demanding one.

The reconstruction does not give conditions corresponding to some semantic intuitions as to how we should restrict the required understanding or knowledge. If we interpret condition 4 as understanding, then we have an immediate delineation of the right technai, for not everything can be said to be the object of understanding. But we can have analytic propositions about anything. It is clear, however, that from Aeschylus to Plato there is a line of thinking that construes technē in quasi-normative terms. Prometheus did not bring down from heaven for humans just any art or skill. Even if he were a Dutch Prometheus, a skill no matter how much it was loved, like bicycle riding, would not qualify. The examples of mathematics, medicine, and music indicate roughly the class of things that Plato had in mind, and the interpretation centering on understanding rather than propositional knowledge can account for this.

With regard to seeing the goodness of technai, there are also differences. Plato does not say much about this "seeing," or insight, in the *Gorgias*, but the metaphors of light in the middle parts of the *Republic* fit much better with an interpretation that construes the required insight as an intellectual analogue of "seeing as" than as a propositional interpretation. We do not know just from definitions that mathematics is good, but reflection on its structure leads to the insight that it exemplifies harmony and order, the Platonic signs of goodness.

Once we opt for the interpretation that rejects the post-Cartesian reconstruction of Plato's notion of a technē, we see that the understanding posited is not just having a concept plus deductive reasoning. Rather, it takes as fundamental the holistic insight and conceptualization involved in seeing how abstract objects are related, how different fields exhibiting order and harmony are related, and what makes theories, proofs, explanations, and the like occasionally deep and insightful. Such understanding can be articulated in a large variety of ways, without any of the articulations ever exhausting the insight on which they are based.

We can now see the link between Plato's positive technē theory and the critique of rhetoric as a purported technē. Plato admits that rhetoric is an activity, but he does not think of the kinds of activities involved in its instruction as genuine teaching. Furthermore, he does not think that the objects of rhetoric – namely, persuasion and the psychological qualities of humans that are relevant to this – have the permanence and abstract structure that would allow them to join the objects of mathematics, medicine, or dialectic, the most fundamental discipline, as worthy companions. Plato also thinks that the knowledge required for rhetoric is merely that of knowing some analytic truths and some empirical general-izations and the possession of certain skills. But these elements together are not sufficient to qualify as Platonic understanding. Finally, rhetoric aims only at meeting subjective standards of goodness. It helps one to learn how to please and thus how to give humans pleasure without helping with the question of which satisfactions are objectively good for us and which ones are not. The epistemic state of the practitioners of the pseudo-technai is that of having merely opinions (*doxai*). As we shall see later, this amounts to having empirical beliefs and beliefs incorporating conventional wisdom. One can also have doxai about the proper objects of understanding, but these are only provisional and can be developed into something deeper (See e.g. *Meno* 97a–98c, which will be discussed in more detail in the next section).

As we noted, Plato gives examples of genuine technai. Thus we should look at how these fit the interpretation of the five technē-making conditions that is being proposed. One of the technai mentioned is mathematics (451b). Its being divided into arithmetic and calculation is not significant for our purposes but is worth noting, since it shows that even though, from the extensional point of view, they have the same objects, two technai or subdivisions of a technē can differ for Plato.

Mathematics is clearly an activity, as Plato's remarks about calculations show. It is teachable, but not merely by giving information. Under-standing of proofs and concepts must be elicited from the learner in ways that are very different from what is involved in practical instruction or mere absorption of conventional definitions of ordinary empirical terms. The objects of mathematics are numbers. Though we do not yet find an explicit philosophical theory of ontology in the *Gorgias*, it is clear that Plato regards numbers as abstract entities with a permanent nature whose inter-relationships exemplify order and harmony. The understanding underlying the activities includes the grasp of the nature of the objects of the discipline as well as their complex interrelations. Whether we include geometry here or treat it separately, it is clear that this kind of understanding is acquired in the context of activities such as proving, calculating, constructing diagrams, and so forth. Again, once the understanding is acquired, it is manifested partly by the performance of tasks involving the aforementioned activities. The activities required for understanding mathematics remain purely intellectual in the modern sense – that is, they do not include the applied mathematics of commerce and so on. The relation between the latter and mathematics is not treated within the theory of technē. The activities lead also to knowing certain necessary propositions to be true. Finally, order and harmony and hence, for Plato, goodness characterize the objects of the discipline. These remarks show that this interpretation of Plato's theory of technē fits mathematics.

Let us now consider astronomy (451c). Astronomy is an activity that includes, for example, the construction of heavenly charts. Its teachability, in Plato's view, is analogous to that of geometry, since, as we know from the *Timaeus*, in Platonic astronomy the heavenly bodies have paths that exemplify geometrical patterns. The objects are the heavenly bodies and their regular movements, which for Plato are entities of fixed, permanent structure. Plato does not think of astronomy as an empirical science in the modern sense of this notion (that is, as consisting of empirical hypotheses and observational confirmation and disconfirmation thereof). Yet some role is given to the senses; Plato does not think that we can deduce the existence of the heavenly bodies from purely a priori premises. The understanding of the geometry underlying Platonic astronomy is similar to the understanding discussed in the previous paragraph, and the goodness of the objects is manifested by the order and harmony that characterizes their arrangement. The technē as sketched here does not by itself guarantee success in "applied astronomy" (navigation).

In the case of music the activity is not the performance as in the modern concert hall, but rather the construction and formulation of tone sequences and harmony. Teaching someone what harmony is, as we know from everyday experience, is a matter of drawing out a certain understanding by patient presentation of varieties of examples and instruction in parts of music theory. In some cases, understanding of harmony in humans comes spontaneously, with minimum aid. But this is also true with mathematics. The objects in the case of music are tone, proportion, and harmony, all of which, for Plato, have the required permanent structure and exemplifying order. Understanding music, as Plato sees it, requires activity, but not the ability to perform well on this or that instrument.

We can see that these examples fit the interpretation proposed. At the same time we can also see that by themselves they do not lead to success in practical application. This is not a problem for Plato. But as we move to two other examples, namely medicine and ethics, the problem of the gap between the theoretical and the practical becomes more urgent. In the case of medicine, mentioned as a technē (e.g. 456b and 459b), the objects are the basic bodily constituents and their interrelations when the whole functions in a healthy way. The understanding of health is itself a formidable problem, since it manifests itself in a variety of ways and cases, depending on age, gender, environmental factors, and so on. Still, Plato seems to be right. For even if we do not articulate it in an explicit way, various world organizations do not seem to disagree on what health is, but only on the best ways for implementing it in different cultural contexts. Thus the genuineness of the objects, their goodness, and the fact that once we understand what health is, we become desirous of implementing it wherever possible, are clear. It is less clear what the entailed activities are. If we construe this technē as analogous with mathematics, then the activities would be those that lead to and manifest an understanding of health. They would include having general conceptions of various states of health and thus the ability to articulate these. They might also include observations that lead to an understanding of what is balance and what is lack of balance in the body. It is not clear, however, that they would include curing people. Curing people is analogous to "applied" mathematics, geometry, and astronomy. We seem to need a number of empirical discoveries and the possession of practical skills in order to cure, and neither of these seem derivable from the kind of theoretical understanding that Plato posits at the heart of a legitimate technē. Thus the sketchy remarks on medicine that we find leave us with two unanswered questions: first, how much of what is useful in practical terms in this field can be derived from theoretical understanding? and second, would Plato agree that the physician needs empirical knowledge and skills not derivable from the theoretical base?

The intuitive pressure to link theory with practical everyday action is even stronger in the case of ethics. Plato apparently wanted to accommodate this, since at 460b he says that in his view the just person not only knows what is just but will also do what is just. In this case, condition 5 is obviously satisfied, and one could think of conditions 2, 3, and 4 as analogous to what we saw in the case of the other technai, the objects being the human excellences and their interrelationships. Their understanding requires the same kind of eliciting procedures as in the case of mathematics and is manifested in certain theoretical activities. Let us note that these activities would involve sketching ideal character types, rather than establishing an "axiom of ethics" and trying to derive all ethical maxims from this. But this still leaves us with the question of whether additional elements might not be needed to enable us to move from the understanding of these ideals and our desire to implement them to actual implementation.

To be sure, Platonic understanding of the nature of the excellences does help to establish our overall orientation. A person who understands what the just and the unjust are will know the difference between the genuine objects of reality and the lesser ones that people wrongly take to be objects of ethics, such as pleasure and satisfaction. This understanding gives us a general orientation with important consequences. One will not imitate any particular human being slavishly; one will not bow to societal custom and convention uncritically; and one will hate the evil in some and admire the good in others rather than hate specific people as such. One will also shy away from manifestations of evil. Still, all of this does not guarantee appropriate attitudes and action in all specific circumstances. We shall discuss this matter further in chapter 3.

We see then that the interpretation of technē proposed fits what Plato wants to say about specific technai. The difficulties that we uncovered in Plato's views on some of the technai seem to be Plato's difficulties rather than problems of interpretation. If we adopt the reconstruction of technē theory according to modern epistemology, the difficulties are even more formidable. What is the relation between knowing analytic propositions and the activities of the technai? How can that kind of knowledge capture even what Plato – and most reasonable people – would take to be the theoretical base of mathematics, medicine, music theory, or ethics?

In any case, the sketch in the *Gorgias* of legitimate technē cries out for further elaborations of conditions 2 and 3. How can we teach understanding, and what are the genuine constituents of reality? The next section is devoted to the second of these questions; the first will be treated in chapter 2.

In concluding this section, we should note the marvelous interplay between the dramatic and the philosophic in the *Gorgias*. The dramatic impact is meant to change our basic attitudes towards power and its importance in public and private life. The philosophical content is the theory of technē and its consequences, for hedonism, for example. The two are masterfully interwoven.

As we shall see in the third part of this book, Plato's stress on the centrality of the mathematical disciplines in our web of insight and knowledge – foreshadowed already in *Prometheus Bound* – became a permanent part of our Western heritage. Other parts of the Platonic conception of what a discipline should be have been lost, however, in some cases for questionable reasons.

How can we Teach Understanding? The Recollection Theory

Plato's technē theory places an enormous burden on the notion of understanding. Its presence separates the real from the pseudo-disciplines. At the same time Plato accepts the conventional wisdom that the technai are teachable. But how can one teach understanding? How can one learn understanding? The very phrase sounds strange to our semantic ear. We can arrive at the understanding of something, but do we really talk about learning to understand something? On those rare occasions when we do, we do not have in mind such standard conceptions of learning as absorbing factual information (leaves are green; the capital of England is London; and so on), learning to act on the basis of practical information (for example, instructions to get from one town to another), or learning definitions of words from a dictionary. Nor is it a matter of reasoning inductively or deductively from premises to conclusion.

Plato seems to be aware of these considerations; in this respect semantic ears do not vary from fourth-century Greek prose to modern English. His suggestion is that teaching someone to understand is like helping someone to recollect. Conversely, the relevant learning is analogous to recollecting.

The recollection theory is spelled out most extensively in the *Meno*. Much can be said about the relevant passages, but here I will restrict myself to showing how the recollection theory can be interpreted as Plato's philosophical epistemology designed to provide the foundations for condition 4 of the account of technē.[6]

This theory has also been interpreted in other ways. Some have seen in it a general theory of how we learn anything; while others have thought that it was meant to illuminate how we learn analytic truths and their deductive consequences. In the following pages I will argue that recollection leads to the kind of complex understanding that also contains a nonpropositional component and that was sketched briefly in the previous section.

The theory is expounded in *Meno* 80c−86c. It begins with an attempt to resolve a paradox. The paradox is stated at 80d5−e5. One can translate its key term as either "understand" or "know". The leading question is: How can we inquire into what we do not understand (know)? If we do not understand it at all, how can we launch an investigation, and how would we know when we had arrived at our destination? If, on the other hand, we understand (know) the object of our search already, what is the point of the investigation? The paradox is stated first by Meno. Socrates' restatement is different in an important way. In Meno's version the paradox concerns inquiry into something totally unknown or not understood by us. Socrates' restatement omits the qualification "totally" (*parapan*). This is important, for, as we shall see, Plato's solution involves the claim that when we seek to develop understanding, in a sense we do and in a sense we do not have in our minds the object to be understood. Plato's solution to the paradox is given in the form of an analogy. Learning of the relevant sort is like recollection (81d4−5).

We need to find out which kinds of cases Plato had in mind. Is he talking about any kind of inquiry whatever? There is a passage that deals with finding out how one can travel to Larissa (97c−98c). A look at this helps to eliminate the unwanted cases. The knowledge sought can be acquired in two ways. One of these is simple practical experience: we can follow a guide along the right road to the city. Alternatively, we can be given good, practical instructions (regarding landmarks, important turns, and so forth) and follow these. In a case like this we do not need anything analogous to recollection. As Plato says, in such a situation, merely having a correct opinion or belief is sufficient. But this case is very different from that given as an illustration of "recollection": namely, a child learning a bit of geometry. As we shall see, Plato has in mind the same cases as in the *Gorgias*: mathematics, ethics, and so on. The concepts needed here cannot be derived from sense experience, and mastery of the subject requires the holistic grasp that we associate with understanding. Thus we can rule out all empirical investigations, as well as the examination of mere conventional definitions, as not relevant to the paradox and its Platonic resolution.

How is the analogy helpful? For Plato, a key feature of remembering is what separates it from thinking of something and then, on the basis of quite different stimuli, thinking of it again. We can think of a person and then later, having forgotten the individual, come to think of him again in a different context. In such a case there is no causal link between the two events of thinking. The case of remembering is different. There is a first experience of acquaintance with an object, abstract or concrete; then there is a temporal interval during which the object is forgotten, but presumably something – a concept or an image – is preserved in the mind. Then there is a second experience, which involves remembering the object. We typically analyze this as having the image or concept that was stored in our mind recalled to consciousness as a result of appropriate stimuli. The key to Plato's analogy is this aspect of remembering: namely, having something that is in our mind brought to consciousness. The mind is not a *tabula rasa*. We have innate structures and potentialities. These enable us to form certain concepts and representations of whole systems of concepts that cannot be derived from sense experience. This is the kind of understanding that is involved in the genuine technai such as dialectic, ethics, mathematics, and so forth.

The skeptic might wonder why we need to invoke this admittedly difficult concept of understanding in order to explain the facts and, in particular, Plato's conception of these facts. Why not just say that we need to have certain concepts, link these by means of analytic connections, and then use deductive reasoning to discover more about our field of study?

Interpretations of this sort have been proposed.[7] In order to adjudicate between rival claims, we need to consider what Plato says about "recollection" (81c–d). His account is as follows. The soul is immortal, and prior to our earthly lives we have seen and learned all things. What we call learning is simply recollecting what we once knew. Furthermore, all parts of reality are interrelated; thus, if one recollects one part, nothing prevents one from discovering all the rest, provided that sufficient effort is made.

What is meant by "all things" (*chremata*) (81c7)? The dramatic context is the search for what excellence is and whether it can be taught. As part of this enterprise, the resolution of a paradox is advised in order to maintain a coherent notion of understanding. Thus it is reasonable to suppose that the "things" are the just, the good, health, number, and so on – in short, elements that Plato would regard as genuine parts of reality and appropriate objects of understanding. They do not include the objects with spatial and temporal location that constitute nature in the ordinary sense.[8]

Plato's statement that all the relevant entities are interrelated and that from understanding one entity we can move to the understanding of all speaks against the interpretation in terms of knowing analytic truths. One could hardly attribute to Plato the view that we can start with one analytic truth and from this be led to understand and accept all the others that are parts of technai. It would also be odd to invoke recollection to explain deductive reasoning. Deductive reasoning involves taking consciously understood elements and seeing what they contain; that is, deriving conclusions from premises. This is very different from moving from a consciously grasped element and relating it to others whose representation is nonconsciously in our mind.

The interpretation of recollection in terms of real understanding can give a better, though admittedly only partial, account of the relatedness of the objects and the ensuing synoptic understanding. For example, the objects of mathematics are numbers. We can take these to be primarily the series of positive integers. It is indeed true that one does not fully understand one of these unless one understands all of them — that is, can place any one in the unending series constituted by these entities. Similarly, one does not understand geometrical shapes in splendid isolation. A full understanding of the objects of this technē requires our grasp of how all the shapes and figures are related. The same can be said about the objects of the other Platonic technai. Astronomy, music, health, and ethics also present us with systems of abstract entities. The movements of the celestial bodies form a system; so do sounds and the ensuing scales and harmonies. Platonic ethics, too, presents us with an interrelated set of entities. These are not — as we shall see in chapter 3 — fundamental rules and derived consequences, but the key excellences which are so related as to provide the foundation for an ideal human character. As we shall see, the *Republic* shows that in Plato's view one cannot understand one excellence thoroughly unless one understands them all. (The systematic links between the objects of the various disciplines also become important in later dialogues like the *Philebus*.)

Still, we are not out of the woods completely. So far, we have shown only how elements within domains of various technai are related. We have not shown how all the objects of all the technai are related. Since Plato does not say much about this in the *Meno*, one can only speculate as to how material from other dialogues might help to fill out the picture. The comprehension of both the Fine in the *Symposium* and the Good in the Republic suggest that the grasping of these qualities as pervading the whole domain of genuine objects exhibiting order and harmony enables us to have a comprehensive view of all the genuine entities in their relationships to each other. Needless to say, this interwovenness does not have the structure of a deductive hierarchy.

Recollection in this dialogue moves on two levels. In 81e3−7 Meno asks

Socrates to teach him that learning is recollection. Socrates replies that, given his own conception of learning, Meno cannot be taught in the ordinary sense of this word that learning is recollection. Socrates can only help Meno in recollecting this. Meno then asks Socrates to help him in any way he can (82a7–b12). The ensuing conversation with the young boy about geometry serves the purpose of helping Meno to recollect what learning is. While the boy is recollecting geometry, Meno is recollecting what learning is. Meno's coming to understand the analogy and hence the resolution of the initial paradox does not take the form of following a deductive argument.

At the end of the conversation between Socrates and the boy (82b–85b), the boy has some understanding of squares of areas determined in relation to the sides and diagonals of a given square. In reviewing the conversation, Socrates and Meno agree that the boy did not acquire whatever he knows through mere information presented by another human being. He gained understanding by discovering things for himself, and this activity resembled recollection.

Socrates interrupts the conversation twice to point out to Meno that the boy is not being instructed in the ordinary sense of this term but is only being asked questions (82e4–5, 84c11–d2). How are we to understand this contrast between instruction and questioning, especially in light of the fact that many of the questions asked by Socrates require only a yes or no answer? For example, at 83b8–c2, we find: "Doubling the size gives us not a double but a fourfold figure? True." Apparently, according to Plato, there is a gap between question and response. We can conceive of the situation in at least two ways. According to one view, the boy is asked to understand analytic propositions and their deductive consequences. According to the other interpretation, the question and the answer are merely surface phenomena. Their role is to stimulate – together with the diagram drawn – recollection or understanding in the boy. This process and the resulting state of having understanding are not observable.

The following consideration speaks in favor of the second view. The questions are raised in the context of studying a diagram drawn in the sand. The boy must understand that the concepts and truths he is mastering are not about the diagram or any other such drawing. Drawings are only aids to recollection. Thus to really understand the basis for the positive answer given to the question is to understand the general and abstract nature of the entities under discussion and their relationships. The gap, then, is between the meager evidence of diagram and speech on the one hand and the abstract nature of what is to be understood on the other.

The conversation with the boy is divided into three parts: 82b9–e1, 82e14–84a2, and 84d3–85b2. The sections are marked off by brief interludes in which the significance of the exercise is highlighted by Socrates. The first few lines of the first section (82b9–c5) help the boy to understand what a square is. He comes to understand that the four sides must be equal and that the size of any given figure is irrelevant to its geometric properties. Understanding all this is not a matter of mere definitions or the grasping of meanings of words. It is, rather, a phase in finding out something important about a part of reality. One could use a variety of words to help the process of recollection. None of these words, in groups or as a totality, can describe exhaustively the abstract relations and entities that we are to understand, however.

In the last part, the boy is helped to understand how to construct a square with an area twice the size of a given square. The diagram serves merely as an aid to understanding a general method of construction. The method is not presented in deductive form.

How do the geometrical constructions lead to understanding? At 85c9–d1 we are told that immediately after the exercise, the boy does not yet have full understanding but only correct opinions. He will attain understanding only after the same questions are put to him repeatedly in a variety of ways.

What is it that can be evoked after repeated questioning of the sort exemplified by the dialogue? It could hardly be a set of definitions. The boy is not learning these; nor is it clear how such questioning could sharpen one's deductive power. Rather, the diagram and the questioning help to form in the boy's mind a representation of the various abstract geometrical entities under discussion and their interrelations. Whether all this can be translated into an axiomatic-deductive form or not is not Plato's concern. (For more discussion, see Appendix 2.)

This sketch shows how the recollection theory of learning and the related conception of understanding fit the technē theory developed in the *Gorgias*. For it explains the kind of genuine understanding that must be part of a Platonic technē and must underlie the activities with which we associate the technē.

This understanding is the most fundamental element in Plato's epistemology. It cannot be defined in terms of more fundamental notions. It can be explained only by illustration and analogy. In face of this deep feature of human cognition, we are reduced to metaphor. But the modern world does not do much better. We are familiar with this kind of understanding from experience in any mathematics or logic classroom. But when it comes to understanding in a theoretically satisfying way, we are just as stumped as Plato was.[9]

From the Epistemological Orientation of Technai to that of a Human Life: The Great Contrast

The recollection theory adds one of the components required by the technē theory. As we shall see in the next chapter, Plato's ontology adds another. In spelling out the understanding required by a genuine technē, we made use of the contrast between understanding (*epistēmē*) and opinion (*doxa*). In the dialogues in which epistemological questions are taken up again, this time in the context of a fully articulated ontology, the understanding–opinion contrast comes to have a central role. Plato builds on this contrast not only a theory of technē, but also a theory about the right and wrong orientations that humans can adopt in planning their ideals and goals for life.

One can see the *Phaedo* as a transitional dialogue between those dialogues that stress the recollection theory and those that stress the epistēmē–doxa contrast embedded in the Platonist ontology. For this dialogue contains both the recollection theory and the Platonistic ontology.

The "great contrast," as we can call the epistēmē–doxa distinction, is laid out towards the end of Book 5 of the *Republic*, where two kinds of humans, or two kinds of orientations of life, are contrasted. The lovers of wisdom (475b) are contrasted with the lovers of sights and sounds (476b–c), the latter being incapable of genuine understanding and hence of pursuit of the proper object of understanding. Thus the famous teachers of Athens, the sophists and the rhetoricians, are not really teachers and cannot help humans acquire what Plato would have regarded as genuine power.

We should note that although the framework is no longer a single technē but a whole human life, the epistemological discussion is still embedded in the context of activity and orientation. The person with the right understanding will pursue the right goals and act justifiably, and the person with the wrong epistemic state will pursue the wrong goals and act without adequate justification.

The overall interpretation that will be defended construes epistēmē as the understanding familiar from our analysis of the *Meno* and the *Gorgias* and doxa, or *pistis*, as the other half of the contrast encountered before. We still need to be more specific about *doxa* as part of the "great contrast" and to examine also the question of how well one can represent this distinction with the tools of modern analytic epistemology.

The lovers of sights and sounds are described as being in a state of dream rather than wakefulness and in a state of being deceived about what is real. These people lack understanding and hence have doxa as their basic epistemic state. We should note that this passage does not say that every time we have a doxa, we are in a state of dreaming, only that when we are in a state of dreaming and take sights and sounds to be the basic elements of reality, then the most we are capable of is doxa. Thus the text in Book 5 of the *Republic* is compatible with the possages in the *Meno* in which the boy is said to have doxa about geometry. One can have doxa about geometry, but can do better eventually. Concerning sensible entities, one can only have doxa which is correct or incorrect but in any case is subject to persuasion and cannot be tied firmly to rational justification.

Is Plato drawing here a distinction between a priori and empirical propositional knowledge? Why is he ignoring the fact that some empirical beliefs are better justified than others? In what sense are all one's empirical beliefs subject to persuasion? A closer examination of the relevant passages shows that the great contrast cannot be reduced to the basic constrasts of modern epistomology.

The key section is 476–479. It is divided into two parts. We have already touched on the first, in which the lovers of sights and sounds are contrasted with the lovers of wisdom. The epistēmē–doxa distinction is used to point to the basic cognitive orientation of the two kinds of people. Thus doxa in this part is characterized in negative terms. In the second part, this account is supplemented by a more constructive description of this state.

The first section, 476b–d, starts depicting the contrast with respect to the understanding of *kalon*, which will be translated here as *"fine"* (as in fine horses, fine buildings, fine proofs, fine paintings, and so forth). The lovers of sights and sounds do not acknowledge the existence of the form of Fine and cannot understand its nature (476b4–8), whereas the lovers of wisdom understand the Fine and grasp what it is (476b9–c). In 476c–d the contrast becomes more general. We are told that the lovers of wisdom are like those who are awake and have understanding (*gnoome*), whereas the lovers of sights and sounds are as if in a dream and have only opinions. The key element of the dream analogy is that the lovers of sights and sounds mistake semblances for reality. Their view of sensibles as genuine reality is mere doxa. This is not a definition of doxa. All who mistake sensibles for ultimate reality have a mere doxa, but not all of doxa must be of this deceptive kind.

In this brief summary, the semblances were identified as the sensible elements. That would suggest that everything not sensible belongs to the objects of understanding. We saw already in our look at the *Gorgias* that this is not so, since, for example, definitions of rhetoric do not constitute genuine understanding. For the definition of rhetoric concerns persuasion, not some genuine constituent of reality. Hence it is an object of *doxa*, not of understanding. The same point is confirmed in *Republic* 479d4, where we also see the conventional views about the Good and the Fine under the rubric of mere semblances. Thus, not all a priori elements belong to the realm of understanding, and not only empirical sensibles belong to the realm of the semblances.

In summary, this section fits with what was said about epistemology in the *Gorgias* and the *Meno*. Not all doxa is about semblances; some is about the right objects, but, as we saw in the *Meno*, these are provisional. The doxa that is about semblances is either about sensibles or about conventional views and definitions. There can be correct and incorrect doxa. The doxa that is typical of the lovers of sights and sounds is false doxa, mistaking semblances for reality.

Since the lovers of sights and sounds do not have an adequate understanding of reality, they cannot orient their lives towards appropriate objects and aims. This is reflected in their activities and cognitive stance.

The second part of the section on epistemology provides a more rigorous distinction between epistēmē and doxa (477b–e distinguishes them as two separate powers). It is then argued that since we distinguish other powers in terms of their objects and in terms of what they accomplish, the same should be true of this dichotomy (477c–d2). It is stressed that the two marks mentioned are the only ones. Thus, for example, one cannot distinguish cognitive powers on introspective grounds or on the basis of what our senses tell us about them.

In 477b10–12 the *natural* (477b10) objects of epistēmē are specified as those which have being in an unqualified sense. This is then contrasted with the objects of doxa, which are "between being and not-being" (e.g. 478d). The qualification "natural" presumably carries over to the whole contrast. The natural, or appropriate, objects of understanding are those that simply are, and the natural, or appropriate, objects of doxa have both being and not-being. With regard to the latter doxa is the best we can do.

With regard to pure being, we can do better; we can attain understanding. This way of making the contrast does not saddle Plato with the view that one cannot have doxa about pure being. He says only that in that case we can do better, for we can eventually reach epistēmē.

A more detailed interpretation of the two realms will be given in chapter 2. Here I shall limit myself to a few remarks linking "pure being" to understanding and the "in between being and not-being" state to doxa. The correlation between being and understanding is given in 479a2–3. The objects of understanding are said to be. This means both that they have being eternally or timelessly and that they have a permanent stable nature, "remain always the same." The latter phrase does not mean, trivially, that they remain identical with themselves, but that their nature does not admit of qualitative change. According to this interpretation, Plato's conception of being cuts across the modern dichotomy between existence and predication. As Plato saw it, any entity is and is of some nature. But some entities have only limited being (that is, existence) and limitations on the permanence of their nature. This way of construing being served Plato's ontological purposes very well. Semantic problems about negative existentials or the status of existence as not one of the predicates arose only much later in the history of philosophy.

This characterization fits the objects that are portrayed in other dialogues as objects of understanding: namely, mathematical, geometrical, or musical entities and those of ethics and dialectic. These are also listed in the educational curriculum of Book 7 of the *Republic*.

The natural objects of doxa are between being and not-being because they have only temporal existence and no stable permanent structure. The predicates that figure prominently in the genuine disciplines apply to this realm in pairs of opposites. Examples of these are attributes of quantitative comparison, mathematical and geometrical attributes, and valuational attributes. For example, conventional opinions are held only for restricted periods of time and are good as well as not good, appropriate as well as inappropriate, depending on the context. Physical objects are never qualifiedly equal but only equal in some ways while unequal in others. This characterization shows what conventional opinions and sensibles have in common. The fact that in modern epistemology we would characterize the first as attempts at analytic truths and the second as backed by empirical evidence does not play any role in the Platonic distinction. (This interpretation of the objects of doxa as temporal and having an unstable nature is supported also by 527b.)

In 477e6–7 the difference in result or accomplishment is treated. Understanding is not subject to mistake, while opinion is. Indeed, if one really understands a proof, a theorem, a set of concepts, a field, and so on, then what one has attained should not be subject to revision. Doxa, on the other hand, is error-prone. In the case of conventional notions about values and morality, this is obvious. In the case of what we call empirical judgments, there are two possibilities. Either the judging subject knows the appropriate ontological status of the object or he does not. If he does not, then his doxa, even if it reflects the sensory input correctly, is partly mistaken. We may identify a brown tree correctly and yet have a deluded doxa because we think of material objects as ultimate constituents of reality. The case of a correct empirical judgment made in accordance with Platonic ontology is more problematic. If I believe correctly that the tree is brown and know that the tree is not an ultimate element of reality, then why should not my belief, when backed by enough evidence, be counted as knowledge? Indeed, at 476d1–3 we are told that understanding a genuine element of reality involves also understanding or knowing the constituents. Perhaps Plato would say that we can know constituents or truths about constituents, but only *qua* constituents of Forms, and hence the doxa, are not strictly about sensible "semblances." This point is never worked out by Plato in exact detail.

Plato would point out that the tree is not always brown; it can change, and hence knowing at a particular time that it is brown is not to acquire permanent information. As to the judgment that something is a tree, the state of being a tree is permanent for any object that is in that state. But the judgment that something is a tree is error-prone; hence this too fails to qualify as genuine knowledge.

These remarks show how the great contrast fits the earlier passages and is a further development of them. The view that one half of the contrast should be regarded as understanding, rather than propositional a priori knowledge, is supported on other grounds, also by Wieland and – earlier – Schleiermacher.[10] The treatment here was designed to deal only with those aspects that are relevant to the overall interpretation as the understanding–opinion contrast and the link with activity and orientation. There are many other important questions that can be raised about the passage, but these are not pertinent to the main thesis of this chapter.[11] The nature of the objects will be investigated further in the next chapter.

So far, we have looked at the great contrast as it is applied to a person's general orientation in life. The *Republic* also contains remarks about some of the technai of the *Gorgias*. These remarks occur mainly within the context of an educational schedule. In particular, we find a number of comments on mathematics and geometry. These comments raise many questions of interpretation.[12] These include Plato's conception of mathematics and axiomatic presentations, the ontological status of mathematical and geometrical entities, and Plato's relationship to the mathematics of his time. The remarks that follow are restricted to showing how the comments on epistemological content fit the general interpretation of understanding that has been developed in this chapter.

In 510c–511b Plato complains about the practices of mathematicians, who are said to argue conditionally, without a thorough examination of their "starting points." Thus, according to Plato, their work needs to be supplemented by dialectic that examines the starting points and allows us then to go back down the path of proofs so as to comprehend the results of this discipline (511b5–7).

For our purposes, the key question is: What are these starting points? The examples given are the odd, the even, and figures (510c3–4). It seems, then, that the starting points are not propositions, but the adequate grasp of the basic elements of the domain of mathematics. Plato could hardly complain that mathematics, like any other discipline, has some basic undefinable notions. Nor is he merely asking for definitions, since some of these were available at the time.

It is more plausible to suppose that he is asking for an understanding of the basic elements in the same sense in which this is demanded in the technē theory of the *Gorgias*. Such understanding would include the ontological status of these entities. We can contrast Plato's views on mathematical understanding with current views on this topic. Today we distinguish between mathematics proper and foundational questions. According to this view, two people can understand mathematics equally well, even if they disagree on foundational questions and oppose each other as, for example, realist and nominalist would. Plato makes no such distinction. For him, no matter how much mathematics or geometry a person knows, if he does not understand the ontological status of the entities inquestion and, like a nominalist, for example, "mistakes semblances for reality," then he lacks real understanding. Thus the starting points are not simply mathematical definitions but include existential claims and ontological characterizations as well.

One might still try to reconstruct all this in propositional terms and simply add ontological propositions to the set of truths that, according to Plato, a competent mathematician should know. We have seen already, however, reasons to doubt that an adequate grasp of ontology and relations between definitions can be reduced to propositional knowledge. One key bit of evidence for this was the "relatedness" condition in the *Meno* discussed above. We find its analogue in *Republic* 531c9–d2. Here too the relatedness of all the domains of genuine disciplines is stressed. It is very dubious that Plato would have regarded the relations between all the numbers, for example, as explicable in propositional terms.[13]

In 525b–c Plato again brings up the distinction between pure mathematics and the applied mathematics employed, for example, in commerce. Once more, the highest achievement is seen as the comprehension of the nature of numbers (525c1–3). If we interpret this passage in the same way as the other remarks on mathematics in the *Republic*, this comprehension will include understanding the ontology, not just definitional and deductive relationships.

The matter of appropriate starting points is mentioned also at 533b–c. Those without adequate understanding do not examine their starting points and cannot give adequate accounts (*logoi*) of these. If we interpret this passage in light of what we saw in the *Gorgias* and the *Meno*, we will not read it as a mere demand for definitions and will not see the giving of logos as a sufficient, but only as a necessary, condition for adequate mathematical understanding. The same interpretation also fits 533c7–d1, where dialectic is described as moving up to the *archai*, or starting points, of our investigations. Illustrations of this move are provided by passages in the *Republic* in which we are led to the understanding of Plato's Forms. As we shall see in the next chapter, these are not merely a series of deductive arguments.

In summary, the passages on mathematics in the *Republic* fit the epistemology sketched in this chapter.[14] They demand not only technical competence but ontological insight and the ability to see how the whole domain of entities with which mathematics deals is interrelated and has relations to the domains of other genuine disciplines.

We shall now turn to the treatment of the "great contrast" in the *Timaeus*. So far we have been looking at the contrast in connection with the technai and orientations towards life in general. In the *Timaeus*, the contrast is drawn in the context of a discussion of key ontological distinctions entailed by the theory of Forms. The distinction is couched in the *nous* versus *doxa* terminology and is presented in 51d3–e6.

The following characteristics are ascribed to understanding:

1   It is acquired as a result of teaching.
2   It is accompanied by true logos.
3   It resists persuasion.
4   Few humans have it.

Opinion, on the other hand, is

1   acquired by persuasion,
2   is not accompanied by logos,
3   does not resist persuasion, and
4   all humans have it.

As the *Meno* shows, opinions can be taught in the normal sense of this term, whereas understanding cannot. Thus, in order to make sense of the contrast, we must assume that teaching is meant to be what is analogous to recollection. With that understanding, the contrast works well. Understanding is achieved by "recollection," whereas, in the typical case, opinions are acquired by persuasion of various sorts: for example, drills in simple mathematics, conventional rhetoric, placement in a variety of perceptual situations. False opinions such as involve "mistaking semblances for reality" are also the result of persuasion.

The contrast with regard to logos centers on its presence or absence. This could hardly refer to some definition or other analytic truth in the modern sense of these notions. Nor could it refer to empirical justification. It we are to render this epistemological distinction consistent with the ontological dichotomy between Forms and sensible participants in the *Timaeus* and with the examples in the *Gorgias* and *Meno*, then *logos* must be interpreted as an account of the genuine constituents of reality of the sort given by dialectic.

The contrast *vis-à-vis* persuasion points to the fact that, according to Plato, genuine insight leaves us without any doubt as to a certain part of the structure of reality; hence no argument can shake our confidence. But, given the changing nature of what perception or conventional wisdom can tell us, opinions on such matters can always be shaken by further argument.

The fourth contrast makes greatest sense if we interpret *nous* as the genuine insight and understanding of the fundamental elements of reality that we have taken it to be all along. It cannot mean merely having knowledge of many analytic truths, or even of large parts of elementary arithmetic, since this is possessed by many humans. Most of us know how to add, subtract, and so on, but, according to Plato, only a few of us really understand what mathematics is about.

It is easy to see why doxa is described as possessed by all humans. In order to get around in the world, we need instructions like the one that would guide us from Athens to Larissa or enable us to make simple empirical discriminations. Since Plato thinks of humans as social beings, he also assumes that all of us are exposed to some conventional notions about law and propriety. It would be quite anachronistic to raise questions about a hypothetical Robinson Crusoe or a wolf-boy from the jungle. Such issues do not come up in Platonic speculations.

It seems from this that the contrast is basically the same in the *Timaeus* as in Book 5 of the *Republic*. The shift is from stressing being mistake-prone to stressing being subject to persuasion. These two notions are closely linked in Plato's epistemology. Persuasion includes a variety of modes of argument, including some that in modern times we would regard as legitimate rational argumentation. It includes everything except what leads to genuine understanding in Plato's special sense. If we are in mistake-prone epistemic states, then further argumentation can shake our confidence. Only if we attain insight that is immune to revision because it allows us to understand ultimate constituents of reality are we no longer subject to change of mind as a result of further argumentation.

In summary, the theory of technē entails a kind of understanding that we associate with the theoretical and normative disciplines, one that is linked to activity in terms of both acquisition and manifestation. This notion is then extended to cover a person's general orientation towards life and not just what a technē needs.

We find doxa as the contrasting notion. Its paradigm cases are finding the road to Larissa and knowing how to cook, rather than the much discussed cases of empirical knowledge in modern epistemology, such as "This is red." We can have doxa about the genuine elements of reality, but such opinion, whether true or false, is always provisional. With regard to what is subject to change and not eternal, such as the sensible elements and conventional views and arrangements, the best we can have is doxa. These cannot be turned into understanding, since, given the nature of their objects, these doxai cannot bring us into contact with the fundamental elements of reality. As we have seen, the world of change includes not only what modern philosophy would regard as the empirical, but also what we would label as the conventional. Thus, the doxai in question cut across the modern empirical – a priori distinction.

Modern epistemology may or may not absorb the Platonic problems and solutions; but in any case it would find this epistemology incomplete. There is no discussion of better or worse empirical evidence, theories of probability, and better or worse structures for empirical explanations. But as we have seen, Plato does not start with skeptical questions about how we can know anything and is not trying to build evidential pyramids, as modern epistemology does. Thus, the issues just mentioned are simply not of interest to him. The question of whether we could graft their treatment onto a Platonic epistemology is beyond the scope of this book.

The interpretation of Platonic epistemology in the dialogues of middle period as having understanding at the heart and more practical instructions, be these empirical or matters of convention, at the other end of the scale, allows us to deal with a couple of problems that have been raised about Platonic epistemology. In an interesting article, Burnyeat raises the question of why we find differences in attitude towards examples in the philosophical analyses of Plato and such twentieth-century authors as G. E. Moore.[15] In the *Meno* and similar dialogues, Socrates is represented as asking for a clarification of the nature of entities like excellence or health. When the interlocutor brings up particular cases or species of the more general concept under investigation, Socrates complains that he is given "many" when he was asking for "one." Philosophers like G. E. Moore, on the other hand, found examples helpful and illuminating in conceptual analysis.

We can account for the difference if we consider the differences in aim and method between these philosophers. G. E. Moore wanted either a definition – that is, a certain kind of analytic proposition – or a grasp of a simple undefinable quality instantiated by members of a class.

Examples, then, help Moore's enterprise, because, if chosen carefully, they present cases in which the quality or quality complex to be analyzed is presented in a clear, unambiguous way. By giving a suitable example, the philosopher engaged in Moore's task can say: "The other instances are all like this."

Plato, however, is not interested in getting clear on just any entity that, in modern times, would be regarded as a quality. His interest lies in understanding certain complex abstract entities that underlie and account for elements in the natures of wide varieties of things. The manifestations of a Platonic Form are very unlike each other. Thus, examples can help if they aid in understanding variety, which is why in some cases, as when in a dialogue something is investigated that within simplistic conceptions admits only of instances within conventionally "elevated" contexts, Plato cites examples from everyday ordinary contexts. But the kind of example giving that Moore engages in is of no help to Plato. If we give a so-called paradigm case of a concept and say that all the others are like it, then either we are wrongly engaged in the investigation of a Form, where the instances are widely different, or rightly engaged in the investigation of what Plato would not have regarded as a Form.

For Plato, examples are useful only if they are presented and interpreted in such a way that they point beyond themselves; not only to something general, rather than particular, but also to a quality that can be seen as pervading the wide variety of manifestations only with a theoretically trained "eye of the mind."

Given the relatedness condition, there are no simple objects of the understanding. Every object is the kind of complex the understanding of which requires nonpropositional mental insight as well. For example, in *Symposium* 210–12 Plato leads us to an understanding of the Form of the Fine. He points to kinds of fineness, but at the end he wants us to "throw away the ladder" and attain a synoptic comprehension of the Fine as it pervades in a variety of ways different kinds of fine things. As we know from the study of other dialogues, he also wants us to comprehend how the Fine is linked to order and harmony and their manifestations. The same applies to other genuine Platonic objects. Plato does not want us merely to know what the different numbers are, but to understand what it is that makes these numbers.

Such reflections on understanding also help with the identification of excellence and understanding. If we render the identification as "Virtue is knowledge," many problems arise. Why should all knowledge of a priori analytic propositions lead to virtue of some sort? How do we move from thought to action and motivation? I would maintain, however, that Plato has in mind the kind of understanding familiar from such disciplines as mathematics. Here indeed one cannot imagine understanding without it entailing competence in some activities. We have seen also that Platonic understanding brings with it comprehension of the goodness of the object. This gives us orientation, the notion in Plato's psychology that comes closest to the modern notion of motivation. Yet some problems remain. As we have already seen, it is not easy to think of medical or ethical activities as analogous to mathematical activities. But at least the interpretation presented provides the basic framework. Further clarification will require a more thorough examination of Platonic ethics. This will be given in the third chapter.

Appendix 1: *Epistemic Vocabulary in Pre-Platonic Literature and Plato*

In modern societies, characterized by the rise of science and the development of technology, the practice of information gathering and information organization plays a key role. It is not surprising that in such a context, philosophical epistemologies assign central roles to propositional knowledge, belief, and the examination of evidence. In other cultural contexts in which prophecy is held in high esteem, moral guidance is given by humans regarded as possessing wisdom. Skills, rather than science, provide the key links to the physical environment and the notions of practical competence and insight may loom larger on the intellectual horizon than the epistemic building blocks of information gathering. Since Plato's predecessors lived in the latter kinds of societies, rather than societies in which empirical science and technology were already developed to a high degree, it is worth taking a glance at their epistemic vocabulary. Some of the evidence will be taken from Bruno Snell's admirable survey of these matters.[16]

According to Snell, *sophos* originally meant "clever" or "knowledgeable." While we might relate these notions to being well informed, their core meaning also includes having good practical sense or good judgment. It is this second sense that the early Greeks seem to have had in mind. Pindar uses the term with a more intellectual conuotation; but even in his writings, it denotes the person who has insights and who bases his activities on these, rather than someone who simply knows many things to be true.

According to Snell, the verb *gignooskein* had as its original meaning noetic seeing and having the right view of human experience.[17] One could interpret this as a state of knowing many propositions to be true; but there is no reason to assume that the early Greeks would have pushed such an interpretation. Snell gives evidence for a shift in the epistemic vocabulary from more concrete objects to more abstract objects and from the purely practical to the more intellectual. But this need not entail an increasing emphasis on propositional knowledge. It could just as well lead from a more limited practical wisdom to a more general intellectual insight and understanding of a variety of important human activities. This second alternative is given some weight by Snell's comments on *gnoome*. He sees the meaning of this word changing from sight and recognition to insight and *intellectual* recognition.[18]

The modern term "epistemic" is derived from the verb *episthasthai* and related nominal expressions. This verb occurs often in Plato. Snell shows that its earlier meaning was that of practical knowledge and skills.[19]

Snell's discussions show that the early epistemic vocabulary centered on practical ability and the kinds of insights, wisdom, and understanding that we associate with more intellectually demanding practical abilities. This conceptual domain can be analyzed by philosophers in a variety of ways. It would be anachronistic to ascribe to pre-Platonic thinkers analyses that seem natural only in a science- and technology-oriented culture.

The same conclusions are supported when we look at dramatic literature. We shall take as our examples *Prometheus Bound* (here after *PB*) and *Philoctetes* (here after *Phil.*). In *PB* seeing the future is regarded as an important skill, but it is not articulated in terms of knowledge of truths and sufficient evidence. Indeed, the issue of evidence is not discussed in the play. Prometheus has a gift analogous to sight, and that is it. No further explanations are given.

In *Phil.* shrewdness in planning a plot, skill with the bow, and skill in warfare are kinds of knowledge which play important roles. No analysis is given of the intellectual capacities underlying these skills. In *PB* Prometheus "sees" the future, and in *Phil.* Odysseus "sees" that the Greeks need Philoctetes if they are to win the war. The nature of any possible rational backing for these claims is not discussed in the plays − a fact undoubtedly contributing to Plato's negative views concerning the educational value of plays like these.

This literature includes cases of what a modern philosopher would describe as knowing a truth, but the dramatists do not seem to have such interpretations in mind. In *PB*, line 104, Prometheus says that we know that the force of necessity is beyond human contestability, using the construction *gignooskoo hoti*; but his description of the situation is more like what we encounter in so-called wisdom literature, such as the Book of Job, than knowing a proposition to be true. Line 379 presents a similar situation. The same construction is used in saying that we know that words are doctors for bad temper. If pressed for evidence, Aeschylus would probably say: "Look at life!"

The verb *oida* is used in more intellectual contexts (e.g. lines 915 and 1041). Prometheus knows, or "sees," what would be Zeus's solution to the problem at hand, and he "sees" already the news that the messengers bring him. Here, too, questions of evidence do not arise.

There are other occurrences of epistemic vocabulary in these plays that support Snell's characterizations. For example, in *PB*, line 62, *sophistes* means "being clever," and *episthasthai* is used in expressing "knowing how to keep one's temper."

Phil. presents us with a similar picture. The meaning of *sophos* as shrewd or clever is exemplified in lines 119 and 1244−6. Many occurrences of *oida* carry the metaphoric sense of "seeing." This word is also used to describe the kind of understanding needed to interpret the condition of another human. For example, in lines 753–4 Neoptolemus is challenged to understand Philoctetes' poor condition, and in line 960 he is described as not understanding what is wrong in the human situation he encounters. The eventual emergence of this kind of understanding becomes part of the foundation of the friendship that develops between these two main characters.

Perhaps one would not expect propositional knowledge to play an important role in a play that centers around human conflict of values and friendship. But let us not forget that Plato's epistemology is used to analyze not only mathematics and similar theoretical disciplines, but also friendship (as in the *Lysis*) and the development and manifestation of ethical excellence. Thus the ways in which these concerns are discussed in drama are not irrelevant to an examination of the ancestors of Plato's epistemic notions.

We shall now look at a survey of Platonic passages, using parts of John Lyons's work.[20] Lyons finds continuity between epistemology in pre-Platonic literature and Plato's epistemology. According to Lyons, the basic Platonic epistemological framework takes for granted basic skills such as healing, calculating, and geometrical constructions, as well as more practical ones like military prowess, and then looks for the cognitive power or state that underlies these skills. The conception of technē that we investigated crops up also in other dialogues. For example, in *Protagoras* 322c6–7 the physician is described as having the technē of medicine, and the treatment of this fact fits the interpretation presented in this chapter. Again, in *Phaedo* 73a9 the person with a certain skill is said to need the *epistēmē* that underlies the exercise of this skill. We find several occurrences of "knowledge of" in this sense (e.g. *Phaedo* 73c2; *Republic* 598c1).

Other parts of Lyons's evidence suggest that the use of *gignooskein* cuts across the dichotomy in English between "knowing" and "understanding." It can express propositional knowledge with the *hoti* construction; and with the direct object construction it can have abstract entities or persons as object, thereby suggesting "knowledge of," or "understanding."[21] But not all cases of understanding are of interest to Plato. His interest seems limited to cases in which explicit teaching and learning play important roles (*manthanein*).[22] This explains why he concentrates more on a case like the acquisition of mathematical competence and less on such currently much-investigated abilities as linguistic competence.

In these remarks, I have merely scratched the surface of the vast field of pre-Platonic epistemic vocabulary and usages. But what has been said should suggest at least two things: first, that there seems to be a continuity between pre-Platonic and Platonic epistemological interests; and second, that full explorations of early Greek epistemology are likely to be rewarding, provided that one approaches the field with an open mind, without presupposing from the start modern epistemological concerns and conceptual tools.

As we shall see, in Plato and in the writings of his successors, we can trace a growing interest in the sentence or proposition as a semantic element and vehicle of truth. But semantic developments do not entail reorientation in epistemology. One may want to focus on what justifies knowledge claims and how we can build up a body of these claims into a texture of laws and generalizations. One can also focus on the question of how various types of alleged insight, understanding, knowing, opinion, and so forth lead to increasing contact with genuine elements of reality. Though the two aims are compatible, we should not assume that they came together from the beginning in the history of Western philosophy.

Appendix 2: *Recollection in the Phaedo*

Phaedo 72e−75d contains an account of the recollection theory. A full, detailed interpretation of this passage cannot be given within the confines of this book, but the following remarks serve to show in rough outline how this treatment, too, fits with the general interpretation of Platonic epistemology given in this chapter.

A series of proofs of immortality provide the context for the presentation of the recollection theory in this dialogue. In the introductory lines, it is pointed out that Plato has stated the doctrine before (72e3−73a2). There is a pun on remembering in this introductory passage. Socrates' friends do not remember the considerations supporting the recollection theory. They ask Socrates to help them remember. Thus we see in the *Phaedo*, as in the *Meno*, two levels of recollecting. Socrates' friends need to recollect the recollection theory, and this theory enables us to "recollect" what genuine learning is (73a4−6).

In 73a−e considerations (*logoi*) are adduced in support of the recollection theory. We are told that appropriate kinds of questioning can elicit understanding from the learner. The use of diagrams can aid such questioning. This reference can easily be taken to be to the *Meno*, and, in fact, some commentators have taken it as such.[23] The result of the questioning is that the learner sees "things as they are." This fits the account of understanding given in this chapter in connection with the *Meno*.[24]

In subsequent sections (73d−e) we are given more details concerning the analogy between remembering and "recollecting." Plato points out that what elicits remembering need not be identical with what is remembered. Pictures, gestures, and so forth may remind us of someone. Furthermore, neither the generalization that like reminds us of like nor the one that unlike things remind us of an original object will do. But apart from this negative claim that neither similarity nor dissimilarity help to capture what can do the reminding, Plato does not provide much in the way of adequate characterization of "reminders." This is hardly surprising, since no good answer to this question has been found up to our own times. A wide variety of things can remind us of someone or something. On the other hand, one's intuition is that not anything goes. If someone says, "I stood on the riverbank, gazing at the Isis, and was reminded of my cat," we demand a great deal of filling in before we accept the claim as plausible. There is a difference between the statement given above and "I stood on the riverbank, gazing at the Isis, and suddenly thought of my cat." But as in the *Meno*, so in the *Phaedo* too, no detailed explanation is given of the difference between thinking of something twice, without there seeming to be any connection, and being reminded of something. Yet Plato could take the fact of there being a difference for granted.

Through analogies and illustrations, Plato gives *logoi* to support the recollection theory. The *logoi*, in fact, give an explanation of understanding by analogy with something that is phenomenologically familiar even though theoretically it might be puzzling: namely, remembering. The analogy is supposed to help us concentrate on the relevant aspect of the cognitive state and surrounding experiences. At the end, the learner is supposed to say: "Yes, it is like that; I see it now."

One could try to recast this material in the form of a deductive argument, but there is no reason to suppose that Plato would have had in mind such a reconstruction, and indeed the poverty of such a reconstructed argument suggests that it is not what Plato intended.

The deductive sketch might look like this:

P1. We either acquire knowledge from the senses, or it
    must be in us already, only needing to be brought to
    consciousness.
P2. We do not acquire knowledge from the senses.
 C. Therefore knowledge must be in us, waiting to be brought
    to consciousness.

The obvious weakness of such an argument is premise 1. Who is to say what all the logically possible ways in which knowledge can be attained by us are? There is no evidence that Plato tried out such mental experiments over logical possibilities. Furthermore, such a reconstruction misses the phenomenological similarities between remembering and the excitement of "recollecting," or attaining theoretical understanding. Plato's proposal that learning is recollection is not meant to be an analytic conclusion. On the other hand, neither is it a mere empirical hypothesis. For Plato, it is a necessary truth about human cognition, given the way the world is and the relevant aspects of human nature.

In his linking of epistemology to ontology in this dialogue, Plato states clearly the role of sense perception in our mental life. One the one hand, it is a needed stimulation; on the other, it does not contain that which we are to know and understand. When we take it as the best link to reality, it deceives us (75e3, 76d9). This theme is reiterated – as we have already seen – in Book 5 of the *Republic* and had already been noted earlier, for example, by Heraclitus.

There is also a link between the epistemology of the *Phaedo* and the *Timaeus*. For in 76b, we are told that only a few people can "recollect" adequately. This is echoed in the fourth element of contrast outlined above in the characterization of doxa and understanding in the *Timaeus*.

What we called the "aboutness" requirement in the technē theory of the *Meno* is spelled out in terms of an articulate ontology that came to be known as the theory of Forms. In 75a7–d5 we are given indications concerning the range of these fundamental entities. The examples are taken from the mathematical and valuational realms, thus showing the correspondence between the range of genuine technai proposed in the *Gorgias* and the domain of Forms as seen in the *Phaedo*. The objects of genuine understanding are also shown, on independent grounds, to be the ultimate elements of reality.

Appendix 3: *The Theaetetus and the Order of the Dialogues*

One of the main themes of this chapter is that for Plato the fundamental epistemic notion was that of a nonpropositional sense of understanding. There is, however, a dialogue, not yet mentioned, which has been typically interpreted in modern times as dealing primarily with epistemology, and in particular with the epistemic analysis of propositional knowledge. Thus we need to relate the content of this text, the *Theaetetus*, to what has been said. My main claim is that Plato has not changed his mind. Even a late dialogue like the *Philebus* suggests the epistemology of understanding, rather than a theory of knowledge with propositional knowledge as the key notion. Still, the *Theaetetus* has to be fitted in.

First, even on the analysis proposed in this chapter there is room, as well as need, for propositional knowledge. For, as we have seen, our deep understanding is articulated, in various ways, at least partly in terms of propositional knowledge. Hence there is room for a dialogue that examines this notion. But is the *Theaetetus* really a treatise in epistemology? Much of it is taken up with an analysis of error. This material, including the suggestions that maybe the mind is like an aviary or a wax tablet, is much more like what we would call today philosophical psychology. It contrasts with the analysis of truth and falsehood given in the *Sophist*, which we will examine in chapter 5. The latter deals with semantic and ontological puzzles; whereas the *Theaetetus* deals with conjectures about how one could account for the mind's "misfiring" – that is, ending up with erroneous judgments.

Secondly, although there are passages which are clearly epistemological, not all of these are about propositional knowledge. For example, some of the arguments – concluding at 185d – show that knowledge is not the same as perception.[25] The argumentation does not hinge on structures of propositions, but on showing that certain concepts are necessary for knowledge – for example, unity and plurality – and that these cannot be derived from sense perception.

Thirdly, the dialogue ends on an inconclusive note. In its last part, efforts are made to explain what we know in terms of propositional epistemic attitudes like beliefs and truths of various sorts. As the final effort, we confront the suggestion that perhaps knowledge is true belief with a logos, or account, of some sort. This proposal is also turned down, on the following grounds. Either the belief in question will be analyzed into its elementary parts, in which case we will not come to know anything that we did not know or believe already, since if what is believed or known is simply the sum of its parts, then grasping the parts does not contribute anything new to what is grasped when one grasps the whole. Atternatively, the "account" added to the belief contains a way of differentiating what is known from everything else. But then, it is argued, such differentiations must be included already in what we believe or know in the first place.[26]

In all this there is an assumption that knowledge or belief can be analyzed as having a "molecular" object: that is, an entity that is the mere sum of parts. The arguments supporting, this assumption lead to a negative conclusion; for none of them allow us to adequately characterize knowledge. One could easily add to this the claim that underlying much propositional knowledge there must be a nonpropositional understanding, but that the nature of this state cannot be explicated with the tools available in this dialogue. Perhaps Plato thought that, apart from the analogies used in earlier dialogues, there is no way to explicate this notion.

I am not saying that one can read this into the ending of the dialogue; only that such a view would be compatible with the content of the dialogue – just as compatible as any of the alternatives¨hat the "propositionalist" might propose. In sum, an analysis of propositional knowledge embedded in material that deals with other issues and that ends with the negative conclusion that we cannot find an adequate characterization does not seem to me to be evidence against the hypothesis of this chapter: namely, that nonpropositional understanding underlies genuine propositional knowledge and that without that notion Plato did not think that propositional knowledge was adequately analyzable.

In the course of this brief discussion, as well as in other places, mention has been made of "earlier" and "later" dialogues. Thus a few remarks concerning chronology and the stance adopted toward it in this book might not be out of order.

The chronology of the Platonic dialogues is a notoriously speculative business. Fairly general agreement can be found only concerning groups, rather than individual items. And indeed, this is the only kind of ordering to which this book is to some extent committed. The general groupings that have been agreed upon have been well laid out by Ross.[27] It is generally agreed that the *Meno* and the *Gorgias* predate middle period dialogues such as the *Phaedo*, the *Symposium*, and the *Republic*. In this book I have tacitly accepted this ordering, but not much of substance hinges on this. The ordering is convenient, because it suggests that Plato outlined his theory of technē and then gradually filled in the details: in particular, that he did not fill in the ontological picture in the first two dialogues mentioned, whereas he did do this in the other three dialogues. But even here the empirical contingency — that is, that the outline came first and the detailed ontology second — is less crucial than the conceptual point that the content of the *Gorgias* and the *Meno* do not entail a fully worked out theory of Forms, whereas that of the other three dialogues do.

Among the *Phaedo*, the *Symposium*, and the *Republic*, one might want to single out the first as the earliest simply on the ground that the psychology it contains seems less well worked out than that of the *Symposium* and the *Republic*, as we shall see in chapter 3. But this is not an overwhelming reason for this chronological hypothesis, and new empirical evidence about the respective temporal priority need not change one's interpretation of the respective psychologies.

Turning to the material covered in the second part of this book, Ross's survey shows general agreement that the *Parmenides*, the *Theaetetus*, the *Sophist*, the *Politicus*, and the *Philebus* belong to the same group, and that this group is later than the groups of dialogues surveyed in the first part. This fits in with the general tenor of the book, according to which, in these "later" dialogues Plato reflects on criticisms and lacunae with respect of the theory of Forms and effects various changes and modifications. Ultimately, this is the key issue that separates scholars on matters of dating. Some think that Plato never changed his views and that the dialogues present a unitary vision, whereas others think that Plato's views did undergo development. An extreme version of the latter view is the hypothesis, that later in life, Plato abandoned the theory of Forms. By contrast, I will argue that Plato never abandoned the theory of Forms; nor did his view become more like that of Aristotle. On the other hand, modifications and extensions were effected in order to uphold the explanatory power of the theory. Within such a conception it is natural to assume that the so-called later dialogues are indeed of later origin.

So far, then, the book does not make any radical assumptions about chronology. There remains, however, the issue of the *Timaeus*. In modern times, as Ross's survey shows, most scholars have taken it to be a late dialogue. A few decades ago, however, G. E. L. Owen argued for including this dialogue with the *Symposium/ Republic* group.[28] His views were challenged vigorously by H. Cherniss.[29] One of Owen's main arguments was the description of the Forms as *paradeigmata*, which suggested to him a conception of the Forms that he thought Plato to have abandoned in the later dialogues. This consideration does not have weight within the conception presented here. For, as we shall see in chapter 2, Appendix 2, Plato uses the word *paradeigma* in such a wide and abstract way that any of the conceptions of the Forms, including those of the *Sophist*, is compatible with it. There are, however, two considerations that would make the earlier dating of the *Timaeus* more in harmony with my interpretation than a late one. One of these is the treatment of time; that given in the *Parmenides* seems more refined. The analysis of time is not in terms of the tenses, as the one in the *Timaeus*. Secondly, the treatment of sameness and difference is more conceptually refined in the *Sophist* than in the *Timaeus*. But this second point could be countered by pointing at the different topics with which the two dialogues are concerned. The *Timaeus* deals primarily with cosmology. Thus it need not cover all the ontological and semantic puzzles that are taken up in the *Sophist*.

Since the ramifications of various new notions introduced in the *Sophist* and other late dialogues are not manifested in the *Timaeus*, grouping if with the middle period dialogues fits more naturally the interpretation of the theory of Forms given in this book. But the absence of certain features, especially in a work dealing with different topics from the ones dealt with in the revisionary dialogues, is not a strong sign of the work having been written before these features were introduced. Thus, even if new empirical evidence were to render plausible the hypothesis that the *Timaeus* is a very late production, this would not be a serious blow to my interpretation, since the latter relies on differences in the contents of the various dialogues, rather than chronological speculations. Philosophers have been observed from time to time in the history of our subject to abandon complicated versions of their theories towards the last parts of their careers and revert to simpler models.

NOTES

1   For an account, see R. Chisholm, *Theory of Knowledge*.
2   For modern traditional accounts of Plato's epistemology, see N. Gulley, *Plato's Theory of Knowledge*; G. Grube, *Plato's Thought*; and I. Crombie, *An Examination of Plato's Doctrines*, vol. 2.
3   T. Irwin, *Plato's Gorgias*, p. 115, agrees that understanding is more than just knowing the meaning of instructions, but he has a different view of what the additional element is from the one presented in this chapter. This difference affects the respective interpretations of what Plato thinks of teaching by example (p. 113). Irwin thinks that Plato would look down on this kind of instruction. On my interpretation, teaching by example is crucial both to teaching via role models and to recollection. In these contexts, teaching by example is good. If it leads merely to the uncritical imitation of another human, then it is bad.
4   B. Russell, *Problems of Philosophy*, ch. 5.
5   For a fuller treatment, see J. Moravcsik, "Understanding."
6   For more details, see J. Moravcsik, "Learning as Recollection."
7   Evidence for this and a decisive refutation of the interpretation that the slave boy conducts an empirical investigation can be found in G. Vlastos, "Anamnesis in the *Meno*."
8   For a differing view, see R. Bluck, *Plato's Meno*, p. 288. Evidence for my interpretation is provided by Symposium 210e5.

9   W. Weimer, "Psycholinguistics and Plato's Paradoxes of the *Meno.*"

10 F. Schleiermacher, *Platon; Sämtliche Werke*, vol. 3, uses *Erkenntniss*, not *Wissen*, for understanding. W. Wieland, *Platon und die Formen des Wissens*, makes the same point (e.g. at pp. 288, 236).

11 For some treatments of these, see N. Murphy, *The Interpretation of Plato's Republic*, R. Cross and A. Woozley, *Plato's Republic: A Philosophical Commentary*; J. Annas, *An Introduction to Plato's Republic*, esp. ch. 8.

12 Annas, *Introduction*, ch. 11; A. Wedberg, *Plato's Philosophy of Mathematics*.

13 Annas, *Introduction*, p. 290, thinks that the distinction between concepts and propositions is not important for Plato's purposes. According to my interpretation, the distinction is important, but in his epistemology, Plato stresses the way in which the nonpropositional is the basis for the propositional.

14 Did Plato think that mathematics can be and should be organized in complete axiomatic deductive form? My skepticism is supported by Annas, *Introduction*, pp. 283–93.

15 M. Burnyeat, "Examples in Epistemology."

16 B. Snell, "Die Ausdrücke für den Begriff des Wissens in der Vorplatonischen Philosophie."

17 Snell, "Ausdrücke," pp. 21–9.

18 Ibid., pp. 32–4.

19 Ibid., pp. 81–3.

20 J. Lyons, *Structural Semantics: An Analysis of Part of the Vocabulary of Plato*, part 2, esp. p. 142.

21 Ibid., pp. 189, 193.

22 Ibid., p. 151, n. 3.

23 See e.g. R. Hackforth, *Plato's Phaedo*, p. 68.

24 Compare Gallop's translation: D. Gallop, *Plato's Phaedo*, p. 19.

25 F. Cornford, *Plato's Theory of Knowledge*, p. 104.

26 Ibid., pp. 158–61. This citation does not signal agreement with Cornford's overall interpretation of his dialogue and its relation to the Forms.

27 W. Ross, *Plato's Theory of Ideas*, pp. 1–10.

28 G. Owen, "The Place of the *Timaeus* in Plato's Dialogues," *Classical Quarterly*, n.s. 2 (1953), pp. 79–95.

29 F. Cherniss, "The Relation of the *Timaeus* to Plato's Later Dialogues."

2

The Forms: Plato's Discovery

───────────────────── ◆ ─────────────────────

According to Plato, understanding must have as its objects genuine elements of reality. Such an epistemology calls for a theory of reality. Are there more and less genuine elements of reality? Does Plato's conception of reality contrast also with appearances or only with the nonexistent or unreal? The answers to these questions are contained in Plato's theory of Forms. This theory has been many things to many people. In modern times, it has been characterized as a conscious recognition of the existence of universals,[1] a philosophic faith which affirms the only alternative to a "flowing philosophy,"[2] a brilliant hypothesis solving at one fell swoop the major issues of ethics, epistemology, and metaphysics,[3] and a postulate justifying the high value placed on dialectic.[4] Given this plethora of interpretations, it is advisable to test a reconstruction of Plato's theory by placing it in the larger context of ancient and modern ontologies, or theories of reality.

We can contrast the real either with what is only apparent or with what is unreal. Some ontologies have one of these contrasts at their center; others have the other. Thus, some ontologies are concerned mainly to give an inventory of all that is in fact real, articulate it into a set of genuine categories, and keep it separate from what can be shown to be unreal. For example, modern ontologies like those of Russell and Moore have this structure. They divide reality into universals and particulars and aim to elucidate the natures of both. Nominalists, too, build ontologies of this sort, but they think that universals are not real. Ontologies of this kind aim at giving an exhaustive inventory of reality. By contrast, no such exhaustiveness need be the aim of an ontology that singles out the most fundamental elements of reality and then shows in terms of these how one can account for much that is less fundamental or merely surface appearance. The conceptual structure of such an ontology is explanatory rather than that of an inventory. It explains the less fundamental in terms of the more fundamental.

Some ontologies combine both interests, but I drew the contrast mainly to show the difference in orientation between an ontology like that of Russell and Plato's ontology, which, like most pre-Socratic ontologies, focuses on radically new ways of making the distinction between appearance and reality and thus should not be expected to aim also at exhaustiveness. In Plato's ontology, we must not expect to find a metaphysical cage for every creature that was construed in Plato's time or our own as real. We do find new contrasts between what is an underlying fundamental entity and what is on the surface. Correspondingly, we also find new explanatory structures.

In recent philosophy, ontological theories have been associated with so-called reductionistic theses. For example, nominalism attempts to reduce mathematics to a foundation in which only particulars are acknowledged as genuine elements of reality. Reductionistic schemes rely on a variety of semantic techniques to achieve the desired result. Underlying such techniques is the conviction that we can explain something deemed problematic by reducing it to, or defining it in terms of, other entities. It would be quite anachronistic to view Greek ontologies as having the structure of such reductionistic, semantically oriented theories. For Plato and his predecessors, the right way to explain something is to show how it is related to other things, in terms of either priority or dependence, not to reduce it to other things.

It would be impossible to take up all the interpretative problems that are raised by Plato's ontology. This chapter is organized around three main claims. The first is that Plato's ontology was primarily designed to account for the relation of appearance to reality in what was at that time a new way. Second, no attempt at a total inventory of all items in reality is being made. As a consequence, there is no general treatment of every item that we would regard as a universal. Plato's Forms are not just universals, and there is no Form corresponding to every universal. Third, it is claimed that Plato's effort to redraw the appearance—reality distinction can be reconstructed without anachronism as having the threefold structure of arguments for the existence of the Forms, characterization of the Forms, and articulations of the explanatory roles of the Forms. We shall examine various passages that have been discussed at length in the secondary literature. The discussion of these passages here will be restricted to their relation to the key claims made about the nature of Plato's ontology.

It may be misleading to call a classical ontology an explanatory scheme, for in contemporary philosophy, explaining is generally thought of as something that people, not entities, do and that the intended products are linguistic entities, subject to variation depending on the intended audience. There is, however, another sense in which it is perfectly legitimate to think of some entities underlying and accounting for – explaining? – others. We think of viruses or bacteria as the underlying elements accounting for a variety of diseases and of atomic structure as underlying and accounting for various dispositional properties of larger objects. In order to understand Plato, all we need do is project this kind of description of relations between things onto a larger ontological canvas.

Plato, then, does not invent or posit, but rather discovers elements of reality underlying and accounting for the realm that he takes to be less fundamental. He is led to such discovery by arguments, and he requires arguments to describe the explanatory roles that the privileged elements play. Discoveries that emerge in the context of theoretical argumentation are thus not matters of simple intuition or of stumbling upon neglected elements of ordinary experience. Only the properly trained "eye of the mind" can "see" the newly uncovered entities. At the same time, we need to stress that, according to Plato, these entities are discovered, not invented. Such an understanding of Plato's speculations helps us to solve a problem brought up by the late John L. Austin.[5] Austin perceived a tension between philosophers saying that universals are among the things we simply "stumble upon" and their subsequently constructing arguments for their existence. We shall see that Forms are not identical with what were construed in later philosophy as universals. But even apart from this, it is intelligible to maintain that arguments about abstract realms can lead us to discover new entities and that such discoveries also help to account for certain salient features of human experience. There is no simple yes or no answer to the question of whether we are acquainted with such entities, either in Plato's ontology or in the work of mathematicians leading to the discovery of, for example, irrational numbers. At the same time, it is misleading to think of Plato's construal of the Forms as analogous to what in the philosophy of science are called "inferred entities," for the latter are often thought of as posits.

If universals are interpreted as common elements among qualitatively identical groups, then it is a mistake to identify Forms with these entities.

We shall see that it is also a mistake to identify Forms with "perfect particulars" – that is, particulars that exemplify a given quality perfectly or to the highest degree. As we shall see, the number two is a Form, and there is nothing "supremely two" about that number by contrast with two points or two lines. Furthermore, since Plato wants to single out the fundamental underlying elements that account for the rest of what we would call real, it is hardly surprising that not all qualities are construed as Forms. Why should all qualities play a fundamental role in accounting for order and intelligibility in what we can know and experience?

As we saw in the Introduction, some of Plato's predecessors like Heraclitus claimed to have discovered the *logos*, or fundamental principle, that governs the workings of nature. The exact ontological status of this principle and its relation to the elements of nature were not stared – at least, not by Plato's standards of clarity and accuracy. We should view Plato's theory of Forms and their interrelations as successors to Heraclitus's "logos," rather than as mere unities corresponding to every qualitatively identical group contained in reality. The latter could be viewed as a "democratic" ontology, with room for every universal. Plato's ontology is neither within this "democratic" pattern nor within the "economizing" patterns of modern reductionistic ontologies; rather, it is within the "aristocratic" ontological tradition of thinkers like Heraclitus, who attempted to discover a relatively small set of privileged elements that combine to give order, harmony, and intelligibility to reality. This feature is retained even in the ontology of the later dialogues.

Some of what Plato takes to be the order and harmony of reality are based on mathematical and geometrical structures. Others are based on structures of natural kinds and those of cosmic values, considered under idealizations. We shall see how Plato finds common elements between these two kinds of structures. The explication of these structures and their ontological status leads to the characterization of explanatory entities in the sense already indicated. As in the sciences of today, so for Plato, a theory of explanatory entities requires the following ingredients:

a   arguments for the existence of these entities,
b   a characterization of these entities, and
c   descriptions of the explanatory roles of these entities.

The first two conditions must be conceptually distinct from the third, or the account will be vacuous. One does not want the account to resemble the proverbial explanation of opium putting people to sleep as the result of its dormitive power. To be sure, Plato never discusses these features of his theory explicitly. We need not attribute to him – anachronistically – a meta-theory regarding ontological explanations. But theoreticians with a "robust sense of reality," as Russell might have put it, do formulate their accounts to meet these formal criteria, even if they are not conscious of them. The claim of this chapter is not that Plato had an explicit theory about the three conditions and their interrelations, but that we can gather from the dialogues material that adds up to a theory of Forms with this formal structure and that he saw that the explanatory roles must be independent of the other two ingredients. The following sections will present the theory of Forms in these terms.

Arguments for the Existence of the Forms

Metaphysical arguments are not constructed in a conceptual vacuum. A metaphysician will take some things for granted, see others as problematic, and construe certain notions as having explanatory power. Different things puzzle theoreticians in different contexts at different times. This diversity of puzzlements is one of the mysteries of the human mind.

Among the things that Plato takes for granted are time, spatial locations, motion, and change. He is not put out by the Eleatic challenge to these notions. As we shall see, he thought that his theory of Forms could meet some of the challenges, and he might have thought others to be more of a problem for those who think of nature spread out over space and time as the ultimate level of reality. He also took for granted – as did several of his predecessors, like Heraclitus and Democritus – the contrast between appearance and reality: that is, the fact that there are fundamental underlying elements that account for the phenomena we humans experience. But the nature of this underlying reality appeared to him puzzling, and he thought that his theory of Forms could clarify it.

Mere linguistic forms do not dictate ontology. One can use terms like "walk" or "read" without having to choose between an ontology that admits only walkers and readers and one that also admits events. The same applies to the use of abstract singular terms. One can use words like "justice" and still have options among a variety of ontological interpretations. For example, one might think of justice as a goddess and her works or as an element of reality spread out over parts of history in the same way as one can think of something perceptible like the color red as made up of red surfaces scattered over space and time. On this view, the various manifestations of justice are parts of one "mass."[6] Indeed, at times, we all talk this way. For example, we say: "There is not much justice left in this part of the world"; "There is more justice now than there was twenty years ago"; and so on. One can also construe justice as a universal or an attribute that has instances or exemplifications.

The "mass" interpretation of qualities corresponding to what are Forms for Plato can be carried quite far.[7] If completely successful, it would render superfluous the conception of Forms as constituents of an independent realm accounting for order and harmony in nature. But such an interpretation runs into difficulties – not surprisingly – precisely in the area of domains like mathematics and geometry, which are at the heart of the Platonic ontology.

Plato had at his disposal some, though not all, of the linguistic devices that in a modern Indo-European language enable one to pick out qualities and other abstract elements. He had to make up – as far as we know – the term *poiootes*, meaning "quality." Still, even this linguistic innovation is not sufficient to ascribe to him a specific ontology of abstract objects. In the light of these observations, we should review two passages in which some commentators have seen the introduction of Forms. One of these is *Euthyphro* 5d1–5 and 6d–e6. Here we find piety described as what is the same in every pious action and an interpretation of everything pious as related to a single "idea." This is also described as what makes all pious things pious and can serve as a pattern (*paradeigma*) that we can look to in judging acts to be pious or not pious. Ross, among others, thought of this passage as introducing Plato's favorite entities.[8] But these lines do not warrant such a strong reading. What is the same in every pious action and serves as a standard or pattern for comparison can be simply the abstract mass piety that pervades everything pious and has some pure manifestations that provide bases for comparisons. Indeed, the lines by themselves do not rule out even a physicalist interpretation of justice, as a force of nature coming with its opposite. The texts do not posit a separate entity with its own specific nature. Even a nominalist could accept the lines from the *Euthyphro* and accommodate them in his ontology (for example, in the manner sketched above).

Similar considerations support the rejection of Gallop's claim that in *Phaedo* 65d4–e5 the theory of Forms in introduced.[9] In these lines, Plato refers to the just, the good, and the fine, and to other notions that have a being of their own and cannot be grasped by the senses. This much, however, could be accepted by a nominalist who does not have an empiricist epistemology and who admits abstract particulars in his ontology, as parts of concrete things. Needless to say, in order to maintain that in this passage the theory of Forms is not yet introduced, we need not assume that Plato or his contemporaries had a very sophisticated and elaborate theory about what a particular is, how something abstract can count as a particular, how abstract particulars can be parts of concrete particulars, and so forth. All we need to maintain is the plausibility of some of Plato's contemporaries having an inchoate conception of justice or the good as entities that can be found in various ways in various places and that a philosophical theory underlying such commonsense notions need not be Platonistic.

In *Phaedo* 74a9–c5, however, we encounter a text that can be reasonably construed as an argument for the existence of very special entities that Plato's ontological speculations claim to have discovered. For in 74a9–12 we are told that the argument to be presented will lead to the discovery of the Equal, an entity that is additional to, over and above, the many things that are equal in one way or another. If Plato thought of equality as a strange mass term or as a mysterious super-particular, then such a description of the Equal would be illegitimate. If, for example, justice is taken to be an abstract mass, parts of which are parts of agents and actions, then it is not something additional or over and above all the just things, but a mere sum of these. Likewise, a super-particular just entity – whatever this might be – would not be over and above all the other just things, but merely an outstanding sample in the same domain. The argument does lead to the conclusion, however, that there is a separate distinct entity which is the Equal and which can be understood only as belonging to an ontological category other than that to which all the many things that are equal in some way belong.

The general structure of the argument is clear. It relies on the non-identity of discernibles. The Equal has a property that none of the many equals, individually or collectively, can possess. Therefore it is a distinct entity. It is equal in some way in which nothing else is or can be equal. The nature of this property has been the subject of much controversy. The treatment in this chapter is restricted to those aspects of the property that are most relevant to showing how the final existential conclusion is drawn and to the subsequent characterizations of the Forms.

But first, two preliminary remarks. The contrast is drawn by Plato between the Equal and the many equals, not between a species of equality and its many instances. Thus, for example, it is not the contrast between equality in length – a perceptible quality – and its many instances. This is brought out by the examples given. We find among these such different things as sticks (logs?) and stones (a10, b5). Presumably, one compares two sticks in terms of length and two stones in terms of either weight or volume. It does not help to say that we can compare both sticks and stones in terms of size, for this only covers up the ambiguity of "size" along the dimensions just mentioned. Is there an unambiguous way of indicating what is meant when one says simply that a stick is equal in size to a stone? The point is that two things can be equal in a number of ways: in length, area, volume, weight, speed, number of parts, and so forth. There is no common perceptual element pervading all these examples, though there may be such within any specification. It is theoretically fundamental, however, to detect equalities and inequalities among all these different ranges of entities. Still, there is just one abstract entity called equality that pervades all the different kinds of equalities found in the world. This gives order to the world. One cannot understand what quantitative measurement is unless one understands this one–many relation.

Secondly, although one can compare two sticks that are equal in length with two others that are not, it makes no sense to compare two objects that are equal in every way. What would that mean? If they are really equal in every conceivable way, would they not be indistinguishable and thus identical? This consideration shows that the argument in this passage does not deal with some ideal particulars.

The argument has the following structure (74b7–c5):

> P1. All the many equals at times appear to be equal in some way (or to something) and not in some other way (or to something).
> P2. The Equal (or "the equals") never appear both equal and unequal.
> The Equal and the many equals are not the same.

There is a problem on the surface, because the premises refer to how things appear, the conclusion to how things are. But in the subsequent passage (74d4–7) the language of appearance is converted into the language of deficiency. The less fundamental elements appear the way they do because they are deficient in certain ways when compared with the fundamental elements of reality.

The gist of the argument, then, is that the many equals are never equal without some qualification, whereas the Equal is equal in an unqualified sense. The nature of the qualifications that Plato had in mind has been the subject of much controversy.[10] For the purposes of this exposition, it does not matter whether the qualifications include only ways of being equal or relational judgments as well. The key point is that the Form discovered is the Form of Equality and not, for example, equality in length, and that it is an entity that pervades all kinds of equalities, even though there is no perceptually common denominator running through all these. Furthermore, there is nothing in this argument that would lead Plato to say that two objects could not be perfectly equal in length, though, given the limitations of our techniques of measurement, we might not be able to verify this fact conclusively. Finally, there are several ways in which the Form of Equal is described in these lines, but there is no strong reason to suppose that these represent more than notational variants. Plato could not be saying that the unqualified equal nature of the Equal is its being equal in every way, since this is nonsense. He is saying, rather, that the Equal is equal in some unique sense that transcends the many qualified ways of being equal, individually and collectively.

In 74c10–d3 the Fine, the Good, the Just, the Holy, and the Equal are indicated as illustrating the range of Forms posited. It is easy to see how the argument applies to each of these. Nothing is simply, unqualifiedly, fine, just, holy, and so forth, but is always so in some ways, and often by comparison with other entities. As we see in *Symposium* 210–12, there are different ways of being fine (aesthetic, moral, intellectual, and so on), and there are many different ways and contexts in which justice is manifested. Later in the *Phaedo*, numbers are also treated as Forms (101b–c) – that is, as entities to which the argument given applies and of which other entities can partake in ways to be explicated. Thus, the range articulated in the *Phaedo* corresponds to the objects of the genuine technai and of recollection as explained in the *Gorgias* and the *Meno*. In a summary way, Plato says that the Forms are entities whose "what it is" is revealed in dialectical discussions. As we have seen, such discussions reveal the eternal and nonspatiotemporal elements that underly order and harmony in nature.

The argument cannot be applied to everything that is regarded as a universal in subsequent philosophical discussions. For example, things are either red (blue, brown, and the like) or not; they weigh 150 lbs or not; they are politicians or not, and so on. Thus, the nature of the argument supports interpreting Plato's theory of Forms as articulating what was called above an "aristocratic" conception of the fundamental elements of reality (more on this in Appendix 1).

The argument in the *Phaedo* is placed within an account of the recollection theory of understanding. This strengthens the thesis that the entities discovered are supposed to be those concerning which recollection is possible; and this realm, as we have seen, does not include all "universals." The dramatic structure and the dialectical form show us that once more we are to see the double application of recollection. The theory is propounded in the context of an articulation of what real recollecting is for Plato, and at the same time the argument presented is supposed to help us "recollect" what the Forms are. This applies also to the characterization of the Forms in subsequent passages. The argument is a vital aid to understanding that there are Forms and what they are.

In 74d5−7 the many equals − by contrast with the Equal − are said to be only "deficiently" equal. Our guide as to what this means is the argument and subsequent characterization (to be discussed in the next section) given just before these lines. Thus, the "deficiency" needs to be spelled out in terms of what the argument gives, since no other helpful material is available. The most natural reading simply identifies the "deficiency" with the qualified being that is introduced in the argument for the existence of the Forms. The many equals are deficiently equal in that their being equal is always qualified in some way, be it in terms of modes or relations. The text of the *Phaedo* in these pages does not give any support for a "perfectionist" interpretation, according to which nature is imperfect and cannot attain perfection in any specific way or in any specific relationship. For example, the difference between the number two and two objects is not that of perfection of the number two in some moral sense, but simply that two objects are not "just two," whereas the number is such that "two" applies to it without qualification.

This "deficient" way of being − for example, being equal − is explained by the fact that the many equals partake of the Equal (100c4−6). (In 100c5 this is applied explicitly to the number two.) This participation enables the many equals to have in some ways the nature of the Equal. For example, equality is a transitive relationship. But we cannot say of, for example, three equally tall trees that they are transitive. Still, what is true of equality can be applied to the many equals and point to an aspect of the order that pervades them. For it is true that if a tree A is equal in length to a tree B and B to C, then tree A must be equal in length to tree C. In ways like these, the "pure nature" of equality can be inherited with qualification by physical objects.[11]

Some of the qualifications affecting participation can be described in terms of an intuitive notion much used in classical Greek philosophy: namely, that of opposition. In many types of cases, the many f's are both F and have the character of the opposite of F. But this characterization does not apply in all cases. It is clearly inapplicable, for example, to the cases which are the clearest examples of genuine understanding and their objects: namely, mathematics and geometry. We need to "slide" in these cases from opposition to negation. The relation between these two notions in Plato's philosophy will be discussed in Part II.

The cosmology of the *Timaeus* requires Forms for certain natural kinds as well. Thus, we should explore how the argument of the Phaedo could be extended to these. Such an extension would require what is, from a modern point of view, an obfuscation. In the natural sciences we specify the nature of various kinds under idealized conditions. Whether we deal with the nature of gases or a species like a spider or a beaver, we aim to find out what its nature would be under idealized conditions, then add the variables that take us from such characterizations to the actual cases. From a logical point of view, there is a great difference between cases involving the qualified–unqualified contrast that we have been investigating so far and those involving characterizations under idealizations with subsequent, qualified accounts of actual cases. But there is no good evidence to show that Plato was aware of these formal differences, and he might very well have fastened onto the similarities between the two kinds of cases.

There is another argument for the existence of Forms, in the *Republic*, and it may be that Plato thought of this as expandable to natural kinds. The argument is given at 596a5–b4 and has the following schema:

P1.   In our customary method is to assume the existence of a Form for each plurality to which we affix a term.
P2.   In the case of artifacts, our customary method applies.
       In the case of artifact-types, we should assume the existence of Forms.

This argument leads to a realm of Forms not covered by the argument in the *Phaedo*. Furthermore, the argument in the *Phaedo* could not generate the Forms discovered with the aid of this argument. A given bed is not also the opposite of bed – whatever that would be – nor is it also a nonbed. It is, however, a bed with qualifications. This should lead us to a careful consideration of what Plato meant by the "customary method." Looking at dialogues like the *Phaedo*, the *Symposium*, and the *Republic*, we do not find any procedure employed that would posit a Form for every plurality marked in Greek by a common noun or verb. We do find in the *Phaedo*, however, the procedure of dialectic referred to. This leads to the discovery of the objects of genuine understanding: namely, a small set of attribute-like entities about which genuine insight can be reached. These are the domains of ethics, medicine, mathematics, and the other disciplines that Plato sees as yielding genuine insight into the fundamental elements of reality. These disciplines are contrasted with those that rely on empirical information only and can reach only what Plato calls conviction or belief. This contrast is maintained, as we have seen, in the *Republic* and the *Timaeus*. Thus, it must be kept in any account of what Plato might have had in mind in *Republic* 596 when he spoke of a customary procedure. Keeping these points in mind, we can reformulate the argument as:

1   Whatever has a nature whose elucidation requires dialectic as the process of discovery is a Form.
2   Artifact-types satisfy the condition of requiring dialectic for the articulation of their nature.
There are Forms for artifact-types.

This interpretation faces the challenge of explaining why dialectic is required for articulating the nature of artifact-types. Plato's conception of artifact-types, like chairs or beds, and his conception of artifact production rests on two key theses. The first is that there is no common perceptual element among all the legitimate instances of a given type. If one went to a furniture museum and looked at all the beds in different historical periods in different cultures and did the same kind of survey on the contemporary scene, one would find a bewildering variety of shapes, structures, and materials used for the different objects that have counted at one time or another as beds. There is no way of delineating the essential nature of beds in terms of perceptible properties. Beds must obey functional specifications, and at different times in different contexts, different materials and shapes will best satisfy these. Secondly, within the Platonic scheme, the functional specifications contain and rely on objective valuations of what is good in reality in general and what is good for humans in particular. This contrasts sharply with such modern notions as manufacturing artifacts primarily to provide something pleasurable for the customers. (Californian jacuzzis would not meet Platonic standards.) The human body has certain needs, and artifacts help meet these needs in the best way possible within any cultural context. This is why it was pointed out a few paragraphs ago that a bed is a bed with qualifications; that is, a certain material object with a certain structure counts as a bed if within a certain context it meets objectively determined human needs and thus should be used in certain ways. The artist producing the artifact must "keep his eye" (b8) on these values as he creates the new object.

Thus, the Form of an artifact is an idealized functional property. The Form of bed is not anything perceptible; it cannot have the shape of a Victorian four-poster or a bed of modern Scandinavian design. It specifies that material, structure, and shape must be such as to facilitate the realization of an objectively given value. Some sleep and some rest is good for humans. The bed in any given context must serve that need. This point of view also permeates modern common sense, though not universally. It can be seen in one of the senses for *bed* listed in the *Oxford English Dictionary*: "a permanent structure for sleep and rest." As soon as we attempt to build something that satisfies this requirement, questions arise. For whom is the bed designed? Children, adults, sick people? In relation to what state of technology is the blueprint to be constructed? The Form provides the functional aim; technology at its best is the means for its realization. This is an extension of dialectic practice as described in the *Phaedo* in conjunction with mathematics, geometry, and quantitative measurement.

These remarks show not only why the Form of bed is not a super-particular of some sort, but also why it cannot be a blueprint; these too, are technology- and use-relative. Furthermore, the qualifiedness of particular beds or even bed-types is not a matter of there not being a "perfect bed," whatever that might mean, but rather a contextuality that is derived from the indirect relation between functional needs and empirical realizations. This qualifiedness is analogous to the one we saw in connection with the argument in the *Phaedo*.

In this way, notions like bed or table contrast with notions like being a brother. The latter is definable in purely biological terms that remain constant throughout history and do not require interpretations under ideal conditions.

The understanding of Forms for artifact-types in terms of functional values shows that it does not make sense to ask for a strict individuation principle among different artifact-types. Do we have separate Forms for airplanes, helicopters, cars, and so on, or just one for means of transportation? Plato does not address this issue, and it is easy to see why. Functional specifications can be sorted and organized in different ways. Understanding them does not rest on being able to see for all times what modes of transportation humans will invent. Thus, the variety produced does not constitute a well-ordered series like that of the positive integers, or even a well-ordered group like the Platonic excellences. At the same time, once within a particular context and faced with the challenge of building artifacts of this or that type, the functional specifications can be associated with the types emerging at any given time and serve as overall guidance.

These, then, are two arguments designed to help us discover the realm of the Forms. The two arguments are distinct and lead to two distinct groups of Forms. One of these corresponds to the sciences of ethics, dialectic, mathematics, geometry, music, and medicine; the other to the production and understanding of artifacts. Natural kinds are meant to be covered in some way by one or the other of these arguments, although it is not entirely clear how. Though the arguments are distinct, they are compatible with each other. In conjunction, they present the realm of Forms whose nature needs to be "recollected" by us.

There is a third argument in the larger section of Book 5 of the *Republic* that deals with the "great contrast" between understanding and opinion. In this argument (475d–476b) the objects of the opinions and beliefs of the lovers of sights and sounds are contrasted with the objects of understanding. Further, the latter are linked to the Forms by the remark that the Forms have the unity appropriate to objects of understanding (476a2–6). The argument for the existence of the Forms can thus be reconstructed as:

1   There is understanding and it requires objects with a certain kind of unity.
2   The Forms are entities with the required unity.
    The Forms exist as objects of understanding.

We shall see later how further specifications of the nature of the Forms enables Plato to spell out in detail how the nature of the Forms helps to explain salient features of understanding and knowledge. We should note here that this argument can cover both the range posited by the first and that corresponding to the second of the arguments we surveyed above.

Characterization of the Forms

In several dialogues Plato offers characterizations of the Forms. When brought together, these can be seen to be consistent with each other. The different dramatic structures and topics of the different dialogues require that the same characteristics are not always stressed in all the texts. The characteristics that Plato ascribes to the Forms can be gathered under three headings:

1 Some key characteristics that all the Forms have, although not only Forms have them.
2 Characteristics that apply to all and only the Forms, but do not provide conditions of individuation for these entities.
3 Characteristics that apply to all Forms and only the Forms and provide conditions of individuation for these entities.

Key characteristics not confined to be Forms

These include the following:

1 They are grasped by thought and not the senses (e.g. *Phaedo* 79a1–3).
2 They are everlasting or timeless (e.g. *Phaedo* 79d1–2).
3 They are not subject to becoming or perishing (e.g. *Symposium* 211a1).
4 Each is "always the same, in itself" – that is, unchanging (e.g. *Symposium* 211b).

Symposium 211a–b and *Timaeus* 27d6–28a4 provide evidence for several of these properties collectively, but we will examine them individually.

The first condition is partly epistemological. It should not be equated with the characteristic of being abstract. For one might take the view that some abstract particulars (for example, the redness of a particular apple) can be grasped by the senses. In any case, the characteristic is not precisely drawn. As we saw in chapter 1, some conventional opinions of the people and some court rulings are objects for the "lovers of sights and sounds." Plato might be assuming that such opinions can be shown to be reducible to views about sensible entities; but the matter is never given a precise, explicit description. Even apart from possible candidates among common opinions, souls are also parts of Plato's ontology, and they are not grasped through the senses, as the arguments for immortality in the *Phaedo* show.

The second condition is ambiguous. Is Plato thinking of the Forms as altogether outside time or as "being always" – that is, eternal? The cosmology of the *Timaeus* suggests the former interpretation, but the evidence is not decisive. He thought of souls as eternal; so on this interpretation, this condition is not unique to the Forms. If he thought of the Forms as timeless, would he not also think this of elements that we would call qualities, corresponding to which there are no Forms, elements that are not constituents of the configuration that gives order and harmony to the world? There is no conclusive evidence that would allow us to resolve this issue. As we shall see in Appendix 2, the same ambiguity affects Plato's treatment of time in the *Timaeus*. But even if we do not ascribe to Plato a precise view regarding the ontological status of all sorts of qualities, the demiurge or creative force of the *Timaeus* provides a clear example of something that Plato acknowledged as real and is either eternal or outside temporal being altogether.

The third condition is apparently meant to separate Forms from living things and from other elements of nature. Taken this way, it is successful. But if we try to take it as applying only to Forms, it fails, since, for example, the space-matter of the cosmology of the *Timaeus*, the "receptacle," also meets this condition. It is more difficult to ascribe a precise status to the soul with respect to this condition. We can interpret the cyclic life of souls in Plato's metaphysics as a series of perishings and rejuvenations or as a series of changes which leave the subject indestructible.

The fourth condition separates the Forms from both the receptacle and souls, since these last undergo change. But it is not clear that it separates the Forms from the demiurge, and it certainly does not separate the Forms from other abstract recurrent elements, those called qualities by later thinkers. Some of the latter are clearly acknowledged in Plato's ontology. For he does include among the "many" over which the Form stands as one, complex qualities like military courage and aesthetic fineness. As we shall see in Part II, within Plato's later ontology, these might be interpretable as parts of Forms.

We need to be more precise in delineating the sense in which the Forms are unchanging. If being subject to change means simply that some temporally dated propositions are at times true of an entity, then the Forms are not unchanging. Two kinds of truths apply to them at different times. One of these concerns humans who come to understand them at various times or lose sight of them. The other kind of truth concerns the changing sets of elements that partake of a Form over periods of time. Thus, for example, it is not always the same entities that partake of justice or the Fine; history shows changes in the participant populations. But Plato presumably does not count these as real changes in the Forms. For, as he might say, these changes affect only the relations that Forms have to other kinds of entities and not their being. Instead of concentrating on modern rigorous definitions of changing and unchanging, it is more instructive to go back to the fundamental Platonic distinction between appearance and reality. For the many who lack understanding, the objects are the appearances. These are entities that change in two ways: they come into being and perish; and they change with regards to properties that are the subjects of genuine sciences – for example, geometrical, mathematical, and other quantitative specifications. The Forms are unchanging with respect to both their existence and those properties that constitute the domains for genuine science and thus endow the Forms with a fixed nature. This nature is what makes them constitutive of the underlying reality.

There are obviously many other properties that all Forms both have and share with other elements of reality – for example, not having spatial location. Within Plato's thought, however, the ones listed above are the most salient. As we shall see, they play a role in the explanatory functions that Plato ascribes to the Forms.

Key characteristics confined to Forms which do not individuate them

There are two characteristics that belong to what we called above the second class of Form characteristics, which apply to Forms only. They are:

1   being "simple in nature" (*monoeides*; e.g. *Symposium* 211b1);
2   being such that things can partake of them (*Phaedo* 101c).

The first of these is difficult to interpret. It can be taken in at least three ways. The crude version would have a Form like the Fine "uniformly fine" – that is, fine in all respects, comparisons, and so forth. But, as has been pointed out already, such an interpretation renders the Forms unintelligible. How could anything, be it a particular or a universal, be fine in relation to everything in all ways, manners, and so on? Thus, unless overwhelming evidence can be produced for this reading, it should not be adopted. Another reading would take this characterization to mean that each Form is completely self-sufficient, with no other characteristic than being "just what it is," the Equal, the Fine, or whatever. This interpretation of "simple in nature" would lead to a metaphysical atomism that has much to be said for it if viewed as helping to explain why Forms should be at the end of the Platonic ontological explanatory chains. Events and objects account for images and sensations, but Forms account for whatever permanent, harmonious nature objects and events have. Forms would be "where the buck stops." Whatever the final explanatory ontological level is for Plato, it should be self-sufficient.[12] But in spite of these attractions, this interpretation runs into difficulties. First, as Plato says in his later works, all entities have several characteristics: they are, and they are the same as themselves. But, as we have seen, this is also true of the Forms. Secondly, we saw in the *Meno* that all elements of reality must be related. Thus, the whole realm of Forms may be self-sufficient collectively, but not individually. Furthermore, in chapter 1, we saw how the elements of different domains of genuine sciences form interrelated collections. Numbers, Platonic excellences, systems of harmony, and so on do not admit of an atomic analysis.

It seems, then, that we should interpret a Form being "simple in nature" as that Form being "what it is" – that is, fine, equal, good, or whatever – in a simple and unqualified way that does not admit of further decomposition and hence having genuine reality, rather than being only part of the world of appearances. Thus, for example, courage is not the sum of military courage, political courage, courage in personal relations, and so on, but rather something that transcends all these kinds of courage and provides that in relation to which all these more specific kinds can be seen as facets of a whole, an ontological unity. We do not come to understand the Forms "bottom up" – that is, from species to genus, but the other way around. The simple nature pervades all the more specific kinds. (We can see this very clearly in the case of numbers. It is in relation to the number two that ordered couples have the structure they have, and it is not the case that the number two is just the sum of being two cows, two institutions, and so on.)

The other property is the possibility of a Form having things partake of it. There are two reasons why in Plato's theory the Forms need not be instantiated. First, if there were such a cosmic rule, then the Forms woud lose their self-sufficiency. Then, as a realm, they could not be at the top of the explanatory chain. Secondly, what reason is there to suppose that all aspects of order and harmony are or will be instantiated in nature? Such extreme teleology cannot be supported from the texts, not even from the cosmology of the *Timaeus*.

What is partaking? The original nonphilosophical meaning is that of sharing, or having a share in something. This need not mean that the part possessed by the participant will be consumed or destroyed in some way. Furthermore, it need not have a very concrete meaning. For example, in *Phaedo* 64e1, Plato uses it to talk about having a share in things helpful to bodily flourishing. In fact, even earlier, Thucydides uses partaking to talk about the relation we have towards certain qualities (e.g. I.84). If one were to interpret the Forms as having "mass terms" as their names and consisting of some one scattered particular spread over all the participants, then partaking need not have a metaphorical or technical use. We see, however, from passages like *Symposium* 210–11 that Plato is working first on a metaphorical and then on a technical use. Partaking becomes the unique relation that participants, or instances (in more modern parlance), have to Forms. As Plato says in *Symposium* 211b2–4, this is a special partaking that does not affect that of which entities partake. Thus it does not affect the Forms; they do not decrease, increase, lose anything, and so on. This characterization requires the separateness of Forms from participants. It would be false of the relation between Forms as abstract masses and their parts.

Plato construes participation as an asymmetrical relation, just as it is in its original nontechnical sense. He would never say that partaking of, for example, justice does not affect the participant. In *Phaedo* 74d4–7 partaking is linked with "deficient being." If an entity partakes of a Form, then it has the nature of that Form deficiently. As we have seen already, this amounts to saying that if x partakes of F, then x is qualifiedly f. This feature of partaking alone shows that we cannot assimilate it to the much more general notion of predication. Corresponding to "x partakes of F in respect z," there will be a proposition of subject–predicate structure, but not the other way around. There will be many statements of subject–predicate structure that do not have, underlying them, the partaking of entities of some Forms.

The "deficiencies" can be spelled out as a variety of qualifications. For example: "x and y are two humans" corresponds to "x and y partake of the Two in respect of being human." Or "x is larger than y" corresponds to "x partakes of the Large with respect to physical size in relation to y."

Thus, we can sum up the salient conditions governing partaking:

1   Partaking is an asymmetrical relation. If x partakes of F, then F does not partake of x in the same way or with regards to being f.
2   When x partakes of F, F is not affected in its nature; it neither increases nor is destroyed.
3   When x partakes of F, x is f with qualifications.
4   Only Forms can be partaken of.

This property of Forms cannot individuate them. That is, from the fact that F and G have all their participants in common, it does not follow that the two Forms are identical. In some cases, the participant classes are distinct: for example, the same entities do not partake of the Equal and the Just. But in some cases this does not hold. For example, according to Plato's ethical theory, the same entities partake of justice and self-control, but the two Forms – as Book 4 of the *Republic* shows – are not identical. Again, if we also take into account some of the examples in later dialogues, the same entities partake of Being and of the Same, but the two Forms are distinct. These considerations lead us to the third type of characteristics ascribed to the Forms.

Key characteristics confined to Forms which also individuate them

It turns out that there is only one such characteristic, and it is related to each Form being unqualifiedly what its participants are only with qualifications. The Equal is the only Form that is equal in this way, the Just the only Form that is just in this way; in short, for each Form F, the F is the only thing that is f in this pure, unqualified way. This property has been discussed under the heading of self-predication, though self-exemplification would be a much better label, since the property is ontological, not semantic. In any case, this property of each Form has had "bad press" in recent literature.[13] In what follows, I shall undertake what is at least a partial rehabilitation.

The linguistic device "the F" does not indicate by itself any specific ontological status, since it can be interpreted in a number of ways: for example, as indicating what answers "What is it?" questions. We know, however, that once this expression-type is used within the context of the theory of Forms, its substitution instances designate uniquely the respective Forms. Since we know now what the nature of a Form is, we know the nature of the *designatum* of "the F."

Shall we now interpret "the F" as a mere proper name, like the ones we give to humans or pets, that single out an entity regardless of its nature? Two considerations speak against this. First, in *Symposium* 211b2 *kala* is used in connection with participation to talk about the "other fine things." This locution makes sense only if it is contrasted with something that is in some sense fine. Secondly, the Forms have explanatory value. Things have their qualified nature by virtue of participation in the Forms. Thus, there must be something about a given Form F by virtue of which participation in it endows participants with the natures they have. The Form cannot be a mere "I know not what," designated by some arbitrary name, from which the participants derive their being. Plato, or a Platonist, might be driven eventually to such a stand if under attack. But the theory could not have been designed initially with that structure, for then it would have already lacked on the surface explanatory force. Thus, in the original form of the theory, the expression "the F" must have been construed as indicating something about the nature of its bearer: that it is a unique entity that is nevertheless linked to the many things that receive F as a constituent in many of their complex predicates. The interpretation of the phrase becomes clearer when we realize that for any Form F, Plato maintains that "the F is uniquely and unqualifiedly f." The predicate explains why there are some truths about each Form that do not apply strictly to anything else and in virtue of which the F can endow the participants with their qualified stable nature.

I will analyze the expression "the F" in two stages. First, there is the meaning it has prior to its being given an interpretation within the theory of Forms. On this reading, "the F" is:

(1)　The entity F, whatever it may be, relating to which enables all the f's to have their f-nature with some qualifications, relations, degrees, and so forth.

We now plug this expression into the presentation of the Forms as worked out in Plato's theory. Thus the "whatever it may be" clause vanishes and is replaced by "unchanging, eternal being, simple in nature, grasped by thought, possibly having participants" to yield:

(2)　The entity F, which is unchanging, eternal, simple in nature, grasped by thought only, possibly having participants, relating to which enables all the f's to have their f-nature with some qualifications, modifications, and so on.

What of the predicate expression "is uniquely unqualifiedly f"? We cannot interpret this as simply "has whatever it is that is shared by all f's," since this would be patently circular when added to the subject expression "the F" on any reasonable reading. The predicate must say something unique about the Form that enables it to be what other entities can qualifiedly share.[14]

As a plausible reconstruction, the following recommends itself:

> Has ("is") in pure, unqualified form the nature which is reflected in many qualified ways, degrees, and relations by all entities truly describable as "f with qualifications."

Joining this with (2) in a sentence expresses a proposition (or, strictly speaking, proposition schema) that is not on the surface vacuous; moreover, it can be seen to apply to Plato's favorite examples of Forms. For example, the number two satisfies the characterization given above under (2) for "the F", and it has that pure unqualified nature (being simply two) that is reflected with various qualifications among all the entities in the universe that can be counted as two in some way. Were it not for the nature of the number two, reflecting it would not give the world of space, time, and thought the ordered structure that it has with regards to counting. "Two" is not just a proper name like "Smith" or "Jones." It singles out an entity that is necessarily the object of many arithmetic truths; for example, "two is an even number," "two and three equal five," and so on. Plato's theory of Forms says that entities like the number two or the virtue of justice have their own natures independently of what goes on in space and time and that these natures are partly reflected among the spatiotemporal entities and endow these with some intelligible structure, some harmony, and some stability.

The claim that numbers are Forms, or that they are only Forms, has not gone without challenge. Already, in the writings of Aristotle, there are indications that some people interpreted Plato as positing an ontological class that is intermediate between Forms and particulars, to which numbers or their basic constituents belonged. This brief discussion of this issue will focus on two issues: first, does Plato need "intermediates" in his ontology? Secondly, how well does the evidence of the dialogues support the hypothesis that he acknowledged such elements?

The strongest argument in favor of intermediates in the recent literature comes from Anders Wedberg. According to this view, intermediates are perfect particulars, which are needed to explain what makes mathematics true.

In response to this argument, it should be pointed out that the truth of mathematics can be read quite well as being about Forms; for example, about the Form of Two of which all couples partake. If these are already posited in Plato's ontology, do we also need perfect particular? Of course, such an interpretation does not give an item by item ontological analysis of a sentence like "2 + 2 = 4." That is, it does not say that there is a 2 and another 2 and that these together constitute 4. It says, rather, that the sentence expresses truly a relationship between 2, 4, addition, and equality. But why should one expect of Plato an item by item analysis? He thinks that sentences and diagrams are only imperfect ways of pointing us towards the appropriate entities and their necessary, timeless relationships. There is no one-to-one correspondence between a geometrical construction and its elements – like the one in the *Meno* – on the one hand and Plato's ontology on the other. Similarly, there is no such isomorphism between ethical Forms and what is true of them. So why expect it in mathematics?

Furthermore, it is crucial to Plato's explanatory scheme that the same entities that satisfy the "aboutness" requirement of mathematics as a techne should also be the ones of which spatiotemporal particulars can partake. Thus, for example, geometrical truths are about Forms, and via participation, the less fundamental parts of reality can reflect partially these truths. Thus the order constituted by the fundamental realm is reflected by the less fundamental realm of daily experience with particulars. This scheme would be disturbed by an arrangement whereby the entities of which mathematically ordered things partake and the subjects of mathematical truths are not identical. Moreover, if numbers are only perfect particulars, then our previous worries about how anything could partake of them arise again.

Finally, all our worries about intelligibility would arise again with regard to perfect particulars. What would it be for something, in Plato's sense, to be unqualifiedly two? We shall see shortly how this notion makes much more sense in Aristotle's scheme.

Of course, to say that Plato does not need intermediates is not the same as to say that he did not posit them. So let us look at some evidence. A key passage is thought to be the simile of a Divided Line (*Republic* 509d), which seems to provide for a slot into which intermediates fit. But that much debated text can be read in other ways. For example, one might suggest that both segments of the middle of the construction introduce the same kind of entity, albeit viewed in different ways: namely, spatiotemporal particulars. A diagram can be seen as just something in space and time, as a final element of reality. Alternatively, it can be seen as what should point beyond itself and lead us to understand the geometrical verities that have Forms as their subjects and do not correspond one by one to geometrical demonstrations and their elements.

Still there is another consideration which favors the positing of intermediates as parts of Plato's ontology. It has its source in a certain ambiguity in Plato's description of philosophy or dialectic.[15] This could be taken as implying either that dialectic has its own special domain of elements or that it views the same elements as the more specific genuine disciplines, but in a different way. Opting for the first alternative, one might posit Forms as the subject matter for dialectic and intermediates as the subject matter for the special sciences. According to the second alternative, by contrast, the Forms are the subject matter for all the technai, including philosophy; but philosophy has a special ontological interest in these entities, presenting a rigorous analysis of their properties and their explanatory functions. Thus there are no special objects for dialectic, and the positing of intermediates becomes superfluous.

Our examination of the general conditions on technai supports the second reading. Mathematics, ethics, and so forth deal with their respective domains of Forms, whereas philosophy deals with all the Forms, concentrating on their general characteristics.

But even if one were to adopt the first reading, the positing of intermediates would not necessarily follow. One could, for example, construe dialectic as dealing with a special subset of Forms – for example, Harmony, Goodness, and Order – and assign other, less pervasive Forms to the special disciplines. It seems, then, that the discussions of dialectic in the dialogues do not provide direct evidence for there being intermediates in Plato's ontology.

Before leaving this topic, it is worth reflecting on why Aristotle saw intermediates as a plausible ontological category and why at least an analog to the "perfect particular" might not have seemed so absurd to the Stagirite. For Aristotle, even mathematics studies some aspect, no matter how remotely abstract, of substances. Thus he is interested in sketching some conception that will explain both what the objects of human mental operations, like calculation or construction, are, and how the relevant aspects of a substance are abstracted. The subject of mathematics is, then, very briefly put, unities abstracted from other more fundamental elements of reality. These units can be thought of as, for example, the unity of this or that horse or, in the case of geometry, as points. These are not only the subject matter, but also what we operate on as we follow mathematical or geometrical instructions. Thus, whereas for Plato there need be no ontology for "Take two parallel lines, dissect here . . . ," for Aristotle the abstracted unities, lines without extension and so forth, will be just that. Thus, from Aristotle's point of view, intermediates might have seemed to be what Plato needed, or would have needed had he viewed mathematics from an Aristotelian point of view. But, as have seen already and will see further in subsequent chapters, Plato's questions about mathematics were very different from Aristotle's.

The ethical Forms also illustrate abstract order and harmony reflected partly among elements in space and time. Some truths – for example, those linking justice to harmony – are true only of Justice, this uniquely and unqualifiedly just entity. These truths are then reflected in various ways and to various degrees by the qualifiedly just institutions, actions, and agents.

In formula (3) the choice between "is" and "has" was left open, there being problems with both formulations. If we just say that it *is* that nature, one might then ask; "But what is that nature?" Just pointing to something, even if only conceptually, is not enough. But if we say that it *has* that nature, then someone might ask whether the Form and its nature are two distinct entities.

It is plausible to suppose that, initially, Plato did not see this difficulty. He was excited to have discovered a new ontological explanatory pattern that had many explanatory possibilities. As we shall see in Part II, one way of reading the *Parmenides* is to ascribe to Plato a growing awareness of this difficulty. We shall discuss later the extent to which Plato or anyone else can deal with it.

This interpretation also sheds light on why Plato says that the participants are "named after" the Forms (e.g. *Phaedo* 78e2; *Timaeus* 52a5, *Phaedo* 102b2). This popular rendering of what Plato says in this regard is not literally correct. *Onoma* in Greek need not mean name; it can mean "noun" or just "general term." Presumably Plato is not telling us that there is a word that functions as a proper name for the Form and then as a general predicate for the participants. This would leave a mystery as to how the two uses are related; it would also create an ambiguity. It is more plausible to assume that a term introducing a Form has a unique descriptive force as applied to the Form and a derivative, general descriptive force as applied to participants. This way we have two descriptive meanings related as primary and secondary. Furthermore, on the analysis presented in this chapter, the term is never a predicate of the participants by itself, but is a common part of many complex predicates that apply to groups of participants.

This unique descriptive force creates problems for modern logic and semantics, for it does not fit the paradigm of either a simple proper name – or individual constant – or a definite description. But in this respect, Plato's framework is in good company. For the same can be said of the way in which the Greeks and people of other cultures characterize some of their deities.[16] The god of war does not have the name "War" as a simple, arbitrary proper name. The word is applied as a unique expression revealing the nature of the god. It is not like "Smith" or like "the most warlike warrior in Greece." Furthermore, from it we can derive the general term "war" with the meaning of "work of the god War."

The names of positive integers are nature-revealing in a similar way. The name "two" for the number 2 is not just like a proper name such as Witherspoon. It is part of a system of expressions that represent the systematic links between positive integers, and it designates an entity whose nature is reflected in a variety of ways by countable collections of any kind, abstract or concrete. The name for the number is related to the predicate "two" that applies with various qualifications to duos. This is probably why for Plato it is a paradigm for how to name Forms. Reflections on Plato's views about names for Forms and our names for numbers show that an adequate philosophy of language should provide more alternatives than just the dichotomy between proper names, and general predicates and derived definite descriptions. Maybe names of concrete things do not indicate the nature of the bearer, but names for necessarily existing abstract entities seem to do so.

In summary, though the special kind of self-exemplification that Plato ascribes to the Forms is not without difficulties, it serves to meet two demands of Plato's metaphysics. First, it explains why Forms are at the summit of the ontological explanatory chain; and secondly, it serves as the condition of individuating Forms. As we shall see, there is reason to suppose that Plato modifies this principle in his later dialogues. But such modifications need to be assessed from the point of view of how the alternatives help to meet the two demands we have just considered.

The characterizations surveyed in this section are compatible with the arguments for the existence of the Forms; but they do not follow from the conclusion of those arguments without additional premises. The characterizations we have seen constitute one way of explicating the "pure and unqualified" being of the Forms discovered through the arguments for their existence. But this is not the only logically possible way. This way of viewing the Forms, however, lays the foundation for their explanatory roles, to which we shall now turn.

Explanatory Roles of the Forms

Two explanatory roles are ascribed to the Forms by Plato. One of these is the ontological explanatory role (e.g. *Republic VI and VII* and the cosmological sections of the *Timaeus*). The other is the epistemological role (e.g. *Republic* V. 474 to the end). Let us first consider the epistemological role.

Epistemological role

As we have seen, both the recollection theory of the *Meno* and the *Phaedo* and the "great contrast" of Book 5 of the *Republic* require that understanding have genuine objects. Let us see how the Forms as Plato characterizes them can fill this role, thereby accounting for the possibility of understanding.

Someone might say that necessary truths could fill this role since these are eternal, or timeless, and unchanging. Nevertheless, these entities do not meet Plato's requirements, for they are not self-sufficient. They depend on their constituents. The *logos* that governs orderly processes and stable quantitative structure in the world depends on its elements. This is a point not faced by Heraclitus, but it is recognized by Plato. The Forms and their relations are what make those necessary propositions that express order and harmony true.

Of course, the traditional gods and goddesses were also eternal and immortal. But for Plato, reference to agency can never replace explanation in terms of qualitative nature especially when it is shown to be derivable from relations within a realm distinct from the spatiotemporal (*Phaedo* 91–100).

It would be a mistake to think of what we understand in the Platonic sense as all propositions about the Forms. As we have seen, there are some changing truths about the Forms, concerning what partakes of them in any given context and who understands them. It would also be a mistake to think that anything later called a universal would qualify as a genuine object for understanding. Some universals — for example, the quality of being a war or of being a successful performance of persuasion — do not provide entities with a nature appropriate to understanding. This became clear in the last chapter in connection with our exploration of the *Gorgias*.

By modern lights, some of the conventional wisdom denounced as what the "lovers of sights and sounds" embrace might also count as concerning universals and being analytic. None of this would move the Platonist to include them in what understanding is about. There are the complex qualities such as "moral fineness" and "military courage." For Plato, their full understanding requires a prior understanding of the Fine and of Courage in their pure forms.

The Forms, however, as characterized, do meet the requirements. Their nature and interrelations are what needs to be understood if we are to grasp whatever order and harmony there can be in the world of space and time; we must see this order as a reflection of another realm in which pure mathematical, geometrical, moral, etc. propositions are true.

We can put this into the following argumentative form.

1   Understanding requires genuine objects with permanence and a rich stable structure.
2   The Forms are grasped by thought, eternal, unchanging, simple in nature, can have participants, and have their nature in pure unqualified form. Thus they do provide such objects for understanding.
     Conclusion: The Forms account for the possibility of understanding.

This argument is not circular. As we have seen, there may be other candidates for some conception of theoretical understanding. Also, the explanatory role does not repeat vacuously the characteristics that emerged from the arguments for existence and the characterizations. Finally, the thesis that the Forms are the objects of understanding is not analytic. One of the reasons for this is that it posits the necessary existence of some entities, and assertions of existence cannot be analytic. Nor is this a "transcendental" argument in the modern sense of this phrase. It is not saying that understanding is necessary. The assertion that humans can occasionally achieve understanding, like the thesis that understanding is recollection, is a general assertion about human existence. Plato takes it to be true and lets the reader decide on the justifiability of this assumption.

Ontological role

Let us turn now to the ontological explanatory role. In *Phaedo* 100c5–7 this role is exemplified. Plato says here that a given entity is fine by virtue of its partaking of the Fine. The qualified nature of the thing's being fine is assumed here. In 100e1–6 this is generalized. When an entity has a quality that is a reflection of order and harmony in reality, x is f in virtue of its partaking of the F, where "is f" is a complex predicate and "the F" is not a normal complex definition description derivable from predicative uses. We must distinguish this formulation from such vacuous accounts as "x is f because it has f-ness," where f-ness is simply whatever all the f's have in common. One can turn this into a nonvacuous statement only if one can supplement it with a separate account of f-ness. Whether this can be done on the usual theory of universals is an interesting question. We shall bypass it, however, for, as we have seen, one cannot identify the Platonic "the F" with the universal of f-ness. What does Plato say about the Form "the F" and about partaking that makes this account noncircular?

First, the entity is not "just f"; it has the property in some degree, way, or whatever that is revealed in its pure, unqualified nature only in the Form. Thus the explanation takes us from the ontological plane of the explanandum to the higher ontological plane of the explanans. Furthermore, there is also a qualitative difference between the two. For example, numbers are on the higher ontological plane, and their interrelations constitute mathematical order. This is reflected partially in the quantitative relations that things in space-time can have with each other. Plato's examples in *Phaedo* 101b–c are $2 + 8 = 10$ and $1 + 1 = 2$.

That the Forms have their own natures can be seen from the fact that there are many truths representing relations between Forms, that are inapplicable without qualification to elements in space and time. For example, the definition of triangle cannot be applied to anything in space and time without qualification.

In the case of mathematical examples, we must keep in mind that they are about numbers, addition, and identity or equality. They are not about what we do when we calculate. If we take two and two and add these, this activity does not require for Plato an ontological analysis; only the true result matters. In this respect, the philosophies of mathematics and geometry of Plato and Aristotle may be quite different. For Plato, it is not what we do that makes mathematical propositions true. Similarly, he is not interested in giving an ontological analysis of what happens when we take two triangles and prove them to be congruent. Rather, he wants to provide the ontology that makes the result of the proof true. Operations of calculating and drawing diagrams are mental activities using physical aids. But the theory of Forms is meant to explain what the calculations and diagrams should lead us to. (See also *Republic* 510b.) A congruence theorem is about the Form of Triangle. Once the truth about the Form is understood, we can throw the diagrams and constructions away, since these are merely aids for recollection, not the subject matter of geometry. The activities are necessary for our learning and – as we saw in chapter 1 – for our manifestations of understanding. But that does not make them parts of the fundamental constituents of reality.

Thus we see that the explanatory roles can be articulated in a non-question-begging way. They do not repeat either the arguments for the existence of the Forms or the characterizations that Plato gives of these entities.

In the introductory part of this chapter, it was pointed out that in an ontology centering on an explanatory structure and the appearance–reality contrast, we do not expect to find an ontological cage for every kind of entity that the philosopher formulating the theory would acknowledge to exist. As our survey has shown, we do not find an ontological treatment of every item that shows up in the Platonic analyses. There is the question of qualities other than those corresponding to Forms. There are also other items, such as facts, propositions, the receptacle or space, and the formal characterizations of Forms (being possible objects of partaking, being eternal, being simple in nature, and so forth), that do not receive explicit ontological classification. Maybe some of these are not needed for Plato's view of reality: for example, facts. Perhaps others can be reduced to elements treated explicitly: for example, being eternal to an aspect of Being.

In any case, none of these items threatens the key contrast that Plato wants to explain or his way of explaining it. Some appearances admit of genuine explanation in terms of the Forms that constitute the fundamental elements of reality, and understanding this enables us to see that some appearances – for example, the conventional wisdom of the lovers of sights and sounds – are illusory and thus unreal.

The poetic language of the similes of light in Books 6 and 7 of the *Republic* show the excitement with which Plato viewed his ontological discovery. He interpreted the Forms as illuminating reality in the way that light illuminates. He also thought of the Forms as enabling things to live, just as light helps organic entities. Finally, he also thought of the Forms as giving us guidance, just as the light of beacons does for sailors. The reality that he thought he had discovered can be reached only by intellectual efforts that are very remote from ordinary experience, and yet – according to Plato – they are implicitly acknowledged even by our everyday cognitive experiences.

Appendix 1: *Not All Universals are Forms*

Republic 523a10–524c12 presents a contrast that provides further evidence for the interpretation presented in this chapter, that Plato did not think of each quality as corresponding to a Form. The contrast is initially between perception that is adequate for dealing with certain kinds of input and perception that needs to be supplemented by thought and understanding to account for other kinds of input. But it turns quickly into the contrast between two kinds of objects requiring two distinct approaches (523c). Finger and color are objects for which perception can give an adequate account. The objects which require thought and understanding for their interpretation include the Large and the Small (523e). Later, other examples are also added: for example, the Light and the Heavy.

According to one interpretation, what makes things qualifiedly large or small or light or heavy are simply comparative judgments. A thing is large compared to this log, but small compared to that building.[17] If we want to maintain the parallel between this passage and the *Phaedo*, as well as the earlier passage of the *Republic*, we can add that other qualifications also enter the picture. A large flea is a small animal, and a heavy brick is a light object for an elephant to carry. We need not ascribe to Plato a conscious recognition of the logical differences between these two kinds of qualifications in order to make the range of "imperfections" alluded to here analogous to those of the *Phaedo*.

It seems, then, that if we take the characterizations adduced from dialogues like the *Timaeus* seriously, we should conclude that there are Forms such as the Large or the Heavy, but that there are no Forms corresponding to those qualities about which perception alone gives adequate information.

In order to save the interpretation according to which there is a Platonic Form for every universal, one would have to construe this passage as dividing our studies of Forms into the more important kind (where thought is needed) and the less important kind (where sensation is enough). But since such a view would contradict the *Phaedo*, one would also have to posit a change in Plato's thinking involving a drastic extension of the realm of Forms.

We have seen that in Book 10 of the *Republic* the realm is indeed extended, but the argument given for the existence of the "new" Forms still would not generate a Form for every universal. The introduction of Forms for artifacts and natural kinds still leaves Plato with an "aristocratic" conception of reality, in which what gives stability, order, and harmony to the world is only what corresponds to a certain subset of theoretically important attributes. Once we reject the interpretation of this passage that would have a Form for each universal, we can return to what seems, in any case, the more natural reading: one in which elements that are intelligible on the basis of perception are contrasted with elements grasped by thought, corresponding to which there are Forms for us to discover.

Appendix 2: *Time in the Timaeus*

Plato occasionally uses original−copy, or real−image, terminology to indicate the relation between Forms and participants.[18] One might think that this requires an interpretation of Forms as super-particulars of some kind, or in any case a type of self-predication that goes beyond what has been expounded in this chapter. The closest thing to evidence favoring such an interpretation would be the fact that Plato uses the word *paradeigma* to designate the Forms in the *Timaeus*. But does this word mean for Plato something like "supreme paradigm" in the modern sense? Do the changes in the theory of Forms in the later dialogues require giving up "paradeigmatism" in Plato's ontology? The *Timaeus* gives us sound evidence for the interpretation of the original−copy, or paradigm−derivative, relation in connection with time. Thus, reviewing this treatment is instructive. It will be seen that the deficiencies of the copies discussed here are not different from the deficiencies of participants discussed in the *Phaedo*. Hence the use of this terminology does not require us to saddle Plato with an ontology of super-particulars or super-exemplars in the *Timaeus*, and thus with an ontology of Forms that must be abandoned in light of changes in the metaphysics of the later dialogues.

In *Timaeus* 37d−e Plato defines time as the "moving image of eternity." At first glance it seems odd to describe time as the image of anything. How could time as such be copying anything? A closer look, however, removes the oddness from the definition. For Plato is not contrasting time in a modern sense, as an abstract property, with some other property, but rather two kinds, or modes, of being: temporal being and timeless, or eternal, being. This contrast is reflected in the uses of the verb "to be" in its several forms. What Plato has in mind by temporal being is reflected in the use of the tenses "was," "is," and "will be." There are many entities whose existence entails their having a past, a present, and a future.

Typically, these are entities subject to change; they were so-and-so, are now a bit different, and are expected to change still further in the future. In contrast with this kind of being, there is eternal, or timeless, being. On hearing that two is an even number, it makes no sense to say either "Yes, but what was it yesterday?" or "Yes, but will it be that in three weeks?" The existence of the Forms and the attributive tie in mathematical statements or certain kinds of definitions point to being that is not relative to the tenses. At this point one can opt for saying that this kind of being is outside time altogether or that it is characterized by the "always is" locution and should be interpreted as eternal and unchanging being. It is interesting to speculate on whether Plato saw this distinction clearly. Would he contrast the eternity of souls with the timelessness of Forms? For our purposes here, the answers to this undoubtedly interesting question are irrelevant. The main contrast in this passage of the *Timaeus* is between simply "is" and the qualified being of the temporal flow, the past, present, and future.

Both G. E. L. Owen and Jaako Hintikka have stressed in seminars that the Greeks saw time primarily in terms of tenses. For a modern person, time might immediately suggest three o'clock or ten minutes past five, but there is no evidence that this was the view of time for Plato, Aristotle, and their predecessors. Thus the distinction we just drew is not anachronistic. Utilizing this construal, we can start reformulating Plato's definition as:

(1)   Temporal being is the moving image of timeless or eternal being.

Temporal being is tensed being: the "was," "is," and "will be" of past, present, and future. This yields the second reformulation:

(2)   Tensed being is the moving image of eternal or timeless being.

Plato's point is metaphysical, not linguistic. It would not impress him if someone were to say that there is evidence that tensed modes of being were discovered by humans and encoded in natural languages before the eternal mode. From the metaphysical point of view, the tensed beings are qualified beings: beings in the past, beings in the present, and beings in the future. Eternal being, by contrast, is unqualified being. It is simply being, without restrictions or qualifications. Thus we see that the original–image relation can be cashed out in terms of the unqualified–qualified relation utilized already in the articulation of the theory of Forms in the *Phaedo*. This shows that regarding something as the image of something else in this very abstract way is to view it analogously to the way Forms and participants as presented in the dialogues in which ontology plays an important role. On the basis of these considerations, we can reformulate the definition as:

(3)   Temporal, qualified being is the moving image of unqualified, eternal (or timeless) being.

This definition does not require an interpretation of the original—image relation that would lead us to interpretations of the theory of Forms other than that presented in this chapter. Paradeigmatism can be simply a restatement of the view encountered in the *Phaedo*.

Why "moving"? There is no eternally fixed past, present, and future. The point from which these distinctions are made "moves along" as history unfolds. The quality of motion in tensed being can be linked to the fact that the reference point from which these contrasts are drawn is constantly changing. In this way, the qualifications of temporal being are linked to change, and thus to the mode of being of the changing world. The unchanging versus changing dichotomy that pervades the account of the Forms and participants – even if it does not single out Forms uniquely – is reflected also in the account of temporal and atemporal modes of being.

We saw earlier how difficult it is to characterize the unique but descriptive way in which "equal," "just," "two," and so on apply to the respective Forms. The analogy carries over to the account of time. Only one thing is uniquely being without qualification: the timeless or eternal. There are many examples of qualified temporal beings, for there are many pasts, presents, and futures. Shall we say that eternal being is or has uniquely unqualified being?

These remarks are not meant to deny that there are various conceptual difficulties that the theory of Forms, as expounded in the *Phaedo*, the *Republic*, the *Symposium*, and the *Timaeus*, faces. They merely show that paradeigmatism is not one of these.[19]

Appendix 3: *Arguments for Forms in the Aristotelian Texts*

There are various Aristotelian texts in which arguments for the existence of the Forms are presented. Here some of these texts will be considered briefly, with the following questions in mind:

1   Do these texts present a clear picture of what were and what were not Plato's arguments for Forms?
2   Is there evidence in these texts for the arguments that this chapter claims to be in the relevant dialogues?
3   Are the arguments contained in the Aristotelian texts in some ways "better" than the ones in the dialogues?

The answers for which I will give evidence in this appendix are as follows:

1 The texts do not give us a clear picture of Plato's arguments. We repeatedly encounter references to "Platonists," which suggests that at a very early date there were supporters of Plato who — presumably either in his old age or right after his death — provided arguments meant to bolster his case. But the bewildering variety of these arguments indicates also a lot of controversy and a lack of clarity and agreement concerning the exact nature of Platonic arguments. Since, according to the view put forward in this book, these arguments were articulated against a background of assumptions about the sciences and about what the explanatory power of a theory should be, this finding is hardly in conflict with our view.

2 The arguments sketched in this chapter for the existence of the Forms can also be found, in various forms, in the Aristotelian texts.

3 The arguments found in these texts, whether recastings of the ones we found in the dialogues or additional ones, are no "better" in any conceptual sense than those expounded in this chapter.

Needless to say, one could fill a book with detailed exegesis of all the relevant texts. Here I shall merely sketch readings of some of the key texts, namely the *Peri Ideoon* and *Metaphysics* A.9.

In what is labelled Fragment 3 in the Oxford text (gathered from writings of Alexander Aphrodisiens), we find all three of the arguments listed in this chapter as supporting the existence of the Forms. We find the argument of Book 5 of the *Republic* in this section (79.3), with the addition that the object of a science is a "pattern." But as the previous appendix shows, Plato uses *paradeigma* in such a wide sense that this hardly adds anything to the unqualified–qualified dichotomy used in this chapter in interpreting this and other arguments. Illustrations like medicine are also provided in this text. But whereas the reconstruction presented here shows why the arguments lead to the discovery of Forms and not merely to what were later called universals, this feature is missing from the Aristotelian reconstruction.

Later in this fragment the argument concerning artifacts is also mentioned and sketched in the barest of terms. In the last two paragraphs, material is presented that seems designed to cover the argument we saw in the *Phaedo*. Equality is used as an example, and the qualifiedness of species and instances is used to mark the relevant difference. Part of the arguments as reconstructed here is said to revolve around "relations"; but it is an open question as to whether this is Platonic material or a recasting of matters in Aristotelian terms.

Throughout the section there are arguments relying on versions of alleged "one over many" principles. As we have seen, these are used by Plato only in certain dialectical contexts, and even there not as arguments for existence. Taking these out of context generates arguments only for universals; thus it is not surprising that Aristotle does not regard these as supporting the existence of Forms.

In Fragment 4 an argument that introduces the "third man" is sketched. It is ascribed to the "Platonists." It bears some resemblance to an argument sketched in the *Parmenides*, which will be discussed in chapter 4. But there it is given not as an argument proving the existence of the Forms, but rather as an argument leading to certain objections to the theory Forms. There is insufficient evidence to determine its relation to what is ascribed by Aristotle to the Platonists. There are several references to the "third man" argument in this section of the *Peri Ideoon*. But it is not clear how they would harmonize with the arguments in the Platonic corpus; it seems to me to be at most an argument for universals.

Other arguments are sketched in the remainder of the fragment, but all in terminology – for example, "first principles" – familiar from Aristotle's philosophy but not equivalent in any obvious way to the Platonic philosophical vocabulary. The discussion of these arguments, as well as the material in Fragment 5, deals – among other things – with the alleged explanatory power of the theory of Forms, thereby providing evidence for the hypothesis that this was already an issue in the early stages of discussions of Platonic metaphysics. This supports the general interpretation of Plato's ontology laid out in this book, according to which it is not the mere existence of entities not acknowledged by common sense that is at issue, but the explanatory power of an ontology.

Metaphysics A.9 supports the general conclusions laid out at the start of this appendix. It starts by questioning the explanatory value of Platonic ontology. It then proceeds to outline what are taken to be arguments for the existence of the Forms. The first three arguments, sketched very briefly, are: the argument from knowledge, discussed in this chapter; the "one over many" argument encountered in the *Peri Ideoon* which here too is presented in such a way as to leave it unclear whether Forms or only universals are argued for; and an argument about "relationals" that can be seen as a – to us – somewhat obscure reference to the argument of the *Phaedo*. In the passage that follows, it is difficult to discern the extent to which Plato is being reconstructed versue the extent to which the discussion presupposes Aristotelian ontological notions. For example, 990b27–29 says that if the Forms are partaken of, there must be Forms of substances only. The explanation for this invokes the essential–accidental predication dichotomy. But, as we have seen, there is no need to ascribe to Plato this distinction either in explicit or in embryonic forms in his ontological passages.

Again, 991b1–10 raises the issue of how the Forms can function as "causes" or explanatory factors. But although the *Phaedo* is mentioned, the analysis in terms of "causes", or explanatory factors, follows the Aristotelian theory of "four causes," and it is not clear to what extent, if any, one can interpret Plato's conception of explanatory power within this framework.

In 992b18–20 the Aristotelian doctrine of the multivocity of being is referred to and is rightly contrasted with the Platonic univocal view. But this contrast does not yield a better, conceptually more adequate argument for the existence of the Forms. It simply points to an important issue which has remained with us to the present day. Authors like Russell and Gödel (discussed in chapter 7) embrace the Platonic univocal view, whereas some proponents of the so-called ordinary language school of philosophy, such as Gilbert Ryle embrace the multivocality thesis.

This brief listing with comments of some of the important passage in which arguments for the Forms are treated gives a fair flavor of the evidence that can be gathered about Platonic arguments from the Aristotelian corpus. Over and over again it is difficult to untangle Aristotelian formulations of Platonic metaphysics from Platonic versions and Aristotelian concerns about first principles, causes of generation, and so forth from Platonic interests in how abstract structure underlies order among the entities of the domains of the genuine sciences and, in a derivative way, whatever order we find among entities in time and space.

It might be thought that philosophers closer in time to Plato are more to be trusted on what Plato's concerns were. But in this century, being closer in time to the author being interpreted does not always yield more reliable interpretations. For example, Wittgenstein's views were interpreted better by those writing later, from a more detached point of view, than by those who reacted immediately, within a contentious atmosphere. Aristotle's insights into the teachings of his teacher were bound to be influenced by his own ground-breaking concepts.

NOTES

1   W. Ross, *Plato's Theory of Ideas*, p. 225.
2   P. Shorey, *The Unity of Plato's Thought*, pp. 27–8.
3   H. Cherniss, "The Philosophical Economy of Plato's Theory of Ideas."
4   G. Ryle, *Plato's Progress*, pp. 213–14.
5   J. Austin, *Philosophical Papers*, pp. 21–4.
6   For explanation of "mass terms," see J. Moravcsik, "MassTerms in English," in *Approaches to Natural Language*, ed. J. Hintikka, J. Moravcsik, and P. Suppes, (Reidel, Dordrecht, 1973), pp. 349–69.
7   For relevant material, which differs in its conclusions, however, see N. Denyer, "Plato's Theory of Stuffs."
8   Ross, *Plato's Theory of Ideas*, pp. 12–13.
9   D. Gallop, *Plato's Phaedo*, pp. 93–4.
10 For a summary, see Ibid., pp. 121–2, 229.
11 This point about the "pure" and the qualified in geometry and mathematics

was called to my attention by Prof. Kenneth Manders; he is not responsible for my use of the idea here, however.

12   This shows that there is really no need for "immanent" universals in Plato's ontology at this stage. Either universals or universal-like Forms are the final steps in ontological explanatory chains, in which case they must be separate, or they are not, in which case a "mass" analysis can reduce them to particulars that are scattered in the world.

13   I argued both in 1971 and 1976 that self-predication has for Plato explanatory force. See also, though with different arguments, A. Nehamas, "Self-Predication and Plato's Theory of Forms," pp. 95–6.

14   For an alternative view, see Nehamas, "Self-Predication."

15   A good discussion of "intermediates" is to be found in J. Annas, *An Introduction to Plato's* Republic, pp. 285–7. We saw evidence showing that in the *Phaedo* the numbers are indeed Forms. See A. Wedberg, *Plato's Philosophy of Mathematics.* I am also indebted to Dr Ian Mason for suggestions.

16   I am indebted for this suggestion to Sir Kenneth Dover.

17   G. Grube, *Plato's* Republic, p. 176.

18   For a detailed exposition, see R. Patterson, *Image and Reality in Plato's Metaphysics.*

19   Hence the use of *paradeigma* to designate Forms should not count as evidence for an earlier dating of the *Timaeus*. A better argument for such a dating is provided by the differences between the accounts of time in the *Timaeus* – still mainly in terms of tenses – and the account in the *Parmenides*, in which the notions of temporal instants or intervals as basic units are hammered out.

3

What We Are and
What We Should Be

————————— ◆ —————————

Plato counts ethics among the activities informed by genuine insight. We saw in chapter 1 that for him, understanding goodness and harmony in the cosmos and in human life is analogous to understanding mathematics or health or musical harmony. The study of such values satisfies the conditions of being a genuine technē. Still, it is not clear from the epistemological passages alone how in ethics theory is linked not only to intellectual activities but also to everyday life. In this chapter I shall survey some key themes in Plato's ethics and see if I can lay to rest this initial misgiving.

Plato construes ethics in a very broad sense. It includes not only matters of duty and obligation, but also considerations of what intrinsic human values we can find, how these are related to the good in all parts of reality, and how these considerations can help us to form adequate goals for our lives.[1] He is not only responding to aspects of popular Greek morality and some philosophical views of his time, but is also widening the scope of ethics by rational justification linked to theories of reality.

K. Dover has recently given us a fine survey of popular Greek morality in Plato's time.[2] In his more general reflections, Dover points out that popular Greek morality – like the popular morality of today's England or United States – was "unsystematic."[3] There were a number of prescriptions for of what to do and what not to do in various contexts, but these prescriptions were not always compatible with each other and were not derivable from a few basic principles or ideals. To be sure, not all popular morality is of this sort. A society may be permeated by one specific religion or ethical view, and in such a case there may be a coherence to its morality. Examples of such moralities would be those of the Jews of the Old Testament, the Puritans of New England, or certain contemporary Islamic societies. But Dover's evidence shows that we should not think of the popular morality of Plato's time in this way.

Given the unsystematic nature of Greek popular morality, we can look at Plato's criticism of it on four levels, representing increasing demands of rationality. First, he wants ethics to be systematic, in the sense of answers to different dilemmas being compatible with each other. Dover pointed out that ethical issues emerge already in Aeschylus.[4] For example, why is ingratitude worthy of reproach? Why do the gods like rulers who behave well towards captives? A minimal demand in answering such questions is consistency. A further, stronger demand would be that the answers admit of rational justifications and be linked to more general principles. But meeting these demands alone will not satisfy Plato. After all, the "basic" principles might be simply that the gods like these things or that this is what the conventions of the particular society prescribe, or whatever.

These considerations lead us to the third and fourth levels, which are distinctive Platonistic contributions. Plato wants our ethical thinking to be informed by understanding relevant objects. This means, among other things, that he wants our evaluations of actions, agents, and institutions to rest not only on how these affect us (for example, cause us to have pleasure) or on the evaluations being given by powerful authorities (politicians, priests, and the like), but on detecting certain objective attributes of the entities being evaluated. Thus the Platonically favored pattern is to assign positive value to x and y on account of their possessing qualities Q_1, Q_2, and so on. According to Plato, objects do or do not have these values, whether we know it or not. Ethical understanding, for Plato, is like mathematical understanding, a matter of discovery, not invention.

Let us assume that we value something on account of the appropriate qualities warranting such valuation. The final level of rationality for Plato is that such valuations should lead us to want to realize things with these qualities, either in our own lives or in the lives of others as well.

These increasingly severe demands on rationality take Plato far beyond popular morality and bring him into conflict with such philosophical views as relativism and hedonism. Plato's response is to point to the analogy between ethics and the other technai.

In order to understand Plato's views on values, let us place it in proper perspective by comparing it with other possible types of ethical theory. This brief survey is restricted to theories of individual ethics, though it could be extended to cover communal ethics as well.

Briefly, and schematically, individual ethics has three components:[5]

1   A theory of desirable or appropriate interpersonal relations. This may be construed narrowly, as merely a theory of duty and obligation, or broadly to include various kinds of cooperation and relations like friendship. Those favoring the narrow interpretation claim that we have peculiarly "moral" intuitions in matters of choice and action, whereas those favoring the broad view claim that such intuitions cannot be separated sharply from the variety of ways in which we assess relations between persons as friendly, cooperative, showing empathy, and so on.

2   A theory of human goods. This includes a principled account of what is intrinsically good for humans (happiness, pleasure, certain kinds of character, and so on), as well as a list of instrumental goods. The theory may be monolithic, having at its summit a single *summum bonum*, or pluralistic. Either way, it must settle priorities in a systematic way.

3   Prudence and practical reasoning. This component articulates ways in which one can reason correctly about ends and means and matters of compatibility among rival ethical claims. Depending on how human goods are specified, prudence may include only inductive and deductive reasoning or it may also include the complex reasoning process involved in selecting an appropriate role model and embodying its desirable qualities in our own lives.

In examining the various ways in which these components may be related, we shall restrict ourselves to relations between the first two since these relations show what is characteristic of Plato's approach to ethics by contrast with most contemporary influential ethical theories. For example, both Kant and Bentham regard the first component as a theory of duty and obligation and see it as independent of the second.[6] Their greatest moral principles are the categorical imperative and the maximization of happiness for the greatest number, respectively. These principles cannot be derived on their views from the second component. They have a separate, purely "moral" source.

According to such a view, ethical principles tell us how to act morally. We may know everything that a correct theory of the second component teaches us and still not be moral. For example, we may want all the human goods just for ourselves. We need additional principles of a different origin to generate fairness, respect for others, and the meeting of obligations.

The independence thesis has both a weak and a strong version. The weak thesis says merely that the first component cannot be derived from the second. The stronger thesis construes the first as a constraint on the second;

that is, if there is a conflict between the two components, the first must prevail.

Utilitarianism and deontic ethics are the most dominant modern types of ethical theories in Anglo-American philosophy. Both maintain the independence thesis.[7] Morality prescribes our obligations, regardless of our interests. Morality is either consequentialist, as in the case of utilitarianism, specifying duty in terms of consequences that accrue, or deontic, spelling out moral action in terms of intrinsic qualities that such actions or motives must have.[8] Kant adopts a monolithic deontic theory, whereas those opting for several equally important basic moral principles of the deontic sort can be labeled pluralists. Some of the intuitionists of this century fall into this category. Both these kinds of theories can incorporate an account of moral virtues. The utilitarian can regard these as what lead to the maximization of happiness; the Kantian can see them either in the same instrumental way or as constitutive of the morally good person.

Historians like Frankena interpret Plato's ethics as a theory that deals with duty and construes virtues as character traits defining the dutiful person.[9] Others have attempted to interpret Plato as a utilitarian, construing his theory of virtues as the best means for acquiring and spreading happiness. Initially it seems reasonable to regard these two approaches as the most plausible ones, since both locate Plato's ethics within traditions that are important today and at the same time attempt to take into account the emphasis on virtues in the Platonic writings. Both these lines of interpretation have encountered difficulties, however.[10]

An alternative to both these kinds of theories becomes available if one denies the independence thesis. Such a denial could be part of a theory of the human good, according to which a person possessing the human goods will also be a morally good person. The possession of the human goods will lead him to be a cooperative, dutiful individual, and, according to such a view, dutiful, cooperative activity is all we need to expect of a morally good person. On this view, moral goodness need not be based on a pure sense of duty as the only appropriate motivation.

There are many possible theories that deny the independence thesis as characterized above. Some of these characterize the human good – which now includes the morally correct – primarily in terms of a set of virtues or character traits, with other goods either necessary for survival or also instrumental in maintaining the virtues.

We shall single out a version of virtue ethics and label it "ideal ethics."

This theory construes the human good as having two key ingredients: an appropriate aim in life and a character structure that has intrinsic merit and is related to the aim by being necessary for its realization. In this chapter I will argue that Plato's ethics is an "ideal ethics" in this sense, thus denying the independence thesis and denying that it is assimilable to either Kantian or utilitarian ethics or to a variety of theories that can be gathered under the general rubric of virtue ethics. Needless to say, "ideal ethics" may include many different proposals as to what the right aim or aims and the right character structures are. In this chapter I will also give an interpretation of what the specifically Platonic ideal is.

Overall aims for a human life range from the simple to the highly complex. The simple include merely wanting to be wealthy, and the complex can include a theory of right aims for human lives and right character traits or life patterns. Within ideal ethics, the overall aim is linked closely with desirable character traits. Both are intrinsic goods. Good character is not just whatever will serve as a means to realizing the correct overall aim. For example, if the aim is to promote and embody certain qualities, then the related character specification tells us the way in which such an embodiment and promotion are to take place. Aim and character are equally important; neither has priority over the other.

Within ideal ethics, the right kind of aim and character can be shown to mold us into human beings who will be cooperative in various ways and will not aim at harming others. Thus, within ideal ethics, the first component can be derived from the second, except that, as we shall see, no "purely moral motivation" is provided.

Interest and utility within such an ethics is relative to the proper ideal. It is not as if there were some basic things that are in our interest beyond any controversy and that we need to formulate ideals within this framework. The priorities are the other way around. First, we need to select an ideal, then define what is useful relative to it.

A particular proposal in ideal ethics will include the need to play certain roles and to enter into certain relationships with others. By entering into these relationships, we also take upon ourselves certain duties and obligations. Thus, there is room for duties and obligations within ideal ethics, but these notions do not enter on the "ground floor" of the theory. It is not the case that there are duties and obligations beyond discussion, within which we formulate our ideals. Rather, we need to formulate and defend an ideal, and then, within it, articulate duties such as those among friends, colleagues, members of political communities, and so forth. Different ideals will yield different duties, or different conceptions of the same duty; for example, filial duty.

Having sketched ideal ethics and contrasted it with consequentialist and deontic theories of ethics, let us turn to our demonstration that Plato's ethics was in fact this kind of ethics.

Plato's Ideal Ethics

As we have seen, an ideal ethics includes a proposal regarding the proper aim for a human life and the proper character of the agent pursuing that goal. According to Plato, the right aim for human life is to understand the order and harmony that characterize the most fundamental part of reality and embody this also in our lives (*Timaeus* 47c1–d2, 90c7–d7). As we have seen, it is part of Platonic rationality that once we understand harmony among the Forms, we should want to create as many instances of it as possible. Some of these will be included in our lives, some in the lives of others.

Plato thought that we should pursue this end while developing a character in which understanding "rules" in a variety of ways. Such an orientation also requires developing certain attitudes, some positive, some negative (*Phaedo* 67–9). Thus, for example, such a person will not enjoy objects of pleasure whose possession hinders the development and use of reason. Plato maintains that intellectual activities bring with them enjoyment (*Republic* 583c–d), but that we do not partake in these activities for the sake of such pleasure. We can see this, for example, in *Phaedo* 68–9, where Plato contrasts the person who calculates the greatest pleasure for himself with the person who opts for virtues, such as wisdom, for their own sakes.

A sketch of the ideal character is given in Book 4 of the *Republic*, where three aspects or parts of the soul are distinguished and correlated with a list of virtues (436a8–444a2). There is much that can be said about this passage,[11] but I shall confine myself to showing how it fits into Plato's exposition of the ideal ethics. The basis of the psychic trichotomy is provided by typical conflicts we experience when making decisions. Appetite emerges at 437d, reason at 439d, and emotion, or the "spirited element" as it is sometimes called, at 440c. Some conflicts involve clashes between reason and appetite, others between emotion and appetite. Plato does not claim that all conflicts fall into one of these two patterns or that one could not divide the soul in other interesting and informative ways. But this trichotomy is important to the characterization of the soul from the agent's point of view. For from this point of view, priorities need be established among the various psychic and physical parts of a human being. An outsider could simply describe human nature and its parts and indicate various ways in which the parts can interact. But when, as agents, we decide to do this rather than that, we are forced to regard some of our parts as more important than others. Some physical parts are more important than others merely because of their survival value. But various decisions and patterns of activity imply that some of our rational capacities are more important than some of our emotional ones. Alternatively, someone might say that the time spent on trying to understand the Forms could better be spent on developing emotional capacities such as love or care.

Plato describes the healthy soul as one in which harmony is established by the "rule" of reason. This "ruling," or guiding, of the other two parts takes place in the following ways:

1   The development and maintenance of reason and understanding have priority over the development of other psychic capacities such as the ability to experience great passion.
2   Reason enables us to understand and recognize goodness in ontologically fundamental entities and thus presents these as objects worthy of pursuit and aspiration. In this way, it acts as a "magnetizer," enabling the appropriate objects to act for us as magnets, attracting our *eros*, or overall aspiration.[12]
3   Reason can transform our desires and interests by showing that previous objects of our desires do not in fact possess characteristics making for what is good, while others do. For example, reason can guide us away from sweets and towards healthy food.

This sketch shows that Plato's attitude towards emotions favors neither unchecked expression nor blanket repression. He recognizes the appetitive and emotional energy in humans, but wants this to be guided by reason in the way indicated.

The virtues related to the various parts of the soul are wisdom, courage or inner strength, and self-control; and the total harmonious functioning of the soul results in individual justice. These virtues guaranteeing inner harmony are noncompetitive and cooperative. A competitive virtue is possessed by some, or by one, at the expense of someone else. It requires superiority of some sort over others. For example, the virtue of being the best warrior can be possessed by only one member of a community. Some virtues are neither competitive nor cooperative; for example, the virtue of being able to fend for oneself. A person's inner harmony is noncompetitive, since it does not prevent others from also having such harmony. Furthermore, given Plato's epistemology centering on recollection elicited by others, the virtue of wisdom is cooperative; we can best attain it and cultivate it by cooperative ventures.

One of the ways in which Plato explains his ethical views is by drawing an analogy between the healthy body and the good human. Health, according to Plato is noncompetitive. (Modern resource problems are not envisaged by Plato; thus it would be anachronistic to expect from him an answer to the question as to who gets the kidney-machine.) Health is a philosophically interesting notion in its own right.[13] Health is both descriptive and normative. It is the condition the body is in when it is at its best. Health cannot be characterized in purely observational terms. The appearances are only the surface phenomena. The real source of health is an inner structure and state that are known on the basis of everyday experience only indirectly. Health cannot be defined in hedonistic terms; a drug addict might experience more pleasure than a healthy person, but we still would not call him or her healthy. Finally, health is manifested in a wide variety of ways. What is healthy for an infant is not the same as what is healthy for an adolescent or an octogenarian. Yet there is a common functional element underlying all these manifestations: namely, the restoration and maintenance of the well-being of the body.

In all these ways, health resembles the other Forms that we discussed earlier. Above all, it resembles the Form of goodness. Thus health is to the body what goodness is to the soul. Being healthy is a function of the body, whereas being good, in terms of aim and character, is a function of the soul.

Characterizations of health surface in different places in the dialogues. *Meno* 72d–e shows that health cannot be analyzed exhaustively in terms of sensible phenomena, and *Gorgias* 464b–c and 521a distinguish concern for health from concern for enjoyment. As I have pointed out already, health cannot be defined as the state in which we experience the greatest amount of pleasure.

In *Republic* 444d3–6 Plato says that health is brought about by conditions under which the bodily constituents are arranged in their natural order. This parallels the account of the soul in Book 4. When the soul possesses each of the four cardinal virtues, its parts are arranged and are functioning within their natural order.

Both health and good character have intrinsic merit for Plato. They are not means to, but constitutive of, human flourishing. This is consistent with Plato's optimistic factual prediction in *Laws* 733e–734c that a healthy and good life will in fact be more enjoyable than an unhealthy bad one. The basis for this optimism is Plato's teleological conception of nature. What is good for us cannot make us miserable. The optimism should be stated with a qualification, however. The good and healthy life is enjoyable for the right kind of individual. Plato is not claiming that it is enjoyable for humans regardless of their psychic and bodily make-up.

How does Plato move from inner harmony to harmony within a community? At *Republic* 442e4–443b5 he says that the good person (that is, one with a proper aim and character) will not want to steal, act in sacrilegious ways, betray others, neglect parents, commit adultery, and so forth. This is the negative link between the good individual and the good community. Within a community of Platonically good people, the members do not have any interest in harming each other. This is because the kinds of acts just enumerated do not lead to realization of the proper human aim or the character that partakes of the four virtues. In fact, being the kind of person who is interested in committing acts of this sort will interfere with aspiring towards the genuinely good things. This approach is quite different from a rule-oriented ethics that adopts the independence of morality thesis. Plato's claim in the passage just quoted is not that he has produced a rule prohibiting all these activities and that we should embrace this rule on "purely moral" grounds. The formulation of rules prohibiting certain actions is a matter for the legislature. The task of ideal ethics is to sketch the right kind of individual: the good person, in a sense of "good" that is neither Kantian nor utilitarian. Its closest equivalent is the use of "good" in characterizations of what makes an entity a good specimen of a species. For such an individual, bad deeds are abhorrent and interfere with his realizing what he takes to be good.

Clearly, this is not enough. We need to see what positive inspiration Plato provides for a good person to be cooperative. This inspiration can be found in our understanding harmony in the most fundamental part of reality and wanting to produce as many instances of it as possible. A positive orientation towards other members of the human community is a matter not of duty but of a love of harmony that carries us from intellectual to ethical matters.

So far, all we have shown is that the good agent will have an interest in creating harmony. But it is unclear how we are to apply this concept to cases where we need to decide between equality and domination, egalitarian and hierarchical structures. Given the Platonic aim for humans, we can derive from the Platonic ideal an interest in educating every potential "recollection" – that is, every "healthy" human being. But it is not clear how on this basis one would deal with the sick or the senile.[14] In the absence of concrete evidence, we can only speculate on a possible extension of Platonic principles. As the passages from the *Phaedo* already cited show, Plato contrasts the harmoniously functioning individual with the person who calculates pleasure or utility in all cases. Thus, one might think that Plato would regard taking care of the senile in view of their achievements and realizations of good in other stages of their lives as part of a harmoniously functioning communal life. But the incurably ill seem to require compassion and sympathy. It is not clear how one could derive these sentiments from the Platonic ideal. As we shall see when we consider the *Symposium* in the next section, Plato thinks that there is a quality of "fineness" (*kalon*) in mathematical, musical, or geometrical structures. It might seem to a modern person, but perhaps not to Plato, that there is something fine, in the same sense, about caring for the unfortunate; but it is not clear how justified we would be in projecting this back into the Platonic scheme.

These considerations show that the Platonic ideal does provide reasons for extending various kinds of cooperation to large segments of humanity. But it does not give – nor does it want to give – a fundamental principle of duty on which all such cooperativeness would be based. Different kinds of respect and cooperation are earned by possessors of different characteristics warranting such respect and cooperation. There is, however, room for duty and interest relative to the various roles and relations into which we enter in a flourishing society. Relationships like friendship, family membership, collegiality, and so on bring with them duties and obligations. These are acknowledged within the Platonic ideal. Thus it would be quite wrong to say that there is no room for duty and obligation in Plato's ethics. There are duties tied to different roles, just as there is utility relative to the ideal and related to the various roles that we play in a flourishing society. But there is no duty and obligation that would be prior to the articulation of the ideal, and, as we have seen already, no sense of utility that is not based on the conception of human good as articulated by the ideal.

One might wonder how one can derive principles of distribution of goods from the Platonic ideal. Some distribution of goods is needed just to maintain the possibility of a community whose life centers on furthering understanding and embodying harmony. It is not clear, however, that from this minimal condition one could derive principles of fairness or equality. Plato does not say much about distributive principles. This is because these principles do not apply to the highest goods as he sees these. He thinks (e.g. *Phaedo* 64–7) that a good person should worry about physical goods only insofar as these are necessary. The intellectual goods are not things that need to be distributed. They are inside us and can be awakened in anyone. It would be anachronistic to raise within Plato's conception questions regarding modern requirements of expensive aids to education that are needed in the ongoing accumulation of knowledge.

Thus, our sketch of Plato's ethics as ideal ethics leaves us with a sense of incompleteness when considered in relation to comprehensive modern ethical theories, which attempt to answer not only the questions with which Plato was concerned, but also the ones that his conception seems to leave out. Should this invite a reconsideration of interpreting Plato as either a utilitarian or a Kantian? Maybe the virtues are simply the best means to happiness, with this notion remaining implicitly assumed in the background. Or alternatively, could we not interpret Plato as a Kantian who thinks that, whereas everyone may pursue happiness, it is our duty to embody the virtues, and that this places a constraint on the pursuit of happiness? There are at least four further considerations which support the interpretation of Plato's ethics as an ideal ethics.

The first is the treatment of Thrasymachus's position in Book 1 of the *Republic*. The topic of discussion is: What is justice? Presumably some of the plausible candidates for a sound definition are that justice is what the gods want or justice is to pay one's debts or justice is what the courts' rules say. Thrasymachus, however, does not want any of this. His view is that it does not matter how one theorizes about justice; for what we call justice in a society is in fact what the strong elements in the society impose on us. This is not a definition to rival the ones just mentioned.[15] Rather, it is an expression of moral skepticism. It regards Socratic discussion of justice as empty (338e1–339a4). It does not matter what we think about justice in our idealistic moods. In the end, the strong elements in society will impose on us their wishes, and these will be called justice. Power, not philosophical reflection, dominates and determines action. If you want to know what counts as justice in a society, undertake an empirical study of the relations of power among the constituencies, don't engage in ethical reflections.

Thrasymachus's reflections parallel those of Callicles in the *Gorgias*. Callicles claims that conventional morality is only a set of rules forced on us by a majority of people in a society who are weak and could not survive in an unfettered struggle for survival (483b–e). The factual analyses offered by the two accounts are different, but the underlying moral skepticism is the same.

Plato seems to see all this. For he does not treat Thrasymachus's proposal as yet another ethical analysis of justice. Instead, he seeks to elicit from Thrasymachus the ideal – in our sense – that he embodies. The same thing happens in the *Gorgias*. There, Callicles is brought to agree that his ideal is a politically powerful person. In the *Republic*, Thrasymachus is led to the same "confession." If Plato were expounding either a Kantian or a utilitarian ethics, these would be strange moves. For exposing the ideal that these dramatic figures espouse does not, by itself, refute moral skepticism. Moral skepticism is compatible with a number of ideals: for example, that of a quiet, retiring individual.

But if Plato is wanting to articulate an ideal ethics, then what he does here makes perfectly good sense. Having an ideal in our sense is unavoidable for all humans. We all have some aim or aims in life, no matter how disjointed, and we all develop some kind of character, reflectively or unreflectively.[16] The ideals elicited from Thrasymachus and Callicles show the kinds of ideals that are likely to be embraced by a typical moral skeptic. Plato then goes on to show what is wrong with the ideal embraced by Thrasymachus; and in the books of the *Republic* that follow, replaces this with his own ideal, both for the individual and for a community. Once the right ideal has been secured, Plato goes on to show – in ways already sketched in this section – that a person embodying this ideal is not a moral skeptic, but embraces many of the fine (*kalos*) attitudes that we expect of a good, cooperative individual. Along the way, Plato shows that there are objectively better and worse ways to opt for ideals. In this way, moral skepticism is not met "head on." Rather, it is shown that once we start with something that everyone must have – namely, an ideal – and become aware of better or worse ways of formulating ideals, we can arrive at a desired life pattern that does not reject morality and in this way can uncover the rational foundation of morality as well as its practical feasibility.

Thus, our interpretation of the treatment of Thrasymachus supports our interpretation of Plato's ethics as ideal ethics.

The second consideration supporting the same interpretation is based on trying to make sense of the overall structure of the *Republic*. On the assumption that in this dialogue Plato is presenting an ideal ethics, the structure can be interpreted in the following way. The first sections are taken up with shallow interpretations of morality (for example, as paying back debts) as well as moral skepticism. In the following sections, commitments to certain shallow ideals are elicited from the participants of the dialogue, and these are shown to be inadequate. Next, Plato embarks on the presentation of his own proposal for an adequate human ideal, on both the individual and the communal level. This culminates in the description of ideal character in Book 4 that we have dealt with briefly already. This character needs to be placed within the framework of an adequate epistemology and ontology, however, since the aim is to further understanding of the fundamental elements of reality and have this understanding inform our lives – hence the epistemological passage towards the end of Book 5 and the combination of epistemology and ontology in Books 6 and 7. The educational scheme in Book 7 is designed to help the individual attain the inner freedom and self-sufficiency that comes with the proper aims and related character. Books 8 and 9 show how the right life pattern compares with inadequate patterns and how it carries with it its own kinds of enjoyments. Book 10 is devoted to topics that supplement the main philosophical content, such as the arts and myths of immortality.

Can we give an equally unified conception of the *Republic* on either the utilitarian or the Kantian interpretations? If we opt for a utilitarian interpretation, then the first half of the dialogue lacks real unity, consisting as it does, first of a discussion of moral skepticism, then of a theory of political communities, and subsequently of an analysis of the good character – that is, one that leads to happiness. The notion of happiness would have to be assumed as a tacit premise in these discussions. Alternatively, one would have to interpret the discussion of virtues as providing that structure which will help maximize happiness for the greatest number. But no such claims are made in this part of the dialogue. The middle books, on this reading, simply deal with new topics. For the epistemology and ontology in the middle books could hardly be related to a utilitarian ethics. The material in Books 8 and 9 would have to be read as the philosophical climax of the dialogue; but these comparisons of life patterns and the comments about greater and lesser enjoyment do not read that way.

They are anti-climactic after the ontological sections. The interpretation of the *Republic* as working out an ideal ethics sees this as natural. We need to understand the basic structure of reality and the harmony that it contains. That such a life is also enjoyable is indeed an afterthought. Thus, on the utilitarian reading, the dialogue lacks unity.

A Kantian reading of the dialogue would require interpreting the first four books as leading to a description of character that articulates either the intrinsically, morally good agent or the condition that is essential to becoming such an agent. But both these readings are problematic. The moral attitudes of not wanting to steal or harm others in other ways are presented – as we have seen – as a consequence of having the right aim and right character, not as the climax of the exposition of the virtues. Furthermore, on this account, as on the utilitarian account, the middle books do not relate in a close conceptual way to the rest of the dialogue. One can have the attitude of not wanting to steal even if one does not have an adequate conception of the Forms. Finally, although one might regard some of the virtues – for example, wisdom and self-control – as constitutive of the good moral agent, it is more difficult to interpret courage, or "inner strength," in this manner.

These considerations are not decisive. One could always fall back on interpreting the *Republic* as a compendium of discussions of different topics. But since it is possible to interpret so many other dialogues as having organic unity, it is a relevant consideration that one can do this with the *Republic* within the ideal ethics interpretation being proposed here.

Another passage supporting this interpretation is *Republic* 357c1–358a3, where Plato says that one of the advantages of his analysis of justice is that it can be shown good both in itself and for its consequences. For a Kantian interpretation, this poses problems. If the virtues are morally good, then they are good intrinsically. That they may be good also in another, consequentialist sense is irrelevant. Furthermore, on that interpretation, Plato is guilty of equivocation. The virtues are intrinsically good in a moral sense and consequentially good in a utilitarian, or prudential, sense.

Difficulties also arise on a utilitarian reading of this passage. For, if virtue leads to happiness, then in what way is it also intrinsically good? If, on the other hand, the virtues are constitutive of happiness, then why are they also claimed to be good consequentially?

By contrast, the passage makes good sense within an ideal ethics interpretation. The virtues have intrinsic value because they constitute one half of the ideal, that of the right character. They are also good in their consequences, since they facilitate the pursuit of the right aim, the other half of the ideal. Both halves of the ideal have intrinsic merit. Thus it is not surprising that one half should be said to have good consequences insofar as it facilitates attaining the other half.

Finally, there is a passage in the *Gorgias* which illustrates how certain dialectical discussions of ethical issues in the dialogues make good sense within ideal ethics. In 497e–499a the relation between pleasure and goodness is examined. Plato shows that in some cases the good and the bad – in this context, the courageous and the cowardly – are not correlated with pleasure and pain. In spite of this, we value the virtues just the same. It has been pointed out that this is not a good argument against hedonism.[17] A hedonist could reply that although in some cases courage does not bring with it pleasure, it and the other virtues often do bring pleasure with them, and thus in the long run these are the character traits that a hedonist should cultivate.

Let us try to interpret the exchange as part of a discussion of ideal ethics. On this interpretation, Callicles is not defining good as pleasure, but is proposing an ideal: a pleasure-loving ideal. For a person embodying that ideal, the overall aim is to have as much pleasure as possible, and the related character type consists of qualities that enhance enjoyment and possession of which leads to enjoyment. Any character type with these characteristics will serve within such an ideal. All that matters is that we should be creatures who both seek and enjoy pleasure. Plato's point, then, can be read as an objection to that ideal.[18] He appeals to our intuition to show that there are contexts in which we value courage or some other virtue even if it does not lead to enjoyment. It seems, then, that there are characteristics other than the tendency to seek pleasure that we wish to include in our ideals. The point of the example is not just that, occasionally, courage does not bring pleasure, but that even in those cases, we assign to it intrinsic merit.

This construal of the argument does not portray it as a good argument for the Platonic ideal, but merely as an argument demanding revision of the pleasure-loving ideal. For the ideal to be adequate, it must include more. It requires further argument – which Plato provides elsewhere – to decide whether the adequate ideal should include pleasure seeking as a character trait having intrinsic merit or have the enjoyment accompanying the embodiment of the adequate ideal merely as a factual consequence of living that life pattern.

These considerations support the interpretation of Plato's ethics as an ideal ethics. In presenting Plato's views, I have made a number of psychological assumptions. The best source for these is *Symposium* 210–12. In the next section, this underlying moral psychology will be summarized.

Plato's Moral Psychology

Virtues play an important role in Plato's ethics. They are the constituents of the good character, and this has intrinsic value. Virtues can be interpreted in two ways.

There is the action-oriented (or behaviorist?) conception of virtue. On this view, virtues are simply dispositions to act in certain ways. Thus, for example, courage is the virtue of courage-exhibiting behavior and activity. The content of this virtue thus interpreted may or may not be specifiable exhaustively in terms of rules. According to extremely legalistic conceptions of courage, a large number of rules could collectively specify all courage-exhibiting behavior. According to other views, the indeterminacy of this large variety of behavior would make such a project impossible.

A mentalistic conception of virtue provides an alternative. On this view, a virtue is both a complex inner state, which includes beliefs, feelings, and attitudes, and the activities issuing from this state. For example, wisdom is an inner state of understanding, a set of attitudes to possible objects of aspiration informed by understanding, and a variety of related activities. Within this conception a virtue cannot be exhausted by a set of rules. How could we have rules for feeling or for forming attitudes? Rules can only govern activities.

Wisdom is one of the virtues, and we saw earlier that it involves recollection. The latter, however, involves a combination of an inner state and mental activities. Thus it provides grounds for claiming that Plato had the second, mentalistic conception of the virtues in mind. This had consequences for moral learning. Since following rules does not suffice for acquiring the virtues and manifesting them, other things must be included in moral education. Plato's holding up of Socrates as a model suggests that, for him, moral learning revolved around what we today call role modeling. The epistemology of role modeling is very difficult. How do we know how to choose the right role model, and how do we know how to steer a happy mean between slavish imitation and the sharing of qualities on such a general, abstract level as to be useless for practical purposes? Plato does not say much about this, and modern philosophy is of no additional help.

A life of virtue is linked to *eudaimonia*, sometimes translated as "happiness" or "flourishing." There are "thin" and "rich" notions of happiness. The "thin" conception of eudaimonia is a very general notion of well-being, whatever that may be. In terms of this notion, it is trivial to say that all humans aim at happiness; for all this means is that all humans want to live well, whatever that is. Agreement on this – as the opening of the *Nichomachean Ethics* shows – leaves us with disagreements on what living well consists of. The "rich" notion of happiness involves a state of being content, satisfied, pleased, happy in the ordinary sense, and experiencing much pleasure. It is far from obvious that this should be the highest good for humans or that we all want to be in this state as much as possible.

Plato uses only the "thin" notion of happiness. He would agree that the life pattern of the human who has the appropriate ideal is a happy one; but this means only that such a person would live well, not badly. This does not make eudaimonia the highest good. We can enjoy a variety of things and can think of ourselves as living well in a variety of ways. Given this situation, the question is: What should we enjoy, what should make us happy?

In view of these considerations throughout dialogues like the *Philebus* and the *Gorgias*, Plato assumes the plasticity of human nature (P1).[19] A human can experience enjoyment in connection with a wide variety of activities and can change his inner state so as to alter the sources of his enjoyment. Thus, for example, if a person enjoys eating a lot and subsequently convinces himself that this is bad for him, he can not only change his eating habits but become a person who enjoys eating only healthy food and in lesser quantities. Or if a person enjoys dominating others and convinces himself that it would be better to lead a life of cooperation and sharing, then such a person is able to change his desires and emotions so that he will come to enjoy cooperating and sharing. According to static conceptions of human nature, we have a set of basic enjoyments that correspond to fixed needs, and our task is simply to find the best means for meeting these needs. Plato's view of humans construes most of our needs as depending on our conception of ourselves. Changes in outlook and character can change needs and hence sources of enjoyment.

But the plasticity of human nature is a psychological hypothesis. It does not lead by itself to a normative critique of possible objects of desire. To support such critiques we need a second hypothesis: that not all objects of desire or attitude are of equal worth (P2).

A rational life includes enjoying those things that one values. P1 tells us that we can change our sources of enjoyment; P2 that such changes can be guided by appropriate evaluations. The way in which desires can be transformed is laid out in the famous ascent passage of the *Symposium*, 210−12. In this passage, as well as others, Plato uses *eros* to denote a generic relation which includes what we today call desire, attitude, love, aspiration, and interest.[20]

In modern philosophy, we differentiate desires and attitudes either in terms of the different causal mechanisms that bring them about or in terms of introspectively registered qualities.

Plato does not regard introspection as a reliable guide to mental topography. He also avoids explanations in terms of alleged causal mechanisms because of his distrust of mere empirical generalizations as adequate explanations, and also because no known systems of such causal accounts can explain all the relevant differences. His conceptual differentiations rely solely on differences concerning appropriate objects. Thus, as was mentioned before, we can call his theory of eros a magnet theory. He sees various objects as potential magnets that can evoke in the well-functioning human being interest and aspiration. Some magnets are more powerful than others for the rational human agent − hence shifts in attention and interest. A central fact that Plato wants to explain is intellectual interest: its awakening and maintenance. This gives modern philosophy and psychology much trouble. Introspection does not provide decisive evidence as to whether we are really interested in a subject, and no known causal mechanisms can explain why, given two equally intelligent, diligent people working in the same environment, one will become interested in, say, mathematics, and the other not.

Finally, Plato can point to what, for the rational human, is a common element among desires, attitudes, and interest. For each of these involves valuing, or "holding dear" (*philein*), an object.

As we saw, a rational eros has for Plato the following general structure: Person P has eros E towards an object x in virtue of x's characteristics C_1, C_2, . . . C_n. These C's are a subset of all the attributes of x. In order to simplify the exposition, we will make the unrealistic, but in this context harmless, assumption that the eros is in virtue of only one of x's attributes. The link "in virtue of," although it may also play a causal role, indicates justification primarily. Thus, this type of eros can be contrasted with those in which the characteristics of the object play only a causal role and considerations of what should be eros-warranting qualities do not enter into the forming of the attitude.

Plato thinks that only certain attributes can function as adequate justifications for any given attitude. For example, one can admire a person for the right or the wrong reasons. One can also take an interest in something for the right or the wrong reasons. In Plato's theory these right and wrong reasons cash out in terms of the appropriate or inappropriate attributes invoked to form and justify a given attitude. In this way, reason "rules" the soul; that is, it reveals the right eros-warranting attributes in objects. Discovering new attributes of an object opens up the possibility of new evaluations and hence new types of eros. This is one part of Plato's theory. The other part involves a progression through four stages, leading to inner harmony. We start with

S1. P has E towards x in virtue of C_n.

We need to consider this case under ideal conditions. For example, we assume that x has no other attributes that would cancel out the magnetism generated by C_n. The history of our relationship with x is also ignored, and so are the possibility of reciprocity, limitations on our energy, and so forth. Understood in this way, S1 leads to x's particularity dropping out of the picture. What matters for E is only that x has C_n. Hence, the rational person will move to

S2. P has E towards all and any x that has C_n.

Once we focus on the attribute that makes x a suitable object for E, we reach a generalization and see that under the right idealizations anything possessing the right attribute will serve as an object for E. Plato expects of the rational agent that understanding S2 should lead to

S3. P has E towards C_n.

This grates on the modern sensibility. One can admire all courageous persons, but how can we admire courage itself? Presumably Plato wants us to accept a wider notion of eros. S3 focuses on a key element in the various kinds of positive eros: namely, evaluation. If I value courageous persons, I must value courage. If I take an interest in and value all beautiful things, then I must value and take an interest in beauty. Within Plato's philosophy, three things support the move from S2 to S3. First, the projected move fits Plato's ontology; we move with our eros towards the

Forms. Secondly, it helps to explain why we should have an interest in a Form even when it is not instantiated and hence want to create instances. That the Forms are instantiated from time to time is a contingent fact, but our eros towards the Forms should not rest on this. Finally, it is S3, rather than S2, that leads to

S4.   If P has E towards C_n, then P wants as much C_n as possible – that is, wants as many instances of C_n as possible.

This thesis is expressed in the steps of creation that we find in the passage from the *Symposium*. It also motivates creation.[21] In this context the creative urge is the aspiration to extend something that we find worthy – for example, the Fine – to all the different levels and regions of reality, from aesthetics to morality to the sciences to the philosophic life.

Given rationality and this motivation, it would be absurd to want the newly created instances all for ourselves. We want more good things as parts of reality. Why should it matter in which particular region the instances come into being? (To be sure, some fine things are better appreciated when they are rare. But one can build this into the description of the object of eros.)

These considerations show that Platonic eros is neither egoistic nor altruistic. In the early stages we may want things for ourselves. But that is because we do not understand fully the object of our eros. As we move through the further stages and our eros, together with our understanding, develops and deepens, we leave the egoism behind. Our object becomes an abstract entity, and it makes no sense to be wanting an abstract object all for oneself. If we have a genuine interest in some attribute, then we would not want to be its sole instance.[22]

The process is cumulative. As we move along, we do not abandon previous objects that warranted desire; rather, we incorporate them into the larger scheme we come to adopt. If I desire healthy food, then, according to Plato's theory, if I function well, I will be wanting healthy things in general – not only for myself, but for everyone in the world. Hence my aspiration is neither selfish nor altruistic. The eros-warranting attribute C_n is in some cases – as this example shows – a species of a generic Form. There are species of knowledge, health, beauty, and so on. We discover these relationships as our eros inspires us to greater understanding. This increase in understanding and the resulting change in eros is

S5. If P has E towards C_n and C_n is a species of a generic Form F, and if P understands this relation, then P will also have E towards F.

We move from eros towards a certain kind of fineness towards eros for the Fine itself, from desire for healthy food to desire for all healthy things and eventually desire for health itself. This leads to an aspiration, *ceteris paribus*, to maximize health in the world.

To take another example, one becomes interested in mathematical proofs because of their abstractness, elegance, and explanatory power. One then moves to eros towards anything with these attributes and will want to maximize the number of entities with these attributes.

The link between eros towards the Forms and the steps of creation is based on seeing the world as imperfect. The world does not exemplify the Good fully, hence the need for creation. Seeing this point helps us to understand why psychology in the *Symposium* does not clash with the account of the good life in the *Republic*.[23] The ultimate state of well-being is contemplation. The person contemplating the Forms is self-sufficient. But this characterization must be understood as referring to ideal circumstances. As pointed out above, in the actual world, we live surrounded by imperfections. The ideal human under ideal conditions would not have the creative urge, since all would be parts of order and harmony. But humans living in the world of time and space, in separate bodies, have to face the flaws of this world. The proper response, according to Plato, is the creative urge, which is neither egoistic nor altruistic. A human engaging only in contemplation in this world is taking a narrow view and is not really valuing the Forms as a rational person living in an imperfect world would.

In interpreting the creative urge, it is important to separate it from other issues with which it can easily be confused. First, the urge to create instances does not apply to all Forms individually, but only to those, or to those complexes of Forms, that constitute order and harmony. This is not spelled out in detail in the *Symposium*, but the *Philebus* – to be discussed later – can be seen as attempting to do this.

Secondly, the contrast between a creative and a passive life should not be identified with another dichotomy: namely, that between a purely contemplative life and an "all-round" life of the sort we have come to associate with the Renaissance ideal. As we can see from the material of the previous chapter, for Plato, contemplation was never a purely passive state.

So our question about the worldly and other-worldly choice should be: which kind of creativity does Plato recommend?

As we saw above, a reconstruction of the moral psychology of the *Symposium* yields what we called S4, a step representing creativity. But one can envisage this functioning solely in terms of theoretical activity. For Plato, understanding involves calculating, proving, coming to see some of the indefinitely many connections between Forms, or discovering for oneself for the first time another way of seeing "parts" or species of a Form like justice. Within the theory of techne spelled out in the first chapter, understanding is a dynamic concept; what falls under it are states of mind as well as cognitive activities. The metaphor of recollecting given in the *Meno* already indicates this. The results of these cognitive activities are instances of the appropriate Forms, though not instances that constitute interpersonal relations or the emergence of processes or concrete things in space and time.

Are these the only creations prescribed by Plato's theory? Even if they were, this would still be nontrivial. For there are many conceptions of the contemplative life that represent it in purely passive terms, simply as seeing final results of calculation and so on. But such a final state is not envisaged in Plato's discussions of dialectic. Even the fragments of some ultimate arrangements that we might represent in our minds need be "recollected" over and over again, in order for these to function as aids to further exploration.

The ascent passage of the *Symposium* that we relied on so much in the previous pages can be read – and has been read through the centuries – in both ways: that is, as telling us that once we reach the "top," we can throw the "ladder," the previous steps, away; and as describing a life in which our horizon is progressively widened so as to allow us to incorporate the previous steps within conceptions of reality that put those previous stages in appropriate perspective. One can think of the agent who arrives at the end of the ascent either as devoting him or herself from then on solely to intellectual activity or as an "all-round" person who exhibits excellences of all kinds: aesthetic and ethical-political, as well as those needed for theorizing. Both these views have been advocated by outstanding individuals through the centuries. I find both plausible and see no evidence to support the hypothesis that Plato made up his mind and committed himself permanently to one or the other or these options. But the key point of my interpretation under discussion here is compatible with both choices. It is to explain how and why Plato thought that the understanding of the Forms leads to the production of instances of the appropriate Forms or Form complexes of one kind or another.

Still, it is incumbent on me to sketch how my interpretation, leaving this question open, is compatible with texts like *Republic* 519c–521b which indicate the reluctance of, for example, the guardians, to "return to the Cave," and educate. In the interpretation being advocated here, this amounts to saying: Why is someone active on the intellectual plane reluctant to educate those who are fundamentally ignorant and thus be active on this more visible plane? One obvious reason is the danger such a person faces, as Plato saw in the case of Socrates. And the reason they require "persuasion" to go into the Cave is not that they need to be made "productive," but because, as stated above, they live in an imperfect world, and their not doing anything about education – an admittedly dangerous field – adds to the lack of order and harmony in this larger segment of the world – that is, larger than their own mind.

Many of our desires today are possessive or consumer-oriented, such as those for food and drink. Romantic love, even if not consumer-oriented, involves degrees of possessiveness that often result in envy or jealously. Aspirations towards Platonic goods lack these features. My gaining wisdom does not destroy wisdom for others; my attaining it does not obstruct others' from attaining it. On the contrary, typically I can attain wisdom better if I cooperate with others in that task. Attaining the Platonic goods – at least in a setting without competing universities and so on – does not set one person against another, and thus issues of egoism and altruism should not arise. This stance is also supported by Plato's ontology. The objects of desire are co-instantiations of Forms and other abstract entities that we would call qualities. So is the aspiring agent. But if I am a set of possible instantiations and so are other objects, Plato sees no reason why I should want the realization of goods to be restricted to those instantiations that happen to make up "me" rather than others.

On a deep level, then, within Plato's philosophy a sharp distinction between the self and others can only stem from confusion. If we are rational and understand reality correctly, then we will not see such a distinction as fundamental, either for attaining understanding or for ethical purposes. Our concern will be primarily with the general and only derivatively with the particular. Only when we fail in this do problems arise. This can be seen from passages like *Republic* 547b7–c4, where Plato maintains that emergence of interest in the self and the accompanying possessiveness are caused by the abandonment of reason and the subsequent degeneration in conduct. The object for reason is always the general.

Plato mentions various considerations that justify his ideal. One of these is the relation between inner harmony and harmony on a cosmic scale. Another is the attainment of real freedom, in the sense of rational self-determination. Finally, a person with Plato's ideal achieves self-sufficiency (*Lysis* 215a). This does not mean a hermit-like life, but lack of vulnerability from environmental factors, including possible lack of esteem by others.

Needless to say, there are many aspects of Plato's ethics that have not been covered in this chapter. I have restricted my presentation to supporting the claim that Plato's ethics is an ideal ethics. It does not allow for independence of a moral component from a theory of human good. Rather, it presents a theory of human good that has appropriate moral conduct as among its consequences. It is a theory of human good that was labeled "ideal ethics" because it singles out our overall aim in life and a character structure that has intrinsic merit and is also required for the realization of the aim as the highest human good. It assigns to virtues an important role, since these specify the good character structure. As we have seen, Plato proposes as the right ideal our having the understanding of goodness and harmony in the world and in human lives, as well as their instantiation, as our overall aim and a character structure in which reason and understanding inform and thus orient our attitudes, desires, and feelings. The resulting ethics is not only neither Kantian nor utilitarian; it is also neither egoistic nor altruistic. The objects of the aspiration of the good human turn out to be among the Forms discussed in the last chapter, and the understanding required to grasp cosmic harmony and goodness is the kind we found in Plato's epistemology in chapter 1.

Plato's ideal ethics has much relevance to our own times. This will be discussed in Part III.

Appendix 1: *Ideal Ethics and the Community*

We have seen that the Platonic ideal requires some cooperation between humans. This raises the larger question of how Plato's individual ethics and his political theory are related. Needless to say, I cannot attempt within the confines of this book to deal with all the complex issues involved in interpreting Plato's theory of political and other social units. I shall simply concentrate on a couple of issues most relevant to the interpretation of Platonic ethics presented in this chapter.

I will consider the following two questions: (a) What kinds of political and, in general, communal organizations can fulfill the requirements of having members with the Platonic ideal? (b) Given that within Platonic moral psychology, the distinctions between self and others, as well as those between the individual and collections of individuals, are blurred, what implications does this have for communal life and organization?

The start to answering (a) must be to recall that the cooperation required by the individual ideal is centered on efforts to increase understanding and create instances of order and harmony. Thus, the cooperative Platonic community is based on shared values and aims. These shared values leave plenty of room for individual variations in personality, habit, and so on. But it is a fundamental presupposition of Plato's notion of a healthy community. To the extent that this presupposition is rejected or regarded as unrealistic by modern political theorists, they and Plato are focusing on different questions.

As we shall see, not only Plato, but also his opponents, assumed that one does not discuss political structures as such, but always political structures within a certain way of life or within the context of shared values. A structure that grants individual members much freedom of choice may be used for good or bad purposes, depending on the values prevalent in society. For example, given a lot of selfishness and hatred, individual freedom will be used to raise the crime rate and to vent anger on minorities or neighboring countries.

It is fashionable in modern political theory to contrast democracy, which allegedly grants individuals much choice, with authoritarianism, which forces structure and edicts on the members of society.[24] Plato's theory of a good community does not fit either of these molds. Given the shared aims and values, it is obvious that not everyone is equally qualified to assume responsibility for decision making. Thus, unequal power distribution, which in this framework amounts to unequal distribution of responsibility, will be accepted voluntarily by members of the community (*Republic* 431d9–e2). Communal life will revolve around agreed-upon educational projects. Within such a conception, the only way to deal with those not sharing the community's values is education. Plato has no good answer to the question of what to do with people who do not share these values and who also reject educational opportunities.

The answer to (b) revolves around the question of what has intrinsic value. For Plato, instances of goodness making up groups and instances constituting individuals are of equal value. For him, it is neither the case that larger units are merely means for making individuals good and happy or that the individual is merely a means to making the larger units (countries, city-states, and so forth) good. Thus, once more we see Plato not fitting either the democratic, individual-oriented conception or the state- or nation-oriented authoritarian model. Since his conception involves both individual and community having intrinsic value, it fits the mold of normative communitarianism.[25] Clashes between the individual and the larger unit are less likely to occur in a Platonic framework, since the aims of both are in accordance with the ideal we sketched.

These brief answers to our two questions will be fleshed out as we compare the best statement in defense of democracy in Plato's time with Plato's conception of individual and communal good. This statement is the famous funeral oration of Pericles, as reconstructed by Thucydides. The following are the philosophically important points of this discourse:

1   Athenians have a democracy, an organization in which power rests with the majority and not with a minority of the people (II.37.1).
2   Athenians enjoy equality before the law (II.37.1).
3   Public office is held on the basis not of social position, but of relevant abilities (II.37.1).
4   Because of the respect and reverence that they have for the law (*deos*), Athenians do not violate it (II.37.10−13).
5   Athenians love fine things, while retaining simplicity (or frugality; *euteleia*), and their love of wisdom does not make them soft or spoiled (opening lines of II.40.1).
6   Athenians believe in the unity of thought (or discourse; *logos*) and action (or work; *ergon*) (II.40.2).
7   Athens is an education for the rest of the Hellenic world (II.41.1).
8   Within the Athenian conception, the happy person is a free person, and the free person is courageous (II.43.4).[26]

Since point 4 follows the points about democracy, the scheme suggests that people will respect institutions if they have ways of influencing them. As John Finley puts it, "This system evokes energy from the individual citizen."[27]

As Solmsen has pointed out, although the word *kalon* does not occur in it, the main claim of (5) is that Athenian life is organized around the pursuit of fine things.[28] (We do have in these lines the occurrence of a related word, *philokaloumen*.)

Much can be, and has been, said about these issues.[29] I shall consider only a few points that are relevant to the preceding discussion. Pericles does not defend democracy on the ground either that it maximizes pleasure or that it is the most efficient way for a state to function and survive. He "rests his claim for democracy on what has become recognized as its principal sanction: its educational value to the human spirit, rather than its mere efficacy as a form of government."[30]

We see from (5) that within this conception, too, a form of government is considered within the context of shared values. It would be odd to find in discussions of political systems today conjectures as to whether in a proposed state people care for classical philosophy, Beethoven, and so on, or not. But for reasons mentioned above, Plato and his contemporaries thought that the nature of the shared values and the presupposition that some values need to be shared are crucial. It is reasonable to suppose, for example, that Pericles thought of (5) as explaining in part the Athenians' adherence to (3) and (4), and the mere fact of (1) certainly does not by itself give ground for supposing that (2) and (3) will hold.

Pericles' conceptions of "fine things" and "love of wisdom" are different from Plato's. Some of the key notions of the Periclean scheme, such as *paideia*, *eudaimonia*, *kalon*, *nomos*, and *ergon* ("education," "well-being," "fine," "law," and "functioning") certainly have their echoes in the Platonic dialogues. But Plato, as we saw, pours new wine into these old skins. The key difference is in the respective conceptions of wisdom and understanding. Pericles did not have in mind the kind of theoretical insight and understanding that Plato regarded as central to rationality. This difference accounts not only for the differences listed above, but also for their differing views on freedom and happiness.

For Pericles, democracy leads to freedom, and freedom to happiness. His notion of freedom is presumably captured in (1) and (2) above; that is, for him, freedom is, roughly, being able to do what one wants. Freedom is also having opportunities and other enabling conditions to be able to realize what one wants. So the people should be able to choose freely what they want; the city should provide means and opportunities. Moreover the city as a whole must be free from enemies. Athens must be free if its citizens are to be free. This is why freedom depends on courage – that is, military courage.

Plato also talks about freedom, but his notion of freedom is radically different from Pericles'. The educational process – described in the Cave analogy and in the tough curricular description that follows – brings freedom to the practitioner as he is released from his chains (*Republic* 515c4–6). This is the freedom of rational self-knowledge and ensuing self-determination. It creates inner harmony and enables a person to pursue appropriate goals.

Thus we need to distinguish three kinds of freedom:

1 Platonic freedom;
2 Being able to do as one wishes, the most commonly invoked notion;
3 Being set free by being enabled to accomplish various things: for example, to be able to avail oneself of an educational system is an enabling condition, and both Plato and Pericles agree that it is important. But they disagree with regard to the most important things to be secured.

The key differences are with respect to the first and second kinds of freedom and the relation of these to happiness.

Pericles stresses the importance of the second kind. Let us reconstruct Plato's response in terms of the following theses. Plato recognizes the importance of this second kind (e.g. *Republic* 557b4–10), but holds that

> giving all citizens this kind of freedom will not guarantee, or even make it probable, that the city will be similarly free (thesis 1).

This thesis expresses Plato's skepticism towards a democratic structure as such. Without shared values of the right sort, it can rapidly degenerate into mob rule and result in as much harm as do many authoritarian governments. Furthermore, it will lack the virtues needed to keep the larger unit free in this way.

Historians writing in the wake of World War II felt that they could assume the superiority of democracy when it came to self-defense. Their grounds, however, would not convince Plato. He would point to the fact that during that war it was necessary to impose many restrictions on civil liberties. He would argue that to the extent that democracies were able to defend themselves, they had to incorporate some features of a government by experts that resembles the Platonically ideal community.

> Plato's second thesis would be that the freedom of a city in the second sense can be assured only by its citizens being free in the first sense (thesis 2).

For a city to be free in this second sense, it must defend itself against external foes. A person leading a Platonically ideal life will understand the value of his city and will want to defend it. Furthermore, a city with that kind of citizenry will have the required knowledge and skill to develop a sound defensive force and strategy. Citizens who are Platonically free will also recognize the need for a leader with the required abilities to take charge in defense of their state. It may happen that a citizenry lacking this kind of freedom will succeed for a while in defending itself from external foes. But in Plato's view, such success would depend solely on contingent and thus easily changeable power relations and not on having the required virtues and skills, which are relatively immune from destruction by shifts in power and prestige.

> Plato's third thesis would read: A city can be free in the Platonic sense only if its citizens are also free in this sense (thesis 3).

This thesis is at the heart of Plato's analogy between the structure of an individual and the structure of a community (*Republic* 368d). The community itself must reflect order and harmony, and this cannot be simply the sum of the order and harmony within individual citizens. On the other hand, the harmony of the community depends partly on the healthy state of its parts – that is, on the harmony within individuals. Plato saw that the good and well-being of the community is not just the sum of the good and well-being of its citizens, thereby anticipating what is today called "the prisoner's dilemma."

It is easy to misunderstand this thesis. Plato does not think that a city-state or some other political community could survive if every citizen devoted all his time to the contemplation of the Forms. If one wants to consider an actual community in which Platonically good humans try to realize a Platonically good community, then one should consider Plato's great creation, the Academy (or at least the way Plato presumably intended it), rather than the sketch of a state in the middle books of the *Republic*. For the sketch is based on the assumptions that not everyone is equally qualified to attain understanding and that a state needs more than just theoreticians in order to survive.

Platonic freedom admits of degrees. It is at the core of Plato's conception of individual and communal good and in what makes Plato's views about communities not fit into any of the ordinary conceptual pigeon-holes which we use to classify governmental structures.

This brief sketch should help us see how fundamentally different Plato's thinking about communal good and political structure is from what we find in contemporary political theory. Does this mean that we should not be concerned with efforts to create an atmosphere of shared values in various layers of social structuring on this globe, and that we should regard freedom of the second type as a fundamental right, regardless of the actual values embraced by members of society? In Part III I will argue for the importance of reconsidering Plato's type of communitarianism today.

Appendix 2: *Aesthetic Devices and the Platonic Ideal*

At the core of Platonic moral psychology, we find intellectual aspiration to attain more and more theoretical insight and the resulting wisdom. This striving is to have a profound effect on character, making us into reasonable and cooperative individuals wanting to live in a flourishing community of the sort sketched in Appendix 1. The Periclean ideal suggests that interest in drama and the other splendid achievements of Greek art should provide the "fine things" to inspire us. Plato's style of dialogue writing and his comments on the various arts show that he was sensitive to the moving power of what we today call aesthetic objects. So how does the aesthetic fit into the Platonic ideal?

We cannot attempt to cover all the difficult interpretative issues that surround

Plato's theory of art.[31] In this brief sketch I shall restrict attention to three questions that are linked closely to the interpretation of Plato's epistemology and ethics presented so far:

1   Some objects that today we would call beautiful, including some works of art, reflect the Forms of the Fine, Order, and so forth so why should aesthetic objects not be given a respectable ontological status?
2   Some of the arts provide educational material in the Platonic curriculum (*Republic* 377b–c, 522a), so why should the poet be dismissed from the ideal community (595a–b)? Is this consistent?
3   If aesthetic devices in literature and the plastic arts are harmful, why does Plato employ some of these in his own dialogues? (e.g. the sun simile in *Republic* 507a, the chariot image of the soul in *Phaedrus* 246a).[32]

Before I attempt to answer these questions, herewith a few general remarks. The modern term "aesthetics" tends to cover up two distinct enterprises. One of these is a theory of art, dealing with such questions as the significance of originality, accomplishment, and so on, factors that also influence the appreciation of art, at least in modern times. The other is a theory of aesthetic beauty; that is, an analysis of an alleged property or properties that parts of nature or works of art possess that makes these objects aesthetically valuable.

In Plato's writings, as well as in Aristotle's, these two enterprises are distinct. But even when considered on their own, the two investigations differ radically from their modern counterparts. Plato, unlike modern philosophers like Kant, does not have a separate concept of aesthetic beauty. As *Symposium* 210–12 shows, what we call the aesthetically beautiful is for Plato "the fine in appearance" and thus one species within the generic Form of the Fine (*kalon*).[33] Viewing the beautiful as a species of the genus that includes fine mathematical proofs, fine character, and so on implies that, for Plato, what makes an object beautiful is the extent to which it reflects the same harmony and order that he discovers in ontologically higher types. (Modern Californian usage seems to accord with Plato. For example, "a beautiful proof" or "a beautiful person" carries with it roughly the connotations of what Plato means by "fine.")

Plato's theory of art also differs from modern theories in its fundamental assumptions. Given the Platonic epistemology, one does not expect to find in Plato interest in or appreciation of individual originality and novelty. We saw in the *Gorgias* how the epistemic possibilities are reduced to the question: Is it a genuine technē or not? A negative answer to this question would leave a modern theoretician with many alternatives, but further divisions of this sort are not envisaged by the Platonic epistemology.

Let us turn to the first question. Plato sees (e.g. *Phaedrus* 250b–d) that the Form of Fine has sensible instances. Combining this with what the *Symposium* shows, we reach the conclusion that although beauty does manifest itself in physical objects, including some works of art, this is, from Plato's point of view, a low grade fineness.

It is low-grade in two distinct ways. First, it is low-grade because particulars are low-grade for Plato. They are subject to change and decay and also contain imperfections. But beauty is also low-grade fineness for Plato because order and harmony can never be embodied in sensible entities to the extent to which they can be manifested in abstract entities. Order among mathematical and geometrical entities is only a certain kind of order, but its limitations do not consist in being affected by "disorderly elements." Thus beauty has an ontological status for Plato that makes it more respectable than, for example, physical pleasure in the *Phaedo*, but less respectable than the Forms and other abstract entities required for philosophical dialectic, mathematics, and so forth.

This answer to the first question helps also in answering the second. The help that some of the arts provide for the educational curriculum is preliminary and preparatory. They help to orient us towards certain kinds of harmony although they not provide the best examples of these.

Not all the arts have the same status. Music produces abstract objects whose structure can be studied by a genuine technē – that is, the study of harmony. It is a mistake to think that just because in modern philosophy the general question "What is art?" is raised, Plato would also have such a monolothic view. His negative views apply mostly to literature and the plastic arts.

To understand Plato's views on these, we need to go back to the point raised earlier, and see not only why these cannot be genuine technai in the Platonic sense, but also why this leaves fewer conceptual possibilities for them than does modern philosophic aesthetic theory. The true Platonically "erotic" person regards all stages of life and their products as pointing towards the understanding of the Forms and the accompanying freedom and self-determination. At the basis of this is the genuine theoretical understanding that is fundamental to any legitimate technē. The poet and the painter need not have this. Their work does not require meeting the conditions necessary for technē. The artist lacks the theoretical understanding that we find in mathematics, geometry, and music theory. This by itself would not be fatal. But we must add to this the basic difference between how the Platonically good person and the artist view products in the world of senses. Noetic aspirations require that we view these as at best leading or pointing to elements of higher levels of reality. But the inspired artist does not regard his or her work as pointing beyond itself to other elements of reality, but rather, sees it as self-contained. Even if ideas or images are conveyed by it, the type of communication is itself viewed as one of the highest human attainments. This clash in attitude between the Platonic philosopher and the poet towards a poem or painting accounts for Plato's wanting to send away the latter. For Plato the appearances – the level at which the poet moves – are helpful only if they point beyond themselves to the underlying reality. But for the poet, the level at which he or she works is self-contained. There is nothing more real than the emotions, conflicts, activities, and sufferings described by his or her work.

So if the artist does not have genuine understanding of reality, he or she must be a mere pleasure-producer, even if some of the resulting pleasures are of a refined type. Plato is only too aware of how much pleasure art can give (*Republic* 603a10–c8) and of its moving power (601b1–4, 605a2–6, 605c10–d5). Given the dichotomy of either having a genuine technē or being a mere pleasure-producer, the artist is located in the latter category and seen, moreover, as an unusually dangerous member of that group.

This austere view cries out for the consideration of other alternatives. One of these is Aristotle's view that while art primarily affects our emotions, it can do something useful with these, even if it is not a substitute for ethical guidance.[34] But even this view is remote from modern aesthetics in its fundamental assumptions.

The main relevant difference is that Plato has no separate faculty of taste or aesthetic capacity that would allow him to separate art both from the theoretical disciplines and from the empirical pleasure-producers. The trichotomy resulting from adding taste to the faculties is exemplified by Kant's Third Critique and has dominated modern aesthetics. It is difficult to compare a theory of art without this trichotomy with one that has it, since the two theories have very different ways of accounting for aesthetic experience. Furthermore, it is an open question whether the addition of taste or an aesthetic faculty really provides a nonvacuous explanation for the alleged uniqueness of aesthetic experience. Aristotle can find something useful for art to do. On a smaller scale, so does Plato. He sees that the successful literary work of art portrays primarily the manifestation of passion and emotion (*Republic* 604d–e), but he admits that in some cases art represents images of excellence (600e5–6). He also thinks that good can come from artistic representations of the deeds of our ancestors (*Phaedrus* 245a2–5). But basically, Plato looks at art as either a mere pleasure-producer or a candidate for giving ethical advice, and by and large he finds art wanting for the latter job. Only a genuine technē can qualify.

There is more room in Aristotle for assigning ethical value to literary representations. For in Aristotle's psychology there is room for the kind of sensitivity to suffering, compassion, and so on that is not derived from theoretical understanding but is still regarded by many as useful for the everyday application of virtues.

Regardless of whether we think of a nonrepresentational painter or a poet writing modern verse or more traditional forms of literature and painting, the artist is, from a Platonic point of view, mired in the world of "sights and sounds" (*Republic* 474–7) even if he or she succeeds in representing what Aristotle would call universals. For Plato, a discipline dealing with sensibles can be of value only if it uses its objects to point beyond these to elements of a higher ontological level.

The last remarks also provide the clue as to how Plato would answer our third question. Devices utilizing what we grasp through the senses are useful if they point beyond themselves and harmful if they cause us to view the sensible realm as self-contained.

The diagram used in the *Meno* in connection with learning geometry is an obvious illustration. As long as it is an aid in coming to understand relations between the Forms, relations that can be represented only incompletely in a diagram, the sensible device is useful. But if viewed as the ultimate object for geometry, then it is harmful and deceptive. Viewing things the right or wrong way is also illustrated – on some readings – by the two middle sections of the Divided Line in Book 6 of the *Republic*. The two sections are of equal length, suggesting to some of us that they represent the same entities – that is, diagrams, but viewed in appropriate and inappropriate ways.

We can illustrate this point in connection with metaphors and similes. Expressions like "the cruelties of April" or "the hawk on fire" call to our attention similarities and analogies that mere literal talk might not reveal. But the elements of the comparison are on the same ontological level. By contrast, Plato's analogies and metaphors, such as the soul being a pilot or the Form of Good being like the sun, take something visible in the wide sense of the term (sun, pilot) and use this to help us to understand underlying reality – that is, characteristics of elements like the soul or a Form that are on a higher ontological plane. Metaphoric ascent can have cognitive and educational value, but a self-contained metaphor that pleases only our sensibility and leaves us on the same ontological plane cannot. The Platonic ideal pulls us towards the realm of the abstract, but an artist would not want to play second fiddle to theory; Plato's "appearances" are his reality.

NOTES

1 For such a broad view of ethics, see also L. Wittgenstein, "A Lecture on Ethics."

2 K. Dover, *Greek Popular Morality in the Time of Plato and Aristotle.*

3 K. Dover, "The Portrayal of Moral Evaluation in Greek Poetry," p. 47.

4 Ibid., p. 44.

5 For a more detailed exposition, see J. Moravcsik, "The Role of Virtue in Alternatives to Kantian and Utilitarian Ethics."

6 I mention Bentham as a classical paradigmatic utilitarian philosopher. Today, there are many versions of utilitarianism, and not everything that I say here about Bentham's view applies equally to all these versions.

7 For an illuminating account, see W. Frankena, *Ethics.*

8 Ibid., pp. 13–14.

9 Ibid., p. 49.

10 See J. Mabbott, "Is Plato's *Republic* Utilitarian?"

11 e.g. J. Cooper, "Plato's Theory of Human Motivation."

12 That reason does not play a merely instrumental role is seen also in J. Annas, *An Introduction to Plato's* Republic, p. 134.

13 J. Moravcsik, "Ancient and Modern Conceptions of Health and Medicine."

14 V. Cobb-Stevens, "Commentary," pp. 32–3.

15 That Thrasymachus's claim is not just a matter of giving a definition has been recognized, though with an interpretation different from that given in this chapter, in Annas, *Introduction to Plato's* Republic, pp. 36–7.

16 This is discussed in more detail in Moravcsik, "Role of Virtue."

17 T. Irwin, *Plato's Gorgias*, pp. 203–5.

18 Dover, "Portrayal of Moral Evaluation," p. 40, seems to support this reading.

19 J. Moravcsik, "Plato's Ethics as Ideal Building," p. 11.

20 D. Hailperin, "Platonic Eros and What Men Call Love," thinks of eros not as love but as desire broadly construed.

21 For other accounts, see G. Santas, "Plato on Love, Beauty, and the Good."

22 The same conclusion with different arguments is presented in Irwin, *Plato's Gorgias*, p. 169.

23 For the relevant passages in the *Republic*, see G. Santas, "Two Theories of Good in Plato's *Republic*."

24 e.g. K. Popper, *The Open Society and its Enemies*.

25 For elucidation, see J. Moravcsik, "Communal Ties."

26 J. Moravcsik, "Plato and Pericles on Freedom and Politics."

27 J. Finley, *Thucydides*, p. 147.

28 F. Solmsen, *Intellectual Experiments of the Greek Enlightenment*, p. 153.

29 See J. de Romily, *Thucydides and Athenian Imperialism*, pp. 134–7; Solmsen, *Intellectual Experiments*, pp. 108–9.

30 Finley, *Thucydides*, p. 145.

31 For a standard treatment, see R. Lodge, *Plato's Theory of Art*.

32 For more discussion, see J. Moravcsik, "Noetic Aspiration and Artistic Inspiration."

33 J. Moravcsik, "Reason and Eros in the Ascent-Passage of the *Symposium*."

34 See J. Lear, "Katharsis."

Part II

The Many-Splendored Nature of the Forms and the Ontology of Order

———————————— ◆ ————————————

Whenever we try to pick out something by itself, we find it hitched to everything else in the universe.

John Muir

4

The *Parmenides*: Forms and Participation Reconsidered

◆

In the dialogues that we considered in Part I, we saw Plato developing the theory of Forms. This theory presents a conception of reality and appearance. That contrast, in turn, is a vital part of Plato's epistemology and ethics. For the epistemology focuses on how we can understand reality and separate it from mere appearances, while the ethics helps us to orient our lives towards the appreciation of what is genuine order among elements of reality and away from the relationships we find among mere appearances.

Plato has to give an account of the nature of the Forms that enables these entities to play the following roles: they constitute the most fundamental layer of reality; they account for stability and order in reality; and finally, they explain whatever derivative stability and order we find among appearances. Does the account of the Forms given in the dialogues that we have looked at so far adequately show how the Forms can play all these roles?

It seems that Plato's way of drawing the reality–appearance distinction and, in terms of this, the portrait of the Forms leaves us with some unanswered questions revolving around the alleged explanatory roles of the Forms:

1 Does each of the Forms have "full being" and self-sufficiency, as required by the accounts of the middle dialogues? If so, how can the Forms be related to each other? Yet the explanatory roles require relatedness. If the thesis that the Forms are at the end of the ontological explanatory chain requires both that they be self-sufficient and that they be related to each other, how is this to be resolved? An adequate answer to this question leads to the next question.

2 Some of the epistemological assumptions about understanding and

some of the ethical assumptions, such as the unity of virtues, demand that the Forms be interrelated. Does the solution to question 1 leave us with relations among the Forms that will serve to fill the roles demanded by ethics and epistemology?

3   Do adequate answers to questions 1 and 2 require reconsideration of the nature of participation? Does partaking of a Form entail partaking of a whole system of Forms and can it play a key role in the contrast between reality and appearance? The need to face this question can be seen by reflecting on the fact that the characterization of partaking in passages like *Symposium* 211b1−5 is primarily negative. Being told that partaking does not affect the nature of the Form of which other elements partake is not sufficient to answer the cluster of questions grouped here.

Answering question 1 requires a redescription of the nature of the Forms. This is done in the *Parmenides*, the first part of which shows what being the Forms must have if they are to play their explanatory roles, and the second part of which spells out, in an indirect way, this mode of being. The articulation of the required relationships is spelled out in the *Sophist*, as we shall see in chapter 5. The nature of the relationships called for in answer to question 2 and proof that these are consistent with what the *Sophist* proposes are given in the dialogues discussed in chapter 6. Question 3 is never faced head on, because Plato at this stage has shown several ways of drawing the distinction between appearance and reality, and he remained unsure as to how much of a burden should remain in this respect on the notion of partaking. Nevertheless, hints towards solutions are provided in the material covered in chapters 4, 5, and 6.

The Platonic contrast between reality and appearance depends on the presentation of the Forms as constituting reality. There are two vantage points from which this contrast can be criticized. On the one hand, one can argue that the gap between reality and appearance is not as great as represented by Plato. This is the tack taken by Aristotle. Roughly, he thought that what is real and fundamental is still in space and time, even though some of its aspects, as Plato saw, are not perceptible. On the other hand, by questioning whether Plato really proceeds in presenting reality as a plurality of intelligible elements, one might try to show that the gap between reality and appearance is greater than Plato thought it to be. If reality has "full being," maybe it cannot consist of a plurality of elements. Maybe it is indissolubly one, and the appearances have no stability or order, being merely illusory. This would be the approach of someone who adhered to Eleatic ontology, developed before Plato, and it is the approach to which Plato responds in dialogues like the *Parmenides* and the *Sophist*. Plato's response can be seen as a series of modifications of the views surveyed in Part I, in particular, modifications centering on the three points listed above. Plato vindicates his conception of reality as a plurality of entities against the Eleatic attack by articulating various relationships among the Forms. The notion of partaking is also modified. The result of all this is that a number of key Platonic notions are now openly seen as "primitives" – that is, basic, indefinable elements. And, of course, the more of these we add to a theory, the less clear it is what the explanatory force of that theory is. Someone steeped in the subsequent history of philosophy might think that, as a result of the modifications, Forms are transformed into the universals of later ontologies, and partaking becomes the predicative tie. We shall see, however, that this is not the case. Even if the realm of Forms is expanded, it does not become co-extensive with that of universals, and the respective characterizations remain different. Furthermore, it is not the case that for every predicative relation, Plato would posit a partaking relation.

Above all, Plato's ontology remains focused on the contrast between reality and appearance and on metaphysical explanations, rather than the mere taking of ontological inventories. This issue bears critically on how one reads the *Parmenides*. Do the arguments contained in this dialogue challenge the explanatory power of the theory of Forms, or do they merely concentrate on the question: Do the Forms exist?

One can deny that the theory of Forms has genuine explanatory power, while still maintaining that the Forms exist. For example, an ontology aiming only at an inventory of what there is could adopt such a stance. But if, as I argued, Plato focuses on the reality–appearance distinction and ascribes to the key elements of reality certain ontological-explanatory roles, then he cannot be satisfied with such a position.

The first part of the *Parmenides* outlines the theory of Forms and its ontological explanations and dependencies. This is presented as a cure for Eleatic monism. It is followed, however, by a series of questions challenging the explanatory power of the theory. Do the Forms and the partaking relations provide nonvacuous explanatory accounts of reality and appearances as collections of intelligible elements? The searching questions and challenges push towards less metaphorical and more purely theoretical accounts of the Forms and of partaking and at the same time raise the possibility of adding a number of primitives, or basic indefinable notions, to Plato's account of ontology. The main claim of this chapter with regard to these passages is that the focus is not on the existence but on the explanatory roles of the Forms and that reflection on these leads to modifications of the ontological accounts of the middle period dialogues.

The second part of the dialogue consists of a series of difficult, convoluted arguments, leading to certain characterizations of "the One." It has been interpreted in a variety of ways. The main claim of this chapter with regard to this section is that in it we find an indirect, or negative, account of the unique mode of being of the Forms and of participation. Though the ontology loses some of its intuitive explanatory power, it retains enough content to stand up against the charge of vacuousness. In this way, it prepares the answers to questions 1, 2, and 3 given in subsequent dialogues.

Many questions can be, and have been, raised about the *Parmenides*. Here we shall confine ourselves to the following issues: What, if any, conception of the Forms emerges in this dialogue? Does it require changes in the conception examined in chapter 2? Does the notion of partaking as presented in the *Phaedo* require modifications? How do these clarifications help us to assess the explanatory power of the theory of Forms?

Addressing these questions is a formidable task. Thus many other questions – for example, the consequences of the arguments of this dialogue for geometry, the analysis of time, and cosmology – will not be treated, although they have been discussed repeatedly throughout the centuries and in our own time.[1]

Eleatic Being or Platonic Being?

The opening part of the dialogue contrasts Eleatic and Platonic being (128e–129d). The Platonic view of Forms and of partaking is shown to account for the partial stability and order of the world of appearances. But if the stability and order of appearances is explained in terms of the nature of the Forms, then it must also be shown that elements on this second level have a coherent nature and that they can serve an ontological explanatory function. This issue takes up a large part of the opening section of the dialogue.

First, Zeno's objections to a conception of reality as a plurality of distinct entities are briefly sketched. Next, Parmenides' positive doctrine of monism is introduced. Zeno and Parmenides are two sides of the Eleatic coin. One shows that pluralistic ontologies lead to absurdities, whereas the other presents a coherent monistic ontology.

Plato shows how the theory of Forms can meet Zeno's objections.[2] As a sample of the Eleatic critique, we are presented with the claim that nothing can be both like and unlike. This is an instance of a pair of opposites characterizing the same thing, a state of affairs regarded as absurd by the Eleatics. Given the Forms and the partaking relation, however, the absurdity vanishes. An element x can partake of the Like in respect of Z to entity y and partake of the Unlike in respect of W to entity t, where it is possible also that y = t. This account of the Forms and of partaking coincides with what we saw in the *Phaedo*. Indeed, there is evidence that Plato had this in mind, for in 129d3–4 the "sticks and stones" that are familiar already to readers of the *Phaedo* are mentioned. Thus Plato explains likeness and unlikeness on level 1 by introducing ontological elements on level 2. This mode of explanation requires the separateness of Forms and participants. In fact, separateness (*choris*) is mentioned repeatedly (e.g. 130b2, 3, 4). The Forms are separate from the world of appearances in the way spelled out already in the *Symposium*. The Forms do not depend on the appearances for their existence and are not affected by being participated in. But now that we have explained level 1 in terms of level 2, can we show that the problems that plagued elements on level 1 will not return to haunt the elements on level 2? In this particular case, this amounts to asking whether the Forms themselves will suffer from being characterized by pairs of opposites (129b6–c3). If this situation obtains, then the same questions can be raised about the explanans as were raised about the explanandum (130a2).

In order for the Forms to be genuine explanantes, they cannot have the properties that make the explananda problematic. The fact that in some ways the Forms are also characterized by some opposites is implicit in the middle period dialogues. But in the *Parmenides* it is faced head on. Thus, it has just been shown that nothing is simply like and unlike; likeness is in some respect and in relation to some other entity. Why not just apply this relativization to likeness among the Forms themselves? This maneuver by itself will not satisfy the Eleatic critique. In the case of the first-level participants, we had to go to a different ontological level to account for the phenomena. The Eleatic challenge demands that in the case of the Forms, the same metaphysical "medicine" can be administered without having to go to a still higher level of ontology. The point, then, is not merely to eliminate what today would be called a conceptual puzzle, but to defend at the same time the claim that the Forms provide the ontologically ultimate explanatory level. One line of approach open to Plato in this context is to attempt a theory within which Forms are related to each other and not to a higher plane, even when we account for opposites applying to them. As we shall see in chapter 5, this, in fact, is the alternative for which Plato opted.

He ended up maintaining the separation and self-sufficiency of Forms, but not as so many atomic elements, rather as parts of an interrelated field. This field has self-sufficiency in a way in which the world of appearances does not. Furthermore, this self-sufficient field has stability and order and is related to appearances in such a way as to endow them with whatever order and stability they have. Thus the Forms retain their ontological explanatory role.

It is important to note that answering the Eleatic objections and defending Plato's anti-Eleatic ontology do not call for a general theory of predication. Plato need not show that all the structures of language that we call predicative are immune to the Eleatic attack. He need show only that those sentences that express truths about the interrelations of Forms are immune to Eleatic objections, and that this can be the case even if there is no ontological plane beyond that of the Forms.

Countering Eleatic monism with a theory of Forms also requires an account of how the Forms are "many" — that is, how they provide principles for individuating these entities. In chapter 2, we saw that a strong kind of self-attribution was intended to solve this problem. But if, in answering the Eleatics, this characterization of the Forms is significantly modified, a new set of devices is needed. We shall see later how Plato responds to this problem. Some commentators like Cornford think that Plato wants us to see through the objections raised and see them as shallow.[3] Others think that the objections raised are so serious as to require a drastic reformulation, if not abandonment, of Plato's ontology.[4] But it seems that neither of these extreme views is called for. Questioning the explanatory power of a theory need not lead to rejection of the existence of one of its key elements; on the other hand, questions about individuation of abstract elements are hardly shallow.

The first critical question raised in this section of the dialogue concerns the range of the realm of Forms. The mathematical-quantitative and valuational Forms mentioned correspond to the range given by the *Phaedo*. Forms for natural kinds are already invoked in the *Timaeus*. But the objector pushes on and asks whether there are Forms for mud, dirt, and hair (130d). Socrates, as defender of the Forms, is represented as not having made up his mind. One can only speculate as to the considerations that are meant to play decisive roles here. If the fact that the newly proposed Form-kinds do not have a valuationally high status seems to count against them, this will be remedied in subsequent dialogues. But perhaps it is the question of whether all natural kinds and significant subspecies of these are to count as Forms. In any case, there is no indication in the text that the question raised is meant to suggest that there might be a Form corresponding to everything that in later philosophy is called a universal. Plato is wondering whether what is true of some might not be true of all; but the "all" here is presumably the extent of all natural kinds, whether highly valued or not, and not the range of all entities that correspond to predicate expressions. The criteria could be, and presumably still are, whether the newly proposed objects constitute a part of a domain of a genuine reality as characterized in the dialogues studied in Part I.

After this preliminary questioning, the debate turns to scrutiny of the notion of partaking (130e5–131e7). Etymologically, the Greek term used relates to sharing. Can Plato's notion be made intelligible by analogies to already understood cases of sharing? This is not a trivial or shallow question. If the answer is negative, we can fall back on having this notion as a basic indefinable concept that is not comparable to any other. But to that extent the explanatory power of the whole theory suffers.

The argument is prefaced by a dilemma. If x shares in y, then x has either a part of y or the whole of it. This is true of such everyday experiences as sharing food and other economic goods. It could also be thought that it is true of less physical goods such as happiness. ("There is just so much happiness to go around".) But, as our examination of *Symposium* 211 has already suggested, Plato rejects both horns of the dilemma for his technical notion of partaking.

Can a participant have the whole of a Form as its share? If so, the whole of the Form will exist separately and also in the participant. This is seen as an absurdity (131b1–2). This argument involves, albeit implicitly, the separation doctrine of the Forms. If the Forms were immanent "masses" like, for example, water or the color red under certain interpretations, then the argument would not apply. But on that construal, neither could one interpret partaking as the participant having the Form deficiently.

Two analogies are brought in at this point to help the cause, but both fail. One of these compares a Form and its participants to a day covering at the same time a large region; the other is that of a sail spread over many members of a crew. In the latter case, we are reduced to the second horn of the dilemma, for only a given part of the sail is over any particular person. But similar considerations apply to the first case. A day is not an indivisible whole as a Form is, and even if we take just a part of it, no region can be said to "have" this in any intelligible sense. The other alternative, that a participant has a part of a Form as its share is reduced to absurdity. How could a participant have a small part of the Large as its share, and so on? The examples adduced here show that in no ordinary sense could we talk about what the participants share as a part of a Form.

Plato, then, is making the point that partaking is not analogous to any of the ordinary notions of sharing. It starts out in Plato's writings as a metaphor, then becomes a calcified metaphor, and eventually a technical term. Why not just have Socrates say this directly, in so many words? Plato's indirect method is forced on him because, although he invents new terms like "quality" ("*poiootes*"), the whole framework of concepts in terms of which we reflect on the formal features of theories was not yet available to him or his contemporaries. For the beginnings of those concepts, we must look to Aristotle's logical writings.

Having questioned the extent to which partaking can be made intelligible, the arguments raise similar questions about the Forms. Of the various proposals formulated and then subjected to criticism, the first one, often labeled the "Third Man," has received the most attention, especially from recent commentators.[5] Yet there is nothing in the text to suggest that any of the arguments in this section is any more important than the others. They all question either the unity of a given Form or the extent to which the Forms can be regarded as both separate from the world of appearances and endowing this world with partial order and stability. Once more, what is at issue is not merely the existence of Plato's ontological discovery, but also its explanatory power.

One could construct an argument against the existence of the Forms on the basis of possible inconsistencies in the underlying assumptions or threats of infinite regress. This is not Plato's intention. He interprets the impact of the "Third man" argument as threatening the explanatory power of these entities. This is often overlooked in modern treatments of the argument, since these take it out of context.

The first argument attempts to show that each Form is not one but is made up of an indefinite collection of entities. This is not an incoherent state of affairs. One could live with it if all one wanted to show is that the Forms exist. But it is hardly an adequate reply to the Eleatic challenger, who insists that the Forms have no more genuine unity than the entities whose nature they are meant to explain. If Plato is to succeed, he needs to show that the elements of reality have more genuine unity than the elements constituting the world of appearances.

The key parts of the first argument (132a1–b2) are as follows: "I think that you judge each Form on the basis of the following. Whenever many appear to you as large, one Form appears which remains the same as you view all the large things. Hence you think the Large to be one."

The next key section runs: "But what if you view in your soul in the same manner the Large itself and the other large ones? Will there not emerge another Large again, in virtue of which the other ones appear large?" The subsequent passage spells out the ensuing regress. If viewing large things a, b, c, and the Large "in the same manner" requires a $Large_2$ in virtue of which elements of this collection are in some way large, then don't we need another element, $Large_3$, to view the collection mentioned and $Large_2$ in the same way? This process can be iterated over and over again. Thus the Large turns out not to be one, but to be an indefinite plurality (132b2).

The crux of this argument is: Are we or are we not either compelled or at least justified in viewing large things a, b, c, and the Large *in the same manner?* Some recent interpreters have suggested that the roots of the problem lie in complex logical principles and distinctions that were not clear to the ancients.[6] But the context, as well as the text itself, suggests that the key question is not one of logic or semantics but a metaphysical issue. Later treatments of issues of self-predication, especially in modern symbolic logic, have led to important proposals in logical theory, such as the theory of types. But what is it about the nature of the Large that would either compel us to view it in the same manner as the participants or block us from viewing it that way? Or does Plato's conception of the Large leave it open as to whether one views the Large in one of these ways or the other? Answering this question is not a matter of modern logical principles, but rather of settling the question of the principle of individuation for Forms and what it is in their nature that gives them explanatory force. Hence, Cherniss's remark that modern interpreters "intended to clarify Plato's text, but tended to whelm it with symbols of modern logic"[7], seems justified.

Within Plato's metaphysics at this stage, there may not be any simple answer to the question of whether we must view large things and the Large in the same manner. Nor is there any evidence that Plato thought such an answer to be available. There are two reasons why one might insist that the

Large be viewed in the same manner as the participants, both linked to what Plato says about the explanatory role of the Forms. One of these is that only by construing the nature of the Large as what can give qualified largeness to participants can we use the realm of Forms to explain order among appearances. The other is that the principle individuating the Forms, which rests on special self-attribution, compels us to do that. Furthermore, faced with the Eleatic challenge, one might try either to interpret self-attribution of the relevant sort as not committing us to viewing Form and participants as large in the same way or to account for individuation and explanatory force without strong self-attribution. We are faced with a number of options.

a   The Large is uniquely large, but not in virtue of its partaking of anything.
b   The Large is uniquely large in virtue of partaking of something else.
c   The Large is uniquely large in virtue of its partaking of itself.
d   Forms partake of each other and in some cases of themselves, but not in a way that would give them a unique unqualified qualitative nature; Forms endow participants with a partial nature and are individuated, but without any assumption of strong or unique self-attribution.

All these options run into some difficulty. For example, is (a) to be taken simply as a basic axiom which cannot be further elucidated? Does (b) not lead to a regress? Does (c) not require revising the notion of partaking? and do such revisions mean that partaking is no longer necessarily cross-categorial? Does (d) not require a new systematic articulation of how Forms are related to each other? and does this option not take away some of the explanatory force of the theory?

We see once again from these considerations that the issue of self-attribution is not a matter of crude reification or the positing of super-particulars, but a difficult, deep ontological puzzle affecting the very core of Plato's way of contrasting reality and appearance in the dialogues surveyed in chapter 2. Which way out did Plato take?[8] There is no direct evidence to settle the matter in this part of the dialogue. The interpretation of the second part, however (see chapter 5), shows that he tended to favor (d).

The next two arguments emerge from reflections on the issues introduced by the first. We need to represent the mode of being of the appearances and that of the Forms in a way that is drastic enough to block viewing the two "in the same manner." We need what in modern philosophy would be called a categorial distinction. But the two sketched here prove to be unsuccessful.

The first (132b3−c11) proposes that the Forms be construed as thoughts. If successful, this would drive a categorial wedge between the Forms and the world of appearances. The suggestion needs to be taken in its historical context and not be confused with subjective, mind-dependent interpretations of universals of the kind labeled "conceptualism." The proposal attempts, like all other classic Greek ontologies, to reconstruct an objective reality. As such, it comes into conflict with an assumption about thought which Plato and his contemporaries and predecessors shared: namely, that thoughts must have objects, and are individuated in terms of their respective objects. The objects may be only myths, but these too have some reality not dependent on individual minds. But given this assumption, the burden of explaining the constituents of reality would fall on the objects that the alleged Form-thoughts have. Furthermore, as we have seen, whatever being the participants are endowed with as a result of partaking in the Forms must originate in the nature of the Forms. But this now has the unwelcome consequence that thoughts become constituents of participants such as concrete things, and we might even be driven to panpsychism, if everything has thoughts in it and these must be interpreted as enabling things to think. Finally, from Plato's point of view, given his general conception of the relation of the mind to the world, the order and stability in the mind are what needs to be explained; they cannot be the explanans.

Another proposal tries to draw the categorial distinction in terms of the original−copy dichotomy (132d1−133a10), thereby embracing proposals discussed previously. The original−copy distinction is asymmetrical and thus gives grounds for denying that the two should be viewed in the same manner. But this attempt, too, fails. For though the original−copy dichotomy rests on an asymmetrical relation, it gives rise to the symmetrical relation of similarity. Being similar is a necessary, though not a sufficient, condition of one thing being a copy of another. This condition, then, provides a ground for the two being viewed "in the same manner." The needed categorial difference disappears.

The exact details of the argument are not relevant to the points I want to make in this chapter and hence will be omitted. Roughly, the argument is shown to be interpreted as generating regress in one of two ways: either because as the collections viewed become larger, we need to add more and more likeness relations, or because of the need to add new originals in the light of which we can detect the necessary condition of likeness that emerges at the first step of the argument sketched above.[9] Either way, the explanatory role of the Forms is threatened.

These sample explorations of drawing a categorial difference between Forms and participants based on analogies from everyday experience all fail. They are terminated by the remark that "many more difficulties" can be raised (133b4). The indeterminateness of this statement suggests that Plato does not have a specific couple of arguments in mind. It is more reasonable to take this as a general comment. There may be many ways of trying to draw the needed categorial difference by analogies with features of everyday experience, but none is likely to lead to illumination. This leaves us with only two alternatives. One is to reject the contrast as unintelligible. The other is to show how the theory as a whole accounts for large-scale phenomena and thus regard the contrast as a basic indefinable concept in the theory. This move, too, reduces the theory's explanatory power.

The final question in this part of the dialogue concerns the knowability of the Forms. The world of appearances is sharply separated from the world of reality. But humans live in the world of appearances. How can such creatures have the contact with a categorially distinct realm of reality that is required, as we saw in chapter 1, for genuine understanding? The Form of knowledge or understanding is relational according to Platonic interpretation, and the relational objects are Forms: for example, understanding of numbers, virtues, elements of harmony, and so on. But an instance of such understanding takes place in space and time. How can such an instance have as its objects that which is not in space and time? Should it not have spatiotemporal entities as its objects if it is like any other natural process? Ultimately, the answer is that understanding and the accompanying "learning" do not constitute a natural process. They constitute a unique *sui generis* process unlike any other, which enables us to have a grasp of the nature of elements of reality. But this admission again adds more primitive concepts to the theory.

The details of this argument are beyond the scope of this chapter.[10] Plato gives as an example of a relational property being a slave of a master. As properties, being a slave of and being a master of are correlatives. So are their instances. We cannot cross the line between the two. How could something like knowledge accomplish this? A modern reply would be that there are relational properties that cross categorial lines: for example, being a slave of Nicodemus. But there is no evidence in the dialogues that Plato considered such properties, and no ground for thinking that he would have posited Forms for these.

In summary, these searching arguments seem to indicate that the basic notions of Forms and of partaking do not admit of noncircular or nonvacuous explanations. This is not what one would have expected as the theory unfolded in earlier dialogues, in terms of similes and metaphors. To view the notions of Form, partaking, and understanding as basic primitives is what the Platonist might be driven to; but this is quite different from how the theory looked to Plato in the first exciting stages of discovery.

Plato adds that in spite of these difficulties it is necessary to maintain that the Forms exist, otherwise one would destroy the power of rational investigation (135c1−3). This is not a claim about the use of language and discourse in general. Plato is not saying that discourse of the type used by the "lovers of sights and sounds" is possible only if the Forms exist. Nor is he willing to defend that kind of discourse against Eleatic attacks. He is concerned with the rational inquiries that constitute the genuine technai, discussed in chapter 1, and with what accounts for order and stability. If the Forms did not exist, then insight and understanding would be destroyed, not rhetoric or poetry. This reading of these lines is in harmony with how we took the claim about the possible extension of the realm of Forms in the earlier passage (130d). There, too, the possible extension is not meant to encompass all predicates of a language. There are no premises anywhere in this dialogue − or those surveyed in Part I − that would justify that kind of leap. Perhaps some things are just as they appear in perception (130d3−5) and thus require no underlying Forms.

Plato hints (135d) that a thinker of exceptional talent can find his way out of this conceptual labyrinth. One way of taking this is to ascribe to Plato the view that it takes unusual philosophical insight to see that in spite of not being analogous to other elements of the world, the Forms can exist and constitute the foundation of reality. Their mode of being can be presented indirectly once we are assured of their existence. We can then see, by understanding what Forms are not, what their mode of being is and how they relate to other elements. Read this way, Plato's comment about the unusual thinker provides a suitable transition to the second main part of the dialogue, to which we now turn.

The One and the Others

The surface structure of the second main part of the *Parmenides* consists of eight arguments, arranged in pairs so as to contradict each other. Furthermore, the second four arguments explore the denial of the first and show that this leads to even greater difficulties than the first four do. The thesis of the first four is that The One is; while that of the last four is that The One is not. An adequate interpretation must answer the following questions:

1 What is the subject; is it the One? Or is it any Platonic Form?
2 Why does this section have this surface structure?
3 If this is just a surface structure, what is the underlying impact of the arguments?

The ostensible subject, the One, admits of several interpretations. It can be the Eleatic One, the Platonic Form of One, a geometrical point, or the unity of some philosophical doctrine about which we have no direct information. Some of the predicates used in the argumentation are spatial, which suggests that we are talking about geometrical points. There is strong evidence, however, that one of the subjects is the Platonic Form of the One. First, in 129c2−4 we saw wonderment about the possibility that the Forms partake of opposites. But if the subject of these arguments is a Platonic Form, then this is precisely what is demonstrated in this section, thereby providing continuity with the discussions of the first half. Secondly, in 135d−e it is said that we should consider not only problems concerning the nature of the Forms but also the effects of the hypothesis that the Forms do not exist. If we adopt the interpretation proposed here, this is one of the key parts of the argumentation of this section. Thirdly, we saw earlier that only Forms are entities of which things can partake. But there are several passages in which the One is presented as an object of participation (157c2, 158b2). In view of these considerations, it is very difficult to avoid the conclusion that the One is a Platonic Form. But what about the spatial attributes? And is the argumentation not in any way an answer to Eleatic ontology?

There is a way of combining these different suggestions. As we shall see, the arguments mostly present unacceptable interpretations of the One. Why could some of these not be showing the untenability of certain conceptions of the Eleatic One, some of them the incoherence of viewing geometrical points in certain ways, and some again the ways in which Platonic Forms cannot be? Plato shows that unities cannot have this or that nature. Such negative claims can serve all three purposes: of refuting the Eleatics, pointing indirectly to the mode of being of the Forms, and clearing up some confusions about geometry. For example, in the first argument Plato shows the incoherence of construing the One as totally unitary. This not only has implications for the theory of Forms; it also serves as a refutation of Eleatic doctrine, at least on one reading. The first three arguments also discuss various spatial and temporal attributes applying to a unity. They can be read as criticizing certain conceptions of spatial or temporal units. Still, in most of the arguments, the One as that of which things partake is discussed. These passages, then, contain a discussion of the nature of the Forms. If we accept the thesis that the surface structure is just that, we can expect that Plato will accomplish all three tasks within this section.

The following are grounds for taking the apparent structure to be just a surface structure. First, there are in fact nine, rather than eight, arguments. After the second argument we are told that matters need to be taken up "for the third time" (155e4), and what follows is an interesting essay about time. Commentators who are mesmerized by the apparent symmetry of eight arguments treat this as an appendix to the second argument. But though it treats fewer topics than the other arguments, this argument is not shorter than some of the others, and it closes out the discussion of time in this dialogue. Since the topic of time is beyond the scope of this book, I will not deal with this argument and will follow the conventional numbering up to eight. But the presence of this essay is already an indication of the superficiality of the paired arrangement. Secondly, not all arguments lead to the One being characterized by conflicting opposites. Though this is the main stream of argumentation, there are exceptions, such as the One being simple like itself and unlike others in the fifth argument. Thirdly, not all pairs contradict each other directly. Arguments 7 and 8 are only in partial conflict with each other.

But if the paired arrangement is only a surface structure, why does Plato employ it? One reason may be that it allows him to divide the material conveniently into two halves: positive and negative arguments. He is thereby carrying out the instruction stated earlier, that one should examine both positive and negative aspects of a thesis. Secondly, although Parmenides claims that in his chain of arguments one can start anywhere and end up with the same monistic view, this structure allows Plato to make the point that starting at different points of assumptions about the One, we reach different conclusions, thereby showing the Eleatic circle to be illusory. For example, we can start by positing a totally unitary One or start by assuming the intelligibility of "The One is" and looking for the necessary conditions of this intelligibility, but we end up with different conclusions. Plato's structuring of the material shows that what appear to be simple notions in the Eleatic arguments are, in fact, highly complex ones.

For example, the One – and other Platonic Forms – must be such that:

1   Each is unique and yet in some sense "many."
2   Each can have participants in lower categories of reality and on its own level.

As we shall see, transcategorial partaking can still be distinguished from partaking among the Forms. Furthermore, the Forms can still be distinguished from the world of spatiotemporal appearances, for the unity of the Forms is different from the unities of the appearances, and only the realm of Forms is self-sufficient.

It is important to note that the arguments lead to contradictions not only if we take them in pairs but also if we take them individually. This leads us to the underlying conceptual points made in these texts. In some unsatisfactory ways of viewing the One, geometrical points and other geometrical unities are dealt with, thus pointing to the correct way of understanding these entities. In other unsatisfactory ways of viewing unity, Forms and the notions of partaking are spelled out, thus again pointing indirectly to adequate conceptualizations of these notions. For example, as we shall see, one argument shows that the Form of One cannot be un-qualifiedly one, yet should not be interpreted as a whole made up of parts analogously to the wholes of everyday experience.

In addition to the surface structure of this part of the dialogue, another consideration that has led some scholars to doubt that there are positive claims in this text is that it is repeatedly described in 135c8–136a2 as an exercise of some sort. We are told that we need the exercise of considering both positive forms of existential claims and their negations before we can attain sound understanding of the nature of the entities in question.

Now "exercise" can mean a number of different things, in ancient Greek as well as in modern English. For example, we can undergo military or physical training, in which case the main purpose is to develop certain skills and abilities. Thus, for example, after an operation the doctor might prescribe the repeated flexing of the knee. This does not lead to the acquisition of new knowledge or important truth. The main point is to strengthen the knee. Similarly, military exercises can include simulated attacks, strenuous walks with full gear and so forth: in short, activities that are designed to build up courage, fitness, and so on and are not meant to lead to the understanding of new important truths.

On the other hand, there are other kinds of exercises, like those assigned in logic classes or classes on formal grammar, where we are meant to develop our abilities to, for example, prove certain kinds for theorems and at the same time are led to discover truths not known to us beforehand.

Reflecting on what it is first to assert something of the form "X is" and see its consequences, and then to do the same with the negative, "X is not," belongs to the second type of exercise. We develop logical abilities and so learn important truths. Thus calling what follows an "exercise" is not incompatible with claiming that it leads to the discovery of certain metaphysical truths, even if these are mainly negative in form. Seeing that assuming the One to be like ordinary objects leads to contradictions, as does denying it any kind of being, can lead to a negative characterization of the being of Forms, and thus to their indirect defense. Let us now turn to the examination of specific arguments, focusing only on the main claims of the interpretation sketched.

First argument

This considers the thesis: "The One is" in the interpretation that the One must be totally and unqualifiedly unitary (137c4–142a8). Thus "The One is" entails that "The One is completely one." This in turn entails that the One is not "many" in any way. But not being many in any way, it cannot have parts in any sense of this notion. From the partlessness of the One, Plato derives the fact that it cannot be a whole, since a whole must be a whole of parts, and thus that it can have no qualitative or spatial delineation of any kind. For such delineations would entail that it has either parts in its qualitative structure or also spatial parts. Thus neither being nor sameness nor difference can apply to it. Nor can such a unit have shape or extension or be in any place. The last of these shows that a geometrical point must not be defined as a completely unitary element.

Not only sameness and difference, but rest and motion (including qualitative sameness and change) are inapplicable to the totally unitary entity (139c4–e5). The key premise in this part of the argumentation is that by its own nature the One is just one, neither the same as something nor different from something (139d1–2). Thus, even if everything partakes of both the One and the Same, the two Forms are not identical. At this point, we can see how the argument applies not only to the One, but to all Forms. If a Form is just what it is – that is, is or has uniquely its own nature – then sameness or difference cannot apply to it; thus it cannot have any distinctness, thereby becoming an unintelligible entity.

From the fact that sameness and difference do not apply to the One, Plato concludes that likeness and unlikeness cannot apply to it either. This is significant for our understanding of Plato's notion of sameness as basically qualitative sameness (and correspondingly qualitative difference), rather than the modern logical notions of identity and nonidentity.

At the end, Plato returns to the premise of partlessness and shows that on that assumption, neither equality nor inequality nor various temporal designations can apply to the unitary, since all these involve having parts. Thus on this interpretation, the One can have no being and cannot be singled out by a term, thus there can be no knowledge or perception of it – clearly an unsatisfactory conclusion arrived at by valid arguments. This is relevant not only to the Parmenidean One, but to other abstract and allegedly intelligible units as well.

Three key premises fuel this series of moves:

1   A completely unitary entity – that is, one that cannot be many in any way – cannot have any "parts" even in the sense of having attributes other than the attribute of being one.
2   If something simply has its own nature – that is, the Equal is just equal, and so on – then sameness, difference, and other such all-pervasive Forms cannot apply to it; thus its nature becomes problematic.
3   Likeness and unlikeness depend on qualitative sameness and difference.

All three of these theses affect subsequent dialogues such as the *Sophist* and the *Politicus*, but only the first two require modifications in the ontology. The Method of Division, as we shall see, imposes some kind of whole–part structure on groups of Forms. Likeness is not a main topic in the *Sophist*, since, as we have just seen, it depends on sameness, which is a main topic in that dialogue. Finally, Forms are interpreted as both being "what they are" and having sameness and difference pervade them, thus being manifolds in some sense. This shows that Plato could not have taken the steps in argument 1 lightly, since they affected his subsequent conceptions of the Forms.

The main conclusion, that there cannot be anything totally unitary in the sense explicated, has consequences for the Eleatic One, for Plato's Forms, and for geometrical points. It is a negative point, and thus simply places constraints on any positive proposal. If the Eleatic One were such a unitary entity, then it could not exist. Geometrical points and Plato's Form of the One do exist, but must be interpreted within the constraint of our result.

We have already seen that a key premise in the argument concerning what a Form is "by its own nature" requires us to extend the result from the One to all Forms.[11] We shall turn now to how a unity can be "many."

Second argument

This argument (142b1–155e3) starts with the same thesis but gives it a different initial analysis. If "The One is" is true, then there must be some combination of the One and Being. Thus, the One is many, and this conflicts with the results of argument 1.

From the One being "many" it is inferred that it has parts. This presupposes a very broad sense of part – namely, one according to which having attributes is having parts. But how are we to understand the union of a Form and Being? Plato gives us only an indirect hint by showing one untenable way to construe this relation. The illegitimate way assumes that if the One has Being, this implies a whole made up of two entities. But since all entities have unity and being, each of the original two entities must contain as parts unity and being. Thus we get the being of the One, the unity of the being of the One, and so forth. On this analysis, the One turns out to be an indefinite collection of parts. Note that this analysis with its obviously unsatisfactory conclusion does not depend on spatial interpretations of the One having attributes. The whole derivation of the indefinite collection takes place on a purely conceptual plane, and the "parts" need not have any spatial location at all.

Given this unsatisfactory conclusion, we can infer that Plato does not want us to think of the union of the One and Being as a molecular complex, whose constituents require the same characterizations in terms of partaking of Forms as the original subject. This point can be applied to the other Forms as well (for example, try "The One is the same", or "different"). Plato indicates this indirectly, the only way open to him, given the state of abstract theorizing in his day. This point can be seen as a prolegomenon to the Communion of Forms, developed in the *Sophist*.

In 143c, he goes back to the original premise and shows that given "The One is" and that this entails that Difference must characterize those two elements, basic foundational elements for the series of positive integers can be derived from the original hypothesis. Thus if the One is, then arithmetic is too. This is an important result, not contradicted later. The details of this argument are of independent interest and will be considered separately (see Appendix 1). But we should note that this derivation has nothing to do with the illegitimate one that led to the unsatisfactory indefinite collection and implied a molecular composition principle.

This concludes the part of the argument from which consequences for the Forms can be drawn. The basic moral is that in a sense all Forms are manifold, but that this nature cannot be spelled out in terms of molecular rules of composition, for we would then lose the wholeness of the unit under analysis. In the section starting at 145a1, there is a transition that leads to a discussion of unities with spatial properties. The transition rests on an illegitimate move. Since the One is a whole made up of parts, we are told, it must have a "limit." This can mean either a qualitative or a spatial delineation. But in the next section it is said that since the One has a "limit," it must admit of a beginning, middle, and end ordering (145a4−b1). From this, various spatial characteristics of the One are derived.

The move is illegitimate, because having a limit is ambiguous in the way indicated, and the beginning, middle, end ordering is applied only to spatial delineation. Justice and harmony also have limits since they have definite qualitative natures, but obviously they do not have the ordering at issue here. To ask of unities like the Forms, "Where is beginning or middle . . . ?" is to commit what in recent philosophy has been called a category mistake. One cannot ask of a stone, for example, what it is thinking about; likewise, one cannot ask of the Platonic One where its middle parts are. Plato uses the same type of move in 150e, where it is said that what is not greater or smaller must be equal, omitting the possibility that this whole range of predicates might be inapplicable to certain entities.

We can only speculate as to Plato's motives here. He may be introducing "category mistakes" in places where they are obvious, thus indirectly leading us to understand the being of Forms as entailing the inapplicability of ranges of predicates and their negatives to them. Secondly, he wants us to reflect on unity and the whole–part relation in such a way as to clarify, indirectly, the nature of geometrical points. The ensuing arguments show that certain ways of thinking about these lead to contradictions. The detailed discussion of this view of geometry is beyond the scope of this book. Roughly, argument 1 shows that points cannot be totally unitary in the Eleatic sense, whereas argument 2 shows that they cannot be very tiny extended things to which notions like containment, size, and the rest apply.

Sameness and Difference enter into this argument, too, but not in the same way as they did in the previous argument. In the first argument, Sameness and Difference raise purely conceptual problems concerning the nature of abstract entities. Here they enter in the context of spatial specifications; hence the conclusions reached here do not contradict the ones reached in the first argument.

Interspersed in this section we find crude, nonrelational treatments of certain opposites. In 146a–c rest and motion are treated in this way, and in 146d we are told that since same and different are opposites, they cannot apply to the same thing. In the *Sophist*, we are shown that nothing is just the same or different. Two things are different in certain respects. Parmenides treats all opposites in simplistic ways. Plato may have wanted to show the absurdity of doing this. In any case, the main, paradoxical conclusions about a point-unit as a mini-substance are independent of this problem of the treatment of opposites.

After the contradictory characterizations, a final summing up is given, starting with 155d5. We are told that the One as characterized has being, and that there is knowledge, opinion, and perception of it; indeed, we are exercising knowledge with regard to it right now.

These final lines must be read as irony. For, first, what we "know" about the One on the basis of argument 2 is intelligible but negative or self-contradictory. If we gain understanding about the One of any positive sort, it is through the indirect process of seeing what does not work. Secondly, as we know from chapter 1, for Plato the objects of understanding and perception are distinct. Thus one can hardly take at surface value the notion that here we have, with regard to the One, all three epistemic states. Any putative state that involves all three must be, from a Platonic point of view, inadequate.

What can we conclude from the first two arguments combined? We see that the One is neither a unity that is in no way a manifold nor a manifold with merely molecular structure. It has parts, but the parts do not function separately. Thus the arguments push us towards other views of unity. Some of these include the notion of a unit that is a whole, the whole being more than the sum of its parts. Such a view of unity is central to the Platonic material that will be discussed in chapter 6, and also to Aristotle's conception of what constitutes an adequate definition.

The next two arguments deal with how the One as an entity is related to the "others." This turns out to be, not surprisingly, an examination of the notion of partaking (see *metechein* in 157c2).

Third argument

This presents what turns out to be an unsatisfactory way of interpreting participation. It starts with reasonable enough remarks. The others have to be one somehow, or how could they be distinct entities? Thus they are not the One, but have to be related to the One somehow. There are many others, and each is one. Without the One entering into their nature, the others could not be one individually or collectively and would constitute only an indeterminate mass. They also have a specific qualitative structure; in that sense, each is "many" and has a "limit." Thus in different ways the others have unity, plurality, delineation, and indefiniteness in their nature. (This is, as we shall see later, spelled out in more detail in the *Philebus*.)

From the conclusion in 158a3−5 − namely, that since the "others" partake of the One, they are distinct from the One − we should not generalize to a thesis about predication to the effect that if X is predicated of Y, then X and Y cannot be identical. Plato has already characterized the "others" as other than the One; hence the conclusion admits only of restricted expansion.

The characterization leads to absurdity when the whole−part dichotomy is pushed and the others are viewed as a whole or as parts of the One. A few pairs of opposites are shown to characterize the others within such a framework, and then it is concluded that all the "standard" opposites will do so.

The difficulty with this line of argument is not only that opposites are not analyzed relationally, but also that being a part or a whole is taken as a nonrelative notion. Nothing is simply a whole or a part. It may be a part of a certain unit and not a part of something else. A whole may be such from a certain ontological perspective, but not from another. All this applies to the partaking relation. A participant is not either a part or a whole as such. He or she may be a whole human and a part of a citizenry. In any case, the part–whole relation is not suitable for spelling out the partaking relation. The participants are not parts of the Form; nor do they have a part of the Form. Indeed, the question "Do they have, or are they, a part or the whole of a Form?" makes no sense. This seems to be the indirect conclusion of the unsatisfactory ending of argument 3.

Fourth argument

This argument (159b2–160b4), like the first, construes the One as completely unitary. The others are, then, completely separate from it; together they do not form a larger whole. If they did, one surmises, they would have to have a common nature. But the totally unitary One cannot have a manifold nature, hence cannot have the nature of having participants. This conception makes participation impossible. It is then shown briefly that if the others cannot partake of the One, they lack unity altogether and thus cannot have any characteristics, including the various pairs of opposites.

This unsatisfactory conclusion has its roots in interpreting the One in a totally unitary way and then attempting to have its nature still reflected somehow in everything else.[12] Again, this argument applies to all the Forms. If a Form is "just what it is" – for example, equal, good, fine, and so on, to the exclusion of other characteristics – then it cannot have participants. Even if we interpret "part" in a unique way so as to cover only the partaking relation, a Form that is completely monolithic in nature cannot have such "parts."

The third and fourth arguments together show that, at least in some cases, interpreting the Forms as having self-attribution in the sense discussed before makes participation impossible. On the other hand, we also end up in trouble if we analyze partaking on the whole–part analogy in transcategorial cases. Thus it seems that partaking is necessary, since without it the manifold of reality and appearance could not have the structure it does. On the other hand, it is one more basic indefinable notion in Platonic ontology.

We have seen, then, that if a Form is to have explanatory power, it must be a unity and be "what it is," yet be so without entailing the consequences of argument 1 and consequently without special self-attribution. It is a unity that is also a manifold, but of the sort that is not subject to the consequences of argument 2, since the basic structure cannot be that of part and whole. The Forms do have participants, but this notion too remains a "primitive," not reducible to, or to be interpreted as analogous to, other concepts such as the part–whole relation.

The arguments do not say anything about genus–species relations among the Forms. As we shall see in chapters 5 and 6, Plato will invoke the part–whole relation after all, but at the cost of making this part–whole structure sui generis.

Can the Forms not Be?

The last four arguments explore the implications of the thesis "The One is not." These arguments show the need to qualify "is" and "is not"; they also lead to a reaffirmation of the claim that the Forms are necessary for order in both reality and *logos*, or theoretical discourse. The arguments center around the One, but can be seen to be extendable to all other Forms as well. Thus the arguments complement the first four, which showed, indirectly, the unique mode of being of the Forms and of the partaking relation. The last four show indirectly why these entities are not only coherent but also necessary ingredients in an adequate ontology.

The first negative argument, argument 5 (160b5–163b6), states the key assumption and then reflects on the fact that it is intelligible and draws some consequences from this fact. The following are the crucial lines:

> What is this hypothesis: "the One is not"? It differs from the hypothesis: "the not-One is not"; in fact, not only differs from it, but is its opposite. What if someone says: "Size is not", or "Smallness is not", and other such things. It is clear that in each case a different entity is said to be that which is not. And so it is clear that even now, if someone says "the One is not", what he is talking about is different from other entities, and we know what it is. So when we speak of the One, we speak firstly of something knowable, and secondly of something distinct, whether we attribute being to it or not-being. That which is said not to be is no less knowable (than what is said to be) and distinct from all else. (160b6–d2)

This passage shows that Plato is drawing certain conclusions from the fact that in these negative existentials – at least, this is what they seem to be on the surface – the subject, as well as the ascription, is intelligible. The problem of negative existentials became a standard topic in philosophical logic, one that surfaces also in the twentieth century. If I say "The golden mountain does not exist," need I ascribe some sort of being to what the subject expression purports to refer to? Various technical solutions have been proposed, showing that such ascriptions can be avoided. We need not go into an exploration of the variety of solutions. It is important to note, however, that no such solution can be found in the Platonic dialogues. As we shall see, Plato has ways of translating various negative existentials into other forms, but no general, purely formal or logical translation is available.

In our text, there is evidence that the issue is not the ascription of not-being to just any entity, since the examples to which the argument is meant to be expendable are found elsewhere in the Platonic texts as standard samples of Forms.

The consequences of intelligibility are interpreted as the subject partaking of various characteristics that today we would call formal: for example, being a "this." This, in turn, leads to the statement: "Thus the One since it is not, cannot have being, but nothing prevents it from partaking of many other entities, indeed it must if it is this and not something else" (160e7–161a2). This strange conclusion seems to "open the floodgates"; for, subsequently, a whole series of characters is ascribed to the subject of our hypothesis. Starting with 161c, it is described in terms of a variety of opposites. We are told that the One, since it is not, cannot be equal to the others and hence must be unequal to them. This is once more an instance of what was labelled above a "category mistake." What Plato is after, presumably, is that the alternatives equal or unequal simply do not apply in such cases as this. But he only has the technical resources to say this indirectly. The subsequent arguments proceed in similar fashion. If the One is unequal, then it must be greater and smaller. As such, however, it must also be equal, since equal lies between greater and smaller. All these incoherent characterizations should force the reader going through this "exercise" to question the implicit claim that with regard to any entity it makes sense to insist that it should have one or another of a given pair of opposites.

Having seen a rich nature built up around the One that is not, we are then told that in some way it must have being too. Thus 162a–b undermines the conclusion about partaking arrived at earlier.

Let us now reflect on what kind of negative existential seems to get us into this morass. Four types of statements need to be distinguished: first, negative existentials in general; second, negative existentials applying to everyday objects; third, negative existentials in which the existence of the object is derived from its essence; and fourth, statements denying what would be necessary existence to entities like numbers and, for Plato, Forms. Different questions and solutions arise in connection with these different types.

First, it does not seem that Plato is concerned with general problems of intelligibility. As the text cited shows, he does not simply conclude from the fact that we can say something meaningful about the subject that the subject must exist. Rather, he posits certain requirements in terms of distinctness and having some intelligible structure, and even then concludes only that some participation is necessary. Only after many other characteristics have been ascribed to the One that is not, do we come to the claim that this One must, somehow, be.

Secondly, he is not dealing with the alleged nonexistence of this or that everyday object. He says that the cases in question are size, smallness, and so forth. Evidence from other dialogues (e.g. *Sophist* 240b) shows that he has resources for dealing with cases like "Homer did not exist." He would say that, maybe, Homer is just an image. As we shall see in the next chapter, he distinguishes between names and bearers of names in several places, but does not discuss the problem of empty names; he is concerned only with cases in which we do not know whether several names designate different entities or the same one.

Thirdly, his concern does not mirror that which we find in connection with the ontological argument. For in order for the analogy to hold, Plato would have to deduce the (problematic) being of the One, even in the hypothesis that it is not, from an analysis of its nature: that is, the nature of unity. But he does not do that. He says, rather, that this is a puzzle we encounter when we try to ascribe not-being to the One, size, and smallness – in other words, to the Forms.

It seems, then, that Plato's problem is like the one we encounter when we consider the existence of entities like numbers. Theirs is a necessary existence, but clearly not a logical truth, or "realists" would have an easy way with nominalists. That their being is necessary follows not from either the respective natures of each such entity or some general intelligibility assumption about subject expressions. Perhaps the way to highlight the peculiar nature of these existentials and their denials is to contrast them with discussions about God. Those who deny God's existence deny also whatever truths the theist wants to ascribe to the deity. But those who deny the existence of numbers do not deny the analogous truths. Rather, they want to account for these with the help of various reductionistic techniques within the framework of a different ontology. So Plato's point might be this: in making assertions about Forms, we are considering material that requires that something should be there: if not numbers and other quality-like entities in the Platonic sense, then entities of another sort.

How are we to express all this within Plato's conceptual framework? Well, one tack is to posit something that has no being but partakes of characters. But this conception cannot really be sustained. In fact, it is clearly rejected in the *Sophist*, as we shall see. On the other hand, argument 5 shows that if we take the distinctness of the one, whatever it may turn out to be, as ground for its being like any ordinary object, we get into the contradictory descriptions that the argument uncovers.

Thus we arrive at the following: that the One must be, somehow, even though it makes sense to say that it might not be; yet, that partaking is some sort of being. If so, how could something not be, yet partake of various characters?

This second point suggests that maybe both being and not-being need to be treated in relational or qualified ways. It seems that in some ways the One might be said not to be, but that in others it must somehow be. The relation between a more primitive notion of being and that of partaking cries out for treatment. Such a treatment is indeed given in the *Sophist* and will be taken up in the next chapter.

The first point suggests that we look at modes of being and not stick to the way ordinary objects in space and time are, as our paradigm. For something to be distinct and have a nature, it need not have the same kind of being as mountains or cities that would allow all sorts of quantitative comparisons in terms of magnitude to be applicable to it.

Are there independent considerations that would push us in the direction of exploring different modes of not-being? Argument 6 (163b7–164b4) provides such. The whole argument concentrates on the meaning of the predicate of the hypothesis: that is, the phrase "is not." On the surface this means complete not-being: that is, the lack of any kind of being. If we try to consider the consequences of the hypothesis that the One is not, using this interpretation of "is not," we encounter formidable difficulties. No characteristic can be ascribed to the subject, not even the "formal" ones encountered in the previous argument as a way of spelling out the intelligibility conditions. From this, Plato concludes that under this interpretation the original hypothesis is unintelligible. This is certainly true, even if we employ the paraphrases that Plato has available and which uses in the

Sophist. Suppose we say: "The One is not; it is only a series of images in the minds of mortals." Even then, we assign to it some being. Thus, within the Platonic scheme, it seems that we should never interpret "is not" as total, complete not-being. Again, we shall see evidence in the *Sophist* that Plato embraced that consequence of the argumentation of the *Parmenides.* This forces us to look for qualified modes of not-being, a task that is not carried out within the negative framework of the second half of the *Parmenides* but is undertaken in other late dialogues.

Let us now consider arguments 5 and 6 together and see what morals can be drawn, other than the surface contradictions. It is easy to see that the surface contradiction between 5 and 6 is precisely that; for the two arguments examine different aspects of the hypothesis "The One is not." Argument 5 considers the status of the subject within the context of this hypothesis, whereas argument 6 centers on the meaning of the predicate. Argument 6 shows the problematic nature of an unconditional not-being. And while this may not be the favorite way of dealing with this problem in modern logic, Plato did opt for solutions that involve the avoidance of unconditional not-being. This is the framework within which the discussion of not-being takes place in the *Sophist*.[13] This conclusion of argument 6 is not contradicted by anything shown in argument 5. The latter attempts to show that what the hypothesis says about the One requires that this entity and others like it, such as size and smallness, be distinct from other entities in some sense. Plato does not say that perhaps the subject does not pick out anything at all, as he might say in the case of certain mythical entities. Implicit in this is a difference between hypotheses about unity, size, and so on and hypotheses regarding what we would call contingent entities, like a building or something possible as a mythical thing.

So there must be something corresponding to the subject expression. At the same time, the argument shows that if we treat that entity as an everyday object and do not relativize the opposites, we end up with an unsatisfactory characterization. The negative moral, presumably, is that we should seek a more subtle analysis of standard opposites and not see the mode of being of the entities in question as we would everyday objects of sensible experience.

All this shows only that there must be something corresponding to this kind of subject. But it does not say what the nature of this entity must be; in particular, it does not say that it must be a Form. We must turn to the last two arguments in order to reach that conclusion.

Just as arguments 3 and 4 explore the relation between the One and other entities, and hence partaking, so arguments 7 and 8 explore the consequences for the same entities and relations of the negative thesis "The One is not." But unlike 3 and 4, 7 and 8 do not stand strictly in the relation of contradictoriness. Argument 7 purports to show that standard opposites appear to apply to other entities even if the One is not. But it does not say that the opposites do in fact apply. The last argument, argument 8, concludes that the opposites neither appear to apply nor do in fact apply. The second conjunct is not denied by anything in 7, and in the case of "appearing" there is good reason to believe that Plato is to some extent changing the meaning of this term.

Why would Plato couch argument 7 in the language of appearance? One good reason would be if he believed that, without the One and the participation of the others in the One, the others cannot have any determinate nature. But if it is the One that endows the others – that is, all entities other than the One – with unity and nature, then the One we have been talking about in the last few arguments is the Form of unity.

Plato's introduction of subjective language is reminiscent of the second half of Parmenides' poem, the part entitled in English translations "The Way of Seeming." There Parmenides presents what he takes to be the world of seeming as interpreted by ordinary mortals with no adequate understanding of reality. By this use of language, Parmenides is not committed to the veridical use of any of the descriptions. By analogy, Plato can employ a similar stratagem. To the *hoi polloi*, the world still seems to be a plurality of entities, even though it can be shown that without the One and the other Forms there can be no reality constituted by a plurality of entities with their own respective natures. The indefinite multitudes surfacing in this argument are the imaginary concoction of mortals (the "lovers of sights and sounds"?). They disappear under careful analysis.

Argument 7 (164b5–165e1) starts in the following way: "Let us see, then, if the One is not, what must be true of the others? Well, they must be what they are, i.e. others, if they were not, we could not say things about the others. And if our account is about the others, these must also be different. For do you not express the same thing with the 'different' and 'the other'? Yes." The argument proceeds to show that since there is no One, the others must be different from each other on this hypothesis. But "they must differ from each other as multitudes (masses?). Since there is no One, they cannot differ as unities. But each, it seems, each is a mass without delimitation of magnitude" (164c7–d1). Whatever there is apart from the One, when deprived of the One, cannot have unity as such or in its constituents. The "others" are just indefinite masses, and even this characterization is merely a matter of appearance. One might add to what Plato says that, without the One, the "others" are just a mass of "I know not what."

Plato then goes on to show how this confusing plurality can appear to have units and pluralities contained with in it, and thereafter the reasoning continues to ascribe to the others the appearances of standard opposites like similarity and dissimilarity. At the end, 165d, we are told that all the standard characters of the sort we have dealt with could be shown to appear to hold of the others if there were no One. In short, without the One of which all else partakes, the rest of reality cannot be a reality at all, but only a confusing mass. Here we have, then, the argument to strengthen what we learned from the previous two. The One that is necessary is in fact the Form of unity. But, one might say, maybe that is premature; maybe we should "bite the bullet" and conclude that reality, or rather what we take to be reality, is just a mirage of indeterminate masses and characters. The last argument, 165e2–166b7, takes away even that desperate option. It starts by saying something that is not denied by the previous argument: namely, that the others cannot have unity and plurality if there is no One. The underlying thought is that only partaking of the One enables things to have unity and plurality. But, starting with 166a1, we are told that not even appearing is possible under those circumstances. "Nor do these appear to be one and many. For the others cannot have any communion with something that is not, and nor can any of those that are not apply to the others, for that which is not cannot have any parts." if the One is not, it cannot have any "parts." We will see in the following chapters that "part" is interpreted by Plato in a very wide sense, which includes the partitioning of abstract elements into their species and into what characterizes the elements themselves. So if the One is not, the others cannot have unity and cannot even give the appearance of being unitary. Is this a switch from a purely subjective sense of "appear" to an objective sense? And if so, is it an equivocation? We have this ambiguity in modern English as well. On the one hand, mirages appear, and we do not conclude that there is something behind these that is or exists. On the other hand, the moon can be said to be increasing, and we regard both the phenomenon and what underlies it as real, even if, ultimately, one wants to describe what happens in different terms. Plato's point, however, need not be taken as equivocation. He is making the general point that we cannot describe our mental life as the presentation of various unities and pluralities unless at least some of these are grounded in reality: no world of appearances without some reality. We can hardly expect Plato to consider versions of solipsism and other purely subjectivist conceptions of thought.

One might paraphrase Plato's conclusion in the following way: if the One is not, then nothing can have its distinctness and nature; and in any rational sense of appearing – where appearing implies objective reality as well – nothing can even appear to have the unity and order that elements of an intelligible reality must have.

This conclusion supplements the conclusions of arguments 5 and 6. We found what that "one" is whose being seems to be assured by the first argument of this quartet. It is that of which all else can partake and hence have some unity, as well as the plurality necessary for having a nature of one's own. That is the Form of the One. Its nature and that of the partaking relation are sketched in negative terms in the second half of the *Parmenides*.

Thus the conclusion is reached: "If the One is not, nothing is" (166c1–2). In the next lines, Plato adds: "Let us say this, and also . . ." and then states that whether we assume that the One is or is not, it and the others will appear and not appear to be and not be "in all manner of ways." The first part of this conjunction – that is, starting with "If the One is not," represents an ontological conclusion derived via valid arguments from premises that are not subject to the fallacious kinds of reasoning we have been pointing out in this analysis. The second half, starting with "Let us say this, and also," wraps up the surface structure argumentation.

One can interpret 166c1–4 in two ways. What we called the first half of the conjunction can be seen merely as the conclusion of argument 8, and the second half can then be seen as the final summary. Alternatively, we can interpret 166c1–2 as part of the conclusion of the whole dialogue, not just of argument 8, hence "Let us say this." What we called the second half is then added to round out the conclusions of the whole set of arguments.

The second reading brings out more clearly what is in any case the moral of this part of the *Parmenides*: namely, that without the One and the other Forms, nothing can be. But this has bite only if we take the first four arguments to show, albeit indirectly, that a coherent account of the unique mode of being of the Forms and of partaking exists.

We have seen that the following features of the positive arguments lead to conceptual difficulties:

1   Insistence that for a "standard" pair of opposites, one or the other must apply to any given entity. This leads to so-called category mistakes.
2   Strong unique self-attribution.
3   Nonrelational analysis of opposites, which construes them as analogous to natural forces.
4   Attempting to force the partaking relation into the mold of part–whole analysis.

If we take the denial of each of these, we arrive at the following analysis of the Forms. Forms are entities to which certain pairs of opposites do not apply; they endow their participants with a partial nature, without having a special self-attributional nature themselves. Their distinctness has its roots not in self-attribution, but in their being related to Sameness and Difference. These relations, however, do not create a third ontological level. Finally, the Forms are related to their participants via a relation that is indefinable and sui generis. Furthermore, the negative arguments 5–8 reinforce some of the conclusions of the positive ones: for example, that self-attribution of the unique sort must be rejected, that category mistakes must be avoided, and so on. These arguments also show why denial of an entity that exists necessarily and constitutes part of the order of the world leads to absurdity. They show too why partaking, though not analyzable further, is a necessary relation between Forms and other elements of reality.

Thus the eight arguments together lead, indirectly, to a coherent position. Is this position incorporated in the theory of Forms? The next chapters will provide evidence for an affirmative answer to this question. But if this was indeed Plato's position, then some changes are required in the ontology developed in the dialogues studied in Part I. Some of the candidates are as follows:

a   If x partakes of F, then x and F must be on different ontological planes. Since the answer to various puzzles is the Forms partaking of each other (for example, the One and Being), this tenet must be rejected.
b   A Form F is unqualifiedly F in a unique way. We have seen how this gets us into trouble with a Form like the One; but the same is true of Being (and also of Eleatic Being) as well as Sameness, Difference, and so forth.
c   If x partakes of F, then x is deficiently F. The notion of deficiency was characterized with respect to, for example, the *Phaedo* "being qualifiedly" F: for instance, equal in some respects and not in others to something.

As we shall see in the following chapters, this needs further refinement. For example, should one say that wisdom is an excellence in some ways but not in others? or that the Same is same in some ways but not in others?

Of course, the possible revisions call for further explanations. How do the Forms endow their participants with a part of their nature if self-attribution of the strong kind is rejected? Is there a uniform notion of partaking that includes examples like Socrates is wise and Being is different from Rest?

If partaking no longer always links items cross-categorially, then it no longer represents the reality–appearance dichotomy. But if elements of reality also partake of each other, how do we draw the reality–appearance distinction? It is no longer that of Forms versus participants.

Have we answered the Eleatic challenges made at the beginning of the dialogue? Yes, for Plato can still distinguish the way in which opposites affect spatiotemporal particulars from the way in which they affect other Forms. For the former involves two distinct ontological planes, while the latter can be explained on a single plane.

Partaking was all along a primitive relation, but the early statement which moved from metaphor to calcified metaphor and simile did not yet imply that this notion would end up strictly as a technical term of ontology. The structure of partaking still remains different from the general structure of predication. What are often simple monadic predications are represented in Plato's theory as complex three-place relations: for example, "Socrates is wise" versus "Socrates partakes of wisdom with respect to certain aspects of this notion." Simple dyadic relations such as "x is as tall as y" correspond to complex triadic relations: for example, Socrates partakes of the Equal with respect to size in relation to Polybius."

Thus the articulation of the nature of the Form and of participation lays the foundation for the fuller account of the modifications of the ontology to be discussed in chapters 5 and 6. The account given in the *Parmenides*, however, already gives indications of how Plato can reaffirm the explanatory roles of the Forms and thus meet the Eleatic challenge discussed in the first half of this dialogue.

As we saw earlier, it is also true that Plato's notion of a Form, even after the putative revisions, is not the same as the later notion of a universal. The exact nature of the differences will become clearer in the next two chapters.

Appendix 1: *The Structure of the Second Half*

The following is a schematic summary of the argument structure of the second main part of the dialogue.

A.   The First Four Arguments. Thesis: "The One is."

Argument	Reference	Topic
1	137c4–142a8	The totally unitary one – that is, such as to exclude any kind of plurality.
2	142b1–155e3	The One as necessarily many.
3*	155e4–157b5	Essay on time.
3	157b6–159b1	The One as "many" and the "others."
4	159b2–160b4	The totally unitary one and the "others."

B.   The Second Four Arguments. Thesis: "The One is not."

Argument	Reference	Topic
5	160b5–163b6	"The One is not" as an intelligible, true proposition leads to contradiction.
6	163b7–164b4	"The One is not" with "is not" as total not-being.
7	164b5–165e1	"The One is not," but what about the "others"? The language of appearance.
8	165e2–166b7	The One is "completely not"; the effect on the "others."

C.   Final conclusions: 166e.

In the main body of this chapter it has been suggested at various points that the apparent overall structure is only a surface structure and that this doesn't exclude the possibility of Plato advancing important substantive metaphysical claims in this text. Here is a brief summary of these considerations.

As was pointed out, the arguments seem to be arranged in contradictory pairs, but this arrangement is not maintained rigorously, and, more important, many of the conclusions are contradictory in themselves. Furthermore, the paired arrangement is broken up by what is listed above as argument 3*, the existence of which cannot be accounted for by the hypothesis that the paired arrangement is essential to whatever Plato wants to convey.

On the surface, the first four arguments are divided into two pairs, concerning what is true of the One and what is true of the "others." But this surface division covers another philosophically more important one. The first and fourth arguments deal with the totally unitary One, while the second and third with the One as necessarily a manifold. Thus the structure is ABBA, with 3* in the middle as an interlude.

The second four arguments have a different arrangement. They are, by and large, shorter than the first four, and yet the conclusions of the individual arguments are at least as weighty as those of the first four. Again, we find a division into a pair dealing with the One (or rather, the One that is not) and a pair dealing with the others. But beneath the surface we again find an interesting division, between arguments dealing with a construal of not-being that enables the One, even on this hypothesis, to have a rich internal structure and those interpreting "is not" as complete not-being, thus echoing that interpretation of the One in the first four arguments that represent it as one in every sense. But from this stand point, the pattern is not the same as in the first four. It is rather ABAB, with the B-pattern representing complete not-being.

Furthermore, the "pluralistic" analyses of arguments 5 and 7 resemble each other only superficially. The grounds for the interpretations are quite different. In argument 5, as we have seen, the nature ascribed to the One that is not emerges as a result of reflections on what it takes for something to be an intelligible true proposition. In argument 7, the many characteristics assigned to the One that is not are the results of concessions to those living in a world of appearances. Moreover, the first few qualities assigned to the subject in argument 5 are not pairs of contradictories. And since the conclusions reached in argument 7 reflect appearances only, whereas those in argument 8 represent how things are in reality as well, 7 and 8 are only partly contradicting each other. In short, the surface structure in the last four arguments constitutes a rather tattered cloth; it tears at the slightest provocation. The real conclusions concern three topics: intelligibility construed in ontological terms, the great difficulties in assigning complete not-being to anything, and the contrast between what merely appears to be the case and what is the case. In connection with the last topic, we noted also the ambiguity of "appearing."

These considerations jointly suggest that the surface structure is not rigorous and that in these texts Plato advances substantial metaphysical claims. The argument that such claims can be seen in the texts and that these are linked to the content of other dialogues from this period – that is, the *Parmenides* and the *Sophist* – is thus not vitiated by considerations of form. This schematic outline should also help one to see quickly the plausibility of the hypothesis advanced in the main part of this chapter: that the surface structure helps us to see why the Eleatic claim that their arguments deal with simple concepts and form a circle that can be entered at any place is untenable. The concepts of unity, being, not-being, motion, and so forth are complex. Depending on which aspects we stress, we arrive at very different conclusions concerning their existence and nature. As Plato suggests before the start of these arguments and after the conclusions of the negative survey of views about the Forms, only a person with exceptional gifts can find his way around these notions. I take this to mean that only a deep thinker can find a combination of the different aspects of these notions that will lead to a coherent and unique conception of the mode of being of Forms, of the partaking relation, and of the explanatory roles of the Forms.

Appendix 2: *The* Parmenides *and the Foundations of Mathematics*

As we saw in argument 2, Plato characterizes the One as indefinite in quantity. His derivation of this conclusion is illegitimate. Thus it is important to note that the argument introducing the link between unity and Number is introduced separately. As Plato says, in this argument we proceed in "another way" (143a). The argument (143a4–144a4) is the following:

Step 1. The One is; therefore the One partakes of Being. The One is not the same as Being (143a4–b2). Thus we have the One and Being.

Step 2. The One is different from Being, and neither the One nor Being is the same as Difference (143b2–8). So we have the One, Being, and Difference.

Step 3. Any two of the above constitute an instance of "both," and each of them is one. Hence we have instances of 2 and of 1 (143b8–d5).

Step 4. Adding one to any of the pairs formed yields 3. Thus we have 1, 2, 3, and addition (d5–7).

Step 5. The collection presented so far provides instances of odd and even (d8).

Step 6. Analysis of 2 as 2 times 1 and 3 as 3 times 1 yields also instances of multiplication (143e).

General conclusion: If the One is, Number is (144a4).

This series of steps starts with reflecting on the ontological configuration of the One, Being, and Difference, a configuration that must exist if the statement "The One is" is true. An analysis of this configuration yields all the basic arithmetic notions that, according to Plato, provide the foundation for the arithmetic of positive integers. In order to see the series of steps as a legitimate derivation, we need an additional premise. This says that if we encounter an instance of a Form or quality, then we can legitimately infer the existence of the Form or quality as well. That is, there can be no instance without that which is instantiated. Thus, for example, when we have instances of odd and even, we can count even and odd as also parts of the ontology. All the arithmetic under consideration can be seen as being about the elements of the series the odd, the even, and the relations revealed by the operations of addition and multiplication. We have the beginning of the series 1, 2, 3 (though 1 might not have counted as a number for some of Plato's contemporaries) and the basic kinds of odd and even, as well as addition and multiplication. Subtraction and division are the negative counterparts of the two basic positive operations, which explains their absence from the passage.

There is, however, another way of viewing this passage. This way is adopted, for example, by Cornford.[14] According to this interpretation, the passage is supposed to show how we can generate the series of positive integers. Cornford himself, however, saw that this task could not be carried out successfully, given only the material provided by the text. For taking as given 1, 2, 3, and multiplication, we will not be able to generate prime numbers. (Cornford refers to other interpretations of a prime, but there is no evidence for these in our text or any other Platonic text.) Cornford thinks that there is a way out. For addition is also introduced in the text. Hence one can always get the primes that way.

But this way out is not satisfactory. It provides either too much or too little in the way of conceptual machinery. If we include addition, as Cornford suggests, then we have too much, for multiplication becomes superfluous; we can get all the positive integers just by starting with 1 or 2 and adding elements. The stress on odd and even also becomes unnecessary. Without addition, however, the original problem of the primes emerges.

These considerations can be taken as indicating that Cornford misconstrued the task Plato sets himself here. Apart from the specific difficulties mentioned, we should also ask how such a generative project would fit into Plato's metaphysics. Forms are given. They are not generated, either from each other or from anything else. Their relationships are also given; they are there for us to discover, not for us to create. Even if someone wants to construe numbers not as Forms, but as Form-like "intermediate" entities, these considerations still hold. Such an in-between category of elements and their interrelations would also have to be given in a timeless way.

This brings us to the alternatives proposed above. Plato's project is "foundational." Arithmetic, as we saw earlier, in chapter 1, is a genuine technē. Hence it must have its own domain of entities that belong to the fundamental elements of reality. Plato not only shows here what these elements are and how they are interrelated, but also how they are related to the most fundamental elements of reality, the Forms. Thus the foundations of mathematics turn out to be parts of the ontological foundations of reality that Plato has been presenting all along.

The Forms play this kind of foundational role for other genuine sciences as well, such as geometry and music theory. The kind of arguments Plato adduces here for mathematics could also be carried out for the other genuine technai. Plato wants to show how the ontology of the One includes the ontology of the basic elements and relations found in elementary arithmetic. This interpretation brings our passage into harmony with the *Phaedo*. As we saw there, for Plato, numbers just are; we don't do anything to them with our operations of adding, multiplying, and the rest. These operations merely help us in understanding eternally fixed relations among mathematical elements. Within such an interpretation the "too little or too much" dilemma does not arise. Of course, we can see how, by addition, all the positive integers are related. But this by itself does not show all the other basic kinds and relationships that mathematics reveals. For those we need the additional notions that Plato introduces.

In calling this approach "foundationalist," we must not overemphasize the similarity between this passage and the work done on the foundations of mathematics in our own century by Russell, Whitehead, and others. The similarity lies in the aim of getting at the basic kinds and relations within arithmetic. The difference is that the modern attempts are also reductionist. They try to find the minimal number of primitive notions needed to define all of mathematics. There is, however, nothing analogous to the drive to reduce mathematics to, for example, logic in Plato's thought. He wants to know what mathematics is about, a legacy of the conditions on technē reviewed in chapter 1. Modern techniques of definability and reducibility are alien to his thinking.

In this way, the passage adds to the positive views expressed in the second part of the *Parmenides*. It shows another aspect of Plato's views of numbers, and as such it is an important early chapter in the history of the philosophy of mathematics.

NOTES

1   e.g. W. Hardie, *A Study in Plato*; W. Lynch, *An Approach to Plato's Metaphysics Through the* Parmenides; G. Ryle, "Plato's *Parmenides*"; F. Cornford, *Plato and Parmenides*.

2   Cornford, *Plato and Parmenides*, p. 80, thinks that Socrates counters Zeno's objections only for concrete sensibles, not for indivisibles like a point. But surely the issue here is conceptual, not physical, divisibility. The latter is given only as an example. A point, too, can partake of opposites with qualifications; for example, it is like another point and unlike a given line.

3   Ibid.

4   Ryle, "Plato's *Parmenides*."

5   The most important of these is G. Vlastos, "The *Third Man* Argument in the *Parmenides*."

6   W. Sellars, "Vlastos and the *Third Man*"; P. Geach, "The *Third Man* Again"; reply by G. Vlastos, *Platonic Studies*, pp. 354–7.

7   H. Cherniss, "The Relation of the *Timeaus* to Plato's Later Dialogues," p. 257; quoted again in J. Moravcsik, "The *Third Man* Argument and Plato's Theory of Forms," p. 57, and Vlastos, Platonic Studies, p. 342; but formal reconstructions keep reappearing.

8   See Moravcsik, "*Third Man* Argument."

9   If a, b, and c are large because they are copies of Large$_1$, then a, b, and c are

similar. But if a, b, and c are copies of Large₁, then all four of them must be similar. If we always account for similarity in terms of the copy–original relation, then we will be generating new similarities and need new originals.

10 For an account, see Cornford, *Plato and Parmenides*, pp. 98–9; for an account much closer to the spirit of this chapter, see S. Peterson, "The Greatest Difficulty for Plato's Theory of Forms; the Unknowability Argument of the *Parmenides* 133c–134c."

11 For other views, see M. Schofield, "The Antinomies of Plato's *Parmenides*." p. 146.

12 Schofield (Ibid., p. 154) writes that the problem of this argument involves predication and its perhaps unavoidable spatial connotations. But the key problem does not seem to me to involve predication in general or allegedly unavoidable spatial connotations of partaking. At issue is precisely the unique, nonspatial nature of partaking.

13 J. Moravcsik, "Being and Meaning in the *Sophist*."

14 Cornford, *Plato and Parmenides*, p. 141.

5

The Eleatic-Proof Theory of Forms of the *Sophist*

———————————— ◆ ————————————

The *Sophist* deals with three main themes: revisions of the theory of Forms after the criticisms and indirect response of the *Parmenides*, a new treatment of the realm of technai, and the defense of meaningful falsehood against the Eleatics, thereby also providing a way of exposing the sophists for what they are. This chapter is restricted to examining Plato's ingenious responses to both his arch-enemies, the Eleatics and the sophists, and his revised theory of Forms. There are many other important issues that a full examination of this dialogue would have to take up but these are beyond the scope of this book.[1]

In this post-Parmenides stage, the main question for the ontology is: Can Plato retain the two-level structure of the ontology that has been used so far? Or must he move on to three or four or even more levels in his metaphysics? The middle section of the *Sophist* is designed to answer this question. At the same time, as the name of the dialogue indicates, this is not Plato's only purpose. To be sure, the middle part of the dialogue defends the Forms against Eleatic attacks. But this vindicated ontology is also used – together with the Method of Division, to be taken up in the next chapter – to wage the battle against the sophists and unmask them as manufacturers of deceit and falsehood. Thus Plato succeeds in forging a brilliant dramatic structure even for this dialogue, which is more technical and dryly didactic than most. In the outer shell of the dialogue, sophistry is discussed. In the inner core, an Eleatic position that might have been used to buttress the sophists' case against Plato is defeated. At the end of the dialogue, with the help of the inner core, the sophist is defeated.[2]

The *Parmenides*, on our interpretation, spells out the unique mode of being of Forms. This entails the failure of spatial and temporal analogies to account for the nature of the Forms. They have to have a certain kind of unity that brings with it plurality. They are wholes that are not the mere sums of parts, and at the same time they do have parts. They have characteristics, but not in the way in which particulars in space and time have these. Their nature and existence is necessary.

There is partaking between particulars and Forms, as well as among the Forms. Partaking does not affect that of which things partake, and the nature that the participant derives from this relation is neither the whole nor a part of the nature of that in which it participates.

Given Parmenides' construal of not-being, there can be no intelligible account of a realm of appearances as a level between being and not-being. Parmenides, however, holds a monolithic interpretation of not being as the total absence of being of any sort, and the second half of the *Parmenides* shows the great conceptual difficulties involved in such a construal. In the *Sophist* this negative stance towards not-being, as no being of any kind, is reconsidered once more and is rejected as not only inapplicable but also unintelligible. Instead, Plato develops a relational notion of not-being and shows this to be paradox-free. This notion then plays a key role in the analysis of negative predication and meaningful falsehood. Other relational notions are introduced as well; utilizing these, Plato upholds the dichotomy between the Forms and the world of appearances and at the same time exhibits the nature of the sophist as a deceiver. The revised theory presents the realm of Forms as a tightly interrelated set of elements, which form a self-sufficient field. As we saw in chapter 1 ("All of reality is interrelated") and chapter 2 (about relations between virtues, numbers, and so forth), such interrelationship was already called for by other parts of the theory; but no explicit view recognizing this network-like aspect of the realm of Forms was developed. In the *Sophist* Plato undertakes this task, and as a result, the sophist does not escape.

The following are the main features of the revised theory of Forms. There are new relationships among the Forms, with a small set of Forms ordering the rest, leaving their nature as a whole made up of interwoven elements, giving them both stability and diversity, and uniqueness without special self-attribution. All this is accomplished without recourse to a regress involving more than the two-stage ontology familiar to us. There are also whole–part hierarchies, but in these, the Forms remain within the same ontological category. The Forms retain their explanatory roles. They are the objects of genuine understanding; they constitute whatever pure order there is in reality; and relations to them enable the less fundamental elements of reality to have natures that are derivative and temporal.

Partaking now includes a variety of relationships. The following constitute some illustrations:

1   Justice is a virtue.
2   The number two is an even number.
3   Mathematics is a technē.
4   Entity x is the same (or different from) entity y in respect of z.
5   Entities a and b are equal in length.
6   Entity e (which could be a particular like Theaetetus or a Form) partakes of Being.

Item 5 represents the familiar transcategorial participation used to account for the contrast between reality and appearance and the derivative and incomplete nature of the constituents of the world of appearance. Items 1, 2, and 3 represent what we will see as part–whole relations. But in these cases, the nature of the participant is not derivative or incomplete as in the case of item 5. Item 4 illustrates a still different kind of partaking, in which that of which elements partake – that is, the Same or the Different – have an ontological ordering role. They give entities their stability and unity, as well as their characteristic of having a nature consisting of diverse elements. But, as we shall see, though the entities of which things partake in these cases are prior to the participants, the relation cannot be reduced to that illustrated by item 5. Finally, item 6 illustrates a general condition constraining every element of what there is, cutting across the real–apparent distinction and involving a Form that Plato thinks of as dependent on some of its participants. In spite of this diversification of the partaking relation, Plato can still maintain the reality–appearance distinction. For the dependencies underlying the partaking relations among the Forms are mutual, while that involved in the categorial difference is asymmetrical.

Furthermore, the Forms are not just the universals or attributes of subsequent philosophy, even in this revised ontology. They are not just what things have in common, but the fundamental natures that make up constituents of the metaphysical order and are reflected in a variety of ways by their participants.

The second main topic is the anatomy of an enlarged conception of technē. As we saw in chapter 1, one can take as fundamental the dichotomy between the "real" sciences and the pseudo-sciences, thus distinguishing, for example, between mathematics and rhetoric. This scheme has at least two shortcomings: first, it does not show what characteristics cut across the genuine–pseudo distinction among the disciplines; second, and more important, if there are more than just two kinds of disciplines, then this framework is not rich enough to represent the facts. As dialogues like the *Philebus* show, Plato thought that there were more than two kinds of disciplines, with something like applied mathematics and geometry coming between dialectic and sophistry or rhetoric. Presumably angling does not quite fit the two extremes either – hence the expanded conception of technē that includes all these under its umbrella, with a rich set of internal distinctions marking out the natures of each.

The third major topic is falsehood. This account, by modern standards, is very brief and sketchy. It is a spin-off of the revamping of the theory of Forms. It centers on defending the coherence and intelligibility of falsehood against Eleatic objections. From the point of view of modern logical and semantic analysis, this may seem a modest enterprise; but in the context of the metaphysical struggles of Plato against his rivals, it is a major preoccupation.

The characterization of the sophist as one who spreads deceitful falsehood harks back to Book 5 of the *Republic*, where, as we saw, the "lovers of sights and sounds" were said to be in a state of being deceived. Plato's goal is to characterize meaningful, potentially deceiving falsehood in a paradox-free way, not just to deal with mere falsehood as such. One might, for example, analyze falsehood as plain nonsense. But plain nonsense does not deceive. It is difficult to represent these facts in Parmenides' philosophy, since the conditions of meaningfulness and those of truth are merged under the notion of "saying something" or, still better, "expressing something." In modern parlance, one could say that Parmenides has both a correspondence theory of meaning and a correspondence theory of truth. As we shall see, Plato retains this general framework, but with very different versions of truth and meaningfulness, thereby avoiding the disastrous conclusion that there can be no meaningful falsehood, on the grounds that this would be expressing that which is not.

As a result of wanting to read into the Platonic text (259–63) something like a modern semantic analysis of falsehood, people have credited Plato with insights anticipating some twentieth-century developments.[3] These include the disambiguation of "is" into the modern trichotomy of existence, identity, and predication[4] and other relevant disambiguations.[5] Recently, these efforts have been criticized effectively;[6] and there has been at least one interpretation showing that Plato's philosophizing here remains purely on the metaphysical plane and meets the Eleatic challenge, thereby demonstrating that what Plato has done here constitutes one of the great intellectual achievements of classical Greek philosophy.[7]

The interpretation of this chapter will portray Plato's work as primarily metaphysical, semantic results about what we can or cannot "say" (e.g. 256a12) being merely derivative. Hence the main stress is on the ontological material between 241 and 258.

Not-being and Blending

The discussion of not-being in the *Sophist* articulates the same position as that reached on a more simply intuitive level in the second half of the *Parmenides* (236e1–239b). The target is once more complete not-being, and three arguments are presented to show its paradoxicality. These are arranged to reveal greater and greater intellectual puzzles. In the first argument (237b6–e7), we are shown that since "that which is not" cannot be applied to anything that is, it is a phrase without possibility of application. But if it is necessarily inapplicable, then how could it express anything? The second argument (238a5–c11) goes further and questions the intelligibility of the conclusion of the first. Its first premise is that nothing that is can apply to that which is not. It continues by pointing out that number and numerical determination such as singularity or plurality are among the things that are. It concludes that such determinations cannot apply to not-being. Thus not-being as such cannot be conceived at all. For it to be conceivable, it would have to be a single item or a plurality of items. The third argument (238d4–239b3) is an interesting example of Plato's use of self-referentiality in argumentation. It points out that the conclusion just reached about inconceivability already presented the subject in the singular, thus violating its own claim. In sum, if not-being is as it is represented in these arguments, in the face of it we are reduced to silence (239b3–5).

This conclusion about not-being itself (*to me on auto kath' auto*) is taken up again later, at 258e6–259a1. This provides evidence for thinking that Plato accepted it and did not give it up even after the subsequent analysis.

In these arguments, not-being is complete lack of being. Therefore it cannot be a relational notion like "not to be this or that." Hence one would expect in the following passage in which being is discussed to also be dealing with being in a nonrelational sense (242c ff.). This is indeed the case. The dialogue turns to various theories of being in the sense of "what is" and shows these to be deficient. The deficiencies are not due to the theories leaving out this or that item, but to the theories not adequately reflecting what it is to say of something that it is – that is, their failure to see that nothing "just is." *Parmenides* 144b1–4 says that it is absurd to think that there can be something that lacks being. Nothing indicates that Plato came to reject this conclusion. It would follow, then, that being is not a predicate in the sense that it could be used to divide reality into items that have it and those that lack it. Being is "topic-neutral," as Gilbert Ryle used to say. The attack on different theories of what there is that follows here supports the view that this is the stance Plato takes up in the *Sophist*. Being is then, within the ontology of the *Sophist*, an all-encompassing Form of which everything necessarily partakes and which cannot be defined in terms of other notions or Forms.

This concept of being seems to correspond to the notion of existence. But some caveats are in order. We should not ascribe to Plato two separate notions of being: being in the sense of existence and being as predication. In modern, post-Kantian philosophy and within the framework of modern symbolic logic such a dichotomy makes good sense. In logic, we have different syntactic devices and symbols by which to indicate that something exists and that a certain property is ascribed to a putative entity. But for Plato, to be and to be something are two aspects of the same Form. If we put aside the modern "formal mode of discourse," it is easy to see that there can be nothing that does not also have some property, or "is this or that," and likewise that there cannot be something with a property that does not also have being in the sense of existence. Thus, within the Platonic scheme, it is reasonable to construe being and being something as two aspects of the same Form.[8]

This interpretation of Being needs to be placed in the context of how Plato decides in general what counts as one Form and what counts as many. It is certainly true that for Plato, to be and to be something entail each other. But this is hardly a reason for him to count these as aspects of the same Form. For example, the virtues entail each other but are distinct Forms, and the same is true of the Same and the Different.

The virtues are distinct, because the argument for their entailing each other is an ethical, rather than a metaphysical or a logical, argument. One could envisage views of ethics within which the necessary links do not hold. Needless to say, I do not wish to foist on Plato the modern distinctions of logical, metaphysical, and ethical; I merely use these to account for Plato's intuitions.

The Same and the Different are viewed by Plato as positive versus negative and as opposites. (Evidence for this is also given by the metaphysical parts of the *Timaeus*.) Thus, these are not just aspects of the same very abstract Form, but two Forms which pervade all reality and complement each other. This is not so with Being and predication.

As we shall see, the two aspects are being and relational being, not predication as such. Relational being is developed in passages which we will be looking at shortly. Thus we have "to be" and "to be in relation to something" as the two aspects. The formula "x is F" is made true by the combination of "F is" and "F is in relation to x" (it is assumed that x is too). Thus, intuitively, this case is different from the other two examined briefly above.

There is another interesting, relevant case, that of *kinesis*. This is only one Form, even though it has as two key "species" locomotion and qualitative change. There is no strictly formal principle on the basis of which one could say why in this case there is only one Form.

We see, then, that Platonic decisions about how many Forms there are in these cases is made by metaphysical intuition, not formal criteria.

This is not an anomalous situation. We have its analog in the ontology of modern semantics. In many semantic theories, logical equivalence is not the criterion for individuating abstract entities called "meanings." That principle is given by the notoriously intuitive criterion of synonymy, a notion much more fine-graded than that of logical equivalence. Yet, this notion is still felt to be necessary by many philosophers and practically all linguists. Of course, once it is decided what is a Form and what is only an aspect or a species of a Form, Plato can give rigorous arguments for individuating Forms. As we shall see, these are based on the principle that A and B are distinct if they have different properties.

The examination of being *simpliciter* is divided into two sections. The first (243d8–245e2) deals with theories telling us that being is "one or many" – that is, they tell us that to be is to be this or that or that to be is equivalent to one privileged notion like unity. Plato calls the theories treated in the second part (246a7–249d4) "qualitative" – that is, they claim that only entities with this or that feature are "really real."

The example used in the first section is "naturalistic" – that is, it claims to reduce being to properties like being hot or being cold. But the logical impact of the argument reaches far beyond the scope of these examples. It affects any theory that attempts to delimit what it is to be to entities that have one or two or three or more of a certain set of privileged attributes.[9] Naturalistic theories are simply a historically plausible paradigm for this sort of analysis. But Plato's claim is not that such thinkers have an empirically inadequate physics. His point is conceptual and thus applicable to any physics. If someone says that all there is are elements that are hot or cold, Plato responds by claiming that this does not explain what it is to be. In modern terms, one might say that even if being were coextensive with such a pair of terms, it would not be intensionally equivalent to them.

The example of a monistic analysis is that of the Eleatics, since they provided a sample of such a theory that presumably everyone in Plato's audience knew. The "unitarian" theory under attack is not spelled out very rigorously. Are the unitarians saying that to be is to be one, or that being is just unity, or simply that there is only one entity in the world? Plato takes the thesis at its best to be the identification of "to be" with such initially plausible candidates as to be one or to be a whole. He proceeds to show that we can identify being neither with one of these nor with the two jointly (244b9–245e7). For a part of the argument, he relies on the tension – seen already in the second half of the *Parmenides* – between being simply a unitary entity and being a whole. A whole must have parts, but that which is simply one is partless. Being as such, however, is not involved in this tension. It is in harmony with both notions. It does not exclude being a whole; nor does it exclude being strictly unitary like a geometrical point. Hence it must be a distinct notion.[10] The main conclusion is that being is indefinable.

In these arguments, Plato was dealing with theses clearly not his own. Thus he cannot presuppose his own theory of Forms. And, as we have seen, in fact none of his arguments presupposes his own ontology. How shall we, then, interpret, for example, the hot and the cold? It is plausible to think of the denotation of such "mass terms" within common sense in mereological terms. The hot is simply the sum of all heat, the cold the sum of all cold (or alternatively, the hot and cold things). Within a naturalistic theory of the sort Plato seems to have in mind, the world is made up of hot and cold items (or fire or air or water?). Reality is exhausted by some such pair or trio, and the items may or may not overlap. Plato restricts himself to pointing out that such a scheme does not say what it is to be, even within a "mass term" analysis of being.

The same mereological interpretation can be applied to the unitarians.

The One or the Whole can be construed as undifferentiated "stuff" in a purely conceptual, mereological sense without implications of materiality. (An example of such abstract mass terms in modern English is "nonsense.") Plato's point, to use more recent terminology, is that, regardless of whether these proposals are extensionally adequate or not, they do not give us the equivalent of what it is to be, within or outside a mereological analysis.

In the next part, Plato attacks what in later philosophy would be labeled "materialism" and "idealism." At least these theories try to say what being is, rather than just delineate its extension. Both these theories say that only entities with a certain salient attribute merit being recognized as existing or real. Plato's point concerning both theories is the same. The materialists are wrong if they think that to be excludes being immaterial, and the "friends of the Forms" err if they think that to be excludes the changing elements. Thus the conclusion is once more the same: being is an all-inclusive and indefinable element of reality. This does not rule out arguing for various ontological priorities; but such should not be at the cost of the ascription of being to the favored items. There are other ways of saying that this is more fundamental than that. As we shall see in the next chapter, Plato does mark off some things as more fundamental than others. But being is there not being used normatively; it is not being reserved for the metaphysical aristocracy.

In 245e–246b Plato attacks those who think that to be is to be a body and to be touchable. Is Plato attacking what he took to be a historically influential position or a possible position to be guarded against? There are difficulties with both alternatives. First, the touchability criterion sounds like empiricism made into a metaphysical principle. It is logically distinct from a "body ontology." One could reject empiricism and still subscribe to a body ontology. What would untouchable bodies be like? And should we label body ontology an early form of materialism?

The most plausible ancestry for materialism is the kind of "stuff metaphysics" that we find in early Ionian speculation. Within this conception, what is fundamental is some scattered mass, or stuff, and everything is derived from the transformations of its various parts. This resembles the Cartesian notion of matter as extension and the picture of extended stuff scattered across space and time and labelled "matter." But this is precisely the view that Democritus opposes. His key insight is that the stuffs are the explicanda, and that we need some primitive fundamental entities that can be counted to explain these, rather than the other way around. Democritus was clearly not an empiricist; but it is far from obvious that we should see him as falling under Plato's label of "body ontology" (see Diels fragments B11 and B125).

Democritus was not an idealist – that is, a believer in an ontology whose basic building blocks are independent abstract domains. But this does not make him a materialist necessarily. His basic elements are atoms (one or two kinds, depending on whether one reads him as also postulating mathematical atoms), their primitive shapes, and the void.

There is no need to try to force Democritus into a conceptual straitjacket of idealism versus materialism, especially since the Cartesian notion of materialism depends on the contrast of the material with the mental, a contrast clearly not in Democritus.

It is unlikely that Plato has Democritus as one of his targets in this section. In fact, it is not clear exactly what the impact of Democritean thinking was on any facet of Plato's thought. The examples that Plato brings up in this section count equally against the empiricists and the "body ontologists." We can leave open the question of whether actual thinkers or possible positions are the target.

One might speculate that Plato regarded Democritus and his followers as falling in the category of those who are confused about being and not-being. For Democritus described the full as being and the void as non-being, even though both are basic constituents of reality. Such a use of non-being would violate Plato's conception of how the notions of being, non-being, and reality are related.

In 247d8–e3, Plato offers a delineation of being as whatever affects or is affected. The exact interpretation of this phrase, as well as the determination of who the "friends of the Forms" are, are matters beyond the scope of this chapter.[11] But there is evidence from Plato's wide use of "affect" and "is affected" that even if the delineation is accepted by him, it does not conflict with the topic-neutrality of being. The attack on the friends of the Forms ends with the conclusion either that both the changing and the unchanging are or that everything both changes and is in some ways unchanging. Both these readings are compatible with the interpretation of Plato's positive view presented in this chapter.

For the understanding of the lines that follow, it is crucial to keep in mind that Plato is still not working entirely within his own framework. His imaginary opponents raise a puzzle after the critical review of all these theories. This puzzle, then, is presumably couched not in Plato's terms but in terms of the ontology acceptable to his opponents. Thus Rest and Motion (or being unchanging and change) should be construed mereologically. Motion is simply the sum of all motions or all that moves, whereas Rest is the sum of all states of rest or all the things that rest. Since on the second interpretation there is a large overlap between the two and the argument to be considered focuses on the tension between the two, it seems more feasible to construe the items as motions and states of change.

The texts surveyed so far do not allow us to say much in a positive way either about being or about not-being. In the face of not-being, we have been reduced to silence, and in the case of being, we have been given only noninformative characterizations, such as that being encompasses both what changes and what does not, and hence are not capable of saying what being is in terms of other notions. Now, in 250a1–c4, Plato presents our situation as a predicament. We ended up with terms – namely, Rest and Motion – that seem to include everything on any account. But Rest and Motion are opposites, and since being is not the opposite of either, it seems "outside" both. On the other hand, it is difficult to see how there could be anything "outside" Rest and Motion.

If we construe this puzzle not within Plato's ontology, but within a kind of commonsense mereology, then it is genuine and lands us in the conceptual soup. For, viewing matters mereologically, the argument with its paradoxical conclusion goes through.[12] We can think of motions and states of rest as two distinct sums, in view of their opposition. But being includes both.

How, then, do we explain the opposition and the fact that being is not affected by it? Can we do this in purely mereological terms? Alternatively, we can think of the two sums as what changes and what does not change. But then the two together make up exactly the sum of the parts of which being consists. So in what mereological sense is being "outside" the two? The only solution seems to be to get away from mereological conceptions in trying to solve this problem.

The conclusion that Plato wants us to come to is that being has "its own nature" and that this is neither to be at rest nor to be in motion (250c6–7). But it is up to Plato to show in the subsequent passages that this state of affairs admits of a paradox-free interpretation. This demonstration, in his view, requires taking up a different conceptual scheme: namely, his own ontology. The change is introduced by the announcement that we find ourselves in the same *aporia* ("puzzlement") with respect to both being and not-being (250d7–e5). But if we add up all that has been said about the two notions, this does not seem to be true. We did not arrive at the same self-referential paradoxes about being as we did about not-being. What Plato must have in mind is that with regard to neither notion have we arrived at the kind of clarification one would normally expect of difficult notions: namely, a demonstration of which items fall under them and which do not and of what other notions can be used to define them. Our inability to accomplish this in either case should not blind us to the differences in the two treatments. There is evidence that Plato was aware of the different status of the two notions in his philosophy. For in 258 he says that we gave up "long ago" talking about the opposite of being, whereas he never makes such a statement about being.

In 250e9–251a1 Plato suggests that in order to arrive at an adequate understanding of being and not-being, we need to consider the two notions together. Such simultaneous treatment makes most sense if we find the two notions intertwined. And sure enough, this is the situation confronting us when we turn to the relational aspects of the two notions. In this way, without any fallacies or misleading moves, Plato turns from the examination of nonrelational being and not-being to the examination of the relational aspects. This is accomplished, in fact, in the lines that follow, without any commitment to a thesis that the two notions have exactly the same nature.

The discussion shifts not only to relational aspects but also to the treatment of these notions as Forms. But of course, to show the relational aspect of Being is to show, in this context, something about the Form of Being, which indirectly illuminates its nonrelational aspect. The text, as we shall see, argues that relational Being must "mix" with relational Not-Being and that this is just as fundamental a fact about reality as the presence of all-encompassing Being in its nonrelational aspect. Thus, to be necessarily involves an entity in its also having a share in Not-being.

The key Eleatic questions that Plato is confronting here are: How can we make sense of Not-Being? And can anything be, somehow, different from Being? By 256e, we have received his answer to the second question: "Yes." We can render Not-being paradox-free and show how many things in some of their aspects are different from Being. The solution entails the fact that all parts of reality are interrelated in certain ways. The next task is to make explicit and explain these blendings and communions. If there is "blending" between elements of reality, then two kinds that "blend" can contain or characterize the same entity. This is the context for the question that is raised in 251: namely, how can one entity be characterized by several common terms that introduce different kinds. This semantic feat can be accounted for only by presenting a coherent ontology of "mixing" kinds. (In these discussions, Plato is still dealing with opponents who do not accept his theory of Forms; hence the nontechnical use of terms like *koinoonia*, e.g. in 251e8.) If mixing is not possible, then any given entity can belong only to one kind, and we cannot form meaningful, true statements of subject–predicate form or of any form that involves some relations between elements of reality. (Plato's claim and example can be taken in more than one way. For a more detailed discussion, see Appendix 1.)

Plato considers three alternatives: either no elements of reality mix, or all mix with everything, or some do and some do not mix (251d). The claim that no elements mix is treated within the examination of the claim that genuine statement making is impossible and is found to be self-refuting (252c2–9). One cannot even state this atomistic claim without blending elements introduced by "being apart," "by itself," "others," and so on. Given the correspondence theory of truth and meaning assumed by the dialogue, this shows that there must be some blending of elements.

The hypothesis that all mix with all is refuted by taking as one of its – absurd – consequences the fact that motion and rest would then blend, and thus motion would be completely at rest (252d–e). If we interpret the two kinds blending as the claim that the Forms Motion and Rest partake of each other, then the conclusion is a non sequitur. But if we interpret it mereologically, then the conclusion follows. For, if the two kinds blend completely, then all motion is rest and all rest motion. Within such a framework there is no way of distinguishing the two totally overlapping entities.

Having eliminated the two extreme possibilities, Plato turns to examining the only remaining, alternative thesis, that some elements blend and others do not. Plato interprets this thesis in terms of the claim that some kinds blend and others do not. Understanding this both in outline and in detail requires a global theoretical science. Such a discipline had already been discussed in other dialogues, where it is named "dialectic." We start, then, with an examination of Being and Not-Being as objects of theoretical understanding – that is, Forms – and this leads us to understanding how the two are intertwined. This, in turn, leads to an understanding of how elements of reality are embedded in a global communion. A detailed characterization of that communion would also be the task of dialectic, although it is clearly beyond the scope of this dialogue. But an outline of dialectic is given in 253. It is worth stressing the turn in the nature of the discussion. Until now, Plato has had to discuss the alternatives and demonstrate the "middle road" without presupposing the theory of Forms. But now that the general thesis of partial blending has been established vis-à-vis his opponents without begging questions, he can use his ontology to clear up the nature of the interrelations and show that this does not lead to paradox.[13]

The Communion of the Forms and the Theory of Connectors

The science of blending is characterized as a technē in 253a10, thus linking this text with earlier discussions of epistemology, as reviewed in chapter 1. Plato thinks that to understand the blending of kinds, it is useful to think of it as analogous to the blending of letters. At this point, we should think of both "blending," as used here, and the notion of partaking as primitive, undefined basic notions. The analogy has two salient aspects. The first is that not all letters harmonize – that is, can be parts of combinations in writing or pronunciation. The second, which is also crucial for Plato, is that there are consonants and vowels and that the latter have as their key function the making of connections. Without them, consonants do not combine. Thus we expect to find vowel-like Forms in the new version of Plato's ontology. Such are indeed involved in Plato's characterization of dialectic. This science is described by Plato in many ways (253a–e). But among its tasks, we find understanding which Forms blend with which others, the reason for separations, and how some Forms pervade all Forms, thereby making blending possible. This last task directs our attention to the vowel-like Forms. (For a more detailed discussion of dialectic, see Appendix 2.)

In 253d1–3 dialectic is also characterized as entailing understanding which Forms are the same and which different. If the text between here and 264 is to be rendered intelligible, we must assume that *auton* ("same") and *heteron* ("different") are used in a qualitative sense.[14] In fact, this is also the primary sense of the equivalent English expressions. The notions of identity and nonidentity are derivative, on a commonsense view. For example, two kinds of animal are the same, since they are both animal species. At the same time, they are different, because they have different characteristics. Of course, if two things are different, they are not identical. Likewise, at least for those who accept the principle of identity of indiscernibles, if two things are completely the same, then they are also identical, or "one" as the Greeks would put it. Being distinct and being one, on such an account, are consequences of certain relations of qualitative sameness and difference obtaining; they are not simply basic notions. Plato uses the notions of qualitative difference to exhibit cases of distinctness and oneness. Some of these, as we shall see, emerge in his proofs that the five greatest Forms are indeed distinct. But it was up to Plato's pupil, Aristotle, to introduce as separate notions qualitative and numerical identity and nonidentity.

The Platonic dialectic described here is not the same as the classificatory scheme of genus and species that subsequently emerged. To be sure, as long as we operate on a purely conceptual level, such relations are included in what the dialectic can exhibit. But we should concentrate on the additional, distinctive feature of Plato's conception of dialectic here: namely, the metaphysical role of the connectors.

Why does Plato need to posit (or discover) connectors? Why can he not simply embrace the following two theses: (1) Some Forms have participant-classes that include the participant-classes of some other Forms, and (2) some Forms can partake of others – for example, the virtues of wisdom and courage of Virtue, or even numbers of Number. A passage like 255e3–6 indicates that for Plato this would not be an adequate account. In this passage he says that it is the Form of Difference that makes each entity distinct, not its own respective nature. This remark ties in with what we have seen in the second half of the *Parmenides*: namely, a distinction between what a Form is "according to its own nature" and what other attributes it must have. In the *Sophist* this distinction is now linked to other salient facts by way of the theory of Connectors. Plato wants to explain the following three facts:

1   (i) Some Forms blend, while others do not.
2   Some Forms necessarily partake of each other.
3   Forms have their own natures.

The first fact cannot be the explanans, since the Eleatics challenge its possibility. It seems to require the existence of some sort of Not-Being, and this is what the Eleatics doubt. This also applies to the second fact. This gives an ontological analysis of the fact that some Forms are attributed to each other. This fact involves qualitative difference and hence Not-Being. Hence this cannot be the explanans either.

The notion of the nature of a Form implicit in the third fact, as we saw in the *Parmenides*, is narrow from a modern point of view. It does not subsume under the nature of an entity all its necessary attributes. Rather, as we saw, the nature of the One is just "to be one," and the nature of, for example, the Different is just "to be different." Given these characterizations, shall we say that when a Form necessarily partakes of another, it both has and does not have the "nature" of the other? These puzzles cannot be resolved merely by distinguishing identity from predication. The puzzle is not: How can a Form partake of another Form without becoming identical with it? Rather, it is: How can a Form partake of another Form without somehow acquiring at least part of the nature of that Form? (This question emerges in a different guise with respect to genus–species relations; see chapter 6.) Plato's response seems to be to see Sameness and Difference as fundamental metaphysical entities, on a par with Being. What enables each Form to have its own nature yet also partake of other Forms, without doing violence to their nature or its own, is its partaking of Sameness with respect to itself and Difference with respect to other Forms. Given the characterization of a Form as having its "own nature," this cannot include being different (except in the case of Difference). So Plato construes qualitative Difference as a universal vowel-Form, which necessarily pervades everything, making it possible for an item to have and (and we shall see) lack, or not have, certain attributes. The existence of the Same and the Different underlies distinctness and diversity, and this in turn makes blending and not blending possible. The fundamental law is the all-pervasive, connective functioning of the vowel-Forms. As we shall see in the next chapter, the Method of Division grafts further laws onto this.

This structure of the realm of Forms makes them the object of dialectic, as described. This presupposes that it is correct to regard the Forms under discussion – that is, Rest, Motion, Being, Sameness, and Difference – as distinct. This is problematic for the Eleatics, especially with regard to the last three. For if everything necessarily partakes of all three, how can the three be distinct? Why not just say that they make up one universal kind and that we have three – or five – names for just one entity? Faced with this challenge, Plato offers a series of proofs demonstrating the distinctness of the five Forms. The proofs start at 254d.

Proof 1 (254d4–12):

    P1.   Take Being, Motion, and Rest among the "greatest" Forms.
    P2.   Motion does not blend with Rest.
    P3.   Being blends with either Motion or Rest.
    C.   Being is not the same as Motion or Rest; hence, there are three distinct Forms.

The conclusion follows, since Being has been shown to have a property that neither Rest nor Motion has. The justification for taking these three Forms is that they have already been introduced earlier. As Plato says in 254d7, we agreed "earlier" that the two do not blend. Blending in the earlier passage was interpreted in this chapter mereologically. Now we can redescribe it within the theory of Forms in terms of classinclusion relations. The point is that, with suitable qualifications, partaking of Rest and Motion can be shown to be inconsistent, whereas no such inconsistency arises by having the same thing partake of Being and of Motion, even if the latter is further specified.

Proof 2 (254e1–255b6):

P1.   Whatever is applied (or attributed) to both Rest and Motion (in the same way) must be distinct from both.

P2.   Sameness and Difference are attributed (in the same way) to both Rest and Motion.

C.   Sameness is distinct from both Rest and Motion, and Difference is distinct from Rest and Motion.

The qualification "in the same way" is to be understood as self-evident. Plato is not considering the application of X to Z and W so that X is identical with Z and only an attribute of W. Indeed, if something is attributed to both Rest and Motion in the same way, it is either not the same as either or the same as both. In the second case, the unwanted conclusion mentioned in 255a10–13 would follow. All rest would be motion, and vice versa. Opposites would have to change their nature – which is impossible.

Proof 3 (255b8–c6):

P1.   If Being and the Same were one, then "it is" and "it is the same" would designate (*semainein*, b11–12) the same thing.

P2.   Thus "Rest and Motion are" would have to be the same as "Rest and Motion are the same."

P3.   But P2 is false.

C.   Being and the Same are distinct.

If Being and the Same were one Form, then in every context "X is" and "X is the same" would have to be synonymous. When we say "Both Rest and Motion are," we are neither saying that the two are the same, or one, or that each is the same as itself. Both Being and the Same can be seen in this way to have their own respective natures.

We now have all but two of the required proofs. One of these – that is, that Difference and the Same are distinct – is never given. Plato takes it to be obvious that if these are opposites, they are also distinct. But the other is presented at the end of this section.

Proof 4 (255c8–e1):

> P1.   Of beings, some are relational and some are "by themselves" complete.
> P2.   Difference is always relational.
> C.   Being and Difference are distinct.

The conclusion clearly follows from the premises. The two Forms do not have all their properties in common. The differentiating property has been the object of much recent controversy, however.[15] I have already suggested that Being has two aspects, corresponding roughly to existence and attribution. Thus it seems plausible to start with these. On this interpretation, Being has these two aspects, but Difference is always relational hence the two are not one.

Someone might object that on this interpretation the argument compares Difference with Being. But P1 talks about beings, not being. In response, one can point to the asymmetry in the subjects of P1 and P2. The first seems to be about beings, but the second is not about different things, but Difference perse. Thus, something must give.

One alternative would be to say that the argument compares things that are with things that are different. But this is no contrast at all; everything both is and is different. According to the other alternative, Being and Difference are contrasted. This would be consistent with the interpretation proposed above. A third alternative would be to take P2 to be about differences – that is, instances of Difference. We would then have to construe P1 to be about "beings" – that is, instances of states of being. But on our interpretation, the existence/predication view yields exactly such a contrast – that is, between the complete and the incomplete occurrences. It seems, then, that this interpretation fits the text and contributes to the overall interpretation of the "inner core" developed in this chapter.

On the basis of these proofs, Plato concludes that there are indeed these five distinct, different Forms: Being, Sameness, Difference, Rest, and

Motion. In terms of the letter analogy, the first three are vowel-Forms, the last two consonant-Forms. Calling them all "greatest" does not mean that, for Plato, these are the most important Forms in all contexts. In different contexts, different Forms are fundamental: for example, from the ethical point of view, the Form of the Good; from a cosmological point of view, the Form of Proportionality.

The way Plato phrases the whole problem of distinctness and his solutions to it show a fine awareness of the difference between names and named things. For example, at 255c8–10, the question of whether Being and Difference are really two items or just two names and one thing is considered.

The proofs also indicate the intensional nature of the Forms. Being, Sameness, and Difference are coextensive; as Plato puts it, everything partakes of each. Still, they are not the same Form, but have their own respective natures. This is crucial for maintaining the ontological explanatory role of these Forms. If coextensionality determined their identity, then they could not have their own nature and could not be more fundamental than the elements which they order into a collection of distinct but interrelated entities. The proofs also give evidence that strong, unique self-attribution of the sort discussed in chapter 2 has been abandoned. For if Plato still accepted such attributions, then these proofs would not be necessary.

The proofs leave us with an interesting metaphysical picture. Each Form has its own nature and also has other distinguishing attributes. Yet it is the pair of Forms, Sameness and Difference that makes everything what it is and different from other things.

From a modern point of view, this might seem like metaphysical overkill. For in post-Platonic metaphysics, the following proposals emerged. One of these would take notions of identity and nonidentity as syncategorematic; that is, the words do not denote any entities, and the notions are defined syntactically. It would then utilize the principle of the identity of indiscernibles to settle matters of identity case by case. It has no additional metaphysical "baggage." Plato would never accept such a view. For him, what in the modern framework are syncategorematically defined notions are precisely the most important building blocks – and plaster – of reality. Needless to say, he does not explicitly reject the syncategorematic view. Such a view might seem very natural to a twentieth-century philosopher like W. V. O. Quine, but it would never have emerged in Plato's time. For the Eleatic challenge is raised on the ontological plane, and Plato, like anyone else at that time, would have assumed that it must be met on that level as well.

Another view would deny the principle of identity of indiscernibles and take the identity of each thing as a simple basic fact.[16] This view would not be acceptable to Plato either. There are many examples of arguments in the dialogues that support the hypothesis that Plato accepted the identity of indiscernibles. Some of these are in the proofs of the *Sophist* to which we shall turn shortly. Plato's interests are quite different from those of people who would argue for the other view. He focuses mainly on the distinctness of abstract nonparticulars, whereas the examples cited by the foes of the principle of the identity of indiscernibles usually involve particulars.

The fact that Plato has a separate object of sameness might tempt some historians to view his theory as resembling later theories which postulate a basic primitive entity called haecceity and see this as what makes things distinct. But this does not quite fit either. For Plato does not say that only sameness is the ground of distinctness. As we have seen, he also has arguments relying on qualitative difference. But what may seem from a modern point of view overkill does not appear that way when viewed in the context of Plato working out an alternative to Eleatic metaphysics. The Forms have their own nature, in the narrow sense discussed already. They also have what we would call "necessary attributes" – for example, relationality. Having all this entails being different from many other things. Plato says that, contrary to what the Eleatics say, this Not-Being is not complete lack of being, but qualitative Difference. Everything necessarily partakes of it. There is nothing that is "pure being." In this way, the combination of giving up unique strong self-attribution, keeping the notion of a Form having its own nature, keeping the principle of identity of indiscernibles, and adding Sameness and Difference as all-pervasive vowel-Forms constitute Plato's answer and alternative to the Eleatic views.

After establishing the distinctness of the five Forms under discussion, Plato illustrates how, with the help of the ontological machinery developed, a number of paradoxes of not-being can be resolved (255e11–256e6). Recent literature has stressed the semantic consequences of these resolutions and has sought the key to the problem solving in disambiguations of key terms. But Plato's main aim is to show that certain ontological entities have a paradox-free nature. This is neither equivalent to nor requires disambiguations of specific words. The discussion centers on the nature of Forms and only derivatively on consequences for particulars.[17] This interpretation of the text on the paradoxes is supported by the fact that, at the end, Plato does not announce that we have now disambiguated various expressions, but rather that we have found a paradox-free way of accounting for how things can be different from Being. The issue once more is not that of nonidentity but of qualitative difference. Plato's proof is not about things being numerically nonidentical with Being, but about things having qualitative natures that differ from the nature of Being. This is what the Eleatics would have regarded as scandalous. But Plato shows that Difference orders all Forms, including Being. Being in turn is necessary, so that Difference can be. This is the necessary interwovenness of the Forms that underlies qualitative diversity. Furthermore, this interwovenness among Forms enables the world of "appearances" to also contain qualitative differences, albeit in a less orderly way.

There are four paradoxes, each of which entails greater surface perplexity than the previous one.

First paradox and resolution (255e11−256a1)

Paradox: Motion is and is not Rest.

Resolution: Motion partakes of Being, and Motion partakes of Difference with respect to Rest. This is a coherent state of affairs. We can derive the first part from the proofs of distinctness just surveyed and the second from earlier passages on Motion and Rest not blending.

Second paradox and resolution (256a2−7)

Motion is and is not same.

Resolution: Motion partakes of the Same in relation to itself, and it partakes of the Different in relation to the Same. Both conjuncts follow from the proofs of distinctness surveyed above and once more constitute a coherent state of affairs.

Third paradox and resolution (256c5−10)

Motion is and is not different.

Resolution: Motion partakes of the Different in relation to the Different. Here we have one complex state of affairs, articulated in terms of interweaving of the Forms, that explains the surface paradox.

This leads to the final climactic paradox.

Fourth paradox and resolution (256d5 – 10)

Motion is and is not.

Resolution: Motion partakes of Being, and Motion partakes of the Different in relation to Being. Both these follow from the account of the distinctness of the "greatest Forms."

Though this may be the most difficult state of affairs for the Eleatics to swallow, it is just an instance of the general law that each Form partakes of Being, since each Form is, and that, at the same time, each Form is qualitatively different from Being. Each has its own nature and its own set of necessary attributes; and at the same time each partakes of Being – that is, has that unique indefinable relation to Being that is spelled out, indirectly, in the second half of the *Parmenides*. As we shall see, relational Being and Not-Being constitute the cement that enables each element to function on its own, bound to all the others. The resolution of the fourth paradox captures that aspect of Not-Being that we have been hunting for since 250 – that is, since we saw that the initial discussions of being and not-being left us in the dark. Once we see how things can be and be different qualitatively from Being, we see the foundation of a metaphysical account of negativity.

With the ontological machinery developed, Plato can explain the earlier puzzle of how Being can be "outside of Rest and Motion." It has its own nature and at the same time has Rest and Motion partake of it, without this destroying either the nature of Being or that of the other two Forms.

In order to explain how Being and Not-Being function intertwined, Plato now focuses on a notion that, according to the interpretation presented in this chapter, was already alluded to earlier as an aspect of Being (255c–e): namely, relational Being. This notion is developed in 256d11–e6.[18] Plato takes two truths already established about Motion – namely, that it has Being and that it has its own nature, which is different from that of Being – and then generalizes to cover all Forms. It is true of all of them that they have Being and their own natures which are different from the nature of Being. It is the nature of qualitative Difference, which partakes of Being and pervades all the Forms, that enables them to function in this way. Thus, Plato concludes that, in relation to each Form, Being is many and Not-Being is indefinitely many (256e5−6). This inference from the preceding material yields an interpretation of relational Being and Not-Being. For the relevant uses:

x is F   = F is in relation to x;
x is not-F = F is not in relation to x.

As we shall see, Plato uses relational Being and Not-Being in these senses in the subsequent passages. We obtain a much less satisfactory interpretation if we try to force the meaning "not identical with Being" on the Not-Being that is discovered at the end of the paradox resolutions.[19]

Given our interpretation, we can unpack the conclusion just reached as:

P1.   Each Form is in relation to many items.
P2.   Each Form is not in relation to an indefinite number of items.

Why the asymmetry? P1 says that each Form can have many items as participants, be these other Forms or non-Forms. The negative thesis says that with respect to each Form there are many items that are not participants. For example, equality is not a virtue. Thus Virtue is not in relation to equality. But qualitative difference also operates on another level, as in the statement "Equality is different from justice." Of course, one must add "with respect of qualities $Q_1 \ldots Q_n$" in a full analysis. If those two Forms are different, then there is some Z that is in relation to justice and not in relation to equality. Each Form is negatively related to many potential participants and is also different from an indefinite collection of entities that make up the rest of reality.

What are the premises on which P1 and P2 are based? Now that the existence and unique nature of each Form have been defended, these entities can indeed be objects in which many items participate. The interwovenness of the vowel-Forms and their all-pervasiveness make this possible. The negative predications are made possible by the functioning of Difference. Thus we can also explain "not blending": for example, why and how the Equal and Wisdom are different and have different participant ranges. In some cases − as with opposites suitably relativized − the ranges even exclude each other.

Are relational Being and Not-Being replacing the notions of partaking and difference? A closer look should convince us that relational Being is not equivalent to partaking. Rather, its introduction complicates the analysis of predication. Instead of just "x is F = x partakes of F," we have "F partakes of Being in relation to x" or the reverse; the text does not say that only one of these is an acceptable analysis. If we substituted relational Being for each occurrence of partaking, we would end up with an infinite regress. Plato's presentation of relational Being confronts us with a dilemma that he does not address directly: namely, are there three equally powerful vowel-Forms, Being, Same, and Different, or is relational Being to be interpreted as the super-connector, linking the other connectors to the items that partake of them as well? Either analysis could be worked out in a coherent way, but Plato does not pursue these matters.

Reflection on relational Being and Not-Being should help us to understand Plato's new account of how the world of appearances reflects the Forms and how attributive relations, not only in transcategorial cases, but also between Forms, are possible. The older, direct relational account is replaced by the connector theory, according to which, positive and negative attributive relations and hence, indirectly, distinctness are made possible by special vowel-like Forms that intertwine with each other and relate subjects and attributes.

This theory also leads to a revised, extended account of partaking. The model for partaking in dialogues like the *Phaedo* and the *Republic* was:

x partakes of F = x is F deficiently = x is both F and not-F.

As we saw in chapter 2, there are two cases of this: first, incomplete attributes, like Equality and the numbers; secondly, cases in which the key truths about kinds hold only under idealizations (various natural kinds and geometry).

The partaking relation thus construed is cross-categorial, linking non-Forms to Forms, and never necessary, but always contingent.

Plato does discuss, however, topics such as ethics and mathematics that require that there should be partaking among Forms. With the connector theory, we can represent these cases as well. They will cover such instances as "Justice is a virtue," "Two is an even number," and, in our dialogue, "Sophistry is an art."

This extension of partaking is far-reaching. The relation is now no longer always cross-categorial. Furthermore, in these cases it is necessary, not contingent. Finally, partaking in these cases does not mean deficient attribution in the earlier sense. Wisdom is not both a virtue and not a virtue; the number two is not both even and not even; and so on.

Let us now consider the cases of partaking that were uncovered as we traced the functioning of the vowel-Forms: for example, "x partakes of the Different in relation to y with respect of Z." Cases like this fall between the first two types discussed above; they are not always transcategorial and are necessary. On the other hand, they have the feature of the earlier model of the participant being both F and not-F. For example, two items are different in some ways and not in others. Again, when some item is not-F, it could become F at some other time, unless the subject is a Form.

These considerations show how much the partaking relation has been widened by the time it is linked with the connector theory.

Let us take once more the simple schema "x partakes of F" and consider the various possibilities for each element. x can be a Form or a non-Form (typically particular). The relation can be necessary or contingent. It can be "deficient" in the relevant sense or not deficient. Does a Form have to fill the F slot in our schema? Even before we consider texts from 263, some of the texts surveyed already suggest a negative answer. As we saw in 255d4, we are told that Being partakes of both relationality and nonrelationality. Are these Forms? Plato does not say.

One can only speculate as to why Plato allows the partaking relation to cover so many different things. Perhaps he saw the second half of the *Parmenides* as showing the unique mode of partaking that no longer requires anchoring to items in specific categories. Perhaps he thought that the connector theory shows how attribution pervades and connects all parts of "reality" in the wide sense that includes both appearances and underlying reality in the narrower sense.

We now have the analysis: x is F = x − connector − F; and once we understand the peculiar connecting function of the vowel-Forms, there is no need to restrict partaking to just some ontological configurations.

From a modern point of view, this may seem an unnecessarily cumbersome ontology. But for Plato, it provided a viable framework for saving a notion of partaking that is not like spatial, part−whole relations and for articulating an ontology for positive and negative attribution that does not lead us to ascribe nonexistence to anything that is a constituent in the analyses and at the same time does not force us to abandon either the correspondence theory of meaning or the correspondence theory of truth.

The connectors are the most fundamental elements in these configurations that underlie truth and falsehood. If, in the cases of necessary linkage, we knew which elements of underlying reality are connected to which other ones via positive and negative ties, we would have a large part of what Plato regards already in the *Meno* as understanding.

This, then, is the general sketch of what transpires in 251–6. We shall now turn to Plato's ontology of negativity as expounded in the subsequent pages.

The Metaphysics of Negativity and the Analysis of Falsehood

The passage discussed at the end of the last section shows how things can be qualitatively different from Being. In the lines following, the converse is shown: namely, that Being is different from everything else, though everything else partakes of it. All this is made possible by the fact that it is in the nature of Forms to have communion with each other (257a8–9: it is the "phusis" of Forms to have "koinoonia" with each other). Since it is necessarily in the nature of the Forms to have communion and we cannot understand them apart from their interrelationships, the Forms are not individually self-sufficient. The whole network, however, is self-sufficient and constitutes the underlying reality that explains the world of appearances.

Plato's account of the ontology of negativity consists of three parts:

Part 1 (257b2–d5): Not-being as qualitative difference; analysis of the ontological correlate of "not-"; comparison of the "parts" of Difference with the "parts" of knowledge.

Part 2 (257d7–258b5): "Antithesis" as a special case of negativity, the contrast between positive and negative predication. The contrast involves equally genuine elements ontologically. Illustrations.

Part 3 (258b6–259d): Final conclusions. Negativity is real and immune to Eleatic criticism. Thus, though we gave up talking about the opposite of Being, negative predication is coherent and rests on the interwovenness of the Forms.

In his account of negativity, Plato points out that when words express something that is "not-something," they need not express opposition, but only difference.[20] That is, when something is not-F, it is qualitatively different from being F; it is not-F, or lacks F-ness, as one might say. This way of construing Plato's account fits the examples that follow. For these include the not-large and not-fine. The only intuitive sense for these is not being large and not being fine, respectively. That Plato has negative predicates in mind is shown by his saying that the not-large includes not only small things but also what is neither large nor small. He concludes this brief characterization by saying that the negation of F does not designate the opposite of F; "not-" designates being different in nature from what is designated by the words that follow.

If x is not large, it is different from large things. How is it different? For Plato, this amounts to the question: In respect of what is it different? The answer is, obviously, in respect of being large. Qualitative difference contrasts the large with the not-large and not with complete not-being. Negative predicates have a coherent structure, and they are constituents in negations.

It is important to stress that this is all that Plato wants to show. This is all he needs in his fight against Eleatic views. Thus his enterprise is radically different from modern logical and semantic analyses of negation. The modern enterprise focuses primarily on sentence negation, rather than on predicate negation, and its key explanans is the systematic change in truth-values between a sentence and its negation. Truth-values in that framework need not be accounted for ontologically.

Even when viewed as an account of predicate negation, Plato's analysis is extremely limited by modern standards. At its best, it handles only singular propositions. It would have difficulty with quantified sentences. How would his account of negative predicates analyze the negations of expressions like "all humans" or "some artists"? But these are limitations only when Plato's work is viewed within the context of a project that was not Plato's.

There have been other proposals for the interpretation of Plato on negativity. One of these would have Plato trying to reduce negative predication to propositions involving only nonidentity.[21] According to this proposal, a statement like

John did not play last Saturday

would be analyzed as

John is not identical with any of the players who played last Saturday.

This analysis is inadequate. If we take it distributively, then the analyzans says that John is not identical with Joe, Tom, Harry, and the rest, who happened to have played last Saturday. This finite conjunction of non-identity statements would be true even if John had played last Saturday. Furthermore, when analyzing statements with predicates like "is wise" or "is fine," we would have to consider in the reduction scheme infinite sets of conjunctions of nonidentity statements. Even modern logicians find such conjunction puzzling. Furthermore, there is no evidence that Plato ever considered it as an explicans. Thus we would have to turn to explications like

> John is not any of the players who played last Saturday,

which would be equivalent to

> John is not identical with members of the class of those who played last Saturday.

But once we eliminate the attempts at reduction dealt with above, this would end up as

> John is not a member of the class of those who played last Saturday.

And while this gives us a true statement, it no longer reduces predication to identity.

Apart from these semi-technical considerations, why should one want to ascribe to Plato such a reduction? There would be a reason if it could be shown that the notion of difference and not-being that Plato uses from 253 to 258 is the notion of nonidentity. But as we have seen there is no good reason to suppose that. Another reason might be the hypothesis that nonidentity is somehow less problematic than negative predication. This is certainly not true for modern analytic philosophy. Should we suppose that it is true for Plato? Plato considers these matters in the context of fighting the Eleatics. For the Eleatics, nonidentity was no less problematic than negative predication. They found the notion of a pluralistic ontology incoherent. This amounts to the claim that they found any attempt at a principle of individuation for pluralistic ontologies incoherent. In this context, nonidentity is no less problematic than negative predication. One cannot reply to the Eleatics by saying that what individuates elements is that they are not identical with each other. The Eleatics want to know in virtue of what such nonidentities can be.

Nor is nonidentity any clearer for Plato than negative predication. For both Plato and the Eleatics the key question is: What enables things to function in their own way? Plato's answer is that qualitative difference enables elements of reality to have their own natures and that this notion is not paradoxical. It is no more or less intelligible than Being, a favored notion of the Eleatics also. Qualitative difference and the respective natures of two elements account for their being distinct, not the other way around.

There have also been attempts to interpret Plato as reducing negation to the incompatibility between certain predicates. Such attempts have already been criticized effectively in the literature.[22]

The whole idea that fundamental notions should be illuminated by reductionist programs seems alien to classical Greek philosophy. It would be anachronistic to think that philosophers of that time would want a "translation manual," as in twentieth-century reductionistic programs in the foundations of mathematics or in epistemology (for example, phenomenalism). In our century, such programs became objects of interest because of the initial sense of success vis-à-vis the program of reducing mathematics to logic. The subsequent reductionist programs were decidedly semantic in their orientation; that is, reducing a set of sentences S', in which the existence of certain entities is acknowledged, to a set of sentences S'', which are equivalent although the dubious entities are not acknowledged. There is no evidence to suggest that this was seen as a viable, interesting paradigm of explanation among classical Greek thinkers. When Thales posited water as a "starting point" (archē), he did not have a reductionist semantic program in mind. When we move on a more purely conceptual plane with the Eleatics, the discussion is still in terms of what entities there must be, not of how to eliminate ontological commitment. From Thales to Plato and Aristotle, the basic ontological questions seem to have been: What must there be? And what is more fundamental (ontologically prior) than what?

Returning to the text, the presentation of negativity continues with a comparison of the parts of Difference and the parts of Knowledge (257c). The parts of Knowledge, or science, are mathematics, ethics, music, and so on. As we have seen, these are defined by Plato objectually; that is, mathematics is the science of numbers, music of sounds, and so forth. Thus, by analogy, the parts of Difference should consist in being different with respect to size, virtue, numerical magnitude, and the like, including the examples used in the text: namely, fine and large. It would be absurd to compare the sciences of number, sound, and virtue with being nonidentical with John, Tom, Harry, and so on, or even with being nonidentical with any of the positive integers. Even if there were such predicates, they would have as their extension an indeterminate collection of heterogeneous entities – not an object for dialectic or Platonic understanding. It would also be strange to interpret these parts as playing the role of predicates like not being identical in statements like "John is not large." Does this mean that John is not identical with largeness? Is it not more plausible to suppose that for Plato this means: "John is qualitatively different from being large," with the relevant respect of difference – namely, largeness – understood?

Thus the comparison between the parts of science and difference seems to strengthen the interpretation proposed in this section. No reductions are effected, but all statements of negative predication are shown to be paradox-free and not to lead to nonexistence. If the Eleatic says, "But I will not accept your Form of difference as an element of reality," then Plato's reply is: "Without understanding not-being, you will not understand being either."

In 257d4–5 we are told that we can see the nature (*phusis*) of difference in its parts. This seems to mean that we grasp qualitative difference through reflection on the meaning of predicates like "is not fine," "is not large," and so on. If everyone were wise, fine, and the rest and no examples of not having these attributes were possible, could we really understand what qualitative difference is? If there were no such contrasts, in the conceptual world at least, perhaps we could have no understanding of qualitative difference, for attributes are contrast-dependent. Those who interpret difference in these texts as nonidentity would have to show that one can tell the same story about identity and nonidentity. To be sure, these two notions are contrast-dependent, but is it true that we learn to understand what nonidentity is by reflecting on such alleged "parts" as not being identical with Paris, the US Constitution, and so forth?

After a more general discussion of negativity and difference, Plato focuses on contrasts between positive. and negative (for example, the large and the not-large, the fine and the not-fine (257d7–258b5)). Before looking at the details, we should consider a difficulty that Plato does not discuss. In the previous discussions it seems that Plato is talking about a negative tie, or negative relational Being. But now it seems as if there were only one, positive, relational tie and negative attributes. Let us consider the statement "This statue is not fine." Should this be analyzed as "This statue is-not fine" or "This statue is not-fine"? Both alternatives are viable.

Neither causes problems for Plato's project as interpreted in this chapter. But it would have been desirable for Plato to indicate which of these two versions he wanted to embrace. Some passages seem to point in one direction, others in the other.

Two things can be qualitatively different in many different respects. Furthermore, the attributes with respect to which we differ can also be contrasted in many ways. The Large is different from the Equal, the Even, the Odd, and so on. Plato now wants to concentrate on a special case of qualitative difference: namely, that between a positive attribute like being large or fine and their negative counterparts, being not-large, not-fine. He calls this special case of qualitative difference "antithesis" (e.g. in 257d7). The natures of the pairs are clear enough; we know how fine things differ from not-fine things and large ones from not-large ones. But Plato wants to emphasize a point about these pairs that is especially important in his fight against the Eleatics. He stresses that in the contrast of fine and not-fine and large and not-large and all other similar cases, we are contrasting equally legitimate elements of being *onta*; (e.g. 258a1−2, 11−13). The point could not be that things that are large are as much elements of being as things that are not large. This would be true even if the quality distributions in the world were different. The point must be about the Large and the not-Large, the Fine and the not-Fine, and all such similar positive and negative predicative elements. Both are legitimate parts of reality. Studying what is wise and what is not wise is the same activity; both Forms are appropriate as objects of dialectic. In the same way, understanding what it is to have a certain weight and what it is not to have that weight are equally legitimate facets of Platonic knowledge.

In 258b6−7 Plato announces that we found the Not-Being that we sought in connection with our task of explaining how the sophist can be a deceiver. The conceptual work done by the inner core helps to answer the question raised by the outer core. The sophists represent things that have a certain attribute as if they did not have it (for example, wisdom as if it were not a virtue) and things that do not have a quality as if they had it (for example, pleasures as if they were good). They represent *onta* − that is, real things − in ways in which they are not. In the last part of the inner core, the nature of this misrepresentation is discussed.

The interpretation of Plato's account of negativity given here proposes that at this stage Plato came to accept negative Forms of a certain kind: namely, those standing for not being fine, not being large, and so on. These Forms underlie negative predicates. This accurately represents Plato's statement that in "antithesis" we contrast elements that are ontologically on a par. There have been scholars, however, who deny that at this stage Plato accepted negative Forms.[23] M. Frede, for example, cites *Politicus* 262 as evidence that Plato rejected negative Forms. In that passage, Plato discusses "divisions" (the topic of the next chapter). He says that the divisions must articulate reality in appropriate ways. The distinctions carved out must be natural. As examples he gives the divisions of numbers into odd and even and humans into male and female. As illegitimate divisions he cites dividing the positive integers into the number 10,000 and, as the other "part," all the rest and dividing humans into Greeks and non-Greeks or barbarians.

The relevance of this passage to the *Sophist* depends on how one interprets negativity in the latter. If we think that Plato's "not-large," "not-fine," and so on are the predicates of not being identical with the large and the fine, respectively, then indeed we obtain predicate pairs that parallel the ones forbidden in the *Politicus*. But if we interpret the negative predicative entities unearthed by Plato in *Sophist* 257–8 as not having the nature of being large and fine respectively – surely the more intuitive reading – then there is no parallel between these entities and the forbidden elements of the *Politicus*. The key point of the latter must be that the divisions leave us with objects inappropriate for theoretical understanding. There are no deep laws about the class of numbers other than 10,000. This is what matters; not whether we describe one of the classes that we have carved out in negative or positive terms. We can say that the number two is even or that it is not odd. In either case, we are dealing with legitimate as objects of understanding.

We should construe Plato as accepting negative Forms in the sense defined. They are just as legitimate as objects of dialectic as positive ones. Furthermore, once we give up strong unique self-attribution, there is nothing problematic about the nature of the negative Forms that would not also be problematic about the positive ones. Finally, it should be stressed that Plato's accepting the negative Forms characterized here would not entail that "anything goes." The putative kinds mentioned in the *Politicus*, as well as many other objects not suitable for theoretical understanding, are as unacceptable to the interpretation proposed as to interpretations like Frede's. And the unacceptable kinds could include the ones, like flattery, ridiculed in the *Gorgias*.

In 258e8 Plato says – as we have noted already – that in the face of the opposite of Being we are reduced to silence. We stopped talking about it "a long time ago," he says, referring clearly to the initial discussion of Not-Being in this dialogue. We have arrived, however, at a notion of not-being that is coherent and accounts for negativity. Plato mentions in 259d that merely to show that opposites in some way characterize each other is not serious theoretical work. The material of 253–8 shows how one can make sense of these relations. Plato's disparaging remarks presumably point to the surface interpretation of the arguments we saw in the second half of the *Parmenides*.

Having refuted Parmenides, Plato applies the fruits of this metaphysical exploration to clearing up falsehood. Once again, before we look at Plato's "essay on discourse" in 259–62, we need to stress what, from a modern point of view, might be seen as limitations on the enterprise undertaken. All Plato wants to do is to sketch roughly the most general conditions on meaningful discourse and to indicate by illustration how we can explain some falsehoods without committing ourselves to positing complete not-being of any kind. What follows is not a theory, with definitions, axioms, theorems, and the rest. Nor is it an in-depth discussion of falsehood in all its forms (for example, universal quantification, conditionals, modal contexts, and so on). Plato's interest in linguistic and semantic matters is secondary. His main interest is metaphysical; he is concerned too with the application of metaphysical matters to intensely felt ethical issues such as the need to cleanse public life of sophistry.

The "essay on discourse" starts at 259e. Plato states once more that without combination among the Forms, discourse would be impossible. It is the interwovenness of the Forms that makes logos possible (259e4–5). The interwovenness (*sumplokē*) is more than mere blending. It is the connectedness of the whole network of Forms made possible by the connectors, the key elements in this version of Platonic ontology. Configurations of elements connected by the connecting Forms provide the kind of ontological complex that can be expressed by simple declarative sentences. Thus, in 261–2 Plato goes on to sketch the most general conditions governing sentence construction of this simple sort.

Earlier, we encountered contexts in which *logos* means theoretical account. But here we need to take it in a much wider sense. Two bits of evidence support the wider reading. First, the account of sentence construction that follows is quite general and is not applicable only to statements expressing genuine understanding. Secondly, the examples of true and false sentences that Plato gives later are not taken from the theoretical disciplines, but express states of affairs that anyone would talk about in everyday discourse.

One might also wonder whether the characterization in 259e should be taken to entail that in every sentence a combination of Forms must be represented. Such a reading is not forced by the text. Given Plato's subsequent examples, it might be better to interpret the condition as a necessary ontological requirement on sentence construction, rather than a condition of what needs to be actually represented. To be sure, at least one Form – that is, a connector – must be represented in every statement. But neither subject nor predicate need be a Form. The examples in 263 are flying and sitting. There is no good reason to suppose that Plato thought of these as Forms.

In the interlude that follows, Plato's opponents are represented as asking whether – even granted that we have proved that there is not-being and that there is *logos* – not-being is contained in *logos*. Clearly this question (260b7 – 11) is not phrased within the framework of Plato's own ontology, a theory that the opponents are reluctant to accept. Thus we cannot give it a precise technical reading. Even the opponents would have to grant that we have shown that logos is an element of reality and that, as such, it is qualitatively different from Being and from many other elements. What the opponents question is whether we have shown that everyday discourse can express the kind of not-being that falsehood entails. In making false statements, we are allegedly misrepresenting reality. Granted that Plato explained how we can make negative statements of subject–predicate form to express what is the case, how do we move from this to an analysis of what it is to misrepresent the case?

This comment on the interlude gives me a chance to comment also on a matter of form and dramatic development. One cannot help but admire Plato's ingenuity and sense of humor in inventing an opponent who combines the views of two such completely different schools of philosophy as the Eleatics and the sophists! "Strange bedfellows indeed!" the audience was bound to say. Plato's audience must have enjoyed the attack on the sophists, which is based on the refutation of the highly abstract theses held by the Eleatics. In this way, even the texture of this dialogue parallels the dramatic structure of a dialogue like the *Phaedo* in which highly abstract metaphysical issues help us to understand eventually the correct answer to concrete ethical questions about how to die. What Plato does in the *Sophist* can be compared in this century with using a thesis of F. H. Bradley to squash the positivists.

After the interlude, Plato sketches very general conditions on discourse. A sentence must be a combination of the right elements; not just any jumble of words make a meaningful sentence. Plato characterizes the basic elements of a sentence as *onoma* and *rhema*, and says that in a sentence we need a conbination of these. Both these terms need to be taken in a very wide sense: *onoma* to include name, noun, and, even more widely, general term, and *rhema* to include not only verb but, more widely, general predicates of a variety of sorts.[24] Plato's examples are of the noun–verb variety, expressing actor–action relationships. It would be a mistake to ascribe to these combinations and the resulting sentences fundamental importance in Plato's own metaphysics and view of language. He merely wants to present the simplest illustrations that even his opponent cannot question. This move reminds one of the practice in earlier dialogues of illustrating deep points by talking about cobblers, carpenters, and practitioners of other such everyday professions.

After the very general, sketchy account of sentential structure (which is there only to show what simple criteria of syntactic well-formedness and meaningfulness are – Plato does not distinguish the two), he turns to the analysis of falsehood (263a–d).

The analysis is very brief. This is understandable, because Plato thinks that he has done all the hard work in 256–9. It consists of contrasting a true with a false sentence and showing how the latter contains an incorrect linking of elements of reality. As an example of a true statement, Plato uses "Theaetetus is sitting," and as an example of a false one, "Theaetetus is flying." The subject of both is something real: namely, Theaetetus. Furthermore, what the respective predicates designate are also elements of reality: namely, sitting and flying. The true statement is about what there is and represents things as they are, whereas the false one represents things that are as they are not. In both statements, relational Being effects the connections. Those making the false statement misrepresent the elements and the linkage. Every element that is designated by some component of the sentence used is something real, but those speaking falsely misconnect them. They connect Theaetetus and flying positively, for example; whereas they should be connecting them negatively. Alternatively, they connect Theaetetus with a positive predicate when they should be connecting him with the corresponding negative one. Plato concludes that this is made possible by the fact that, "as we said" (referring to 256e), with relation to any entity there is much that is and much that is not (263b11–12). There are positive and negative configurations that can underlie a statement, and those speaking falsely weave together the wrong elements. The wrong interweaving is done by us, not by some force in a part of reality that is independent of us. There are no true and false facts flying around. There are only elements that can be represented by words, and the words can be picked and interwoven correctly or incorrectly. The account is adequate and does not lead to positing something that is not in the complete – or existential – sense. (For more details, see Appendix 3.)

Theory of Forms and of Partaking, Quo Vadis?

Having examined Plato's struggle with Eleatic positions in the *Sophist*, we should note how much he concedes to Parmenides. The correspondence theories of meaning and truth are never called into question. Furthermore, at the end, Plato too turns out to be a kind of monist. The underlying reality is the realm of Forms, and this is now a field in which qualitatively different elements are interwoven. There remains a big difference, however; for Plato's monism – or holism? – allows him to retain a conception of a world of appearances that has some order and harmony and the nature of which is accounted for by the underlying reality.

What happened to the Forms in this "struggle"? First, there is no trace of the strong, unique self-attribution that we saw in the version of the theory in the *Phaedo* and the *Symposium*. To be sure, some Forms partake of themselves. Being partakes of Being; the Different partakes of the Different in relation to other things; and so forth. But in these cases there is nothing special about the participation. That is to say, the subject partakes of the Form-predicate in the same way in which anything else would partake of the same entity.

What about the characteristics we saw Plato assign to the Forms in chapter 2? Forms are still entities that can be partaken of; but it is not clear that they are the only such entities. (See the question about relationality in 255c.) *Contra* the earlier version, Forms, as well as non-Form-like entities, can also be participants. Forms are still timeless abstract entities; but this characterization also fits things we would call "universals" that are acknowledged in Plato but, as far as one can see, are not regarded by him as Forms. An obvious example is the universal discussed already: namely, "not being identical with 10,000." What remains true of Forms only is that they are the object of dialectic and understanding. But having that function no longer implies for Plato that they are the only entities of which things can partake, that they do not do any participating themselves, and so forth. Plato needs a new characterization of the universals that qualify as Forms. We shall see in chapter 6 how he deals with this problem.

Let us recall that the Forms were introduced in the context of the reality-appearance distinction. This feature of the theory is retained. But whereas before, one could more or less identify the world of appearances with what the "lovers of sights and sounds" accept, now the world of appearances is a much more heterogeneous realm, which includes abstract as well as concrete elements and is distinguished from the tightly interwoven set of elements that represent the "right divisions," or "natural kinds," that serve as the objects of the genuine sciences. Further, although Plato's doctrines already required relations between the Forms, an explicit working out of these relations is effected only in the *Sophist*, where it is linked with giving an account of negativity.

In the earlier model, partaking was the link between appearance and reality. This is no longer the case in the *Sophist*, where elements of reality partake of each other. Partaking has become a many-splendored thing, as we have seen. There is still the deficiency-involving type of participation, but there are other kinds as well. As we saw, partaking is still not equivalent to predication or the copula. Since it also connects subjects with relational Being, it covers relations that the copula does not. Furthermore, relations other than participation enter into the articulation of the realm of the Forms.

The part—sum relationship as exhibited in spatiotemporal complexes has not played an important role in Plato's ontology. But other part—whole relations have surfaced:

a   parts as in the parts of science and Difference;
b   parts that are carved out by Divisions; and
c   parts of definitions, as, for example, the last one of sophistry in the *Sophist*.

In the next chapter we shall see how Plato combines all these into a coherent ontology. But it is apparent already, from our survey of the "inner core," that the structure of the realm of the Forms has become more complicated.

We shall ask also how, in the "new version," the being of the Forms differs from the beings of particulars and other non-Forms. The key difference that remains is that there are only contingent links among particulars, necessary relations being anchored in relations among Forms. But it is not clear that all relations that Plato would regard as necessary involve Forms and do not involve also other abstract elements. One might simply speculate that necessary relations involved in linkage between non-Forms – as, for example, the definition of flattery in the *Gorgias* – were not given an explicit analysis in Plato's ontology. So perhaps it is not so much that a distinguishing characteristic now falls by the wayside, as that issues not faced explicitly before are now confronted and accounted for in a more complex theory.

Plato still thinks that the Forms account for whatever order and stability there are among appearances. It is just that more primitive concepts and more primitive relations have been introduced into the theory of Forms, and the theory's explanatory power can no longer be indicated by anything as simple as the similes of light in Book 6 of the *Republic*.

It became clear to Plato that to account for order, more structure must be added – or rather, discovered – among Forms. Each Form is one, but also "many;" that is, it has a manifold nature and is indefinite in terms of the kinds that fall under it. It also retains its own nature in a narrow sense, as we have seen; but this is no longer explicated in terms of unique self-attribution. It is left as a primitive, perhaps as a result of reflection on the kinds of considerations we saw unfolding in the *Parmenides*. In chapter 6 we shall examine the additional structures that Plato discovered among some of the Forms.

Appendix 1: *Naming and Stating*

In 251a–b Plato seems to be concerned with what the world must be like for us to be able to form meaningful declarative sentences, some of which are true. In order to understand the positive account, we must get clear on what exactly Plato's opponents are denying when they say that "the one cannot be many." As the example shows, the so-called late learners deny that one can apply to the same human several descriptions such as shape and color (251b7–c2). Apparently, we can rationally apply to a human only "human," to something fine only "fine," and so on; and it is assumed that the kinds designated by these expressions do not overlap. Given the brevity of the text and the fact that classical Greek does not mark use–mention distinctions with some explicit device, the evidence is compatible with a variety of interpretations.

One obvious alternative is to construe the opponent as denying the possibility of any kind of statement making. Statement making involves the combination of elements. Without the view that some elements are syncategorematic, one might think that there is an ontological correlate to all the combined elements, hence that any statement making requires combinations. What we are left with is naming in the wider sense, which includes not only giving proper names to particulars, but giving names to kinds, which will presumably be treated mereologically and thus also as particulars of a certain kind. So the only permissible language-game is naming. We attach labels to kinds, and with the use of such labels are able – contextually – to refer to any given part of a kind.

The view that a part of a kind can be labeled with only one kind-name is counterintuitive. We typically give more than one label to any particular, as Plato's example showed. But this implies that a given entity can belong to more than one kind. This, in turn, constitutes an example of the "blending" of kinds, the state of affairs that Plato needs to show to be coherent. Furthermore, once we allow more than one label for a particular, then statement making becomes possible. For we have a state of affairs that can be expressed by, for example, "human and heavy" or "both human and heavy," when pointing to a portly gentleman. But this already involves more than naming; it involves the combining of sentential elements.

Let us consider other alternatives that have been presented in the literature. Cornford takes the moral of the example given at 251b9–c2 to be that statements of subject–predicate form are allowed, but only where subject and predicate are identical, as, for example, in "A man is a man."[25] But this interpretation leaves the late learners with a nonatomistic view of language. As we have seen already in connection with the initial treatment of not-being, Plato regards the ascription of singular or plural as an element in a statement mode. This means that he should have the same objection to the view ascribed by Cornford to his opponents. Cornford thinks that Plato is concerned only with statements that involve at least one Form.[26] But if any version of the theory of Forms is presupposed by this discussion of extreme semantic atomism, the reply will be question begging. Plato must meet his opponents on their own ground. Moreover, some of the examples that come up – for example, the statement of the doctrine of the late learners – are not about Forms. Finally, as we saw in this chapter, this final examples of true and false statements are about Theaetetus, not Forms. Could it be that the defense of statement making employed by Plato in this early part does not cover the statements used by Plato to refute the Eleatics?

Other scholars such as Ross and Hamlyn construe the late learners as denying predication and allowing only statements of identity such as "Man is man" and "Good is good."[27] If this were true, one would expect Plato to remonstrate and explain that statements of identity are highly complex entities involving linking elements of some sort, as well as the kind to be described. Plato could make this point in a preliminary way, even without bring in the connector theory that is developed in the subsequent passages. But he does not do so.

The identity interpretation has also been criticized by Michael Frede, who thinks that the late learners allow statements of subject–predicate form, but only of the type "This is a man," "This is good," and the like.[28] This interpretation suffers from the same defect as the other two. As we saw already in 238, a statement of the accepted sort would be analyzed by Plato as a complex entity with a number of ingredients. Plato, however, does not reply to the late learners by saying that their own privileged class of statements refutes their atomism. Rather, he points to the self-refuting nature of any statement of their general view.

Thus it seems that the interpretation sketched at the beginning, which contrasts naming and statement making, has as good a grounding in the text as any of the others, is philosophically deeper, and fits better into the overall structure of the inner core of the *Sophist*. For the contrast between mere naming and statement making is, as we have seen, also at the core of the "essay on discourse" that starts with 259e. Plato's ontological theory serves also as a defense of the possibility of statement making. The denial of both ontological and semantic atomism are preconditions for the removal of puzzles about falsehood.

Appendix 2: *Dialectic*

The discussion of dialectic is linked to the letter analogy given in the immediately preceding lines (252e9–253a6). I have already discussed the general impact of this analogy. But let us look in more detail at the analogy between vowels and connecting Forms. The vowel-like Forms are responsible for all linking, positive or negative, in the world. They should not be viewed like, for example, glue connecting pieces of paper, havever. Paper and glue are quite different materials. By contrast, the links between Forms are effected by Forms – though of a different kind. Furthermore, at times the vowel-Forms play the role of consonant-, or brick-, Forms – that is, as items to be connected. For example, Wisdom and Equality are different, but Difference is the same as itself; hence it requires an element to link it to others as well as to itself. The Forms are more like brick and cement. Cement connects bricks; but in solidified form, it too can play the role of a brick to be linked to other bricks. This is important for the understanding of dialectic. The vowel-Forms serve as all-pervasive connectors; but they are also the subjects of the kind of theoretical propositions whose understanding is part of a legitimate technē.

In 253 we see several characterizations of dialectic. To begin with, we are told about the resemblance between the communion of Forms and the harmonizing of letters (253a1–10). The implications are spelled out. First, some Forms harmonize, whereas some do not. Secondly, some Forms are primarily linking Forms. Thirdly, without a connecting Form, there can be no linkage. All this is true also of vowels.

We are also told that this realm of entities with this structure constitutes an appropriate object for a genuine technē (253a10, b8–c5). Since this science yields genuine theoretical understanding, the objects must be Forms. Hence, from here on, Plato can utilize his own ontology to solve the outstanding puzzles about negativity and communion.

We encounter the notion of dialectic several times in the dialogues. Dialectic is whatever Plato, at that stage, thinks of as a crucial aspect of philosophical investigation. It is not the same procedure in every dialogue. Here it is the understanding of which Forms blend, which ones connect, and which ones are the reason (*aitia*) for separations in the division according to kinds.

Still another description is given in 253d1–3. We need to understand how to divide correctly, according to kinds, and to grasp which Forms are the same and which ones are different. An example of the latter activity is the set of proofs of distinctness of the "greatest" Forms, which is given subsequently.

The most detailed description of dialectic (253d5–e2) is given, not surprisingly, in terms of its objects. Attention to gender in the descriptions given helps us to discern four relationships that the dialectician must uncover in the realm of Forms:

1   There is the case of one Form pervading many scattered entities. The contrast between the feminine gender used by Plato for the Form that does the pervading and the gender of that which is pervaded suggests that this is the relation of one Form having many particulars as participants, the relation that plays such an important role in the earlier delineation of the Forms.

2   There is the relation of one Form surrounding many others. The feminine gender is used for both what surrounds and what is surrounded; hence it is reasonable to suppose that this is the relation of blending that obtains in the case of correct divisions: for example, Art surrounding the acquisitive and productive arts.

3   The third relation is described as a Form made into a whole through the contribution of many others. The language used here (d8–9) resembles that used in 253a4–5, c1–2, e3–6, and 259a5–6. In all these passages, Plato seems to be talking about the vowel-Forms connecting others. The Different is the "different from . . . ," made into a whole by the completion of all its parts – that is, the elements that yield negative predicates. Art, basically, is not a relational Form like Difference.

4   The fourth relation is that of many Forms entirely separate. This refers, presumably to opposites or to the contrast between the Equal and Wisdom, which come from different realms of objects for science. By the time Plato explains the connector theory in the subsequent passages, we have seen that no two Forms are entirely separate in a technical sense. At this stage, Plato is relying on the intuitive notions of opposition and different subcategories, notions that can be made precise within the communion and connector theories.

Among these relations, the dialectic of the *Sophist* concentrates on the second and the third. A detailed knowledge of all these relations in specific cases would give an articulation of what results from the wisdom already envisaged in the recollection theory of the *Meno*.

Appendix 3: *The Analysis of Falsehood*

Plato has sketched the minimal conditions required to produce meaningful declarative sentences. Now further conditions have to be added, in order to distinguish the true from the false.[29] Plato first repeats the formula familiar from other dialogues, which, presumably, is acceptable to his opponents as well. The true statement describes things that are as they are, whereas the false one describes them as they are not. Plato now shows how, within the theory of Forms as developed in this dialogue, he can give a paradox-free interpretation of this formula. The examples, as we noted, are "Theaetetus is sitting" and "Theaetetus is flying." Plato's text analyzing the differences can be divided into five parts.

> T1. The true (statement) says about you things that are as they are in relation to you (263b4–5).

This description says that what underlie the true (statement) are *onta*: that is, elements of reality in the wide sense. Furthermore, the true (statement) represents the correct connection between these elements. It says that sitting is in relation to Theaetetus, and this is in fact the case. The elements involved are subject, connector, and predicate. There is no need or ground for thinking that Plato's analysis also involves an ontology of facts, a notion that originated in philosophy much later.[30] Some might wonder about the plural usage in Plato's reference to what is ascribed rightly to the subject. One can take the line either that this need not be taken literally or that Plato had in mind both sitting and relational Being as what is attached to Theaetetus.

> T2. The false (statement) expresses things that are different from what is (in relation to you) (263b7).

The false (statement) also has elements underlying it: namely, Theaetetus, relational Being, and flying. But these are not related in reality in the way the statement represents them. What is related to Theaetetus is sitting and, most relevantly, not-flying, as well as countless other attributes. What is in relation to Theaetetus – namely, not-flying – is different from what the statement claims to be related to him. How is it qualitatively different? We saw Plato's answer – or, for that matter, any commonsense answer – in his remarks about "antithesis" as a special case of qualitative difference. As the fine contrasts with the not-fine and the large with the not-large, so flying contrasts with not-flying. To show that the misrepresentation involved in the false (statement) does not lead to assuming that there is something nonexistent, it is sufficient to point out that the basic difference between what the true and the false (statements) say is qualitative difference of a certain kind, not unqualified not-being. If the modern reader becomes impatient with the constant linking of every relevant linguistic item to an ontological correlate, he or she should be reminded that this is what it takes to refute the Eleatics. If Plato says that there are these combinations and that maybe we need not assign a designatum to every main linguistic element, then the Eleatics will reject the reply. In any case, there is no evidence that syncategorematic treatments of the elements in question here was available or was contemplated by Plato. The conclusion from T2 is that qualitative difference is the not-being required in the analysis of falsehood.[31]

> T3.   The false (statement) says things that are not (in relation to you) as if they were (related to you) (263b9).

T3 restates T2 in terms of relational Being. The parenthetical material inserted in my presentation is what Plato would have taken to be understood. This interpretation can be justified both on structural grounds and by the fact that the phrase "in relation to you" occurs again in T4.[32]

> T4.   The false (statement) expresses things that are, but are different from what is in relation to you (263b11).

T4 describes in a paradox-free way how what the predicate designates both is and is not. That is to say, this element is part of reality in the wide sense, yet at the same time it is not related to Theaetetus; it is qualitatively different from what is in relation to Theaetetus.

At the end, Plato reminds us of the result obtained earlier that justifies this analysis.

> T5.   For, as we said, in relation to any one thing, much is, and much is not (263b1–12).

The reference is to 256e5–6. As McDowell has pointed out, in that earlier passage the assertion is only about the Forms. Hence T5 is more general.[33] The expansion, however, is justified by what has been shown between 256 and 262. Qualitative difference permeates all the Forms. This helps to carve out positive and negative Forms. These in turn can be linked also to entities that are not Forms; hence the general conclusion in 263b, which underlies a general analysis of falsehood and is not restricted to statements about the Forms.

Both true and false statements of the sort illustrated here represent configurations of elements that exist. Furthermore, they contain the right combination of linguistic elements. In view of these two conditions, we can see that both kinds of statements can be meaningful. But in interweaving the elements of one of these in our discourse, we represent a configuration that does in fact obtain, and with the other misrepresent what would be the appropriate links. The misrepresentation is done by those who interweave words; it is not in need of a metaphysical posit of not-being.

With this, Plato justifies his belief in the existence of meaningful and, at times, deceptive falsehood. This opens the door to the final characterization of the sophist as a deceiver.

NOTES

1   See e.g. J. Moravcsik, "Being and Meaning in the *Sophist.*"
2   The notion of an inner core was first proposed by Hermann Bonitz, *Platonische Studien*, pp. 152–209.
3   e.g. G. Ryle, "Plato's *Parmenides.*"
4   J. Ackrill, "Plato and the Copula."
5   M. Frede, "Predikation und Existenzaussage."
6   F. Lewis, "Did Plato Discover the 'Estin,' of Identity?"
7   J. Roberts, "The Problem of Being in the *Sophist.*"
8   Some people have attacked the claim that Plato has the notion of existence and an existential "is"; but for a defense of this view, see R. Heinaman, "Being in the *Sophist.*"
9   The argument is quite general and does not depend on the examples of hot and cold. Plato says that the argument applies to any such pair (243d), and in fact to all who think that Being is more than one (244b1–4). Thus it is difficult to accept F. Cornford's claim (1934, pp. 218–20) that Plato is arguing here solely against physicalist theories.
10   For details of the argument, see J. Moravcsik, "Being and Meaning in the *Sophist.*"
11   For more discussion, see ibid., pp. 39–40.
12   G. Owen and M. Frede think that this argument is invalid; but see Roberts, "Problem of Being in the *Sophist.*" section 6.
13   J. Kostman, "The Ambiguity to 'Partaking' in Plato's *Sophist*," pp. 351–2 argues that there is a break in terminology and that after 254, partaking becomes a technical notion for Plato.
14   W. Ross, *Aristotle: physics*, p. 491, notes re *Physics* 189b32 that *heteron* means qualitative difference, whereas *allon* is used more to mean numerical distinctness.
15   See Kostman, "Ambiguity of 'Partaking'," section 4, on views by G. Owen, G. Vlastos, and M. Frede.
16   J. Moravcsik, *Thought and Language*, part 1, ch. 1.
17   K. Sayre, *Plato's Analytic Method*, p. 197, n. 72.
18   This passage is discussed in Moravcsik, "Being and Meaning in the *Sophist*," pp. 52–3; Frede, "Predikation," pp. 52–3; and J. McDowell, "Falsehood and Not-Being in Plato's *Sophist*," p. 122.

19 For this reading, see O. Apelt, *Sophistes*, pp. 7–8, 148; also F. Cornford, *Plato's Theory of Knowledge*, pp. 290–2.

20 Instead of "express," Cornford, *Plato's Theory of Knowledge*, p. 290, uses "speak of," and A. Taylor, *Plato*, p. 164, "assert" – both infelicitous versions.

21 W. Ross, *Plato's Theory of Ideas*, p. 116.

22 e.g. J. Kostman, "False Logos and Not-Being in Plato's *Sophist*."

23 Ross, *Plato's Theory of Ideas*, p. 168; Cornford, *Plato's Theory of Knowledge*, p. 293; M. Frede, "Predikation," p. 93.

24 For evidence concerning the wide sense of *rhema*, see Moravcsik, "Being and Meaning in the *Sophist*."

25 Cornford, *Plato's Theory of Knowledge*, p. 254.

26 Ibid., p. 255.

27 W. Ross, *Plato's Theory of Ideas*, p. 112; D. Hamlyn, "The Communion of the Forms and the Development of Plato's Logic," p. 295.

28 Frede, "Predikation," p. 61.

29 For separation of meaning and truth by Plato, see R. Hackforth, "False Statement in Plato's *Sophist*," p. 56.

30 For a defense of the "fact" interpretation, see D. Wiggins, "Sentence, Meaning, Negation, and Plato's Problem of Not-Being."

31 For a different view, see E. Lee, "Plato on Negation and Not-being in the *Sophist*," and for criticism of that view, Lewis, "Did Plato Discover the 'estin' of Identity," pp. 257–8, n. 19.

32 This is defended in Moravcsik, "Being and Meaning in the *Sophist*," pp. 76–7.

33 McDowell, "Falsehood and Non-Being in Plato's *Sophist*," p. 123.

6

The Ontology of Order
Reconsidered: The Divisions
and the *Philebus*

◆

In the previous chapter, we looked at *Sophist* 253d and saw that the so-called Divisions are also included in Plato's notion of dialectic. This helps to explain the unity of the dialogue. In the inner core, the ontological presuppositions of Divisions are explained, and in the "outer shell," the method is applied to the analysis of sophistry. The theory of connectors explains how Forms are pervaded by sameness and difference. But this by itself is only a precondition for the other relations, such as that of part and whole, that are involved in the Divisions. In the Divisions of *Sophist* and *Politicus*, two disciplines – namely, sophistry and statesmanship – are explained by revealing their many characteristics. In this chapter we shall explore the anatomy of these structures.[1] The Divisions are also introduced in the *Philebus*, though the examples are quite different. In this dialogue, an attempt is made to characterize the good human life in terms of a ranked order of its ingredients. Thus, to a large extent, the examples involve qualities within which quantitative comparisons can be made. Furthermore, in that dialogue some of the Divisions are linked to an ontological trichotomy that results in a specification of abstract mixtures which underlie order and harmony.

A great many issues can be raised concerning this material. In this chapter we shall limit ourselves to an examination of what ontological structures underlie the Divisions in the *Sophist* and *Politicus* and how these are related to the ontological structures underlying the Divisions in the *Philebus* and to the trichotomy that is articulated in that dialogue. Finally, we will ask what implications these structures have for the theory of Forms.

This focus requires our not touching upon many interesting questions that have been discussed in the literature concerning these dialogues.

Our investigation will center around the following questions:

1   What are the key ontological relationships between generic Forms, their "cuts" — that is, their species resulting from Divisions, or "cuts," and the art to be characterized or defined? We have seen already that each Form is "one and many"; how is this dual nature elaborated in the Divisions? Why must there be more than one Division explaining the same art?

2   What structure underlies the good mixtures of the *Philebus*, and how does this structure relate to the theory of Forms as developed so far?

3   How do Divisions and the trichotomy affect the explanatory power of the theory of Forms, and does the redescription of the explanatory power require a reconsideration of the conception of appearance and reality?

When viewed as a version of the universal–particular distinction, it is tempting to see Plato's contrast between appearances and reality as the contrast between empirically accessible particulars and abstract universals not knowable via empirical methods. In this part of the book, we have already seen evidence that this identification yields an overly simplistic picture of Plato's theory of Forms and other elements of reality. The dialogues under consideration in this chapter give further support to wanting to draw a more elaborate picture of these matters. Being an abstract entity is not, for Plato, a sufficient condition for something being an object of a genuine discipline and hence for being one of the fundamental elements of reality. We also see in these dialogues extensions of the realm of Forms. Within this larger realm, Plato finds an important subset of Forms that play special roles vis-à-vis order and harmony. Thus the explanation of law and order in the universe has two stages: first, it is shown that there are Forms and that law and order in this world depend on reflecting the natures of these; secondly, it is shown that among the Forms a certain subset constitute special configurations, the "good mixtures," and that the existence of these accounts for order and harmony among elements of the domains of the key sciences. Thus, within what is genuinely real there are further distinctions of fundamentality, and within the realm of appearances we find both abstract elements that are not Forms and sensible particulars.

The Ontology of the Divisions

Many of the Divisions in the *Sophist* characterize the sophist in several ways: for example, as a hunter of men, as a merchant of commodities allegedly nourishing the soul, as a seller of products of his own manufacture, as an athlete in eristic contests, and as a producer of deceptive images (223c–231e and, for the final characterization, 268c). There is also a characterization of the sophist as a purifier of the soul; but this has been interpreted, reasonably, as an ironic interlude, referring to the nature of Socratic activity, as misunderstood by the contemporaries.[2] Each of the divisions starts with cutting up the generic Form of techné into parts which are then cut further. Each series of cuts, or divisions, results in a characterization of the sophist.

The general conceptual topography of these cuttings suggests that Plato is presenting the outline of a classificatory system. But caution is in order. One would want to compare these classifications with Aristotle's classificatory schemes in terms of genus and differentia for biological kinds. Aristotle's classifications deal with dynamic, causally connected phenomena. What links successive generations of a species together? How can classifications capture the variety of distinctive biological activities that separate species? However, Plato's domain for classification is quite different. It includes arts, number, sound – in short, entities that have abstract elements as their instances and do not constitute dynamic fields. One obvious resulting difference concerns the need for instantiation. It is plausible to interpret biological classifications as being concerned with species that have members in the actual world. But Plato's divisions have intrinsic merit, even if what is delineated does not in fact have any instances, or at least no completely adequate instances. Thus, for example, Plato hints in various places that by his method one should be able to come to understand what philosophy itself is. Plato would regard this as an important intellectual task, even if it should turn out to be the case that there are no good particular instances of this discipline in the actual world.[3]

The ontology of the divisions is characterized as cutting a whole into parts. This is not incompatible with the generic Form being divisible in different ways. The same whole can be articulated into different collections of parts. In different contexts, we might want to stress this or that articulation of a generic Form.[4]

As our examples show, the divisions result in descriptions of certain abstract entities that are claimed to be necessarily true. At this point, we should note two implications of this way of describing the end results of divisions. First, there are many such descriptions applying to a given abstract entity. For example, the number two is necessarily an even number; it is necessarily the successor of one; and so forth. Some of these characterizations may be more important and revealing than others. Mere truth is not sufficient for achieving insight.[5] Furthermore, some of the characterizations are uniquely true of sophistry, such as the production of false images in terms of *logos*, whereas others, such as being hunters of men, are true not only of sophistry. Finally, let us also note that there is no reason why all the delineations mentioned could not be true of sophistry. It seems that they are in fact all true, though some are more revealing than others.

There are, however, additional complications. Not only is sophistry described via different divisions; it is also placed in different main cuts of technē. Thus it is described as acquisitive in one division, yet as productive in another. Cornford thought that maybe Plato was describing different kinds of sophistry.[6] But another, less speculative solution is at hand.

Even a cursory glance should convince us that sophistry, like many other disciplines, has both acquisitive and productive aspects. Why should it not do so? All arts concerned with the production of artifacts have a productive aspect, but also involve acquisition, such as payment, fame, the embellishment of the beauty of the surroundings in some cases, and so on. Philosophy too has this dual nature; it produces logoi, explanations, and leads to the acquisition of wisdom, insight, and so forth.

One might object that there are some arts, like angling (219a–b), that are purely acquisitive and do not produce anything. But there are many others that are more like philosophy. Plato describes learning as the acquisition of knowledge; but as we saw in chapter 1 in our review of parts of the *Meno*, this activity also produces, for example, diagrams and arguments.

Sophist 223c6 and 226a5 produce evidence that Plato wants us to see the arts, and especially sophistry, in this way. For in these passages the sophist is described as *poikilos*, or "multi-faceted" in nature. Presumably Plato would want to say the same about the arts he regards as more beneficial, such as mathematics and medicine. It is not surprising that the most revealing delineation of sophistry is given in terms of objects produced. The genuine sciences are described primarily in terms of the objects given

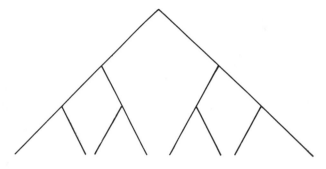

Figure 6.1

independently of the activity of the technē to which they relate. So here, too, the most revealing characterization of sophistry is in terms of its objects; but the objects are not parts of an independent reality; they are produced by the sophist himself.

We can see by a comparison of the *Sophist* with the *Politicus* that Plato does not regard the acquisitive–productive dichotomy as the only "natural" division of Art. For in the latter dialogue the arts are divided into those that are theoretical and those that are practical. Putting the two together gives us a cross-classification, or even more complicated structures, when we realize that the same technē can be both productive and acquisitive. These observations show that Plato's divisions are quite unlike the Aristotelian classifications. For not only is there the difference in terms of need for instantiation, there is also the difference of Aristotle needing to carve out nonoverlapping species and hierarchies of genera, whereas in Plato's scheme the intermediate cuts can crisscross the generic Form of Art in a variety of ways. To be sure, Plato is aware of biological classifications, as, for example, in *Sophist* 220a–b; but these serve only as auxiliary devices to secure some of the *differentiae* used in the main lines of divisions.

Not only is sophistry a many-splendored thing, so is the generic Form of Art. No one part–whole analysis can capture fully the complex nature of a Form. Thus we should not think of the divisions as giving Aristotelian structures of the kind shown in figure 6.1. Rather, we should think of the parts as overlapping, crisscrossing, yielding a conceptual quilt, articulating the complexity of the generic Form and also the different facets of the specific technē to be delineated. We can expect the divisions to yield structures like those shown in figure 6.2.

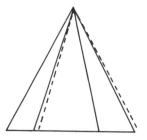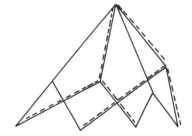

Figure 6.2

This interpretation explains the metaphor of cutting and gives an answer to the epistemological puzzle of the *Meno*. As we saw in Part I, the *Meno* called for an ontology that would provide the background for an epistemology in which the object understood has a unity of its own but is necessarily related to other fundamental elements of reality as well. Dividing and cutting the generic Form yields both unity and interrelatedness. What is cut is the generic Form of Art, or Number, not classes of participants. The parts overlap in various ways, thereby yielding different conceptual paths from the generic Form to the specific discipline, or groups of sounds or numbers. One cannot represent the ontological configurations underlying the divisions in what today would be called an "extensional" way.[7] This aspect of the theory of Forms has been pointed out already in connection with the greatest kinds of the *Sophist*, since these kinds are coextensive but intensionally distinct. This interpretation of the ontology of Divisions supports the same point of view.

The smallest parts are still abstract, attribute-like entities. They are not particulars or extensionally defined classes of particulars. Platonic science is purely Platonistic; that is, it deals only with intensional elements. Even the bad cuts and the bad final entities are on the level of the abstract. Whether statesmanship has actual particular instances and, if so, how many is a practical concern, not a concern of the Divisions. We saw already in chapter 5 that there are good and bad ways of cutting, yielding either natural or nonnatural parts. Thus, in addition to the natural parts, like odd and even, male and female, we need to take account also of the indefinite variety of bad parts, such as "not identical with 10,000," "pottery in Sparta," "non-Greek," and so on. There are also an indefinite number of nonnatural parts on the same level of specificity as sophistry, statesmanship, and the like. These constitute the indefinite collections into which we can let the objects of successive cuts go, once the task of understanding a certain technē has been accomplished. Sophistry is an ultimate natural part. The pseudo-arts such as "pottery in Athens" or "half of statesmanship mixed with aspects of flattery," elements that are analogous to the unnatural parts of not-Greek and not-10,000 mentioned by Plato explicitly, can be "cut" further, indefinitely.

The "quilt" interpretation is not standard, and indeed clashes with what we can see as Aristotle's reconstruction of Divisions in Plato. Aristotelian classifications in terms of hierarchies of the genus–species sort yield ontological "tree" structures, as do biological classifications today, at least on a realist reading of these. Dividing animals into mammals and non-mammals or birds and insects does not yield cross-classifications.

Aristotle's main interest was biology, since this was paradigmatic for this ontology of substances, as individuals, as species, and eventually as genera. It is quite natural for an original philosopher to see the work of his predecessors as consisting of imperfect approximations of what he is trying to do. Thus one need not place much weight on Aristotelian reconstructions of Platonic divisions.

In order to place classificatory "trees" and "quilts" in proper perspective and to strengthen the "underdog" quilt interpretation, let us place classifications in a larger philosophical perspective. Classifications come in many sizes and shapes. In biology and some of the other natural sciences, tree-like structures are useful for understanding relations between kinds and sub-kinds. But in other disciplines, such as anthropology, linguistics, and philosophy, cross-classifications are also important, and for some of these the modern successors of Plato's "quilts", so-called feature systems, are useful. For example, in philosophy we can "divide" the genus declarative sentence not only into singular and general, but also into that involving opaque contexts and that which does not. Hence we have a cross-classification; since more complexities can be added, a feature system containing the features singular + − and opaque context + − as ingredients is useful. Platonic quilts serve well those structures that are analyzed today by means of feature systems, such as phonological units or kinship relations in anthropology.

The subjects of Aristotle's biological classifications are very different from the generic notions that Plato divides. Classifications of arts and sciences lend themselves to quilt structures, or feature structures, as much today as in Plato's day. Sciences can be pure or applied, with subsequent subclassifications; they can be natural or social; they can have a mostly mathematical structure or a mostly qualitative one; and so forth. There is much room here for cross-classifications. Thus it is hardly surprising that Plato's divisional structures lend themselves to a quilt-like interpretation. This also fits well with Plato's Forms being intensional entities. For the same person can be both a mathematician and a physicist, but the same animal cannot be both a horse and a tiger; we need extensionality for the second kind of division, but not the first. Needless to say, we can get mixed structures as well: that is, structures containing some tree-like cuts with feature systems within them or the other way around.

Plato's other examples do not lend themselves to the tree system either. Pleasures are good or bad, differ in intensity, in the parts of soul they involve, and so on. This cannot be expressed by a single genus–species hierarchy. Sounds also admit of many divisions; for example, divisions into letter sounds constituting alphabets and musical sounds resulting in scales and harmony. Mathematics and geometry are different again; for here, species like odd and even numbers can be distinguished, but different methods are needed to present the whole series of positive integers or the different geometrical shapes involving angles. Reflection on examples such as these may have been what inspired Plato to move on to the determinate–indeterminate–mixed classifications of the *Philebus*, to which we will turn shortly.

Was Plato clearly aware of the difference between tree-like and quilt-like divisions? There is not sufficient evidence to answer this question. Tree-like structures emerge in auxiliary divisions; that is, those needed to establish a given "part" along the way. But in any case, the quilt-like structure outlined here captures his thought and examples much better than the tree-like structures familiar from Aristotelian ontology and modern biological classifications.

Finally a *caveat*. The realization that Aristotelian tree-like structures do not capture adequately the complexities of Platonic divisions might tempt some to link this with the issue of "realism": that is, the issue of whether Plato thought that ontological configurations underlay his divisions and that the divisions at their best approximate reality and are not affected by classificatory interests related to human need and interest. But whether the quilt interpretation is sound or not is quite independent of the question of realism versus skepticism. Those who think that classifications are not "realistic" but are rather related to human interest can raise this claim equally against tree-like structures or those captured by feature systems. Again, feature systems and their ancestors, quilt-like structures, and any combination of hierarchy and feature can be defended as realist structures, just as well as any genus–species-type, pure tree-like structure.

There are, then, two basic relations linking elements of configurations that underlie the divisions. One of these is partaking, and the other the part–whole relation. The Form to be understood – for example, statesmanship – partakes of the generic Form of Art. Statesmanship is an art. It also partakes of the natural parts whose articulations yield paths to it. Statesmanship is an art of such and such a nature. We shall postpone the difficult question of differentiae as entities to be partaken of until later. There are also whole–part distinctions. The parts, in turn, can be natural, in which case these too are wholes, or nonnatural, in which case they are not wholes. These distinctions have as their basis the discussion of wholes and parts in the *Parmenides*, discussed in chapter 4.

The fact that a generic Form like Art can be divided in a number of different ways strengthens the interpretation according to which it is a whole that is greater than the sum of its parts, a view of wholeness explored in chapter 5. This helps to explain Plato's analogy (*Politicus* 278b–d) between the knowledge of divisions and the knowledge of the letters of the alphabet. In the latter case, what is most important is our knowledge of how to combine the elements correctly. The resulting units – that is, syllables and words – are wholes that are more than the mere sum of parts. The analogy forces us to think of the knowledge of divisions and the objects of this knowledge in a similar way. The objects are a generic Form as a whole, with natural parts that are themselves wholes and nonnatural parts that, for Plato, are not wholes – that is, have no real unifying principle (263b).

Plato's key notion in assessing divisions and their end result is that of adequacy, or self-sufficiency (*hikanoos*; e.g. *Sophist* 221b2, 221c4). This notion, like that of insight, admits of degrees. If the divisions were to end in the delineation of separate species falling into different classes, then the emphasis in assessing a division would be truth and falsity. Either our definition picks out the right class, or it does not. Hence the evidence given here is in harmony with the point made above, that divisions have to result in logos that is not only true, but also adequate and insightful. Clearly, some are more so than others.[8]

The final characterization of the Form under investigation – for example, Statesmanship – is constituted by an interweaving of terms (*Sophist* 268c5–6). For example, the final characterization of sophistry (268c–d) is that it is a productive art that produces semblances by mimicry through insincere ignorance. This logos is itself a whole and not just the sum of its parts, as the discussion of "interweaving" in the *Sophist* shows (see chapter 5). So we have two kinds of whole–part relations in divisions. The generic Form is a whole. We understand it when we grasp the variety of ways in which it can be articulated into natural parts. The characterization of an art is also a whole. We understand it when we can locate the art within the conceptual map of the generic Form Art under which it falls.

Having distinguished two part–whole relations, let us summarize the ontological notions and relations that underlie divisions. Since Plato does not do this explicitly, any attempt of this sort must be to some extent a reconstruction. The reconstruction has to capture the following facts:

a   All Forms are wholes, and all wholes in divisions are Forms.
b   Some Forms are wholes and not parts.
c   Some Forms are both wholes and parts.
d   Some parts of Forms are not wholes.
e   Some Forms are parts of Forms and also wholes and have no parts except in the sense of having participants.

(a) captures the distinction between the right divisions that always involve wholes and those that include nonnatural parts – that is, parts that are not wholes. (b) singles out the generic Forms like Art, Sound, and Number. (c) collects the appropriate intermediates, those that characterize correctly a specific Form under investigation. (d) singles out the unnatural. (e) describes the specific Forms like Statesmanship or Sophistry. These have no more specific Form as a part, and the nonnatural parts are not their parts either; they belong to a higher node on the division scheme. As we have seen already, we can find an indefinite number of nonnatural parts, such as "not identical with 10,000," "not identical with justice," and so on, on the same level as the specific Forms that Plato wants to illuminate.

Within this scheme, partaking between Forms is a relation between wholes. It is not equivalent to predication; for if it were, it would also link more specific units and nonnatural parts. With the help of this construal of this relation, we can define

D1.   A whole within divisions is either something that has participants or something that has parts which have participants. (The disjunction is to be taken in the inclusive, rather than exclusive, sense).

We can also give a delineation of the "part" relation.

D2.   In the divisions, "x is part of y" is definable only over attribute-like entities. Within this constraint, x is part of y = possession of x entails possession of y.

These definitions enable us to assert:

T1.   Some parts are also wholes, but others are not.

We thus distinguish the natural from the nonnatural elements in divisions. The definitions and explanations still leave us with a primitive notion of both naturalness and genuine unity, which inform the whole ontological scheme.

Are the differentiae used in the divisions Forms? Do they combine with the Form Art to constitute Forms? Plato does not give explicit answers to these questions. I will survey here some of the difficulties that arise if it is assumed that Plato does think of a differentia as a Form, as well as others that arise if he is thought not to take this view.

A similar problem arises for Aristotle in *Categories*, chapter 5. If the differentiae are in the same category as the substances, then the unity of these is preserved, but how can differentiae be qualities? If they are genuine qualities, then the essences of substances are cross-categorial, and so do not preserve the unity of the nature of substances. Furthermore, if the differentia is in the same category as the genus, how does one distinguish the two in a nonarbitrary way?

Some of the examples used by Plato suggest that the differentiae should not be regarded as Forms: for example, "using short arguments" (*Sophist* 268b) or various ways of striking fish, as in the delineation of angling. It does not seem that these notions satisfy the Form-making characteristics surveyed in the previous chapters. It is difficult to think of various ways of striking fish as an object of theoretical study. Furthermore, if a differentia like productivity is a Form, how will Plato distinguish the differentia from the genus? Is it arbitrary whether we call Art or productivity the genus?

The other alternative is to construe the differentiae as attribute-like entities that combine with a generic Form like Art to build parts of Art that are wholes, and thus Forms. But it is not clear from what Plato says about Forms and about Division how these constructions are built up.

Reflecting on the end results of the divisions takes us to the treatment of this methodology in the *Philebus*. For apparently an art like that of statesmanship is a complex, many-faceted element, with a variety of features. Can we say anything more informative than that an adequate understanding shows the features of statesmanship combined "in the right way"? Statesmanship, like most disciplines, is a mixture of many ingredients. Can Plato say anything informative about these mixtures and their goodness?

Before we turn to the *Philebus*, however, we should show in more detail how Divisions answer in part the question that surfaced in the epistemological passages of the *Meno* examined in chapter 1. There we encountered the claim that the objects of understanding are interrelated. Division provides the ontology for the explication of this claim. At the end of several divisions characterizing the same specific Form, we not only learn much about the specific Form; we also learn about the generic Form under which it falls. The logos at the end of a division and the way it is developed do not isolate an abstract entity – that is, a Form – from everything else in the universe. Rather, they illuminate it by showing how it is related to many other "parts" of a generic Form. Thus we also learn much about generic Forms. These are not defined. We come to understand them by coming to see the different wholes that their correct "cutting" reveals.

Still, one wants to know how relatedness in divisions is linked to the specification of mixtures in the *Philebus*. Is it merely a precondition? And if so, what must be added if we are to understand not only relatedness, but the variety of structures that, for Plato, are at the core of order and harmony?

The *Nova Scientia* of the *Philebus*

The *Philebus* inherits two problems. One of these is the ontological problem that the mere existence of the Forms, even when supplemented by the connector theory and the relatedness condition articulated by Divisions, is not sufficient to explain the kind of order that Plato sees as crucial to mathematics, ethics, and the other key disciplines mentioned earlier. The other, an ethical problem, arises out of the treatment of pleasure in earlier dialogues like the *Gorgias*. The main topic of the *Philebus* – at least as far as the "outer shell" is concerned – is whether the Good should be identified with pleasure and enjoyment or with knowledge and understanding (11b4–8). In the *Gorgias* and the *Republic*, Plato construes the disagreement between himself and the hedonists as being mainly about the correct ontology (e.g., *Republic* 476a ff.). The hedonist is represented as suffering from an intellectual disease. He believes only what his senses tell him. His blindness prevents him from understanding Goodness and the whole range of the other Forms as well. Plato seems to suggest that if the hedonist were to understand the correct ontology, he would change his views on ethics.

However, in the later stages of his career, Plato encountered someone called Eudoxus, a fine mathematician who presumably worked in Plato's academy and who expounded a view of goodness in which pleasure and the good are closely connected.[9] Plato could hardly dismiss Eudoxus as someone who did not understand the higher regions of reality. Eudoxus was probably just as committed to the existence of abstract entities as Plato.[10] Furthermore, as we saw in *Sophist* 254e, Plato admits that two abstract singular terms might name the same entity. Why could a sophisticated thinker like Eudoxus not avail himself of this insight and claim that "the good" and "pleasure" name the same entity? Plato needs a deeper, more subtle reply. He needs a conceptual examination of both pleasure and knowledge in order to determine what places they should have within a good life (12c4−5) and how both can be Forms. We are shown that pleasure has many types and that some of these are even in conflict, as opposites. Thus pleasure, too, proves to be a many-faceted entity. There is no reason why it should not be regarded as a Form, to be investigated dialectically, just like knowledge. Within the treatment of the *Gorgias*, it is enough to construe pleasure as a nonconcrete mass which is scattered around in the universe and named by the term "pleasure," which in this context would function as a mass term. This will not do for the more elaborate treatment of the *Philebus*. Pleasure is both one and many. It is one Form, with many natural parts. Since there are an indefinite number of kinds of pleasure (pleasure of this smell, that color, and so forth) and many of these do not enter into the formation of what Plato would regard as natural parts, these constitute a collection of the "indefinite," or an abstract plane, analogous to what we saw when we scrutinized divisions in the *Sophist* and the *Politicus*.

With this in mind, I shall examine the key ontological passages in this dialogue. My interpretation will be tested in the light of the following questions:

1   What is the ontological theory of the *Philebus*? Does it require supplementation of the previous ontology with new categories of entities?[11]

2 How is the Method of Division expounded in this dialogue different from that of the *Sophist* and the *Politicus?*
3 How should we interpret the questions raised about the Forms in the introductory part of the dialogue? And are these questions related to the ones in the *Parmenides* and the *Sophist* (13e–15c)?
4 How can we relate the initial description of Divisions in this dialogue to the examples given (17a–18d)?

These four questions deal with the general structure of the ontology of the *Philebus*, as well as a few passages that provide important evidence for this. The most crucial question for an interpretation of the ontology is:

5 Is partaking no longer the only important ontological relation explaining how Forms combine to constitute order and harmony? What additional ontological relations did Plato discover in this dialogue?

Finally, we have two questions concerning the interpretation of the ethics in this dialogue and the relation of ethics to ontology.

6 How does the Method of Division and the ontology relate to the characterization of the good life given towards the end of the dialogue?
7 Can we give a coherent account of the methodological passages up to 18d, the ontological passages in 23c–26d, and the final ethical passage of the dialogue?

It has been argued already that the indefinite plurality with which we leave an analysis of a generic Form is not the domain of sensible particulars, but the many abstract, specific, attribute-like entities that arise on the same level as the specific Forms that we are trying to delineate. For example, the indefinitely many tones, or speech sounds, are for Plato, as for modern everyday discourse, indefinitely many sound or tone types, each of which can have many sensible instances, or tokens. Similar considerations apply to pleasure. There is an indefinite variety of types of pleasure. These differ in source, degree of intensity, and in many other ways. This class comprises the final elements of the generic Form of pleasure that Plato is investigating, rather than the indefinitely many actual experiences of pleasure that humans have had, have, and will have. These illustrations show once more the thoroughly Platonistic nature of Platonic science.

Thus we should not assume that the "one over many" configuration referred to by Plato in several places is always that of Forms and participating particulars. Already in the earlier dialogues there are passages that defy such a reading. For example, in *Meno* 71e–72c Socrates' demand for an explication of excellence is met by Meno not with an illustration via a particular case, like Achilles, but with descriptions of different kinds of excellence. Socrates' ensuing complaint that Meno is offering "many" in place of one amounts to objecting that in place of giving an account of a generic entity, Meno offers only references to species. The *Philebus* confronts us with the reverse situation. Plato's interlocutors focus on two generic notions, whereas Plato want to stress the important differences among the parts of the respective generic entities. As passages like 62d5 ff. inform us, there are intellectual as well as physical pleasures; some are necessary, and some are not.

Two additional facts strengthen the hypothesis that the Divisions, as described in the *Philebus*, move always on the level of abstracta. At one point (12e) pleasure is contrasted with color and shape. Within this contrast, Plato talks about color as such, and specific colors like red and blue, and also about shape, and specific shapes like a triangle and a square. He does not contrast color and shape with their sensible instances. Furthermore, he insists on the need to distinguish the "many," referring to these as "parts" (*meros*; 12e7), thus using the same vocabulary as that examined earlier in this chapter. We saw that in the other passages, *meros* refers to abstract, attribute-like parts, not to sensible instances. In the *Philebus*, it is stressed that not only is it necessary to recognize the proper parts of larger abstract units, but also to realize that in some cases the parts under consideration may be opposites (12e–13a, 13e–14c).

With the aid of this interpretation, we can take the main point of the introductory discussion of the *Philebus* to be that different kinds of pleasures may have very different natures, and thus we cannot assume that all kinds of pleasures will have the same relation to the Good. Nor can we assume that all kinds of pleasures must be inferior to all kinds of knowledge and understanding.

After these introductory remarks, Socrates announces that we have stumbled upon one aspect of the old puzzle about "the one and the many" (14c). He goes on to distinguish different facets of this puzzle. With respect to particulars, he distinguishes two puzzles (14d–e):

P1.   How can one particular have many properties?

P2.   How can one particular consist of many parts?

He then says that these puzzles do not confront us with difficult conceptual challenges as long as they arise only with regard to particulars, but that they do present important challenges when applied to unities like Human, Ox, the Fine, and the Good. These puzzles are said to come to light in connection with Divisions. The examples are chosen in such a way as to invite analogies to P1 and P2. Applied now to the abstract unities under consideration – that is, Forms – we obtain the following restatements of the puzzles.

AP1.   How can one Form fall under several higher, or more generic, Forms?

AP2.   How can one higher, or more generic, Form have many abstract parts?

AP1 is illustrated in divisions in which Human or Ox are to be delineated, not divided, whereas AP2 is illustrated in divisions in which the Good and the Fine are divided, not defined.

One would expect what follows to be a thorough discussion of AP1 and AP2. Instead, at 15b1–c3, three questions are raised about abstract units, and these questions seem to be about the existence of the Forms and their relationship to particulars.[12] Thus, in this passage, *apeirois* at 15b5 can be taken as referring to particulars. The three questions do not receive detailed answers. Instead, at 15d4–6, we are told that this identity of the one and the many crops up in connection with discourse in general.[13] This remark echoes what we are told at the end of the first half of the *Parmenides* (135b8–c3). Thus it is reasonable to interpret it as being about the kind of theoretical discourse that Plato is interested in throughout. Having raised the three questions and then stated that these cannot threaten the legitimacy of theoretical discourse, Plato turns back to the methodology of dialectic that involves dealing with AP1 and AP2.

The structure of these passages has worried modern commentators. If we were to take the preliminary discussion to be about pleasure and its particular instances, then the whole of 11–15 would have to be seen as leading up to questions about the Forms and the sensible particulars. But on this account, it becomes puzzling that Plato treats these problems so briefly and why he launches into a discussion of dialectic, a method that deals with relationships among Forms. Either there is a sudden, inexplicable break in the flow of the argument, or Plato is guilty of not noticing the difference between the relationship that particulars have to Forms and that which more specific Forms have to more generic ones.

Let us briefly compare three lines of interpretation of 11–16. According to one of these, Plato introduces in 11–14 a debate concerning hedonism, and this concerns the relationship of pleasure to its many sensible instances. This account of the debate sees it as culminating in a passage in which questions are raised about the reality of the Forms by contrast with particulars. Then the whole matter is dropped, and Plato turns to the discussion of divisions. Since that discussion cannot answer the questions raised just before it about the reality of the Forms, this reading cannot bestow unity on the whole passage.

Another interpretation bridges the gap between different parts of the text by assuming that Plato makes no distinction between the relationship of particulars to Forms and that between the most specific Forms and the generic Forms under which they fall. But we saw already in our examination of the second half of the *Parmenides* that some of what Plato presents as surface paradoxes result from not seeing the difference between these two fundamentally different relations. Furthermore, in juxtaposing P1 and P2 with AP1 and AP2, Plato is calling attention precisely to this difference. Why should we interpret the larger chunk of text in such a way as to assume that Plato is ignoring a key distinction to which he calls attention in a part of the same text?

The third interpretation is the one that I am adopting in this chapter. Relying on what has been shown about the one–many relation, it claims that both the introductory passage and AP1 and AP2 deal solely with relationships among Forms and other attribute-like abstracta, the "bad parts" of the divisions of the *Sophist* and the *Politicus*. Thus the interlude is really the brief passage in which questions about the reality of the Forms and their relation to particulars are raised. Given the parallel already noted between the brief dismissal here and the similar move in *Parmenides* 135b8–c3, we can assume that the same view is being articulated. There are problems in spelling out and understanding the mode of being of the Forms, but their existence is a necessary condition for the foundations of the genuine theoretical sciences. Further conditions are added in the dialogues that I am considering in this part of the book. In the *Philebus*, as we shall see, Plato works out these necessary conditions that some of the Forms fulfill in constituting the most important structures of order. These configurations are the "mixtures" discussed in this dialogue, such as combinations of sounds in musical harmony, the appropriate proportions of ingredients constituting good health, and that which yields the pattern for the good life. The mixtures demand further relations in addition to those of partaking and the part–whole relation. Given the whole scheme, it is natural for Plato to describe the Forms as units – that is, constituents in more complex configurations determined by measure, proportion, or, at least, priority.

Thus the discussion of the methodology of Divisions is not an interlude, but a natural continuation of the discussion of different kinds of pleasure and knowledge in the introductory section.

Divisions are first characterized, then illustrated by Plato in this dialogue. The description starts at 16b5, and the path to be followed is regarded as dialectic. But what Plato regards as dialectic depends on the context within which he is dealing with any given theoretical issue. The conception is cumulative, however. Thus, we need to give an interpretation to his description that covers both the divisions of the *Sophist* and the *Politicus* and those given here in the *Philebus*. The examples given here are musical sounds and harmony and speech sounds and their combination, thus presenting us with abstract complexes that are different from the examples of the *Sophist* and the *Politicus* – that is, from the examples for which a Platonic version of genus–differentia analysis seems to suffice. The following points are made in Plato's initial description, and an adequate interpretation must account for all these.[14]

According to Plato, the path is such that (1) he always loved it; (2) it has often escaped him (16b6–7); (3) it is easy to indicate; but (4) it is difficult to use; and (5) it underlies all the sciences (16c1–3). The first two points show that the method is not something entirely new, while the last three show that the method cannot be exactly the same as that employed in, for example, the outer shell of the *Sophist*. If we can come up with a characterization of Divisions that applies to the *Sophist* and the *Politicus*, as well as to the *Philebus*, then all five points will have been shown to apply. The path Plato always loved is dialectic in its most general sense. It has often escaped him in the sense that he is puzzled at times as to which facet of dialectic is most applicable. For example, how do different aspects of dialectic apply to the outer shell and the inner core of the *Sophist*? It is easy to indicate in general how divisions are made by "cutting" generic Forms, but in practice it is difficult to come up with the right articulation of generic Forms like Pleasure and Knowledge. Finally, Plato is confident throughout that the methods he uses in the middle period dialogues, as well as those examined in this part of the book, provide the foundations for all the genuine technai.

The difference between the examples used in the dialogues examined earlier in this chapter and those of the *Philebus* can be seen by invoking a metaphysical distinction hammered out only in later philosophy. We have seen that the cuttings of the generic Forms in the other two dialogues are effected by the invocation of differentiae. But in the case of sounds, colors, and quantitative dimensions like length or weight, such distinguishing characteristics are not available. We can divide sounds into high and low and colors into light and dark. But when we consider the indefinitely many shades of color or sound, there are no distinguishing characteristics to separate these.

If there were differentiae to mark off each of these parts, there would have to be an infinite number of them, corresponding to the infinite number of parts; thus the whole domain would lose any semblance of orderly structure. By imposing measurement on these domains and having the elements of measurement derived by rules from a finite number of entities, Plato comes close to the modern scientific ideal of explaining an infinite collection on the basis of a finite set of fundamental elements. (I am indebted to Alan Code on this point.) The difference between the parts is basic primitive qualitative difference. They constitute ranges of determinables within which they occupy the places of determinates.[15] In some cases, we can order the determinates by defining units of measurement and then constructing an order with the help of these. In others, we can order the determinates along some dimension like loud and quiet, high and low. The determinable–determinate configurations allow Plato, on the one hand, to avoid the ontological problem of the differentiae, to which I have referred already, and on the other, to introduce notions of measurement that can in some cases replace the role that differentiae play in the other divisions. The characterization of divisions that is presented here in the *Philebus* is general enough to include both kinds of divisions, genus–differentia and determinable–determinate.

Plato says in 16c9–10 that everything has in its nature the one as well as the limit and the unlimited.[16] We need to find one unit and, via the repeated divisions, establish not only that the original unit is one and indefinitely many, but also "how many" it is; that is, establish the intermediate parts of the original unity, as well as the final, specific, appropriate parts (16d1–e2).[17] Only after this intricate articulation of the original unity has been established, can we let the unit dissolve into an indefinite plurality. This characterization fits both the kind of division, in the *Sophist* and the *Politicus* and that in the *Philebus*. For it leaves the ways in which the intermediates and the final appropriate units are determined sufficiently general to include genus–differentia–species configurations as well as those of determinables and determinates – that is, relations like color and all the colors, length and all the lengths, and so forth. The shift to the second type of division enables Plato to introduce into this part of the ontology measurement and what he will later call "mixing."

In line with what has been claimed already, the indefinite plurality referred to in this characterization of divisions is interpreted in this chapter as the indefinite good and bad parts that surfaced already in the *Politicus*. Here this helps to explain yet another feature of Plato's method. For if the indefinite collection were one of particulars, then direction would matter in the divisions; that is, the move from the indefinite to the intermediates and the generic unit would be an upward move from one ontological category to another; whereas the move from the generic to the specific would be a downward move between categories. But if we assume that all three levels include Forms and abstract, attribute-like parts of Forms, then directionality does not matter, since, either way, we are moving on the same ontological plane. With the help of this interpretation, we can explain how, later (55c–59c), Plato can distinguish disciplines that deal with the appropriate genuine objects from those that deal only with particulars. Furthermore, we can explain the irrelevance of directionality illustrated by Plato in his treatment of phonetic sound. One articulation moves "top down" (17b), whereas the second, more detailed treatment (18b6 ff.) moves "from bottom up" – that is, from generic to specific in the first case, specific to generic in the second. Section 18a–b4 gives direct evidence that, for Plato, directionality does not matter. Thus our interpretation can make sense of these passages without accusing Plato of failing to distinguish empirical induction from conceptual analysis and also construes the *nova scientia* as remaining on the Platonic plane.

In the case of musical sound, the same considerations hold. Although when we talk of our offspring's early efforts at the piano, we may talk about the sound tokens produced, when we turn to music theory, even on the commonsense level, the domain with which we are concerned is that of types, not tokens. The composer must select scale and harmony; thus he faces choices involving types. Only the performing artist need be concerned with the tokens to be produced, and Plato in the *Philebus* is not talking about performing artists.

In 16c9–10 Plato says that determinacy and indeterminacy are inherent (*sumphuton*) in the nature of the Forms. This reads better if we take it to mean that generic Forms have a determinate structure and indefinitely many abstract parts, rather than to claim that it is in the nature of Forms to have an indefinite number of sensible particular participants. The latter fits Aristotle's characterization of form better than the Platonic Forms.

Partaking does not play an important role in divisions with respect to sound, which lead to specifying good mixtures like harmony. To be sure, every sound-type is a sound – "good" ones fitting into the harmony, "bad" ones constituting inappropriate combinations. Thus the right basic tones will partake of Sound. Furthermore, they partake of Low or High. But the structures yielding the separate units that make up the sound range, as well as those that yield harmony, are not mere matters of partaking, but rather of applying measure and proportion to the range of sounds. In this context, measure and proportion have normative implications for Plato. Their application must result in good mixtures and harmony. Furthermore, what coustitutes a good mixture and what is appropriate harmony depend on the intensional aspect under consideration. We would say today that it depends on the point of view of the science that we are pursuing. Hence this aspect of Plato's conception of understanding can be seen as a forerunner of the Aristotelian idea that each science has its own domain and its own good.

As Gosling saw, on the accepted modern interpretation there is a problem about why Plato thinks that we need to search for the original generic unit to be analyzed.[18] After all, everyone knows that there are sounds and that they have something in common, so why the mystery?

The quilt interpretation of Divisions can solve this problem. For though in some sense everyone can recognize sounds, it takes some discernment to see phonology and music dividing the same Form. Not only are the intermediate "parts" different; so are the final most specific elements and the structures that one can build out of these. Words, complex expressions, and sentences are quite different from harmonies and melodies. But the dialectician should see also the common generic qualitative element. To give a modern analogy, it takes discernment to see that physics and chemistry divide the same generic qualitative notion, that of matter, in different ways.

According to the interpretation presented in this chapter, the surface impression that the illustrations provide three divisions of one Form is misleading. In fact, there are two divisions of one Form, but for one of these Plato provides two analyses, in order to illustrate the irrelevance of directionality. Vocal sounds are divided at 17b and again in the story of Teuth at 18b5–d5, whereas musical sounds are divided at 17c–e. No elaborate mathematical theory is required to see that, after the initial dichotomies, proportional notions are used to characterize scales and harmonies. Furthermore, we distinguish musical tones within systems of sounds, and these constitute a range of determinates according to the dimension of high and low. What we know about Greek music of this time suggests that Plato could have come to these conclusions on his own, without expertise or any particular background in music theory.[19] There is no need to invoke conjectures about Pythagorean theories and influences to explain what Plato is doing here. This is of considerable comfort to the interpreter, since evidence for the alleged Pythagorean theories of that time is scarce indeed.[20]

Finally, we can explain our interpretation of 17a1–3, where Plato says that some people move from the one to the many too slow, some too fast. As an example of those who move too fast, one could cite Meno, who moves immediately from the generic notion of excellence to its many varieties. Philebus, on the other hand, is a good example of a slow mover. For he insists in the early section of the dialogue that pleasure is one and is reluctant to recognize that the many kinds of pleasures have different natures and that these differences matter when it comes to determining the role of pleasures in the good life.

Let us now review the similarities and differences between the different levels of elements discussed in the *Sophist* and the *Politicus*, on the one hand, and the *Philebus*, on the other. There are two schemes under consideration: the genus–differentia scheme and the determinable–determinate scheme utilizing measurement. The *Sophist* contains only the first scheme, whereas the *Philebus* has both. In both schemes we find generic Forms: in one, the Form of Art; in the other, Forms like Speech, Sound, Pleasure, and Knowledge. But in the second scheme, some of the generic Forms are determinables in the sense specified. There are intermediate "cuts" in both schemes. But whereas in the first scheme, the intermediate parts are specified simply in terms of differentiae, in the second, some intermediates admit of mathematical specifications – for example, complexes exemplifying certain proportions. As we shall see, further ontological discussions in the *Philebus* introduce so-called mixed elements. These can arise within a division either as intermediates or as the final, most specific entities.

There are an indefinite number of the most specific entities within both schemes, at the bottom of the divisional "trees," or "quilts." Some of these are genuine unities, hence objects of dialectic, and "good parts," or natural parts, whereas others are not. Many pleasures, sounds, art forms, collections of numbers, and so forth do not qualify as natural parts.

The partaking relation and the part–whole relation govern the configurational structure in both schemes. But the *logos*, or governing principle, in the divisions of the second scheme is not purely qualitative in all cases, as it is in the first scheme.

The second scheme cries out for further specification. To say that for the right unities we need to have various ingredients in the right proportion or order is not enough. We want to know the nature of the ontological configurations that underlie the good, well-ordered unities. We said before that a Form is one, has many kinds as parts, and has an indefinite number of most specific abstract parts, some of which are natural, others not. But this does not say enough about the nature of the good mixtures. The One–many–indefinite trichotomy needs to be supplemented by the introduction of further ontological distinctions and relations. This is in fact what we find expounded in 23c–27d. However, this section raises many questions. We could ask about the "mind," or creative force, that is posited as being behind the main ontological trichotomy to be explained. We could also ask about many issues of philosophical psychology that are raised subsequently. But we will focus strictly on the ontological configurations and on the question of how these modify or supplement the theory of Forms.

In this passage, Plato talks about three elements as the key ingredients of reality. As we shall see, the trichotomy cuts across the Form–sensible particular distinction. The three elements are a limiting, or balancing, element; the indefinite, or unlimited; and mixtures of these two. The unlimited or indefinite, is characterized as admitting the more and the less (24e–25a), and the examples cited are hotter, colder, stronger and milder, faster and slower, larger and smaller (25c). Thus we see immediately that this is a much narrower class than the indefinite collections that emerged in connection with the divisions that we discussed. Some of those – for example, all the arts and the pseudo-arts – fall outside the trichotomy that is now introduced. The examples of the limiting, or balancing, factor are double, half, equal (25a). The third type is the result of limit, or balance, being applied to the indefinite, or unlimited, element (25b). One must add "applied in the right way"; for within this scheme, as we shall see, there are no bad mixtures. If a mixture does not capture a genuine unity or a natural part of reality, then it does not count as a mixture; it must be unbalanced in some way and thus still falls in the class of the unlimited. This is brought out by the fact that the examples of the mixed class cited are good health (25e7–8), the combination of high and low, or fast and slow, yielding the right musical elements (26a), good temperature, and the good quality combinations of soul and character (26b). We shall now examine, in greater detail, each of these ingredients.

Let us consider the unlimited, or unbalanced, element (*apeiron*). It is an element that can exist both by itself, as a strong wind in a howling storm, or as an ingredient – for example, the low in a sound that is part of a harmony, contributing to a complex.[21] The indefinite encompasses both Form and particular. There is the Form of Strength, and there is also the particular strong, howling wind that wreaks havoc with Greek shipping. There is no good English translation for *apeiron*; we need the modern disjunction of indefinite and unbalanced, since Plato will include in this category not only speed and heat, but also the badly constructed chair, the sick body, and the howling wind. What we would today regard as quite determinate, such as the measurements of a building, even if it does not adequately serve the functions that it was designed to fulfill, falls for Plato in the same class as that which does not by itself admit of precise measurement. The reasons for this will be given below.

The distinguishing mark of admitting the more and the less characterizes for Plato not only extensive quantitative dimensions like length or weight, but also intensive quantities like pleasure. It would be anachronistic, however, to construe the distinguishing mark as a linguistic test. By the purely linguistic criteria for comparatives, the better and the worse, as well as knowledge and intelligence, would fall in this class as well. But Plato, does not regard such items as quantities in the sense in which pleasure, weight, and so forth are. He has an intuitive sense of "quantitative," in which being more or less wise or more or less virtuous are not matters of quantity.

This interpretation contains the claim that Plato would characterize some concrete entities as indeterminate in length. Is this not odd? Today we tend to regard anything that has length as having a determinate length, whether it serves a good function or not and whether we can measure it or not. This could be called "the principle of the determinateness of nature." It is part of modern common sense. There is no evidence, however, to suggest that this was part of the common sense of Plato's time. This is not to say that the principle was consciously considered and rejected, but that its consideration did not arise. One can understand this when one considers the state of measurement in Plato's time.

Measurements of both length and area were imprecise by our standards and included subjective elements.[22] Intensive quantities were not measured, and the measures used for some extensive quantities included parts of the human body and what one could accomplish with an artifact like a plough. There is evidence of more precise measurement, perhaps using some reliable unit, in the case of weighing things involved in commercial exchange and payment. But these are not the things one has in mind when attempting to characterize what is good and orderly in nature and in human lives. On the other hand, considerable technology evolved using heat. Examples of this include the wherewithal to heat baths and buildings and to cook. But only proportional measurement was required in these cases, and no nonrelative unit of measurement underpinned these proportional specifications.[23] Sameness of temperature and proportionate increase or decrease can be effected by control over the means of production of heat. Such procedures do not require an exact scale of measurement.

The notions that covered phenomena in connection with which there were no exact scales of measurement were those that played a part in what Plato regarded as theoretical sciences. As mentioned above, measurement of weight was more refined.[24] But weight does not play an important role in what Plato regarded as the theoretical *technai*.

These considerations help to explain why what we take as a subjective aspect of measurement – namely, the normative notion of a right standard – and what we take as an objective aspect – namely, measurement of length or weight by whatever means are available – seemed very different to Plato and his contemporaries. Today what we think of as proper heat or good weather are matters of subjective evaluation, whereas the length of a line or the area of a surface is a matter of objective fact. But in Plato's time, it was natural to view these things the other way round. Good weather and good bodily temperature can, in theory, be specified by principles determining proportions among the needed ingredients. Measurement of length or area entailed applying procedures involving less mathematics and notoriously unreliable perceptual means. Plato thought that the former could serve as the basis of a discipline with a strong theoretical component, whereas the latter could not.

In view of this and in view of the fact that the principle of the determinateness of nature as mathematically precise determinateness was not explicitly considered, one can see why it is anachronistic to ask what Plato would have said about a temperature of 65 degrees Fahrenheit or a length of two meters. These specifications and the conceptual frameworks that they assume were not parts of the phenomena and explanatory frameworks that Plato and his contemporaries were considering.

To understand Plato on these matters, we must reverse our intuitions. This will also help us to understand what Plato says about measurement in *Politicus* 283d ff. and to see how what is said there is in harmony with the passage in the *Philebus* that we have under scrutiny.

In the *Politicus*, Plato contrasts measuring quantities in terms of more and less with measuring in relation to standards of fitness (284d–e). He sees the latter as more fundamental and as providing foundations for theoretical understanding for some domains. This type of measurement is said to underlie good weather, good health, and the good life. This coincides with what Plato says about applying "limit" to the unlimited, or indefinite, in the *Philebus*. Here, too, the key notion is hitting on the right proportions of ingredients. The other kind of measurement in the *Politicus* orders elements in terms of the greater than, equal to, and lesser than relation. According to Plato, this is the less reliable, less theoretically interesting kind of measurement. Borrowing from the *Philebus*, we can supplement this. In a sense, the view emerging from both dialogues ascribes a kind of determinateness to nature. That is, in terms of comparisons along a certain dimension or set of dimensions, elements can be ordered as greater, lesser, or equal. But this is not a mathematical determinateness. For there is no absolute unit and thus mathematical determination underlying the orderings. The application of mathematics to quantitative structures comes with the determination of proportional mixtures and hence the good natural elements of reality. Thus the two dialogues supplement each other on these points and present a coherent picture that helps us to understand the nature of the *apeiron* here and why Plato can also include in this category the "unnatural," or "bad" mixtures. In his sense, the latter are not really mixtures, since they do not contain the correct proportions. Thus, from the point of view of the correct proportionality, they are unbalanced, and the fact that such an entity may be six feet long or be an area of such and such dimensions is irrelevant to the Platonic ontology.

In sum, this category includes what are, from a modern philosophical point of view, three kinds of entities. First, it includes Forms for certain natural forces and generic quantitative properties, as well as instances of these. Secondly, it includes ingredients in proper mixtures, a complex expression which is redundant from the Platonic point of view. Thirdly, it includes bad temperature, bad health, and other such entities that, from a modern point of view, seem to be quantitatively determinate mixtures but lack the property of having the Platonically correct ingredients and proportions.

To say that everything partakes of the Indefinite is not to say that all Forms, such as Art, do. Rather, it is to say that everything in our experience, and among the Forms whose interrelations our experience partly reflects, is characterized by something that falls into the kind Indefinite. What artists do they may do quickly or slowly; the picture may be larger or smaller; and so forth, even if the Form of Art itself does not partake of the more or less.

We can thus make sense of this category and avoid confusing it either with modern philosophical notions of quantity or with the much weaker, less restricted sense of indefiniteness invoked earlier in the characterization of divisions.

The second category of reality is called the Limit. The meaning of *peras* in this context also includes the sense of being a balancing factor. As we have seen, the examples given are primarily proportions. But as we look at the applications of this notion to good health or the good life, we see that, in addition to proportionality, factors such as priorities among ingredients are also included under *peras.* The Forms under Limit also have participants, in this respect mirroring the unlimited class. We must avoid associating this notion of Limit, or Balance, with what would first come to mind in modern contexts in thinking of applying mathematics to empirically accessible quantities: namely, measurement in terms of basic units such as millimeters or square inches. For the reasons sketched above, that is not what Plato saw as the interaction between the mathematical and the sensibly given that underlies order in the world. One might press the matter by saying that even if measurement in terms of precise units is not the key to Plato's view of how mathematics underlies order, why not say that every proportional determination of ingredients in complexes is part of that underlying structure? But, as we have seen, Plato combines the use of proportional specifications of ingredients with normative considerations. The right proportions specify what is good or fit. From that point of view, what is governed by the "wrong" proportions can just as well be described as being unbalanced and thus belonging to the category of the unlimited.

The mixed class is described in modern translations as the combination of the limit and the unlimited (25b). Our brief survey shows that a more felicitous rendition might be: the combination of proper constituency-determining factors, such as proportionality or priority, with the constituents of complexes that manifest order. This already has built into it the Platonic notion that there are no intrinsically bad mixtures. We listed above the examples given by Plato. In the cases of music and health, the ordering structure is that of proportionality. Its application presupposes that the appropriate ingredients have been singled out, and in some cases ordered along some dimension, such as high and low. In the case of the good human or the good life, the ordering structure, as we shall see (Appendix 2), is that of priority.

The category of mixture, too, includes both Forms and their participants: for example, Health and instances of health, or Human Good and instances of this in lives and characters. Although Plato does not work this out explicitly, it is clear that hierarchical structures are included in this category. For example, good health is in the mixed kind, and it is, in turn, an ingredient in the good human life, which also belongs to the mixed kind. This passage does not introduce new ontological elements not found in other dialogues; nor does it eliminate the Forms already posited. What it does introduce are new ontological configurations for what Plato took to be the most fundamental aspects of order. Forms are not reduced to either numbers or ratios. One could not look at ratios and read off from these alone what good health, good life, and so on are. Rather, the application of ratios already presupposes that the right ingredients have been distinguished and that we can associate ratios governing the combinations of these ingredients with various Forms.

One might wonder whether the purely qualitative divisions of the *Sophist* and the *Politicus* could be replaced by the kinds of mixing expounded in this ontological section of the *Philebus*, but there is no textual evidence to indicate how Plato viewed this issue.

We can view 23–7 as having links both to the discussion of divisions that precedes it and to the sketch of the good human and the good life in the final sections of the dialogue. The mixing described here can be seen as a further development of the divisions in which, "somehow," the right elements are combined into harmonious wholes. The link to the later passage is established when we see the good life as having various kinds of knowledge and pleasure as ingredients and these being arranged according to principles of priority.

We must not misinterpret the language of mixing and producing in these Platonic contexts. Just as there is no "generation" of numbers in the *Parmenides*, but rather a timeless domain in which we can define various relations, so here there is a timeless domain over which various relations are defined, using the metaphor of "mixing" in the same technical way in which the metaphor of partaking is used to introduce the technical notion of being a participant or an instance.

Seeing the good human as analogous to what is "mixed" in everyday life helps also in thinking of this specification as an ideal that can be approximated, by reflecting it in more or less "pure" form. In this way, constructing a good life is similar to constructing a beautiful building.[25]

We are now in a position to answer the questions with which we started the review of some parts of the *Philebus*.[26] The ontological theory is that of the theory of Forms, as developed in other dialogues discussed in this part of the book, with additional structures defined on a subset of the domain of Forms. The questions raised about the Forms in the early part of the dialogue are about the reality of the Forms and about their interrelations. The former are treated briefly, as at the end of the first half of the *Parmenides*, and the latter are worked out in the passages on divisions and in 23–7. Divisions are given a general characterization that embraces both the divisions in *Sophist* and the *Politicus* and those in the *Philebus*, with the latter having more structure and not merely qualitative differentiae. As we have seen, the initial description can be related both to the genus–differentia and determinable–determinate structures. Partaking is still one of the relations that is fundamental to the ontology. It connects particulars with Forms and also Forms among themselves. But it is not the only key relation among Forms. The good life as Plato sketches it does not have the mathematical order that good health and musical harmony presumably have; but it does have an ordering relation – that of priority – and it is compatible with additions of proportional specifications of the various ingredients.

Appendix 1: *Collecting and Naming the Right Units*

Already in *Gorgias* 454e3, 464b6, and 466a6, there are mentions of the relevant part–whole relation and the positing of kinds, but no self-conscious explicit treatment of the Divisions. Such treatment surfaces first in the *Phaedrus* (265d–e). Thus it is appropriate to make some remarks here about this passage. It is divided into two parts. In the first, a procedure called "collection" is described, which refers to bringing a plurality together under a Form (265d3–4). The neuter used to designate the plurality to be collected suggests that Plato is describing here the gathering of a collection of particulars under a Form. On the other hand, the neuter could also be used to designate what we saw in this chapter as parts under a generic Form. In the lines that follow, this procedure is said to present an object for dialectical examination. Thus we see that the passage leaves open the questions with which we have occupied ourselves in this chapter. If collection is only the collecting of particulars under a Form, then it is indeed preliminary to divisions, and directionality matters.[27] If it is meant to describe the collection of specific Forms under a generic Form, then directionality – as we saw – does not matter. Again, the object of dialectical discussion can be sophistry, statesmanship, or philosophy. But it can also be one of the generic Forms, such as Art or Love. We cannot use this passage to decide between these alternatives.

The second part of the passage states that divisions must be in accordance with natural articulations of kinds (265e1–2). This could mean that we are to divide a collection of particulars according to some of the Forms of which they partake, or it could mean that we divide a generic Form itself into parts. The two procedures together are called "collection and division" (266b4), and their practitioners "dialecticians" (266c1). The second section, then, leaves open the same questions that the first section does. The passage as a whole cannot be used to decide between the interpretations of Divisions that we have considered in this chapter.[28]

Still, even here there is a stress on carving out natural units. This is a matter of what abstract entities we single out by a name. Thus we should look at the passages in which the naming of abstract entities is discussed. For example, *Sophist* 223a4–5 says that a certain kind (*genos*) of art deserves its own name, and in 225a8–10 a certain type of combat is named. In 229d1–3 Plato wonders whether a certain kind of instruction is so specific as not to allow further divisions into units that would be worth naming.

There are passages suggesting that what we name are pluralities. For example, *Sophist* 219a10–15 discusses whether a number of arts should be considered worthy of being called by a single name, "productive art." The criterion, however, seems to be whether these arts share a common function. Thus we single out what today would be called a class, but we do so via the function they share. Similar considerations apply to 224b1–2, where the discussion is about what the term "merchant" should cover. In sum, these passages are consistent with the interpretation in this chapter according to which what we cut is an intensional entity, the generic Art, and not extensionally definable classes. At the same time, the passages by themselves do not offer sufficient evidence to establish this interpretation.

Naming in this context is a matter of finding the right abstract entity, not a matter of formulating propositions. However, in *Politicus* 281a12–b1 Plato considers a situation in which a certain art might be described by some as weaving, and he concludes that this would be a case of naming something falsely. To a modern philosopher it seems odd to think of namings as true or false. The names under consideration, however, name property-like entities and also have predicative uses. Thus we can explain true and false namings as singling out an entity with a name that is *true of* that entity or *false of* it. It is false of it if the parts that fall under the entity to be named cannot be described by a predicative use of that name.

Finally, in many passages, such as *Sophist* 221b2 and 221c4 and *Politicus* 278c3, 265d1–2, 267c8, 277c8–9, and 280b1, Plato asks whether we have named accurately and correctly. In each case, the issue is whether we have separated off a natural part of a generic Form or whether what is named – part or generic – has sufficient unity. If not, then what we took to be a genuine element of reality is not that; it is only a nonnatural part of something.

The namings, as was shown in the chapter itself, can be more or less illuminating. In *Sophist* 233d1–2 a complex naming, or characterization, of the sophist is said to be "most proper." The section in the *Phaedrus* and the passages on naming are compatible with the interpretation proposed, but do not rule out other alternatives.

Appendix 2: *The Harmonious Soul of the* Republic *and the Mixed Good of the* Philebus

A comparison of chapter 2 with the chapters of Part II reveals developments in the theory of Forms. Whereas the inner core of the *Philebus* contains ontological passages, which we have examined, the outer shell is about goodness and the good life. Thus it makes seuse to look back at chapter 3 and to compare the ethics sketched there with some of the ethics of the *Philebus*, to see whether we can find change or development. Even a cursory glance shows that there is some similarity between the *Republic* and the *Philebus* on ethics, since in both the key to goodness is harmony of some sort.[29]

The contexts in which ethics is introduced in the *Republic* and the *Philebus* are different. The context in Book 4 of the *Republic* is moral psychology. It concerns how humans should respond to certain characteristic types of mental conflict. The *Philebus*, by contrast, sketches goodness in the context of adjudicating rival claims concerning the roles of pleasure and knowledge as constituents of the Good. Goodness turns out to have several components, and these are ordered according to certain priorities. As noted in the chapter, the basic objection to hedonism can no longer be that it ignores reality and deals only with appearances. In fact, 60b ascribes – hypothetically – to Eudoxus just the kind of view we mentioned already: that is, taking pleasure and good not as distinct abstract entities but as only one, albeit with two names. The new response acknowledges pleasure as an object of dialectic and distinguishes several kinds of pleasures. Some of these are admitted as components of the good life, though they do not receive high priority. Thus, extreme anti-hedonism, too, is shown to miss the mark. Indeed, this is obvious from the *Republic*, which admits pleasures of the mind. But the *Republic* does not offer an explicit theory that would incorporate that insight. In the *Philebus* we can account for the flaws in extreme anti-hedonism as ignoring some of the components of a good life. Thus it is analogous to the view of those who try to reconstruct human speech without the admission of consonants, on the grounds that the vowels are the elements that make speech beautiful.

Thus we see that hedonism is rejected both in dialogues like the *Gorgias* and the *Republic* and in the *Philebus*, but on different grounds. The practical outcome in terms of the good life to be lived or the character to be developed may be the same, but the *Philebus* provides a richer ontological framework for accounting for this. Furthermore, although the respective contexts for ethics differ, they are compatible. The good person as characterized in the *Philebus* would presumably react in cases of mental conflict in the same way as the good agent of the *Republic*.

The roles of reason in the *Republic* and the *Timaeus* were understanding order and harmony in reality and being able to see how this can be mirrored on a smaller scale in a human life and in human communities; setting aims for us; and informing (in the way sketched in chapter 3) our desires and attitudes. These roles are ascribed to reason in the *Philebus* as well. The importance of understanding order in the universe and in humans is stressed again (64a1–2). But in the *Philebus* this task is mentioned in the context of a more precise analysis of the ontology of order. We are shown how mathematical elements can contribute to the harmonious units which we study in a variety of disciplines. In the *Republic* and the *Timaeus* we do not find such articulations. We find only references to the realm of Forms in general terms, presumably as a set of interrelated elements, and the need to turn to the Forms, without any explanation of how to distinguish and relate these.

The moral epistemology remains the same. According to the *Philebus*, too, we need insight into the Good; that is, into the order and harmony in reality as such and in the possibilities of having this reflected in human character and life, both on the individual and the communal level. The difference is that the object of understanding is described in more detail in the later dialogues than in the *Republic*. We need to grasp the right mixture of the appropriate elements. This is spelled out only in terms of priority among the relevant items. We do not know if Plato thought it possible to spell it out in more mathematical terms. In Book 4 of the *Republic* we have a sketch of the good agent. In the *Philebus* we have sketches of the Good (64a1–2) and of the good life (60c7, 61e8). Thus, in terms of the patterns of good lives and aims, the ethics remains the same, but the task of reason is spelled out better. Similarly, the right attitudes towards pleasure do not change between the two descriptions, but the ontological analysis of pleasure, as well as its roles in psychology (which we could not cover in this chapter) is described in much more detail, with the addition of complexities that are consistent with the earlier sketch but go way beyond it.

The ethics of the *Republic* requires links between Forms. The Forms standing for the key excellences and their relation to the Good involve ontological relationships. These are, not spelled out in that dialogue, however. One could apply the techniques of divisions, as well as the principles of mixing of the *Philebus*, to make these relations explicit. The good, harmonious soul of Book 4 of the *Republic* could be accommodated by the *Philebus* where it would be located in the mixed class. So would the right combination of pleasures. As was pointed out in the chapter, the structure of the *Philebus* allows for hierarchies of mixing. We need to combine pleasures in the right way and different kinds of knowledge in the right way and to combine both these in the right way to reach a characterization of the good life.

The mixing of ingredients, as explicated in the *Philebus*, has only a superficial resemblance to the doctrine of the mean in Aristotelian ethics. For Aristotle, hitting the mean between excess and deficiency is a matter of empirical sensitivity; for Plato, understanding the principles of proper mixing is a matter of theoretical insight. The Aristotelian mean is patterned after the balance of natural forces in living organisms, whereas the Platonic proportionalities have the static harmony of music as their paradigm, even in the case of health and weather.

Finally, just as the trichotomy of the soul in Book 4 of the *Republic* does not exclude other genuine or natural articulations of the good human agent in other contexts, so the specifications of the roles of pleasure and knowledge in the good life, as given in the *Philebus*, do not rule out the possibility that other equally revealing accounts of the right mixture could be given with different additional ingredients entering into the considerations. In the *Philebus* the issue is the role of knowledge and pleasure. Perhaps in other contexts, Plato would talk about how what is called *thumos* in the *Republic* enters the mixture, or our *eros*, or overall orientation.

Still, the basic analysis of the good life as a mixture – be it in terms of priority or proportions – of the right ingredients would hold even for discussions that center on entities different from knowledge and pleasure. The ontology of cosmic order also underlies the order in human lives and communal activities.

Concluding Remarks about Reality and Appearance

The review of the theory of Forms in Part I of this book left us with certain questions and tensions. The main tension is between the commitment both in the epistemology ("All elements of reality are related") and in the ontology (for example, the unity of virtues) to a network of relations among the Forms and the repeated emphasis on the need to look at any given Form "in itself." To be sure, the latter exhortation surfaces typically in contexts in which the one Form is contrasted with the many particulars that partake of it. Still, the scheme is crying out for an articulation of relationships among the Forms. We saw also that, apart from the insistence on "the F itself," the very contrast between the Forms and sensible particulars as intelligible reality versus partly intelligible appearances requires that principles of identity and individuation be clearer for Forms than for particulars. But individuation in terms of unique self-attribution brought its own problems. Furthermore, the appearance–reality distinction was not drawn very sharply. It is clear that the Forms constitute reality and that sensible particulars constitute at least parts of the realm of appearances, with the nature of the former being reflected imperfectly or incompletely in the latter. But this leaves out the status of other abstract elements, as well as that of elements of common sense, such as the opinions encoded in popular morality or the law that seem to be parts of the realm of appearances but do not fit the paradigmatic cases of the sensibles.

In Part II we saw Plato defending his views primarily against Eleatic attacks. In the course of doing this, he addresses the issues just enumerated. There are three ways in which links between Forms are introduced. First, Forms are interrelated via of the all-pervasive links provided by the connector theory. This also affects the issue of individuation. There is no trace of strong, unique self-attribution in the dialogues we surveyed in this part of the book, but individuation is supposedly provided by three factors: (1) partaking of the Same and the Different; (2) each Form standing for a "nature" – for example, what it is to be one; (3) each Form occupying a place within some network that articulates the ontologies of various divisions and mixings. Secondly, Forms are interrelated within divisional structures. As we have seen, these structures can be given strictly intensional interpretations, thereby preserving coherence between conceptions of the Forms in the connector theory and those in the Divisions. Thirdly, some Forms are related by the structure and constituencies of good mixtures. These mixed units are the backbone of order and harmony that Plato detects in reality.

The reality–appearance distinction must be drawn in a more complicated way within the revised scheme. First, the notion of partaking cannot do the job, since this relation applies not only to Forms and particulars but also to relations among Forms. Secondly, it is clear that many abstract elements – that is, the parts that are not wholes but are nonnatural units in divisions – are also parts of the realm of appearances. Thus a lot of burden lies on the notion of what is or is not a genuine unity, or a "natural cut" within divisions. One cannot use mere mathematical and quantitative specification to eliminate the bad mixes, since these too admit of some proportional specifications, although not "the right ones." The deceptive nature of at least some of the appearances is retained in the revised theory. Certain abstract parts of concepts seem to have genuine unity, but dialectical investigation shows us that in fact they do not.

Although the range of the Forms is expanded, the reasons for regarding an entity as a Form are not. Pleasure is now an object of dialectic, but, all along, being such was one of the Form-making characteristics. Thus it is still true that the Forms are not simply what corresponds to any predicate expression. The theory of Forms is not a general theory of predication, either in its earlier or in its later form. Not all predicates stand for Forms. Furthermore, the Forms are key parts of Platonic explanatory schemes. They stand for natures of abstract elements, and these natures can be reflected more or less adequately or more or less completely by participants, both abstract and spatiotemporal.

The explanatory scheme becomes more complex. The existence of Forms is a necessary, but not a sufficient, condition for order and harmony in reality. The unique mode of being of the Forms and of the partaking relationship needed to be spelled out. Furthermore, on the level of the self-explanatory and thus at the end of explanatory chains, we find the whole interrelated realm of the Forms, not just the Forms one by one. As we have seen, something like this was implied all along, but it was not made precise or explicit. Yet, the interrelations are shown not to require yet another level of reality. In this way, the Eleatics can be answered.

Plato's defense is primarily against the Eleatics, because he is so sure about the existence of a realm of reality that is independent of space and time and he thinks that the real challenge for his ontology is not to lapse into Eleatic monism. As we shall see, this aspect of Plato has not been properly understood in the twentieth century. It is worth stressing it here, so that we do not fall victim to the mistake of supposing that the revisions in the theory of Forms anticipate Aristotelian objections and concepts. None of the questions and objections raised concerning the Theory of Forms would be answered by requiring that, for example, Forms be "in things" – that is, necessarily have instances. In fact, our interpretation has shown why Plato's fundamental orientation requires that the Forms constitute a separate domain. It is not just an arbitrary choice on Plato's part to insist on instantiability but not necessary instantiation. The key truths of mathematics, music theory, geometry, and ethics are not about spatio-temporal particulars; if we interpret them that way, they are false or meaningless. Requiring the Forms to have instances would not help in making these truths more intelligible.

Finally, in addition to the existence of the Forms, their unique nature, and their interrelatedness, there is another layer in the explanatory structure that for Plato makes all these conditions both necessary and sufficient for explanation. This is the discovery of the mixed elements: that is, configurations of some of the Forms (reflected also by particulars) that underlie order, proportional descriptions, harmony, and hence goodness or appropriateness. Plato thinks that this key structure cannot be explained adequately except within a theory of Forms. But it is a distinct explanatory layer. It is no longer enough simply to appeal to the realm of Forms; the special configurations constituting the right mixtures are the final steps in the relevant explanatory chains. Thus the reality–appearance distinction becomes more complicated. There are important differences between various parts of reality from the point of view of fundamentality, and the appearances include not only the observable and the visible, but also some of what is abstract and related to theorizing. The notion of technē is enlarged to include, for example, sophistry but the genuine technai are still kept separate, since only these are concerned with the good mixtures. These modifications, sketched only sparingly in the *Philebus*, should recall to the mind of the reader not so much the modern universals of Moore and Russell, as the logos of Heraclitus that governs what Plato would have called the "appearances." It is small wonder that Plato seems to have reacted mostly to Eleatic and Heraclitean philosophy. The Eleatics, though they located reality in the right category, did not allow for a plurality of entities and hence rational order and intelligibility. Heraclitean thought saw correctly that there is an overall governing logos to be discovered, but Heraclitus failed to give this what Plato thought he could provide: namely, an adequate ontology.

NOTES

1 For more detail, see J. Moravcsik, "The Anatomy of Plato's Divisions."
2 For discussion of this view, see F. Cornford, *Plato's Theory of Knowledge*, pp. 181–2.
3 For further arguments that the Divisions are not like Aristotelian classifications, see K. Sayre, *Plato's Analytic Method*, pp. 186–90.
4 That this is done at times is seen by S. Minardi, "On Some Aspects of Platonic Divisions." Unfortunately, he sees this as incompatible with taking the Forms to indicate more than "family resemblances" among activities.
5 The fact that one can construct more than one division ending with the same specific kind does not show that the method is of mere heuristic value. See H. Cherniss, *Aristotle's Criticism of Plato and the Academy*, p. 46.
6 F. Cornford, *Plato's Theory of Knowledge*, p. 173.
7 For an attempt, see M. Cohen, "Plato's Method of Division"; for criticism, see Moravcsik, "Anatomy of Plato's Divisions."
8 For arguments against taking the Divisions to be deductive structures, see Cherniss, *Aristotle's Criticism*, pp. 28–30.
9 See J. Gosling, *Plato's* Philebus, p. x.
10 See the introductory remarks in R. Hackforth, *Plato's Examination of Pleasure*.
11 For an interesting discussion of this question, but with different conclusions, see R. Shiner, *Knowledge and Reality in Plato's Philebus*.
12 My proposed reading of 15b1–c3 construes the first question to be about Forms and the second about how these can retain their identity even though they undergo no regeneration process. For other discussion, see A. Mourelatos, "Heraclitus, Parmenides, and the Naive Metaphysics of Things."
13 *Logos* in this passage need not be translated "sentence"; such a reading causes difficulties. In *Parmenides* it can mean "discourse."

14 For a different list, see Gosling, *Plato's* Philebus, p. 155.

15 For a good explanation, see W. Johnson, *Logic*, part 1, p. 174.

16 For a discussion of different readings, see G. Striker, *Peras und Apeiron*, pp. 20–2.

17 *Hoposa* refers to the many intermediates and not to their number. See also *Sophist* 242c6.

18 Gosling, *Plato's* Philebus, p. 162.

19 On ancient music theory, see *Oxford Classical Dictionary*, pp. 706–12.

20 Gosling, *Plato's* Philebus, pp. 179–80 and p. 86, presents a different interpretation, which includes conjectures about philosophic schools concerning which we have very little evidence. Moreover, he fails to see the thoroughly intensional nature of the Forms.

21 For this reading, see Striker, *Peras und Apeiron*, p. 50.

22 On measures for length, area, and capacity, see *Oxford Classical Dictionary*, pp. 659–60.

23 R. Forbes, *Studies in Ancient Technology*, vol. 6, sections on heat and cold in Greek and Roman technology.

24 D. Hahm, "Weight and Lightness in Aristotle and his Predecessors."

25 The example of architecture, in which the Greeks achieved so much without exact units of measurement, was suggested to me by Harold Delius.

26 For more details, see Moravcsik, "Forms, Nature, and the Good in the *Philebus*."

27 Cornford, *Plato's Theory of Knowledge*, pp. 184–5; J. Skemp, *Plato's Statesman*, p. 69.

28 See Hackforth, *Plato's Examination of Pleasure*, pp. 142–3.

29 For more on ethics in the *Philebus*, see J. Cooper, "Plato's Theory of Human Good in the *Philebus*."

Part III

Platonism, Ancient and Modern

◆

It seems not unreasonable to require . . . that if Plato is to supply a philosophy for us, it must be a philosophy which can be expressed in our own language; that his system, if we hold it to be well founded, shall compel us to deny the opposite systems, modern as well as ancient; and that, so far as we hold Plato's doctrines to be satisfactorily established, we should be able to produce arguments for them, and to refute the arguments against them. These seem reasonable requirements of the adherents of any philosophy, and therefore, of Plato's.

William Whewell, *Of the Platonic Theory of Ideas* (1856)

7

Platonism in the Philosophy of Mathematics and General Ontology

◆

Mathematical logic . . . is a science prior to all others, which contains the ideas and principles underlying all sciences.[1] This statement by Kurt Gödel in 1944 echoes the statement, reviewed in chapter 1, found in Aeschylus about the art of numbers being the chief art. Gödel talks about mathematical logic, whereas Aeschylus speaks about numbers. But this difference is not fundamental; it merely reflects the difference in time and intellectual context. Aeschylus could not have known about mathematical logic providing the foundations for the art of numbers. Both authors think that what is most fundamental to mathematics is also most fundamental to all the other domains of reality. Aeschylus's comment reflects an attitude that was articulated by Plato into a full ontology and epistemology. This, in turn, influenced modern philosophy of mathematics. Thus we can see Gödel's comment as an echo of Plato's view.

Such a historical claim can be challenged on several grounds. Is it not the case that the differences in intellectual context between Plato's time and Gödel's are so great as to render the similarity between the statements only a surface phenomenon? After all, they had different conceptions of what a science was. The examples available to Plato were mathematics and geometry. Gödel, by contrast, had the whole range of empirical sciences, such as physics and biology, available for inspection. Thus it could be argued that the two authors make their respective statements on the basis of very different evidence.

Secondly, what were the alternatives confronting the two authors? There are at least two possibilities open to someone wanting to disagree with Gödel. He or she could say that the most fundamental concepts in the sciences are ineliminably qualitative concepts. It could also be claimed that the various sciences are quite different, with different explanatory schemes, and that they do not have anything substantial in common. Plato's alternatives are different. He is fighting against the view that all sciences are merely practical know-how and the view they deal only with sensibly accessible phenomena.

Furthermore, fundamentality could be spelled out in 1944 in terms of logical reduction techniques that were not available in Plato's time. For Plato, fundamentality in this context probably meant being needed in all other rational disciplines or being the paradigm for all other disciplines.

Gödel's Platonism was a conscious choice over other available ontologies, principally nominalism and conceptualism. Plato did not have in front of him carefully worked out alternatives of this type. For example, modern conceptualism, the view that mathematical entities are mental constructions, is a response to paradoxes in logic. As we saw in chapter 4, in the *Parmenides* Plato considers the possibility that Forms are just thoughts, but the grounds for such a view at his time seem to have been no more than a hunch that perhaps psychological entities have a more ontologically secure status than mind-independent abstract entities. Again, modern nominalism is based on sophisticated reduction techniques showing that an ontology of particulars without universals can accommodate mathematics. The closest to this in Plato's time would have been the guess that mathematics could be viewed as being about sensible particulars in time and space.[2]

These are formidable objections. Nevertheless, I believe that we can see a nontechnical notion of priority and ontological importance in the ancient and modern conceptions of mathematics just sketched that justifies looking at some of the modern work as echoes of original Platonism. Qualitative notions are important in science and philosophy, in that these often have to serve as bridges between technically different developments. A word like "fundamental" has a complex meaning with several semantic layers.[3] One of these is the nontechnical, intuitive notion of being independent of all else and — somehow — having all else dependent on it. We can detect this notion in Plato, as well as in the modern writers we shall consider. This notion can be connected with a variety of diverse technical conceptions.

We can find similar, perennial intuitive elements in science, philosophy, and ethical conceptions. These include the notion of one entity bringing about the existence of another (in modern times, causality), the notion of rational accounts requiring generality, and the contrast between appearance and reality. Some of these concepts play roles in Plato's claims; others do not. We shall consider parts of Plato's thought that involve some of these notions. One could consider Plato's views as theories or theory fragments and, following Whewell's admonition, compare them to contemporary theories. Alternatively, one could trace what has been called throughout the centuries "Platonism" and attempt to show a thread of continuity. This was done in Shorey's magnificent book, the title of which has been borrowed for the title of this part of my book.[4] Finally, one can single out themes in Plato's thought and try to find echoes of these in contemporary philosophy. This approach seems to be a prerequisite for the first one mentioned. Hence this is the one adopted in this part of the book, leaving open the possibility that, on the basis of these considerations, the stronger tie demanded by Whewell could also be forged eventually, at least in the form of a reconstruction.

In selecting themes that one might expect to find echoed a couple of millennia later, one needs to sail between the Scylla of formulating something so general as to be almost vacuous (for example, philosophy deals with experience; Plato tries to make sense of what we encounter in reality; and the like), and the Charybdis of topics that are too closely tied to recent developments, such as the notion of ontological commitment or essentialism in the form of quantified modal logic.[5] One must take the golden mean and steer between the too broad or vague and the anachronistic. There is no hard-and-fast rule for doing this. One must use one's historical and systematic judgment; and concerning such matters there is room for disagreement among informed practitioners.

Still, there are some guidelines; or at least, some such have governed the choices made in this book concerning the utility or lack of utility of viewing a Platonistic theme or technical phrase in modern terms. What I have regarded as anachronistic usually has one of two sources. One of these is to force on Plato's thought concerns that are central to some modern school of thought, but were not central to his. An obvious example is the treatment of falsehood in the *Sophist*. Plato's interests are primarily metaphysical. He wants to show that the notion of falsehood can be defended against Eleatic criticism and can be shown to be paradox-free. He needs this in order to keep the notion of truth as a significant quasi-normative concept, used in his metaphysical theorizing. This is totally different from current modern efforts to present formal theories of truth and falsehood as parts of general theories of logic. It is also a mistake to view this aspect of Plato as "leading in the direction of" current modern efforts.

The roots of current formal semantics do not lie in deep metaphysical struggles with Eleatic monism, although those of the work on the foundations of mathematics, at least in the first half of this century do.

The second source is the effort to reconstruct what in Plato are informal qualitative concepts in terms of modern formal concepts. Often, though not always, such efforts distort. For example, the material on the various relations among different kinds of Forms cannot be reduced to modern set-theoretical logic. Partaking, for example, is not the same as being a member of a class. Furthermore, there is no uniform ontological relation that would be equivalent to modern notions of predication.

When is it useful, then, to view Platonic speculations in modern terms or as leading to modern notions? One such class of cases includes those in which one can trace a genuine development in terms of refinement, with certain concerns underlying the whole historical time slice under consideration. An obvious example is the logical concept of negation which can be traced from opposition to purely conceptual opposition to term negation and so on to formal developments in symbolic logic. In this case there are no dramatically diverging interests, and one can see the sequence of change that led eventually to the emergence of logic as a distict sub-part of philosophy. The same point can be made with regard to explanatory schemes. Amid the variety of such schemes that we find in the pre-Socratics and in Plato's dialogues, we might look for the ancestor of modern concepts of causation. It is also reasonably clear that early notions of necessity and necessitation eventually led to the development of modal logic, without drastic shift in concerns and orientation.

At times it is helpful to recast Platonic arguments with the help of modern notions such as extensionality and intensionality, because in this way we can articulate the logically sound sequence of steps that led Plato to conclusions that were important to him and affected his concerns. At times, this kind of reconstruction may reveal flaws that are of interest not only from a purely technical but from a philosophical point of view.

In general, the main danger in Platonic studies today comes from the temptation to assume that Plato's concerns in all subfields of philosophy were the same as those of certain leading modern schools of thought. In the first part of this book, the chapter on epistemology and that on ethics were both written with the firm conviction that Plato's main concerns and starting points in these two fields were different from those of leading modern traditions. But this does not mean that awareness of these differences might not serve as a corrective to today's systematic philosophy and could not lead us to address ourselves to these concerns of earlier times, which in some cases apply to facets of modern experience as well.

In the last two chapters of this book, we shall consider echoes of Plato's views on mathematics, the relation between the theory of Forms and subsequent theories of universals, and the relation between Plato's Ideal Ethics and what ideal ethics might look like today. Other suitable topics for such treatment would be Plato's epistemology and modern epistemological views on insight and understanding[6] and Plato's political theory and recent attempts at theories of communal life that take into account the need for shared values among the participants. It is my hope that, if successful, this part of the book will stimulate further work on the topics treated, as well as on the topics only listed and other suitable ones.

What is Mathematics About?

As we saw in chapter 1, Plato's interest in mathematics focuses on the nature of the objects with which this discipline deals. This is in line with Plato's general approach to the genuine disciplines, defining these in terms of their objects. The investigation of these entities is carried out by examining how we interact with them, what the results of these interactions are, and what evidence we have concerning the existence and nature of these entities. Plato believed that we discover mathematical entities and proofs; we do not just construct or invent them. On the other hand, such discoveries are not like suddenly glimpsing a mountain peak or a remote island that no one has ever stumbled upon before. Our discoveries are like empirical discoveries in the sense that we become aware of objects that we did not know existed before; on the other hand, such discovery is possible only after much training. It is not like ordinary direct acquaintance. It is more like the insight into the nature of a substance that is not directly accessible to sense experience, but about which we gain a lot of information, with respect to both its relation to the empirical and its relation to other real things that are beyond the surface of observation.

Plato's conception of mathematics includes several themes. These are logically distinct. Thus it is worthwhile looking at them one by one. At the end, we will see why and how Plato put them together into a harmonious account.

1   Mathematical entities are pre-existent; that is, they exist independently
    of the human mind or the mind of any other intelligent being.
    According to this conception, mathematics would be true and would be
    related to the functioning of entities in space and time even if there
    were no existing knowing subjects.

2   Mathematical theorems are discoveries of a certain kind, not inventions
    or constructions. As was pointed out above, this does not mean that we
    just stumble upon them, as we stumble upon empirically accessible
    entities. This is not entailed by thesis 1, which is compatible with a
    variety of ways in which we could come into contact with entities.
    Plato thought, as we saw earlier, that mathematical theorems are
    already there, waiting to be discovered. An alternative could have been
    to say that mathematical entities are pre-existent, but that our math-
    ematics represents these entities not in their own right but as they
    relate to human interests.

3   Mathematical entities have a certain generality, which is expressed by
    Plato as their having possible participants and by more modern authors
    as their having possible instances. As we shall see, not all so-called
    Platonistic philosophers of mathematics agree with this, but the dissent
    centers on certain technicalities.

4   Mathematical entities need to be abstract, because the theorems of
    mathematics (and geometry) cannot be applied directly to spatiotemporal
    reality. Geometrical theorems are about lines without width and points
    without extension; mathematical theorems are about entities like 2 or
    15, and one cannot find such entities in space and time.

5   Mathematical activities like calculating and proving are best studied
    under idealization. This is not true of many empirical phenomena –
    for example, the distribution of fauna or the digestive system. The
    argument for studying mathematical activities in this way rests on the
    actual activities being infected by errors and by human limitations such
    as those on memory, which are irrelevant to the characterization of the
    important features of the activity.

Not all five of these themes need be endorsed by all Platonists, and Plato
does not discuss all of them together. To be sure, the thesis about discovery
entails the thesis about pre-existence, but not the other way round. The
thesis about the generality of the entities is independent of both thesis
1 and thesis 2. The thesis about abstractness and that about idealization are

also independent ingredients of Platonism. Plato himself would add two more themes:

6 Mathematics is about the genuine, or more fundamental, elements of reality. It explains only indirectly the salient intelligible aspects of entities in space and time.
7 Mathematical entities, together with other Forms, are at the highest level of the ontological explanatory hierarchies that constitute reality.

For Plato these two themes underlie the other five and link his views on mathematics to his general ontology. Once we invoke the reality–appearance distinction and see how it applies to mathematics, the various theses merge into a unified account. If mathematics is about reality and the actual activities that enable us to interact with these entities are a part of the world of appearances, then it seems reasonable that we should study mathematical activities under idealization; for we thereby abstract from those factors that tie the human realization of these activities to aspects of our nature and life that are not germane to showing how the activities can lead to the discovery of the true nature of mathematical entities. Also, once we locate mathematical entities as parts of reality, the pre-existence condition can be derived from this, as well as the discovery theme. Theme 4 also fits into this account, since it shows how mathematics is about reality, and theme 3 shows how it can also be related to the world of appearances. As we saw in our review of the *Philebus*, Plato thinks that mathematics has a special role in relating and ordering qualitative notions or properties. We shall now turn to showing that these themes are shared by Plato and some of the most important recent philosophers of mathematics, such as Frege, Russell, Gödel, and Bernays. The concern of these thinkers with these themes is expressed in their work on what have been called "foundational" questions. This raises the question of whether we can say in any nonanachronistic sense that Plato, too, was interested in foundational questions.

Foundational work on mathematics consists of two distinct ventures. One is to see if mathematics can be reduced to another discipline; in particular, to symbolic logic. This entails that all the statements of mathematics be translatable into the language of the other discipline. In modern times, this project has taken the form of attempts to translate all mathematics into logic and set theory. One can have two motives for such an enterprise. One is a desire for simplicity and conceptual economy. The other is the belief that the elements constituting the domain for the other discipline are in some ways clearer and more intelligible than those of mathematics. It is fairly obvious that Plato was not engaged in such a project; nobody in his time was.

The other type of foundational work entails a search for the appropriate ontology for mathematics. For even if people agree that, for example, mathematics can or cannot be reduced to logic, they might disagree as to what the proper ontology for logic and set theory is. In some sense it is clear what mathematics is about: it is about numbers. But this leads to the next question: what are numbers? In the context of this type of work, that question is not about how numbers function in theories, proofs, and so forth, but about which established ontological category they belong to. In this sense, Plato is working on foundational questions. He has a proposal about the realm to which numbers belong, even if his ontological categories do not coincide exactly with those of twentieth-century philosophers.

We can see this concern expressed in several passages already discussed in the first two parts of this book. It also becomes clear in *Republic* 510c–511b. Here, Plato makes the following statements:

1   The mathematicians posit the odd, the even, the figures, and so on (510c3).
2   They do not give an account of these.
3   They treat them as evident.
4   They treat them as starting points (510c6–d1).
5   They use diagrams and other constructions to talk about, for example, the square itself (510d6–8).
6   They lack understanding of their starting points (511b5–7).

We need to interpret these remarks and the criticism they contain in light of Plato's theory of technē as discussed in chapter 1. Statement 1 presumably refers to the mathematical practice of assuming notions like odd, even, certain shapes, and so on as given and then proceeding to use them in proofs and constructions. Statement 2 shows that Plato finds this practice unsatisfactory, because it leaves something out. What is left out is – as the subsequent statements show – an account of the starting points. This could be interpreted as a failure to recognize the systematic nature of mathematics and geometry and to see what the fundamental axioms are. But such an interpretation is unlikely, because a search of this nature was already going on in Plato's time. One might also think that Plato demands definitions for everything. But this, too, is unlikely, since he would have seen that this leads to an infinite regress and would not square with his own practice.

In view of Plato's conception of technē, it is plausible to interpret the demand as asking for an ontological account of the elements of the domain that compose mathematics and geometry. Such an account is provided by the theory of Forms. Plato is not saying that one cannot do mathematics without raising such ontological questions. He is insisting, though, that we do not fully understand what we are doing until the mathematical work is supplemented with ontological work. Plato claims to be able to show that the objects of mathematics necessarily exist, and he is certain that he knows what their nature is.

In recent times, Frege, Russell, Gödel, and Bernays – among others – seem to have adopted conceptions of mathematics that incorporate themes 1–5. We shall shortly see evidence for that. Thus, even if they do not accept items 6 and 7, their views can be seen as echoing original genuine Platonism vis-à-vis mathematics. At least three of these thinkers also accepted a conception of numbers that makes these attributes of a special sort. Thus, for example, the number three would be the property shared by all collections that have three members. We shall see how similar this conception is to the one Plato entertained. We shall adduce evidence from both ancient and modern sources for regarding themes 1–5 as common themes in Platonism.

We have seen much evidence in dialogues like the *Meno* and the *Republic* for construing Plato as holding the pre-existence thesis. Both the recollection theory of understanding and the approach to technē in terms of objects entail this. For understanding and genuine science to be possible, there must exist a domain of objects that have unique properties and are independent of the human mind. This, however, is not enough. On a realist conception, trees, mountains, and sounds also exist independently of the mind. Philosophers like G. E. Moore would have said that the sounds of the forest exist even if there is no one to hear them. Likewise, mathematics exists even if no one knows it. Furthermore, a real Platonist believes that mathematics exists regardless of whether it is instantiated in a world of space and time. As we have seen, this is certainly Plato's view. Let us now look at some of the relevant modern evidence.

Paul Bernays wrote: "Euclid speaks of figures to be constructed, whereas for Hilbert, systems of points, straight lines, and planes exist from the outset. Euclid postulates: one can join two points by a straight line; Hilbert states the axiom: given any two points, there exists a straight line on which both are situated."[7]

Again, "the tendency of which we are speaking consists in viewing the objects as not in any way dependent on the thinking subject."[8]

The first statement is about geometry, but one can apply it easily to mathematics. The objects in this discipline, within Bernays' conception, "exist from the outset." They exist apart from human understanding. It is our task to discover their existence and come to understand their nature and interrelations.

The second statement, too, considers the independence of the mathematical and geometrical entities from the knowing subject. It does not say anything about the empirical world. This coincides with the classification of views already suggested. The pre-existence theme can be accepted by both Platonists and nominalists with regard to the relation to the mind, but Platonists add a strong second clause asserting the separateness also from the empirical world.

Reflection on the pre-existence condition and the nature of mathematical activities leads the Platonist to the second theme: namely, that mathematical results and proofs are discoveries. For Plato, this is part of the general thesis that finding out about the nature of Forms is a matter of discoveries that start with much detailed theoretical work, gathered under the name of dialectic, and end with wondrous insights. The language of *Symposium* 212 and the similes of light in the *Republic* bear witness to the excitement and awe with which Plato regards results in these fundamental disciplines. How amazing that the human mind, under certain conditions, can grasp such notions and such truths! The path to these discoveries, as the passages referred to show, is arduous. It is not like enjoying the sights of the landscape of the American continent on a flight from San Francisco to Boston; it is more like snowshoeing for hours in Colorado at 9,000 feet and then coming to a spot from which one can see three peaks over 14,000 feet in height. We see evidence for this conception in Plato in the conversation with the young boy in the *Meno* (reviewed in chapter 1), where it takes real struggle and the abandonment of a false start to begin to understand what a certain geometrical theorem is really about.

For Plato, the excitement of discovery moves on two levels. First, there is the excitement generated by coming to understand a truth of mathematics. Then there is the even greater excitement of coming to understand the ontological status of the entities whose interrelations one is trying to learn. Separating these two levels of discovery and excitement helps us to understand why Plato thinks that, in one sense, everyone knows the Forms, whereas in another, they do not. We deal with numbers, quantitative relations, values, and value comparisons in our everyday lives. Indeed, without such activities, human life would be inconceivable. But we can do this without having an adequate conception of what the objects we interact with really are. We can even have true views (gathered under the label of "true opinions" in the *Republic* and the *Meno*) about some of the relations between these objects without understanding their true nature. In this respect, the study of mathematics and geometry, from the Platonist point of view, is not unlike the situation in astronomy. We can know a lot about the movements of the celestial bodies without having an adequate conception of what these entities are. In fact, this was true of much of ancient astronomy.

These, then, are the considerations that lead both Plato and the modern Platonist to think of mathematics and its ontological foundations as in accordance with the pre-existence theme and the theme of the results being discoveries by the much trained, informed mind.

There are, however, considerations that seem to tell against this conception. These center on certain paradoxes discovered in modern times which suggest that we need to limit and regulate the kinds of abstract entities that are admissible in an adequate ontology of logic and mathematics.[9]

One such paradox involves the application of predicates to themselves. For example, we can formulate the predicate "heterological" and define it as designating the property of a predicate not applying to itself. We can then raise the question of whether "heterological" is heterological. Both the affirmative and the negative answers to this question lead to contradiction. This has led some logicians to posit hierarchies of properties and predicates, or even hierarchies of languages. According to such conceptions, each property has its appropriate domain of instantiation. Elements of that domain are on the same level, and that level is lower than that on which the predicate or property stands. This regimentation could be viewed as a restriction on Platonism if we think of Platonism as including the principle that there is a property associated with any plurality of entities or that there is a set made up of any such plurality.

On the basis of these considerations, Bernays regards "restricted Platonism" as the most viable statement of the Platonistic position.[10] But the restrictions need not be interpreted as human, mind-dependent constructions that interfere with a pre-existent domain. One could view the restrictions as human interventions regimenting sets, or properties. However, one can also view the needed modifications as showing that, initially, we misunderstood the nature of mathematical and logical entities. We thought that what were out there were sets of any plurality. Now we know that we were wrong. We need to reconsider. This seems to be the spirit of Gödel's remark that the logical paradoxes show our logical intuitions to be self-contradictory.[11] Thus Platonism need not be restricted in any sense in which it becomes mind-dependent, but we cannot trust all our logical intuitions when attempting to understand the whole pre-existing realm of logical and mathematical entities.

So far we have dealt with themes 1 and 2. We shall now turn to themes 3 and 4. One way of combining the demands of abstractness and generality in the objects is to interpret geometrical and mathematical truths to be about properties that are not directly represented by the senses. The truth that the angles of a triangle add up to 180 degrees is about relationships between abstract properties. Its unqualified instantiation would have to be a figure bounded by lines without width. There are no such lines in sensible experience. Thus the application of this truth to particulars in space and time always involves some qualification. The same holds for mathematical truths. Thus the proposition that two is an even number is interpreted as linking the property whose instances are all doubles with the property of being divisible by two. There is nothing in space and time that is simply two.[12] At the same time, we can use this truth in making sense of statements about collections of things known via the senses. We can pick out instances of two, suitably qualified, such as two cows, two birthdays, two sunsets, and so forth and apply the principles of arithmetic, suitably modified, to these pluralities.

This brief sketch provides the intuitive ground for the construal of numbers as properties of a certain sort, referred to above. It is shared by the authors cited, except for some writing of Frege in which – for various technical reasons into which we cannot enter here – he wants to draw a very sharp line between concepts and objects, and numbers fall into the latter category.[13] In general, then, we can regard the thesis that numbers are properties of equinumerous sets as a characteristic view of modern Platonism.[14]

But what are these "equinumerous sets"? Frege points out that they cannot be delineated apart from construing some plurality of sensible particulars as instantiations of a property (or universal). Nothing is just 24;

it must be 24 molecules or pieces of silver or whatever. We saw in chapter 2 how this point is crucial for Plato's understanding of mathematics and its ontology. It is thus very interesting to see similar thoughts expressed by a modern Platonist, Frege.

> It marks, therefore, an important difference between color and number that a color such as blue belongs to a surface independently of any choice of ours. The blue color is the power of reflecting light of certain wave lengths and of absorbing to varying extents light of other wave lengths; to this, our conception of it cannot make the slightest difference. The number 1, on the other hand, or 100, or any other number, cannot be said to belong to the pile of playing cards in itself, but, at most, belong to it in virtue of the way we have chosen to conceive of it; and even then not in such a way that we can simply assign the number to it as a predicate.[15]

We would need to add several other passages from Frege in order to show that in the context of his writings these lines can be read as not having the conceptualist flavor that at a first, cursory glance one might attribute to them. The various properties of playing cards are, both for Frege and for Plato, "out there" in a reality that is independent of the human mind. It is not so much a matter of how we choose to conceive of the playing cards, but more a matter of which of their features we attend to, that determines how we apply mathematical descriptions to them. The mathematical descriptions apply in an objective sense, but always as instances of this or that attribute.

Here, then, we see elements common to how Plato conceived of numbers and how recent Platonistic philosophers of mathematics conceive of them. The similarity is on an intuitive rather than a technical level. We cannot ascribe to Plato a full understanding of the property of being equinumerous or the distinction between sets and properties.[16] Furthermore, as we have seen, it is an oversimplification to identify Forms with properties. At the same time, there is enough similarity between properties and their instantiations on the one hand and Forms and partaking on the other to regard modern views on this topic as echoes of Plato's thought.

Someone might say that the "aboutness" condition invoked may be a part of the Platonic technai concept but, by itself, is not enough to justify moving to the construction of numbers briefly sketched. For this condition only justifies having propositions, or facts corresponding to these, as parts of the independent realm that mathematics represents and illuminates. We need an extra premise to move from the propositional level to the level of sub-propositional elements. In Plato, this means moving from the level of *logos* and whatever makes that true to the elements that Plato thinks *logos* is about. We find a tacit acceptance of such an extra premise in both Plato and modern Platonists. Propositions are complex entities. They have many elements in common, and one should regard the recurring common elements as more fundamental than the propositions. One can hold such a view and still maintain that a proposition – or, for Plato, logos – is not just the sum of its parts, but a holistic entity. The view that perhaps we need to accept propositions but should regard other abstract elements as merely abstractions from propositions is likely to emerge only in the context of a philosophical climate in which abstract elements are regarded as suspicious and a need is felt not to multiply them beyond necessity. But for the Platonist, not only is there no such suspicion; there is the conviction that we understand the nature of abstract entities better than the nature of spatiotemporal particulars. Abstract realms are not admitted grudgingly, as extra baggage, but are regarded as more fundamental and as what account for whatever order we find in the world of everyday experience and the natural sciences.

The fifth theme concerns the study of mathematical activities under idealization. There is not much evidence that would support ascribing this to Plato as a view he held explicitly and consciously. But one could argue on the basis of absence of evidence of his being concerned with what people actually do when they calculate or prove theorems. On those rare occasions when such matters are treated, as in the recollection passage of the *Meno*, the error-filled actual performance is presented only by way of contrast with what Plato is interested in: namely, the resulting clear understanding. So Plato's position could best be summed up as the conjunction of three claims: what matters most is the nature of the objects; the required understanding and insight must be characterized in the light of the characterization of what is unique about the objects; and that if we consider the actual activities that lead to insight at all, we must consider them under idealization, without regard to the lawlike or accidental blemishes that characterize actual human performance.

Thus recollection is characterized in terms of what it accomplishes. One could imagine an account of recollection or some roughly equivalent modern conception – for example, the normal maturation of our notions of number, addition, and so forth – that takes into account basic human limitations of memory, attention span, and so on. But we do not find this either in Plato or in modern echoes of him. Proving theorems in modern times is considered under idealization. To the extent that theories about proving theorems take into account hypotheses about computing time, length of statements that can be understood, and so forth, these theories depart from the Platonistic tradition – for better or worse.

In the above account of the five themes, mention was made of modern discoveries of problems concerning certain types of self-predication that have led to recognizing that only certain structured collections should be seen as falling under genuine properties, not just any plurality. We saw earlier that some forms of self-reference or self-predication emerge in Plato's writings. There is what we called the problem of unique self-exemplification, and then there are the cases of self-application that seem straightforward and indeed, necessary, such as the Same being the same as itself and the Different being different from everything else. It is worth comparing the ancient and modern problems. As we shall see, the similarities are rather superficial; above all, the kind of remedy that was regarded as feasible by Russell and others does not do at all in Plato's system.

Modern theories of logic and semantics include attempts to construct a general theory of predication. A typical theory of this sort posits a class or property corresponding to every predicate expression. Thus we explain predication partly in terms of the ontological correlates of predicates. As has been mentioned already, there is no evidence to suggest that Plato was interested in constructing a general theory of predication. He was interested in the ontological preconditions of meaningful discourse and in analyzing declarative sentences of subject–predicate form in such a way as to admit also the thesis that such sentences are wholes that are more than the mere sums of their parts. But this does not commit him – or his pupil, Aristotle – to a "unitarian" theory of predication: that is, to saying that the same type of ontological element (for example, a universal?) must be correlated with every predicate.

In modern theories, the remedy is taken by many to be a hierarchical structure of properties. Within such a system we cannot have a property whose instances range across several levels, including the level of the property in question. But in Plato's case, there are strong reasons for not wanting a solution with such consequences.

Many of the Forms are transcategorial, in the sense that their possible participants can be on different ontological levels and be from very different kinds constituting reality. The Fine can have as participants actions, material objects, humans, human souls, institutions, sciences, and other Forms. The same is true of the Good. In general, the key valuational Forms of Plato cannot be restricted to type and natural kind. This is not an accidental feature of the theory of Forms. What has positive value either constitutes the most fundamental layer of reality or has this value as a reflection of the order of higher realms. In order for this theory to work, there must be entities whose presence can be reflected across different levels and categories, such as event, object, character, institution, and so forth.

One solution would be to have many Forms of Fine, with a system of assignments restricting any one of these to a certain type and category. But, as we saw in the *Parmenides*, this would rob the theory of what Plato takes to be its explanatory power. It would destroy the unity of a Form, and this is precisely what Plato thought to be crucial if his ontology were to be an adequate reply to the Eleatics.

We find even worse problems if we consider another group of Forms, the "greatest kinds" of the *Sophist*. These Forms are at the heart of what was labeled in chapter 5 the connector theory. Two modern devices recommend themselves as ways of regimenting the "greatest kinds." One of these would be to have many elements of sameness and to have each function within one type and one category. This would be unacceptable to Plato, for the same reasons that exclude similar treatments of the Fine, the Good, and the rest. An additional conception suggests itself if one reflects on recent treatments of identity. Why not treat identity and nonidentity or sameness and difference as syncategorematic elements – that is, as elements that are defined only syntactically, without ontological correlates?

Such a move would not merely be anachronistic. It is not simply that Plato would not have thought of such a technical maneuver. More important, such a construal would be the exact opposite of what Plato demands of these Forms. These Forms do not simply provide logical structure. They are the super-connectors; they are the key elements of reality that order everything according to qualitative sameness and difference and, in virtue of this, also into a distinct, intelligible plurality of elements. Far from being ontologically posterior to the ontological correlates of theoretically important descriptive predicates, these Forms are the most fundamental elements in an ontology that is primarily a response to the Eleatics. They are needed so that Plato can insist that being, sameness, and difference are inextricably interwoven. Understanding this represents the three as paradox-free and as providing the pluralistic order that the Eleatic One cannot provide.

Thus we see that hierarchical regimentation cannot be the answer to the logical paradoxes within a framework that captures not only themes 1–5 but also themes 6 and 7; that is, the Platonistic framework of how reality accounts for appearances. This still leaves much in common between Plato's conception of mathematics and that of the so-called Platonists of the late nineteenth and the twentieth centuries. But if one were to embrace all the Platonic metaphysics, then a different alternative solution would need to be found to the modern paradoxes.

These reflections bring out once more the key point that Plato sees as his main philosophical rivals the Eleatics, not a philosopher of nature like Democritus or subsequent modifiers of his system like Aristotle. Democritus may have worked out a conception of nature that for most practitioners made it a viable object of study and understanding and at the same time provided what was seen as a viable "model" for the world of space and time. But his efforts do not meet what Plato took to be the heart of the Eleatic dialectic: namely, deep conceptual problems regarding any plurality of elements, be these abstract or concrete. Again, restricting the nature of Forms and the extension of this realm might meet some qualms originating in a more empirically oriented epistemology or in new insights into the dynamics of power in the biological parts of nature, but it does not meet the challenge of providing an intelligible alternative to the Parmenidean One.

At this point, one might suggest trying to remove from Platonism those parts of the theory that are designed primarily to meet the Eleatic challenge and then mold the remainder into a viable theory that would resemble in its intuitive parts, though not in the technical ones, some modern views about the ontological foundations of mathematics. In my view, this would be a trivialization of original Platonism. The Eleatic challenge is indeed the most powerful challenge that philosophies have to meet. It is thus interesting to note that this view is represented in the writings of some of the great modern Platonistic philosophers of mathematics.

First, a preliminary point. In construing the central debate to be between Plato and the Eleatics, I am setting aside conceptualism, in both its ancient and its modern forms. In doing so, however, I am in distinguished company. One of the modern versions of conceptualism is intuitionism in the foundation of mathematics. It regards the relation between the reflecting and knowing subject and the science as fundamental. But Bernays, writing of this, says: "This is an extreme methodological position. It is contrary to the customary manner of doing mathematics, which consists in establishing theories detached as much as possible from the thinking subject."[17]

It seems, then, that at least in this respect, most mathematicians are what we might call "closet Platonists." Thus it is not arbitrary to regard some of Plato's techne conditions as setting up conditions for genuine rational enterprises that subsequently became permanent themes in philosophy and science, and to see what Plato took to be most problematic in his metaphysics as not this aspect but the reply to monism.

This way of construing the impact of Platonism in the ontology of mathematics is represented by Bernays as well. He writes:

> In the system of *Principia Mathematica*, it is not only the axioms of infinity and reducibility which go beyond pure logic, but also the initial conception of a universal domain of individuals and of a domain of predicates. It is really an *ad hoc* assumption to suppose that we have before us the universe of things divided into subjects and predicates, ready-made for theoretical treatment.[18]

To deny that the universe comes ready-made as a plurality of intelligible elements means either going back to some version of conceptualism or embracing – no matter how reluctantly – Eleatic monism. Plato saw that his philosophy faced two tasks: first, he must argue for there being something independent of the human mind that must be the object of knowledge and understanding; second, he must show that this objective domain is indeed a plurality of elements. He thought that the latter could be done in two steps: first, by showing – as he tries to do both in the *Parmenides* and the *Sophist* – that the Eleatic notion of being is incoherent; and second by demonstrating that his conception of being, sameness, and difference as an interwoven whole both is intelligible and can serve as the foundation of mathematics in particular and logos in general. Whether these steps can be justified is one of the perennial problems of philosophy, as much alive today as it was 2,400 years ago.

Bernays is not the only recent philosopher to see Platonism as facing Eleatic challenges. Eleatic themes are also seen in recent foundational work by Gödel. In discussing views concerning the reference of true sentences, Gödel sketches an argument showing that all these must have the same reference. He then writes:

> Frege actually drew this conclusion; and he meant it in an almost meta-physical sense, reminding one somewhat of the Eleatic doctrine of the

"One." "The True" – according to Frege's view – is analyzed by us in different ways in different propositions; "the True" being the name he uses for the common signification of all true propositions.[19]

It is easy to see how the Eleatics would have construed the Fregean view. They would have said that, indeed, there is only one reference, "The True," and that although the various sentences are differentiated by what Frege would call their senses, these do not have any grounding in reality; they represent only the error-prone opinions of mortals attempting to make some kind of pragmatic sense of the world of appearances in which they necessarily find themselves. Furthermore, they would find the positing of "the False" as the reference for false sentences incoherent.

Frege's positing of these two objects has been retained only in certain approaches to formal semantics; it is not a path followed by many contemporary metaphysicians. But whatever problems one might have with the nature of the two entities posited – or discovered? – there is this profound aspect of Frege's system. It is an honest attempt to come to grips with the Eleatic challenge; it yields monism on the level of the reference of true sentences and the pluralism we intuitively want on the level of the senses. In this way of struggling with Platonism and the Eleatic position, Frege can be seen in terms of his basic intuitions and their technical embodiments as indeed echoing Plato's thought.

On the basis of these reflections, we can see significant echoes of Platonic themes in modern foundational work on mathematics, and also, in the case of a few, most thoughtful philosophers, an echo of the view that the key challenge to a metaphysics of mathematics comes from the Eleatics. Seeing this much should set the stage for further reflection on the deepest claim of Plato's metaphysics: namely, that it can lay the foundation for some pluralism in reality in the case of the domain for mathematics.

Forms and Universals?

Platonistic metaphysics has been identified in this century not only with certain views on the foundations of mathematics, but also with an ontological "realism" that results in the theory of universals. In this section, we will seek to determine whether theories of universals like that of Russell and Moore are in any interesting sense echoes of Plato's thought. Instead of looking for definitions of "universal" that are bound to be in need of qualification as soon as we look at the works of particular philosophers, we shall adopt the technique used in the previous section and consider quotes that give us themes characteristic of realist ontologies. Let us consider the following:

> 1:   "that which many different thoughts of whiteness have in common is their object, and this object is different from all of them."[20]

Whiteness is an example of a universal. Many of our thoughts are about instances of that universal. We have thoughts about a white surface, a white blanket of snow, a white shirt, and so forth. Our thoughts of whiteness are different from these thoughts. They are about the universal whiteness of which the particulars just named are instances. We see here several "one–many" structures. We can have many different thoughts of the same instance of whiteness. We can have also many different thoughts of whiteness. The object in both types of cases unites the class of thoughts. Then there is the ontological one–many relation: one universal, whiteness, and many instances of this.

Universals constitute a very broad category. Some universals, like whiteness or redness, are part of everyday experience, and their instances are directly perceptible. Others, like the universal of being a court procedure, are also part of everyday experience, but their instances can be perceived only in the context of low-level theoretical descriptions. Law courts do not come ready-made, as do instances of redness or whiteness. Colors and other secondary qualities, as well as, for example, pleasure, are closest to perception; notions like those involving legal and political practice are less closely linked to mere perception. Both these classes of universals seem to be included under what we saw Plato describe in Book 5 of the *Republic* as the objects for the "lovers of sights and sounds."

There are other universals that lead a kind of double life. Universals like number, shape, and health are part of what we encounter in everyday experience; but within such experience we obtain only a very superficial conception of their natures. It requires considerable theory to gain an adequate comprehension of the full nature and ontological status of these entities. Finally, other universals like those of energy or being an atom, are for us strictly theory-laden. We can understand these only on the basis of having learned theories of physics or some other science.

These brief reflections show universals – or attributes or qualities, as these are sometimes called – to be a heterogeneous class. Further quotations will be needed in order to understand better what is claimed to be a common nature within this wide genus.

It is, however, worth stopping at this point to ask ourselves whether there is anything in the Platonic material that we reviewed earlier that could be interpreted as echoed in the quote given. Is Plato's realm of Forms extensionally equivalent to the realm of universals as suggested here? And is it intensionally equivalent – that is, are the arguments for their existence and the conceptions of the two types of entities identical?

Although in Parts I and II it was argued that the Forms make up a smaller class than universals, here we should keep in mind especially the intensional differences. How do we know whether our thought is a thought about whiteness or a thought about white things? Presumably, introspection should tell us. But, as we saw in chapter 1, only extensive theoretical and dialectic reflection enable us to understand what it is to have a thought of a Form and furnish tests for whether we have at any given time such a thought. As long as we interpret colors purely on the phenomenal level, as these seem to be presented in the *Republic*, sensation is sufficient to enable us to form an adequate concept of them, and since one can interpret a color as a "mass" spread over particulars, we need no theoretical apparatus to assign to it its proper ontological status. Thus the quote seems to have something more extensive in mind, in contrast with the narrower range of cognitive processes required for understanding.

Having considered a quote linking universals to thought, let us now consider an attempt to link universals to language:

2:   "No sentence can be made up without at least one word which denotes a universal."[21]

To simplify things, let us restrict our attention to sentences of subject–predicate form. Presumably the claim is that in any sentence of that form, at least the predicate must designate a universal. But does this apply to every predicate? Since we are dealing with an ontological claim, it cannot be language-relative. It cannot be restricted to predicates in English, or in any other language. But this drives us to think of "every possible predicate" in any language. What could this be? One could make up a predicate to cover any plurality of entities. Thus the following chain seems to underlie our second quote. Descriptive sentences contain predicates; predicates cover some plurality (actual or possible) or entities; and there is a universal connected to any plurality. Hence there is a universal connected to any descriptive sentence.

No such general link between Forms and language can be found in Plato's writings. To be sure, the existence of the Forms will make the existence of any sentence of subject–predicate form possible, since each such sentence expresses some aspect of sameness and difference. But there is no argument claiming that there must be a Form for every predicate. In chapter 5 we examined the analysis of falsehood in the *Sophist*. This required that subject-and-predicate expressions designate "things that are" (*onta*), not that the predicate designate a Form.

There is evidence both from the middle period dialogues and those surveyed in Part II that Plato does not want to link a Form to every predicate. The treatment of rhetoric in the *Gorgias* and the characterization of the lovers of sights and sounds in Book 5 of the *Republic* suggest that at this stage in Plato's development he did not think that there was a Form for rhetoric or for everyday court procedures. Whatever one might see as happening to these examples in the theory of Forms of the later dialogues, there are further examples from that corpus which show the gap between being a predicate in general and being a Form-introducing expression. One such set of examples is provided by the "bad parts" of the *Politicus*: that is, parts that are not also kinds (*eide*). Not being identical with 10,000 is a case in point. Then there are the "bad mixtures" of the *Philebus*: the ones in which the appropriate elements are not mixed according to the right proportions. These, too, do not correspond to Forms.

It is clear from these reflections that statement 2, at least at first glance, leads to positing a universal for any plurality; this is too wide a realm to correspond to the realm of Forms. But perhaps it is even too wide a realm for universals. Perhaps we should consider other statements that would limit what a predicate in a language might introduce, and thus offer a narrower construal of statement 2.

Something like this seems to be envisaged in the quote below; that is, some constraint that might render statement 2 more restricted, and hence more in harmony with our pre-theoretic intuitions about "genuine" descriptions.

>   3:   "A universal is anything that may be shared by many particulars."[22]

This suggests that it is not enough to be a plurality of entities; something needs to be shared among these. The question arises, however, how much weight the notion of sharing can take? How do we characterize a plurality of entities that do not share anything and contrast it with a plurality in which there is sharing? The latter kind of plurality must share a common element. This may or may not help with the theory of universals; but it clearly does not help with the identification of this with the theory of Forms, since we are now back to the examples cited already; phenomenally conceived qualities and conventional institutions or "bad parts" will qualify even under statement 3, but not under Platonic strictures.

The notion of not sharing something can be made quite clear and usable once we restrict it to kinds. Thus one can say that three red squares have a color in common, whereas a green square, a blue square, and a yellow square do not have any color in common. Of course, both collections have in common the universal of being colored. Thus one might want to modify the example to include collections whose members are not all colored or do not all have weight or any other such universal in common. But since there does not seem to be a limit to the generality of the universals that we can invoke to indicate something that is shared, even among entities that on a commonsense level seem quite disparate, this conceptual chase does not really help us very much.

We need some other notion to help capture what is meant here intuitively by "sharing." Some philosophers have thought that the notion of similarity might provide some illumination. We need to consider this since, as we have seen, Plato himself considers this notion in connection with his survey of criticism of Forms.

As we saw in chapter 4, Plato shows that given the original–copy analogy as an explanation of the Form–participant relation, we will be saddled with a series of similarity relations, since these are entailed by the analogy. The analogy cannot be the final explanation, since it pushes matters back to consideration of the Form of Similarity. This passage cannot be used to support the claim that for Plato any plurality of entities exhibiting similarity in some way leads to the positing or discovery of a Form. From the fact that some conceptions of the Forms might lead to there being similarities among the participants, one cannot draw the conclusion that for any similarity there is a corresponding Form. Even if for each Form there were a similarity relation, it does not follow that for each similarity relation there is a Form.

Furthermore, the discovery of Forms, as chronicled in the *Phaedo* (reviewed in chapter 2), does not square with the picture of a Form for every similarity relation. The Equal and other quantitative and mathematical Forms were introduced on the basis of reflection between the qualified and unqualified uses of their names. Only where there is a certain similarity and dissimilarity do we see Forms and participants. (Similarity in this context is interpreted as having a predicate in common, dissimilarity as lacking such a predicate, with certain qualifications.) Thus this line of reasoning cannot be assimilated to the one we borrowed from a modern conception of universals. The conception of a Form for every group of similar things is both too simplistic and too wide in extension to correspond to Plato's conception of the Forms. This can also be seen by reflecting on the explanatory role of Forms and universals respectively. The Forms are supposed to represent the most fundamental aspects of reality. They are those elements whose interrelation gives order and harmony to the world. It would be implausible to argue that a realm of universals, corresponding to all the similarities, could fill the role Plato assigned to the Forms. That there are similarities in the world guarantees a minimal intelligibility, but not the robust notion of order and intelligibility that Plato demands.

To highlight the differences between Forms and universals, let us consider the Form of Justice. Whereas justice is simply that, according to Plato, nothing among the participants is simply just, but always just with some qualification. Some of this can be captured by the theory of parts and wholes introduced in the later dialogues. There is military justice, the justice of the courts, justice in the family; or again, justice in the state and justice in the individual. Thus there is a Form of Justice, and many "crisscrossing" parts. Spatiotemporal particulars partake of the Form of justice via its parts. Even this might not exhaust all that Plato has in mind when he thinks of being just requiring qualification. But we shall let that pass.

In a theory of universals, there will be a separate universal for every complex predicate involving justice. Thus there is a separate universal for each of what, above, we called parts of justice. Furthermore, there will be an additional, infinite class of universals corresponding to every conceivable qualification involving social or psychological context.

Thus we are left with three issues. First, how can one capture the Platonic notion that we can partake of Justice more or less adequately? Second, how can we restrict the notion of similarity so as to leave us only with "real" similarities? Thirdly, how can we gather together the many universals involving justice so as to capture the Platonic theme that these have something fundamental in common?

The answer to the third question would be a molecular conception of complex universals. Why not just take all the complexes that have justice in them and construe them as making up, by conjunction, the universal of justice? This is "molecular" in the sense that the generic universal is simply the conjunction of all the more specific ones.

It turns out to be the case that, even apart from the cases that interest Plato, there are reasons for thinking that the simple conjunctive picture of universals is not correct. Let us consider briefly adverbial constructions in a natural language like English. The universal corresponding to "walks slowly" cannot be decomposed into a conjunction of walking and being slow. The walking agent may be an instance of walking and may not be an instance of being slow; in fact, perhaps she is fast in most everything she does. Slowness modifies the walking. It can also modify many other activities, with different interpretations of what it is to be slow resulting from the different combinations. By invoking complex relations between first-order and second-order attributes, logicians like Reichenbach have shown how this problem can be solved within a framework of an ontology of universals.[23] But it would be senseless to attribute such a theory to Plato. In any case, his examples are different; they involve relations between generic Forms and their parts. As we saw in chapter 6, for him these do not involve molecular structures. The generic Form is a whole that is more than a mere sum of parts. The holistic conception dominates Plato's conception of Forms. For Aristotle, too, the holistic conception is important. It plays a key role in his account of the so-called unity of definitions.

We see, then, that for Plato and Aristotle, the whole–part relation is more fundamental for the representation of relations among Forms with important common elements. Modern logic works more with conjunctive complexes. The theory of universals as developed by "realists" of this century is couched in terms of modern logic. Thus here, too, we see an important difference.

As was shown above, if similarity is to play an important role in either Platonism or modern theories of universals, it needs restriction and refinement. If x and y are similar every time they have an attribute of any sort in common, then the notion is too wide. Let us consider ways in which the notion could be narrowed.

4:   "Universals are what make entities qualitatively different."[24]

What are qualities? Sweetness, being red, and being a number are qualities, presumably; whereas the predicate "being identical either with the Empire State Building or the Battle of Waterloo or the first laugh of Woody Allen" is not. Intuitive contrasts like this can be multiplied at will. But it is difficult to draw a theoretically satisfying differentiating line between the two types of cases. Even if it turned out to be the case that people from different cultures all over the world would sort the cases in the same way, this would show only something psychologically revealing about humans; it would not suffice by itself to warrant ontological conclusions.[25]

Let us suppose that we had found an adequate way of narrowing down universals to the realm of qualities. This realm would have to include all the secondary qualities even in the phenomenal sense; thus, once more, we would have a realm that is too wide and not sufficiently motivated as an order-creating realm to be equivalent to the Platonic realm of Forms.

What all this shows is that universals are entities resembling many ontological elements in Plato's ontology, but that they also include elements that, though not particulars, are not included in the realm of Forms. We can add to this that the Platonic Forms have some of the characteristics that universals have, but also have additional attributes that the universals of the modern realist lack.

The most important differences will surface when we compare the two theories in terms of their purported explanatory power. First, however, we shall turn to a sketch of how at least some realists see the epistemology of the theory of universals.

5:   "We know sensible qualities and the relation of similarity by acquaintance."[26]

The notion of acquaintance plays a technical role in Russell's philosophy. Knowledge by acquaintance is contrasted with knowledge by description. The former is direct knowledge, analogous to seeing; whereas the latter is inferential knowledge. Some Platonic passages support the hypothesis that this modern notion of acquaintance is an echo of Plato's views about how we know Forms. There is the sudden vision of *Symposium* 212 and the similes of light in the middle parts of the *Republic*. Yet this comparison requires major qualifications. The epistemology of Russell and Moore suggests that we can stumble upon at least some universals in everyday experience. There is an anecdotal story about G. E. Moore having a nightmare in which he could not distinguish universals from furniture in the room. But as we have seen, Plato conceives of genuine understanding as coming to have an adequate representation of abstract entities that do not have unqualified instances in space and time. In a way, we do have "contact" with some of the Forms even when we live in the epistemic realm of mere true opinion, since navigating, calculating, and making decisions with normative impact are necessary parts of human life. But, as was pointed out above, we do not understand what we are dealing with. The real understanding comes only after activities such as dialectic and proof construction, which enable us to enter the required frame of mind.

Comparison of the modern with the ancient is made difficult by the fact that the epistemology of Russell and Moore is empiricist, whereas that of Plato is not. Take seeing in its natural sense and consider special types of cases, such as being able to see something spectacular only after hiking or being carried to special vantage points (the moon, unscaled mountains, and so on) or having been trained to make extremely fine discriminations between shades of a color. None of these is really adequate as an analogy to Plato's interpretation of discovering a proof or understanding the true ontological status of an element of reality.

The same point can be made by contrasting the role of the senses in the respective epistemologies. In the modern view, the senses provide the data which reason is to organize – basically along lines of similarity. But there are also other data: universals that are not abstractable from sense experience. These are known to us by direct intuition.

By contrast, for Plato, the senses primarily play the epistemic role of providing stimulation that triggers off a variety of complicated intellectual processes which result in the optimal case in understanding. Perception does not provide the fundamental data. What the senses present must be interpreted in terms of concepts that we acquire only by recollection.

In view of these considerations, it does not seem felicitous to think of the conception of knowledge by acquaintance as an echo of Platonic conceptions. This epistemological difference has serious consequences for the respective construals of self-knowledge. According to the empiricist view, much of our mental life is known to us directly, by introspection. According to Plato's view, most of what is important for the life of reason takes place on the nonconscious level and is known to us only indirectly.

For example, we need the complex of processes labeled dialectic not only to discover what is fundamental in reality, but also to discover what our own beliefs and convictions are.

This contrast allows us to characterize conceptions of mind as "deep" or "shallow," without attaching any evaluative implications to these expressions. A "deep" theory construes the important cognitive processes that result in understanding and belief about values, self, and others as nonconscious; a "shallow" theory interprets these processes as open to introspection. Needless to say, all theories of mind cannot be conveniently divided into two groups according to these labels. Rather, the labels indicate the extremes of a continuous scale, with much room for intermediate positions.[27] There is room for introspective acquisition of information about ourselves in Plato's scheme, but it is much more limited than what we find in other, empiricism-inspired views.

The choice among these kinds of theories has not been merely a matter of empirical evidence. In the Western traditions, moral, religious, and other psychological factors have heavily influenced the choices. By and large, these factors have made the "shallower" conceptions popular.

In the Judeo-Christian tradition, notions of belief and intention play important roles in our moral and religious lives. Much of one's religious worth is determined by one's beliefs and intentions. This makes it attractive for people to think that their beliefs and intentions are directly observable by them. Direct access seems to suggest the possibility of control and change. Thus, for example, a phenomenon like repentance may seem easier to assimilate if one adopts a shallow theory of the mind. For then, the things we regret are things we can inspect and know. Needless to say, no religion entails the shallow view. Repentance remains an important ingredient in a religious life even if one opts for the deep view. Given that conception, one must reconcile oneself to the fact that much of what one regrets is part of the nonconscious level of one's psyche. But those elements, too, are subject to change; influence on oneself need not be direct influence.

Similar considerations arise in connection with certain moral phenomena. Promising something involves both belief and intention. One feels more comfortable with accepting the binding power of promise if one feels that the psychic ingredients involved can be known directly by the agent. But this comfort need not accompany the acceptance of the binding power of a promise.

Deep theories, like that of Plato, construe the workings of the mind as analogous to how other substantial elements in nature work. In cognition and physics alike, "nature does not wear its essence on its sleeves." This does not prevent the rational agent from understanding the workings of his or her own mind; nor does it make self-control impossible. Indirect self-knowledge is quite sufficient for our being able to dedicate ourselves to a Platonic ideal in our lives. Mathematical and moral knowledge may yield certainty; but our assessment of how well we have mastered these types of knowledge does not.

Plato, like anyone else, would make room for conscious states of professing beliefs, making decisions, and drawing conclusions. But he would question the claim that these give us certainty with regard to our knowing in all cases what we really believe and decide. The more we train ourselves and the more we learn to make the right inferences, the more confident we can become with regard to claims of self-knowledge. But many of these cannot be entertained with complete certainty. We might think we believe that justice is harmony within ourselves and within the community, only to be subjected to experiences in the face of which we discover some of our "dark side" and our correspondingly less enlightened views on justice. Likewise, we might think that we really understand the nature of certain mathematical entities, only to be confronted with new evidence showing that our grasp was only partial. As we shall see in the next chapter, this lack of certainty does not rob the Platonically ideal individual of peace and contentment.

So far, we have considered several claims made by philosophers in this century who are regarded as Platonists. These claims are logically independent of each other; one could hold any one of them without holding the others. Still, when put together, they form the sketch of a general theory of universals that can be seen as promising to answer many philosophical questions. Two of the statements describe the nature of universals; they are what can be shared by a plurality of entities and account for qualitative difference. Two further statements link these entities to thought and language. Universals, as characterized by the other two statements within this conception, underlie predicates and thus enable these to function descriptively. Universals can be the objects of thought, thereby allowing us to think not only about particulars but also about these entities, thus reaching a higher level of generality. Finally, the statement about acquaintance gives the beginning of an epistemology of universals.

As we went along, I suggested that, individually, the statements are not sufficiently similar to what Plato says about Forms to be interpretable as echoes of Platonic themes. When we look at the statements together, combined in a theory sketch such as the one just given, the differences seem even larger. A theory of universals, if it follows the lines just drawn, is very different from the theory of Forms as we have seen it in Parts I and II of this book, both in terms of arguments for the existence of these entities, as well as terms of characterization, and in explanatory power.

We can say, however, that Plato – at least by the time he composed the dialogues surveyed in Part II – has in his ontology entities that have universal-like natures. These would include all the many abstract "parts" of generic Forms. One can also say, for example, that being an entity in which many particulars can share is one of the Form-making characteristics, but that the overall characterizations of a universal are at once too broad and too thin to capture Plato's rich notion of what a Form is.

This, however, is not the conclusion one finds in influential modern works on Plato's metaphysics. As an important case of dissenting opinion, we shall consider a statement by Sir David Ross. He writes:

> The essence of the Theory of Ideas lay in the conscious recognition of the fact that there is a class of entities for which the best name is probably "universals", that are entirely different from sensible things. Any use of language involves the recognition . . . of the fact that there are such entities; for every word used except proper names . . . is the name of something of which there are or may be instances.[28]

Ross identifies here Forms and universals and offers the following characterization of both: (1) they are distinct from sensible particulars; (2) they may have many instances; and (3) they provide entities to be named by predicate expressions. Even at a cursory glance, one can see that this set of descriptions fits the conception of universals that Russell and Moore had. Statements 1 and 2 say some of the same things that Russell and Moore wanted to say about universals, and statement 3 provides the same link between language and universals as the one forged by the Russell–Moore conception. Our concern here, however, is with whether these characterizations fit Plato's Forms. Are these statements true of the Forms; and if so, do they single out Forms in a unique way?

The first statement is surely true of the Forms. But it is true also of many other types of entities; for example, souls, some of the bad mixtures of the *Philebus*, and so on. The second statement is true of the Forms only with the qualification that we overlook the difference between partaking and instantiation. As we have seen, partaking as introduced in the *Phaedo* and exemplified by the relation of the Equal to the many equals is quite different from mere instantiation. As Plato develops his ontology, additional types of participation are introduced. Some of these, for example, that between entities to be defined by division and the generic Form and intermediate genuine parts, resemble instantiation. So here we have a closer link. Bue even then, as we have seen, it is not clear that in the later dialogues Plato consistently holds the view that Forms are the only entities of which things can partake.

Statement 3 offers a unitarian conception of predication. We have already had several occasions for claiming that this was not Plato's conception. Not all predicates are on the same ontological level for Plato, and though every predication presupposes the existence of some Forms, namely the Same and the Different, it is not as if Plato thought that there must be a Form corresponding to every predicate expression. The reliance of language on the realm of universals as conceived by "realist" theories of universals is very different from the view presented in chapter 5, according to which descriptive discourse presupposes the connector theory.

We see, then, that Ross's characterizations are move in keeping with the Russell–Moore theory of universals than Plato's theory of Forms. They do not account for the Forms being objects of the genuine sciences, their providing via the connector theory an answer to the Eleatics, and their constituting the kind of good mixtures that Plato sees in the *Philebus* as the foundations for order and harmony in reality.

Nevertheless, as much by omission as by commission, Ross's statement is a good corrective to certain interpretations of Plato's ontology. First, it implies that universals – or Forms – need not be instantiated. Thus his statement clashes with the views of those who think that in the later dialogues Plato is leaning towards a conception in which Forms are immanent: that is, in things. In more technical terms, within such a conception, Forms must be instantiated. It would be a mistake to think of Plato as contemplating the alternatives coined in medieval times: namely, whether universals are *ante res* (that is, not in need of instantiation) or *in rebus* (that is, necessarily instantiated). This dichotomy emerges only once the notion of a universal has been clearly articulated, and a realist might opt for the second conception as a less strong version of universals as part of a defense of these entities against skeptical attacks. Plato's interest was in ontological explanatory chains. Within such a conception the notion of an immanent Form or universal does not make sense, because we need self-explanatory, self-sufficient entities at the end of such chains. He was also interested in explaining how mathematics could be true but not be about spatiotemporal entities. Again, immanent Forms or universals do not help here. Indeed, on either Ross's account or on the account sketched in this book, the notion of an immanent universal does not play an important role in solving any of Plato's key problems. It enters crucially into Aristotle's ontology, because Aristotle has different ontological priorities in his metaphysics and yet wants to retain something of the Platonic conception of "Form" — that is, as the subject of certain necessary truths.

At the other end of the Platonic ontological hierarchy, we find the sensible particulars mentioned also by Ross. These are presumably objects, animate agents, and events. Some interpreters have wanted to interpret this level as also including entities like the tallness of Simias, the generosity of a landlord — or the smile of the Cheshire cat? These are abstract particulars, and one can think of the more robust individuals either as composed of these particulars or as having a crust composed of these particulars surrounding some kind of core. In any case, Ross's account leaves out these "little fellows." To be sure, there are expressions like "the tallness of Simias," used, for example, in the *Phaedo*. But that by itself does not mean that Plato intended these phrases to introduce a genuine class of entities within his ontology. Again, the question would have to be asked: To what Platonic puzzle would the existence of the little fellows be a part of the answer? Plato is anxious to present an analysis within which elements of reality either have a clear structure that individuates them or derive whatever stability they have from connections with the entities whose stability is clearly intelligible. But what would individuate the little fellows, except their relationships to the particulars of which they are parts or to which they are otherwise related? They could not be fundamental in a Platonic framework. And taking them to be primitives would not do in an ontology that is meant to be an answer to the Eleatic challenge.

Finally, Ross says nothing about perfect particulars as a part of Plato's ontology. This, too, is a welcome feature of Ross's description. Perfect particulars could not do the job the Forms are meant to do: that is, have participants. As for explaining how the objects of the genuine sciences differ from the objects of everyday sense experience, the notion of a perfect particular does not arise. There could be a use for this notion if one wanted to spell out the idea that various participants can exemplify a Form more or less adequately by positing a perfect particular that exemplifies it completely and then have all participants approximate this entity. But, as we have seen, it makes no sense to talk of an entity that is, for example, perfectly just (or perfectly two?) in every way.

These reflections do not show that Plato could not have had within some of his conceptions immanent universals or abstract particulars. They do show, however, that he did not need such entities, either within the schemes in which the Forms are characterized or account for other phenomena or in his defense of his theory against what he thought to be the strongest objections.

The key difference between theories of universals and the theory of Forms is that between the alleged respective explanatory forces of the two kinds of theories. Thus we turn to a few comments on these.

The following is a rough outline of how universals are supposed to account for regularities, and thus a certain degree of order, in the world.

1 Entities a, b, c are similar in some respect.
2 This similarity is interpreted as their having a common element.
3 The common element is not a part, but something to which he entities relate in a unique way.
4 The common element accounts for qualitative sameness.
5 There are universals, characterized as in the quotes above, and two entities instantiating the identical universal accounts for their being, to that extent, qualitatively the same.

Whether this scheme has explanatory force depends on how much we can say about similarity, qualitative sameness, and, above all, universals, apart from their alleged explanatory roles. The same also holds for the notion of instantiation. Of course, something needs to remain undefined in any such account or a certain set of notions need to remain interdefined. A modern "realist," Whitehead, is reputed to have said that in some contexts there is nothing wrong with circular definitions as long as the circle is big enough.

This scheme of universals based on the argument sketched above cannot by itself capture Plato's picture of an abstract realm of order and its being approximated by the partial order of entities in space and time. But perhaps one can add further conditions to a realist theory and thereby capture Plato's picture. For example, one could select a subset of universals that do not have instantiations in the sensible world and take these and their necessary connections as capturing Platonic order. But such a scheme would differ from Plato's in crucial ways. For, according to his theory, it is not just being a universal that guarantees being a constituent of fundamental order, but its having other additional attributes. In Plato's scheme, to be a Form is to be an object of a genuine science and a constituent of the fundamentally harmonious and orderly. He does not need additional assumptions in order to have in his ontology a realm that constitutes order and harmony.

Let us, then, place side by side universals and Forms and compare them in terms of range and explanatory value. Within both the theory of universals and the theory of Forms one can distinguish between natural units such as male and female, even and odd, and nonnatural units such as barbarian or not-10,000. Within the theory of Forms the unnatural is simply not a Form; whereas within the theory of universals it is a universal, but not a natural one. Both Forms and universals need to be distinguished from extensionally defined sets such as that consisting of Magdalen Tower, World War II, and the US Constitution. In the last case the notion of a qualitative common element becomes a purely formal, intuitively empty notion.

In terms of range, Forms and universals differ. Universals, as we have seen, are defined in terms of qualitative sameness among elements of a group. Thus the schema for representing a universal is: x, y, z are all, as well as the only, elements that have F; hence we have the universal F-ness. Thus universals include qualities that have no significance for abstract theories: for example, smells and laziness. On some assumptions these qualities have no teleological significance either.

There are Forms corresponding only to those properties that are objects of genuine science, where the latter is construed as the study of order, harmony, and teleological structure. This will be spelled out in more detail below.

The explanatory roles of the two kinds of elements is construed in quite different ways. For universals the fact to be explained is that there is a collection of elements x, y, z that constitute all, as well as the only, entities that have quality F in common. The theory says that it is in virtue of their being instantiations of the universal F-ness that they have this qualitative sameness. The universal F-ness does not cause the elements to be F; but it has the ontological explanatory power of making possible the collection having F.

The argument in the case of Forms is quite different. The fact to be explained in this case is that there is a collection of elements x, y, z making up the class of all and only elements that have F with various qualifications;

thus x, y, z are F with qualification 1, qualification 2, and so forth. Nothing is just F, in the case of F being a Form. This fact is explained by there being a Form F-ness of which x, y, z partake and so have the nature they have. Order and harmony are relations among the Forms. In the world of appearances there is only partial or qualified order. Again, the Forms are not the cause of this partial order; but their existence, nature (as spelled out in chapter 2), and partaking make the partial order in space and time possible. This is, then, their ontological explanatory power. The point is not only that none of x, y, and z are identical with F-ness, but also that none of them is simply F. As we have seen in our discussions, it is not clear whether Plato wants to say only that the Form just is F-ness or that he also wants to say that it is the only entity that "is F" without qualifications, in some unique sense.

We have, so far, two characterizations of the Forms with respect to their explanatory role. One is that participation in them enables particulars to have certain properties with various qualifications. The other is that their interrelations constitute pure order and harmony. We need to see how these two are linked together. Clearly, in some ways even universals enable the world to exhibit some order. Let us start with a minimal kind of order and work our way towards more complicated notions.

First, there are mere regularities exhibited by groups of objects, events, or processes. The regularity is captured by qualitative sameness, and this in turn can be given ontological grounding by universals. Second, there are regularities that admit lawlike projections. These are relations between qualities that do not just happen to hold in the world, but would hold also in possible cases. The most general of such lawlike regularities can be regarded as laws of nature. Again, universals can be seen as making these possible in the same sense as described above with regard to the first kind of regularities. Third, there is the explanatory priority of sturcture over disposition and disposition over event.

This is how, in general, we give causal explanations. We explain an event in terms of the disposition of which it is the manifestation, and the disposition in terms of underlying structure. For example, water froze last night because of its own propensities and the weather conditions, and its disposition to freeze at a certain temperature is explained ultimately by its H_2O structure. Note that this notion of order can no longer be described in strictly formal or logical terms. It would be logically possible to turn the chain around and have events as the ultimate level, but no scientist would do that.

So why is this not enough for Plato? For one thing, the priorities have to do with causal chains, but Platonic order and harmony are static, the paradigm case being the set of obviously noncausal structures of mathematics. Second, one can have cases falling under the third category of order that are not related to either mathematical structure or teleological considerations.

To say that Plato's notions of law and harmony are not formal notions is not to say anything that is not already true of this third category. He thinks of mathematical, geometrical, and teleological structures, and other structures that can be derived from these, as constituting order and harmony in a special sense that does not admit further analysis. Today we see a similar conception even among those who do not embrace a Platonistic ontology. These are the scientists who think that a science whose conceptions admit of mathematical analysis is more insightful than a science that contains almost exclusively purely qualitative notions.

We can now link the two conceptions: that is, order and harmony on the one hand, and the contrast between the qualified and unqualified characterizations on the other. The kind of order and harmony that Plato has in mind cannot apply directly to things in space and time. In its unqualified form it holds only in the abstract realms; hence the need to describe harmony in the world of appearances always in qualified form. Hence, too, the need to have separate entities – namely, the Platonic Forms – as the constituents of order, and not immanent structures.

As mentioned before, the obvious illustration is mathematics. $2 + 2 = 4$ is not about particulars or groups of particulars. It represents relationships between numbers. In this book these are interpreted as Forms; but this way of looking at the explanatory role of Forms can also be accepted by those who disagree with that reading but at least admit that there is a Form, Number.

The same construal applies to harmony. Harmony is determined by numerical ratios, and its application to any kind, music, heavenly constellations, and so forth is always qualified. There is no such thing as pure harmony or pure goodness, in the world of appearances. We have seen that the same thing applies to health and other Platonically privileged notions, including those for biological natural kinds, where teleological considerations come into play. The modern conception of an idealized specimen or process would not do as a substitute for Plato's Forms, for these are possible particulars and do not have the attribute-like generality of the Forms.

Whether this noncausal explanatory scheme gives Forms enough non-vacuous explanatory power depends on how conceptually sound the notions of being a Form and of partaking are. This is independent of the fact that – as we have seen – there is also a partaking among Forms, without the "qualification" requirement. Any Form involved in this second type of partaking relations to others must also have the first kind of partaking relations to some actual or possible entities.

The Platonic scheme accounts in one fell swoop for the fact that there are true statements in mathematics, geometry, value theory, and so forth that have subjects not in space and time, but are nevertheless useful for explaining the partial order that we find in the realm of particulars. This is not true of the realist framework sketched.

In confronting the problem of assessing the explanatory powers of theories of universals and that of Platonic Forms, one could be "driven" to a third position: namely, that of not saying that the entities in question either do or do not have explanatory power, but insisting that they are necessary entities, so fundamental as not to allow characterizations except as they relate to each other and less fundamental entities, that are needed to account for order in reality and the nonempirical disciplines, regardless of how much or how little we can say about them. As we have seen, there are indications in the *Parmenides* and the *Philebus* that Plato in his later, more defensive stage may have been tempted to look at the Forms in this manner. One could also look at universals in this way, provided one could show the nature of universals to be coherent. In this connection, it is relevant to note that in recent times there have been several attempts to lay out the realm of these entities in systematic, rigorous ways.[29] This shows that an ontology containing such entities is not saddled with incoherent elements. Presumably the same can be done for Forms.

In summary, then, we can say that while recent foundational work on mathematics contains elements that are echoes of Platonic conceptions, both in spirit and in terms of the claims made, the same cannot be said of recent "realist" ontologies. Yet these ontologies capture what are, from a modern point of view, prerequisites for the existence of Forms: namely, the possibility of the existence of attribute-like entities. This possibility is required for what was called in the Introduction the third explanatory pattern in the development of Greek philosophy. Furthermore, both universals and Forms face similar challenges from skeptics demanding what one demands of fundamental entities in any rational explanatory scheme:

namely, independent explanatory power or arguments supporting the unconditional need for, and the coherent nature of, the posited or discovered entities.

NOTES

1   K. Gödel, "Russell's Mathematical Logic," p. 211.
2   For an introduction to this topic, see N. Goodman, *The Structure of Appearance*.
3   See J. Moravcsik, *Thought and Language*, ch. 6.
4   P. Shorey, *Platonism, Ancient and Modern*.
5   For an introduction to these topics, see W. Quine, *Methods of Logic*.
6   For a recent echo, see K. Manders, "Logical and Conceptual Relationships in Mathematics."
7   P. Bernays, "On Platonism in Mathematics," p. 275.
8   Ibid. This rendering, which is my own translation from the German original, is slightly different from the printed version.
9   For an introduction to these topics, see articles by Ryle and Lawrence in M. McDonald (ed.), *Philosophy and Analysis*, pp. 37–53.
10 Bernays, "On Platonism in Mathematics," p. 277.
11 Gödel, "Russell's Mathematical Logic," pp. 215–16.
12 I am indebted to Kenneth Manders for helpful discussions.
13 G. Frege, *The Foundations of Arithmetic*.
14 C. Menzel, "Frege Numbers and the Relativity Argument," p. 87.
15 G. Frege, as quoted by Menzel, "Frege Numbers," p. 90.
16 For an introduction, see e.g. A. Farris, *Plato's Theory of Forms and Cantor's Theory of Sets*, pp. 10–11.
17 Bernays, "On Platonism in Mathematics," p. 282.
18 Ibid., pp. 282–3.
19 Gödel, "Russell's Mathematical Logic," p. 214.
20 B. Russell, *The Problems of Philosophy*, p. 99.
21 Ibid., p. 93.
22 Ibid.
23 H. Reichenbach, *Elements of Symbolic Logic*, §51.
24 G. Moore, *Philosophical Studies*, pp. 285–6.
25 See N. Goodman, *Fact, Fiction, Forecast*.
26 Russell, *Problems of Philosophy*, p. 102.
27 For further discussion, see Moravcsik, *Thought and Language*, ch. 2, 5.
28 W. Ross, *Plato's Theory of Ideas*, p. 225.
29 G. Bealer, *Quality and Concept*; C. Menzel, "A Complete Type-Free Second-Order Logic of Properties, Relations, and Propositions"; E. Zalta, *Abstract Objects*.

8

Platonistic Ethics: Effecting Reorientation and Sustaining Ideals

◆

It is more difficult to relate Plato's ethics to contemporary moral philosophy than it is to relate his ontology to the material surveyed in chapter 7. In that chapter we saw a close connection between Plato's way of thinking about the ontology of mathematics and the thoughts on the same topic of some outstanding philosophers of this century. We saw also that although the "realism" with regard to universals developed by philosophers like Moore and Russell differs both in spirit and in terms of specific proposals from Plato's theory of Forms, the former can be seen as a development from the latter. Furthermore, Platonism of some sort, in competition with nominalism and conceptualism, is still one of the main ontological options today.

The same cannot be said of Plato's ethics. Two of the main schools in modern ethics are consequentialism and deontic ethics. These both share what was described earlier as the autonomy thesis: that is, that an adequate theory of moral obligations is independent of theories concerning the human good. The moral psychology underlying these theories also differs in fundamental ways from the Platonistic one. Thus one could not characterize Plato as the ancestor of a main school of ethics in this century. To be sure, we have seen recently the emergence of "virtue ethics": that is, ethical theories in which virtues and character play prominent roles.[1] But there can be ethical theories with such a focus that are compatible with either consequentialism or deontic ethics. Thus, merely having this focus cannot be what is essential to the Platonistic ethical outlook.

In view of these considerations, my strategy for trying to find echoes of Platonistic ethics must be different from that adopted in the last chapter. First, I will outline what are, from a modern point of view, the most strikingly distinct features of Plato's ethics. Such an outline will inevitably include among other features of Plato's thought those it has in common with many other classical theories. Still, they deserve our attention. As I pointed out earlier, Plato's ethics is one of many ways in which an ideal ethics can be formulated. Within such a framework, the key questions are: What will sustain the right ideals in a human? And how can we, through rational understanding, effect a reorientation in the minds of those with wrong ideals? These questions are very different from those raised by thinkers who conceive of moral philosophy as being primarily a set of instructions for reasoning about and formulating our moral duties.

After sketching what is striking from a modern point of view about the Platonic, I shall look at some remarks by two twentieth-century philosophers, F. H. Bradley and Ludwig Wittgenstein, in order to show and give a flavor of samples of ideal ethics that do contain some echoes of Plato's thought. In this century, orientation and reorientation tend to emerge either in religious contexts or, at their worst, in fanatic ideologies. It is thus important to show how these notions can constitute the foundations for a secular rationalist ethics.

Before we embark on this project, let us reflect on the links between Plato and the philosophers to be studied. Plato's ethics of ideals, in the sense explained in chapter 3, was carried on, if not in details, certainly in terms of its key conceptual features, by Aristotle and by some strands in Hellenistic ethics, such as the early Stoics. After that a separate tradition of ideal ethics joined the Greek line: namely, that of the Judeo-Christian tradition. In this tradition too, overall aim and related character determine both what is good and what should be reflected in our relations to others, and there is no autonomous moral component. The two traditions were united in the medieval period by philosophers like Thomas Aquinas. In the modern period such approaches were pushed out of the limelight by approaches centering, roughly speaking, on the problem of how to establish moral rules for societies within which we find fundamentally different conceptions of what constitutes the human good. Still, the earlier tradition lived on, especialy in religious thought, and can be seen clearly in our century in neo-Thomistic writings. Similar thoughts about ethics are also found in some non-Catholic writers, such as Josiah Royce. The fact of pluralism suggests to the more recent tradition the conception of morality as "traffic laws" guiding ethical movement among entities heading in different directions. For the older, classical tradition the pluralistic picture of many modern societies suggests the need to include with tolerance within ideal ethics and to find deep underlying common elements in the various traditions, then reinterpret differences as lying more on the surface.

Thus, although the ethics of Bradley and Wittgenstein do not occupy central places in the ethics textbooks of modern Anglo-American analytical philosophy, they do have a place in a long tradition whose relevance today can be highlighted both by looking at them and by comparing them with Plato.

Distinctive Themes in Platonistic Ethics

We shall consider Platonistic features under four headings: (1) the content of the ideal ethics, (2) moral psychology, (3) moral epistemology, and (4) individual versus communal values.

In order to place the Platonic content in proper perspective, I shall draw a number of distinctions of increasing specificity; thus emulating to some extent the Platonic divisions. First, I will consider the division of moral philosophies into a class whose members maintain the separateness of moral theory from theories of the human good and a class whose members deny this separation and attempt to derive the former from the latter.[2] Plato's theory falls squarely in the second group.

Within the second group, we can distinguish theories that assign to overall orientation, aim, and character a special place among human goods and theories that do not. Plato belongs in the first group. Within this group there are theories specifying overall aims for human life on more or less concrete levels and as more monolithic or more disjunctive. These are collectively labeled "ideal ethics."

Within ideal ethics, some theories specify the adequate overall aim for humans without linking it closely to desirable and objectively good character traits. Others insist, however, that the adequate overall aims can be realized only by humans with such-and-such character traits. Thus, for example, a fanatic version of ideal ethics might specify the overall aim as the realization of a certain political unit with much power and leave the character specification as purely instrumental; that is, any character will do as long as its possession enables a person to contribute to the realization of the political – or religious – unit. On the other hand, there are ideal ethics, – both secular and religious, – in which both the aim and the ideal character are thought to be of intrinsic value and are conceptually linked.

For example, the aim can be to fit into the larger order of the universe; but, given the nature of this task and of the human soul, only persons with a certain character structure or character structures can realize this aim, and within this class, some character structures are of intrinsic value.

Plato's ideal ethics belongs to the class just exemplified. As we saw in chapter 3, the aim is the understanding and mirroring of the order and harmony of the larger, more fundamental parts of reality, but this – as Plato understands the task – can be accomplished only by persons with a certain character structure that incorporates some noncompetitive and cooperative virtues, and these have intrinsic value. Since ideal ethics of this sort links so closely overall aim and character, humans adopting such an ethics find the ethical pervading their whole life; thus they see meaning in their lives. If the aim and character are articulated within a larger, more general scheme of values and reality and the human good can be placed within such a scheme, then our lives have objective value; we do not only find meaning *in* our lives, we also find the meaning, or meanings, *of* life.

One way of bringing out the difference between having meaning *in* life and having found the meaning, or one of the meanings, *of* life, is to contrast coping with contributing. If we have an overall aim and can continue to be focused on it, that helps us cope with life, its vicissitudes, its many circumstances that are beyond our control. It gives us direction and hope. We can say, "Yes, there is purpose in my life, and I try my best to realize this under the circumstances." There may be other ways of coping, but this is certainly one of them.

Alternatively, one might shift the emphasis from coping to contributing. Instead of concentrating merely on that aspect of being purposive that helps one to cope, one can focus more on how realizing one's purpose will contribute to values and their realization in larger units of reality. If one can see one's life as contributing to some larger objective good, then one can see the meaning of life, at least in one of its versions.

Plato's ideal ethics belongs to the class that interprets the ideal as linking us to larger, fundamental parts of reality. Another such ethics emerges from the Judeo-Christian tradition. The overall aim revolves around having a certain relation to the most fundamental element of reality: namely, God. This relation enables us to see the meaning of life and gives us a life plan that pervades all aspects of our existence. The similarity between this ethics and Platonism, however, should not blind us to the great difference between the entities which Plato wants us to relate to – namely, the Forms – and the fundamental entity in the Judeo-

Christian tradition. Needless to say, there have been historically important traditions which have tried to forge a unified conception from these approaches. My purpose here is to stress the differences in the original versions of these theories in order to understand the Platonism of the dialogues better.

We can consider, then, many ideal ethics as prescribing for us certain relations to fundamental elements of reality (such as love, understanding, and so on) and distinguish each such theory in terms of what it takes to be the fundamental entities to which we need to be related and what this privileged relation is.

In summary, then, Platonic ethics belongs to that group of ethical theories whose members deny the automony of moral obligation, assign to aim and character a special role among human goods, regard aim and character as closely linked, and interpret the adequate human aim as the task of attaining a certain relation to a fundamental element of reality. For Plato, the relevant elements make up the realm of Forms, and the required relation is understanding and mirroring.

Let us flesh out the Platonic conception a bit. First, as was said earlier, the harmony and order that Plato has in mind do not have their paradigm in the dynamic order of change and rejuvenation that one sees in the lives of biological specimens and species, but rather in the order and static harmony exemplified by mathematical and musical structures. When in the cosmological sections of the *Timaeus*, Plato draws an analogy between the cosmos and something that has life, he is thinking of the holistic organization, not the rhythmic sequence of birth and death that we associate in modern times with the subject matter of biology, an association that was already hammered out by Aristotle.

The notion of finding our good through our relation to this kind of harmony is key to the similes of light in the *Republic* and is still present in the *Philebus* (e.g. 59d1–5, 62a, 66a–c). The task of mirroring what is good and orderly in the cosmos is stressed also in the *Timaeus* (e.g. 90d4–7). To be sure, the phrase "meaning of life" has no strict equivalent in the Greek prose of Plato's time. The relevant phrase from the Platonic corpus, *telos biou*, means literally "purpose of life": that is, having a purpose in one's life. It can mean merely having what was called above meaning in life. Plato, however, bases his account of what is an adequate purpose in life on the objective evaluations of his ethics and his hierarchical conception of reality. Thus he suggests as our purpose aiming at what is objectively good. In Plato's view, this entails wanting to contribute to the goods of larger units. This conception gives content to the notion of "meaning of life."

The Platonic ideal, in the sense defined, gives meaning to life. Thus our ethical lives should center around the sustaining of this ideal. This will occasionally include formulating rules of conduct and applying these; but these are not the most fundamental ingredients in the project of sustenance. To sustain the Platonic ideal is analogous to sustaining interest in, for example, mathematics, music, or philosophy. It is to keep a certain orientation in our attitudes, beliefs, and activities. As we shall see, Plato's moral psychology and epistemology are geared to this task, rather than to formulating very general principles of conduct and applying these.

Within such an ethics, reason cannot be merely instrumental. It does not merely seek means to predetermined ends, but rather seeks insight into the fundamental elements of reality and, in view of such insights, sets aims for us. This is also how Joseph interprets Plato.[3] Taking passages like *Republic* 505d7–e1, he interprets Plato as thinking that human rationality at its best includes search for purpose and sense in reality. Furthermore, according to Plato, this rationality is imperishable and is separable from individuals. This causes problems for some interpreters. They complain about "the regrettable vacillation of Plato on the question of conscious personal life and its significance in the face of an all-embracing idea."[4] The answer to charges of vacillation, has been well stated by W. F. R. Hardie: "For the disembodied soul is without lower parts; and hence it would not have the function of exercising control over a human soul; hence the exercise of such control cannot be the essence of a rational soul."[5]

This sketch of ethical content points to a problem. Rationality is defined partly in terms of the correct setting of aims. But this notion, like all other cognitive notions in Plato, is defined objectually. Thus we move from rationality to its proper objects: the Forms and their interrelations which yield order and harmony. But what makes these objects and their inter-relations good and worthy of embodiment? As we have seen, part of the answer to this question lies in the fact that their nature makes them objects of genuine understanding. Thus we seem to have arrived at a "Platonic Circle": rationality defined partly in terms of the proper setting of aims, this defined in terms of a set of objects, and these defined in part in terms of their suitability as objects of understanding, and hence, rationality. In reply, the Platonist can take either of two routes. He can bite the bullet and say that this kind of circle is unavoidable; that here we have a collection of basic philosophical notions which can be explained only in terms of each other and which illuminate each other. Alternatively, he can say that the objects are also defined in terms of such properties as yielding order and harmony. So we still reach "rock bottom," but in another way. Within this conception we need to view the claim that order, harmony, and imperishability are good as analogous to axioms in a formal science. Other ethics also have axiom-like assumptions: for example, that enjoyment is good or that duty has an unconditional claim on us. These other assumptions deal with compartments of reality such as human psychology or human interaction. Plato's "axiom" deals with some of the most general features of reality. From his point of view, that is an advantage.

The last part of our discussion of ethical content touched on some properties of rationality and hence poached already on the domain of moral psychology. This is hardly surprising. Platonic ethics presents an ideal to be sustained. The ideal is for humans, hence it must assume some conditions governing human nature. Unless these are viable, the ideal may be beyond implementability for humans.

In turning to moral psychology, let us take up a few more threads concerning the setting of aims. This process is in part conscious, giving rise to conscious decisions and commitments, but in part a matter of development, taking place on the nonconscious level. Attitudes, dedication, orientation are complex matters and require nonconscious maturational periods just as much as do the development and exercise of basic intellectual capacities like reasoning or language development.

The aim-setting role of reason must be brought into harmony with another Platonic claim: namely, that reason can give rise to feelings and action. It is hardly controversial to hold that reason is a causal factor in the emergence of feelings and activities, but Plato wants a more direct link. For example, one might say that through the use of reason we discover that health sustains life; we have a built-in desire for the sustenance of life, so set ourselves the goal of maintaining health. This, in turn, is a matter of action. Plato would not deny that sequences of this sort occur. But he also wants a more immediate contact between reason and action. For him, it is a matter of understanding to realize that harmony and order are good. Thus when reason uncovers manifestations of these phenomena, Plato expects us to be immediately drawn to them. Once that happens, our attitudes and actions can be informed in virtue of such insights, in ways sketched already in chapter 3; for example, such insights allow us to formulate lists of qualities that warrant approval, admiration, respect, and so on. Having feelings and performing actions presuppose the capacity for desire and enjoyment. But reason will give the desire and enjoyments objects in the way just sketched.

We see this in everyday life in connection with the development of certain intellectual interests. A person studies mathematics, perceives the beauty of it, develops an interest in pursuing various facets of the subject, and orients his life, or at least part of it, towards this pursuit. His modes of enjoyment, some of his desires, and his conception of what is useful will be molded by this overall interest. As we said earlier, mathematics functions like a magnet, drawing the individual. It is very difficult to translate this account into a framework in which the basic notions are desire and instrumental reasoning. Can we say that a person has a general desire called, for example, "intellectual curiosity," and one day discovers that studying mathematics is a good means to satisfy his or her desire? This suggests that the person views mathematics as merely a means to satisfy an antecedently given desire. This does not seem to square with the phenomenology of intellectual life. When one is immersed in a subject, one will not give it up just because an expert psychologist predicts that another subject will be an even better means of satisfying an antecedently given desire. According to an alternative conception, one that we can associate with Plato without undue anachronism, we have a general capacity for developing intellectual interests. We can channel this into something shallow like solving crossword puzzles or something deeper. Reason and understanding present possible objects and evaluations thereof along relevant scales. Such presentations and evaluations evoke from us attitudes, feelings, desires, and action. When the interest disappears, for whatever reason, what we end up with is not just lack of enjoyment, or pain, but boredom. Interest and boredom are opposites, and so are enjoyment and either pain or plain lack of enjoyment. But these are distinct contrasting pairs, and Plato's moral psychology centers around the first, not the second. A person bored with intellectual battles is not a person who merely stops enjoying; rather, he is the weary "Don Juan" of intellectual encounters who does not enjoy them because he has become bored and can no longer summon the energy and interest to participate.

This moral psychology results in a very plastic conception of the non-cognitive aspects of human nature. Instead of a set of "basic," rigid needs and desires, Plato interprets what is in a sense "basic" as very general psychic capacities and energy waiting to be given orientation, objects, and modes of expression and manifestation.

When humans are functioning at their best, the proper objects and orientation will be given by conscious rational search for values in larger spheres of reality and their reflections in human lives. When we are at our worst, according to Plato, these tasks are not addressed in a conscious systematic way and are carried out unreflectively by beliefs, likes, and dislikes formed accidentally and left unexamined.

It is this extremely plastic view of human nature that is also responsible for the other crucial element in Plato's ethics: the drastic reorientation of humans with the wrong ideals. The typical encounter in the ethically oriented dialogues is not between people who calculated the good things and appropriate interactions in the right way and those who were mistaken in their calculations, but between those like Socrates who had the right ideal and others who embrace misguided ideals like hedonism, inordinate power, the desire for domination and such like. Plato asks of such people not only that they accept new rules of conduct, but also that they reorient their whole lives around a new ideal. This requires some restraint, but restraint and the adoption of new principles are not at the heart of the new ethical life that Plato demands. New insights and new interests have to be awakened, and then the plastic noncognitive capacities must be given new objects, new modes of expression. Such people must be "reprogrammed," as some might say today. The transformation of aims leads to a drastic transformation of the individual. It is not simply a case of the competitive individual restraining his aggressive tendencies; with some psychic work, he can become the kind of person who enjoys more cooperative and intellectual activities.

The difference between the more rigid and the more plastic conceptions of our appetitive nature can also be illustrated with respect to planning one's life. One can say, "Given that I have these likes and dislikes, these talents, these preferences, desires, and needs, what kind of life will give me the greatest satisfaction and enjoyment?" Alternatively, one can ask, "What things in life are really worth pursuing? Which of these are such that, with some effort, I can orient my life around them and let such orientation structure the objects for desires and attitudes and determine utility for me?" The second is the Platonic approach. The first seems more appropriate for contexts in which we are already fairly well settled and are considering more short-range goals. But even if not so much in professional philosophy, in everyday life today we repeatedly come up against the need for an ethics of reorientation; for example, in connection with drug or alcohol abuse or in confrontation with the fanatic.

The fact that within the Platonic framework, the overall setting of aims can affect any aspect or facet of human life helps to account for there not being any sharp distinction between moral and nonmoral qualities, or virtues, in Plato's theorizing . In a moral theory that upholds what was called earlier the autonomy thesis, there are moral virtues like honesty and fairness and nonmoral virtues like intelligence, being able to get along well with others, determination, and so on. They refer to distinct domains: the first with duties, the second with whatever is either a good means to or constitutive of our good. Within the Platonic scheme, having the right attitudes toward others and acting appropriately toward others come from sustaining the right ideal. To be sure, one could make a distinction among the Platonic virtues between those that affect our relationships with others and those that do not. But for Plato, this is not a crucial distinction. Above all, both kinds of virtues have the same source; there is no distinctive "moral" source for virtues like fairness. The source for all the virtues is the sustaining of the ideal of understanding the fundamental elements of reality and trying to mirror the order and harmony in oneself that one finds in the higher realms.

This brief sketch has revealed five points in Platonic moral psychology which, from the point of view of many contemporary moral philosophies, stand out as distinctive. The five are connected. First, humans are creatures who set aims. Their understanding of reality can cause feelings and attitudes to emerge. Secondly, reason has noninstrumental as well as instrumental roles. This follows from the first. Thirdly, since we can follow or become attracted to what pure reasoning reveals, our nature includes the psychic category of interest and orientation, notions that, within the Platonic framework, cannot be reduced to a combination of desire and belief. Moreover, having psychic elements like dominant interest and overall orientation playing a key role requires the fourth Platonic thesis: namely, what we have called the plasticity of human nature. This needs to be posited in order to allow orientations of very diverse sorts to have the power to restructure needs, desires, and conceptions of utility. Finally, within this and other similar conceptions of ethics, there will be no sharp distinction between moral and nonmoral virtues, in terms of either how a virtue functions or what its source is.

Within this theory, the question Why be moral? boils down to the question Why have an adequate ideal for ourselves? This assumes that there are objective, rational ways of assessing ideals which give these at least a partial ordering. If this is so, then the question about morality in the modern sense loses its bite. Once we have an adequate ideal, our reply will be: Why not?

The question Is it rational to be moral? is transformed into the question Is it rational to choose an ideal the sustenance of which includes the development and practice of cooperative virtues? Given the possibility of objective assessment of ideals, this question should admit of an answer; Plato thinks it is the affirmative.

Given the key points in the content of Platonic ethics and moral psychology that we have seen so far, we can formulate the key questions for Platonistic moral epistemology as follows: How do we come to understand what the adequate (or an adequate) ideal for humans is? and How do we know how to embody this ideal? These questions are very different from the sorts of questions that one might take to be fundamental to morality, such as How do we know the fundamental principle of our obligations? and How do we know how to apply this principle so as to yield more restricted ones which, eventually, will enable us to pass adequate judgments in particular cases?

The answer to the first question is found in the characterization of the kind of understanding and reasoning that were described in chapter 1 as entailing a dialectical cognitive process. The second question can be rephrased as: How do we know how to embody virtues?, since sustaining the Platonic ideal is not primarily a matter of applying more general moral principles to less general ones, but rather the development and maintenance of virtues. Within the Platonic scheme, virtues are complexes of concepts, beliefs, attitudes, feelings, and dispositions to act. Thus mere propositional knowledge and behavioral training or conditioning are not sufficient for acquiring and maintaining virtues. Plato's answer, as we know, is some form of "imitation." Given the developments in dialogues like the *Phaedo*, the *Meno*, and the *Republic*, we can interpret the required "imitation" in modern terms as role modeling. Role modeling involves selecting someone who exemplifies in high degree the virtues to be embodied and then modeling ourselves after such a person in the relevant respects. This process can be broken down into three tasks: (1) selecting the right role model; (2) perceiving the relevant aspects that are to be embodied in our lives; and (3) acquiring the relevant virtues as these are manifested in practical contexts.

Within Plato's philosophical psychology, the first two tasks are closely linked. As we have seen, Plato wants us to be able to see humans as participating in various virtues and other characteristics. If we agree with the admittedly difficult thesis that the kind of theoretical insight needed to understand the Forms will also enable us to recognize instances of these – more plausible in mathematics, more difficult in ethical contexts – then we select the appropriate person on the basis of his or her participating in certain Forms. Given this way of interpreting others and ourselves, it should not then be difficult to select the relevant aspects to be emulated. If we admire someone in the Platonically correct way, then we admire them for having qualities Q', Q'', and so forth. Thus we should be able to lock in on the appropriate quality in a given context.

The third task causes the Platonist the most difficulty. For even if one accepts the psychological and epistemological premises listed above, it is still unclear what it is that enables us to make our own the virtue we see well practiced by someone else. Theoretical insight and analysis of others in terms of their qualities may be necessary conditions for the acquisition, but, as Aristotle was not slow to point out, it is not very plausible to assume that they are jointly sufficient.

Still, role modeling is something that we occasionally do successfully in our lives. The notion may not be central to current professional philosophical discussions, but it is a key concept in discussions focusing on medical education, learning how to teach, and character building in general.

Role modeling requires cooperation among humans. It is best achieved in a communal setting; that is, among people with values that are at least partly shared. This brings us to another key feature of Platonic ethics: namely, the relation between the individual and the community. As we saw in chapter 3, Plato's view stands between individualism, which assigns intrinsic value only to individuals, and authoritarianism, which assigns intrinsic value only to the larger political unit. Given the notion that wholes have intrinsic value and that the world, at its best, mirrors a structure of smaller wholes making up larger wholes, Plato's scheme acknowledges the intrinsic value of both individuals and the community. The kinds of value and the extent of the autonomy assigned to either individual or community depends on the state in which one finds these elements. Furthermore, the attitude that connects members of the Platonic community is neither one of enlightened self-interest nor one of altruism, but a dedication to goodness and its instances in whatever form they may appear. Since this goodness involves harmony within whatever participates in it, it is not a mass notion like the enjoyment of the hedonist or the happiness of some utilitarians. Destroying some enjoyment in one person may increase enjoyment everywhere else in some rare cases, but destroying Platonic harmony will not increase harmony elsewhere.

Finally, pervading all these Platonic conceptions we find the distinction between appearance and reality. It is applied on different levels. Forms are reality, and the world of space and time, the appearances. Within that world, the underlying elements of human nature are more real, and the behavioral manifestations are the appearances. This explains why Plato's ethics is agent-centered rather than action-centered.[6] For actions are the surface manifestations of the underlying human character, and the Platonic ideal, as we have seen, is articulated in terms of conditions on the underlying character.

The reality–appearance dichotomy is not only a theoretical concept for Plato, but also a very practical one. Indeed, it is very easy to think of applications for it today. For example, it is said at times that news telecasts are a good thing because they help to spread information to large segments of the population. But a contemporary Platonist would immediately raise the question: What kind of information is being spread? And is it the kind that enables people to get at underlying realities rather than just being "dazzled" by appearances? For example, seeing a lot of action on television often obscures rather than helps our understanding of what ideas, tradition, thinking, and feeling underlie what people are doing. An obvious case is the appearance of a political candidate on the screen. This clearly gives more information than just hearing his voice over the radio; but the additional information may get in the way of a sound evaluation of the person's ideas and character. The same applies to televised war scenes. These show a lot of action and thus information one might not get in other ways, but often this prevents us from understanding the underlying causes of a war, rather than helping us to grasp these.

The last few reflections show us at one and the same time both the enormous difficulties of restating in contemporary terms the Platonic ethics of ideals and reorientation and the obvious relevance and applicability of such a theory to the problems of today.

In the next few sections, I shall prepare the way for such an undertaking. First, I will contrast the conception of goods in ideal ethics with conceptions of goods in Rawls's influential writings. Then I will consider themes from Bradley and Wittgenstein which, though leading to non-Platonic ideals, mirror in some striking ways some of what we singled out in this section as distinctive features of Plato's ethics, and in this sense are echoes of his thought. The fact that one should turn to these philosophers indicates already the flavor of the kind of philosophizing that genuine contemporary Platonistic ethics would have to embody.

Goods and Ideals

A philosopher might describe the human good as "happiness and whatever leads to it," or "whatever enables people to live a life of enjoyment." These are rather thin conceptions of the human good, since they do not contain a plurality of distinct elements. In contrast with these, Rawls's theory is a substantive theory of goods.[7] It contains descriptions of several kinds of goods. Some are primary, including self-respect and whatever is required for this good; others deal with the satisfaction of basic physical needs; and still others involve opportunities to develop our talents. Rawls's theory starts with generally agreed upon common sense, empirical conceptions of parts of human nature, and constructs a list of goods in light of this. In this respect it differs both from Plato and from many religious theories of goods. The latter start with assumptions about human nature that cannot be derived from common sense and are subject to controversy. Similar considerations apply to assumptions about the world in general. Rawls assumes a minimal layer of common sense, whereas the Platonist assumes his own view of reality.

As an illustration, let us look briefly at what Rawls says about happiness. He bases his conception of happiness not just on humans enjoying themselves but also on their developing their talents and capacities. In this respect, his conception is closer to classical ones like those of Plato and Aristotle than to, for example, hedonism. Rawls describes the happy person as one who is "in the way of a successful execution (more or less) of a rational life plan drawn up under (more or less) favorable conditions, and he is reasonably confident that his plan can be carried through."[8]

This characterization of happiness is consistent with what we have called the plasticity of human nature. It assumes that humans can plan and can have capacities for enjoyment and talents of various sorts as well. But it leaves open the question of how wide the range of enjoyments and capacities that humans can develop is. On the other hand, by leaving to rationality, defined in non-Platonistic ways, the role of constraining the range of plans, Rawls allows a far larger number of plans as rational than would Plato, and thus allows a far larger range of ways of achieving happiness.

More specifically, there are three key differences between Plato's and Rawls's conceptions of happiness. First, although Rawls requires a rational life plan for happiness, he does not link happiness to questions regarding meaning of life and special types of understanding, thus differing in this respect from Plato. Secondly, the notion of aim does not get "top billing" with Rawls, as it does with Plato. Rawls's conception of happiness is compatible with both the hypothesis that humans can have a wide variety of aims and be happy with these and the hypothesis that there are just two or three "basic things" that all humans aim at. Thirdly, nothing in Rawls's characterization of happiness ensures that the happy person will be cooperative and will behave towards others in acceptable ways. Plato, by contrast, thinks that one can derive cooperation from an adequate specification of happiness. Rawls, of course, would not regard this as a disadvantage of his conception. For he has a separate component – namely, morality – that acts as a constraint on ways in which we can realize our happiness. Plato, as we have seen, has no such separate component. Thus the topic of happiness is a good case for focusing on the difference between "two-stage" moral philosophies like Rawls's and the unitarian conception that thinkers like Plato advocate. As we shall discover later, the two types of moral philosophy can be seen as attempts to answer different fundamental questions.

The conception of happiness in both Rawls and Plato includes developing some of our distinctively human capacities. But the two philosophers give different answers to the question of why this should be so. For Plato, such developments fit into the larger picture of harmony, order, and appropriate functioning through the various layers of reality. Rawls, on the other hand, links such developments to certain kinds of enjoyments via what he calls an "Aristotelian principle," which says: "Other things being equal, human beings enjoy the exercise of their realized capacities (their innate or trained abilities) and this enjoyment increases the more the capacity is realized, or the greater its complexity."[9] The Platonist would say that this is true only of people with certain character structures, and that it helps humans only if they have the right conception of which capacities should be developed and which ones should not. Again, Rawls wants a very broad principle, consistent with the realization of many life plans, rational in his sense. Plato – and later, Aristotle – want something more restricted. But this is partly because, for them, this principle must contribute to a well-functioning human who is also "moral" in the modern sense of the term.

Another important notion for Rawls, as has been mentioned, is that of "primary goods." The key element among such goods is self-respect. This notion has for Rawls two aspects. It "includes a person's sense of his own value, his secure conviction that his conception of his good, his plan of life, is worth carrying out. And secondly, self-respect implies a confidence in one's ability, so far as it is within one's power, to fulfill one's intentions."[10] From this we see that self-respect is an important motivating factor for Rawls. "Without it nothing may seem worth doing, or if some things have value for us, we lack the will to strive for them."[11] Rawls sees self-respect as also helping towards the appreciation of others. "One who is confident in himself is not grudging in the appreciation of others."[12] As this account shows, self-respect does not depend on the respect that others may or may not have for us. Socrates presumably had Rawlsian self-respect, even if very few people in Athens respected him. At the same time, this kind of self-respect psychologically prepares the ground for the respect of others, and thus eventually for fairness. If we appreciate others, it is easier to start reflecting on what, if any, intrinsic value they have.

Rawlsian self-respect, as the quotes show, is an individualistic virtue. The respect that I develop towards myself is respect for me, the individual. It is not primarily respect towards a certain kind of being. In this way, this notion of self-respect differs from respect in a Platonistic scheme. For the Platonist, the first question would be: In virtue of what characteristics am I justified in having respect for myself? Once we had answered this question adequately, Plato would insist that a rational person should generalize. If I deserve respect from me in virtue of certain characteristics, then everyone with those characteristics, *ceteris paribus*, deserves my respect. If self-respect is interpreted as respect towards the agent as a unique individual, then there is no room for it in the Platonic scheme. If it is interpreted as a quality-dependent attitude, then it is "earned" by all those people who possess those qualities.

This contrast bring us to another key notion in ethics: namely, rationality. Rawls describes the instrumental roles of reason, and also rationality, as these contribute to the notion of a rational life plan in the following way: "A rational person should be able to see which are the effective means for carrying out her life plans."[13] Such plans involve rational choice. "A rational choice involves preferring plan A to another if the first includes all that B can realize and some other desirable objectives."[14] Furthermore, "a rational choice must include matters of likelihood."[15] These remarks yield basically the conception of instrumental reason that emerges from the literature of rational decision making in economic contexts. We must consider means, value distribution, value inclusion, partial ordering, and likelihood distributions.

One of the shortcomings of Plato's discussions of rationality is that he does not devote much thought to the instrumental role of reason. Is it that he did not have it worked out, or that, given his main project of sustaining and reorienting ideals he did not deem it to be of much importance? We will never know; his pupil Aristotle was not slow to fill the gap.

Rawls's other conditions on rationality are linked to what it is for a life plan to be rational. The following conditions must hold: "(i) It is one of the plans that is consistent with the principles of rational choice when these are applied to all relevant features of his situation, and (ii) it is that plan among those meeting this condition which would be chosen by him with full deliberative rationality, that is, with full awareness of the relevant facts and after a careful consideration of the consequences."[16] The first condition shows that the agent choosing a rational life plan must see intrinsic value in certain cognitive processes, such as consistency and consideration of relevance. The second condition places key value on the notion of "full deliberative rationality." The two conditions jointly would not rule out the Platonic idea; at the same time, they include a great deal more than that.

If we look at this characterization and compare it with Platonic epistemology, as discussed in chapter 1, we see why Plato could not have given Rawls's account. For, as we saw, Plato characterizes rationality in relation to objects. Rawls's characterization, like most modern characterizations, is procedural. Plato describes reason and insight as what establish contact between us and the Forms. To be sure, he would add that the process requires the construction and understanding of proofs, definitions, and so on. But for Plato these are just addenda. For Rawls, by contrast, these are the core of the characterization. Rationality is induction, deduction, recognition of relevance, and reflection on the state in which one is as decisions are being made.

This contrast also helps to explain the difference between Rawls's reflective deliberative state and Plato's notion of wisdom. In the state described by Rawls we can consider any problem, plan, or task, and should be able to come up with as rational a verdict as possible under the given circumstances. Plato's notion of wisdom is like hitting the mark in bringing ourselves into the right relation with the rest of reality, rather than a set of procedures that help us to approximate a certain state of mind that is necessary regardless of the objects of cognition at any given time.

These remarks also help set the stage for looking at another difference between Rawls and Plato. Rawls's conception of rationality is metaphysically neutral, whereas Plato's is not. This is part of a larger point that Rawls stresses; he says that in general his ethics does not invoke metaphysical or religious principles.[17] To be sure, pedantic readers would insist that this is not strictly speaking true. Rawls's list of goods presupposes time, space, human bodily existence, certain psychic states, and so forth. But within a sympathetic reading it is clear what Rawls has in mind. His ethics is neutral with regard to such metaphysical issues as dualism, materialism, nominalism, and the like, and it is also neutral with regard to such issues as atheism, agnosticism, and theism.

Rawls and many others would regard this feature of his ethics as a distinct advantage. It is easy to see why. Just as his moral theory is independent of different conceptions of the human good and can thus serve as a common ground for people with different aims, conceptions of goods, needs, and so on, so the theory of primary goods and rationality can serve as a common ground for people with different metaphysical and religious views.

Would Plato think, if confronted with the alternative just sketched, that his not being metaphysically neutral is a disadvantage? Should he think so? There is no simple answer to these questions. Rawls's project and Plato's project are very different. Plato, as has been stressed already, wants to formulate an ethics of correct ideal specification, sustaining of ideals, and ways in which humans can drastically reorient their lives. It is difficult to see how one can have an ethics of this sort which is metaphysically neutral. Ethics of this kind involves seeing the world in a certain way. Presumably those who accept the ethics in question think that this way is the right way. Rawls's type of ethics, on the other hand, serves our needs when the problem is to work out satisfactory ways of cooperation among people with very diverse conceptions of human nature and goodness and diverse world views. Plato admits some variety, but as we have seen, this is merely surface variety. As to deep underlying differences between people, Plato's only response would be: education. But can this really meet all the concerns that Rawls attempts to address? At the same time, can we really be content without a viable ethics relating to the choosing of ideals and possible drastic reorientation?

Many readers may find these sketchy remarks comparing themes in Rawls and Plato unsatisfactory. They may claim that either one should single out just one or two themes and give these detailed treatment or one should not make the comparison at all – hence the need to stress the aim of this section. This is not to compare in a detailed way Rawls and Plato or to settle who is right about any given topic like rationality or happiness, but rather to show that a certain way of articulating comparative ethics is wrong. According to that approach we can assume that there are fixed concepts central to any ethics or moral theory, such as rationality, happiness, lists of goods, and so forth and then compare different philosophies partly in terms of how successfully they deal with these topics. But my admittedly sketchy comparison shows that this cannot be done. Rawls and Plato have different questions at the core of their ethical philosophizing, hence different projects are outlined by them. Notions like rationality, happiness, and so on do not remain fixed across the two projects. Rather, they are given different interpretations within the two different enterprises. Neither set of conceptions is either psychologically or metaphysically incoherent. Can we join them in one picture? I shall say a few things about this at the end. In the meantime, I shall turn to themes in two philosophers who were closer to Plato in philosophical orientation than either Rawls or other Anglo-American philosophers working in utilitarian or Kantian traditions.

Plato and Bradley on our "Stations"

It would hardly be an exaggeration to say that today F. H. Bradley is not widely read by professional philosophers in England or America. This is not only because he linked ethics to metaphysics; it is also because in his metaphysics he was an idealist, and a modern statement of Eleatic monism is no more likely to gather support in today's technologically successful society than it did in the Greek world of Plato. Yet, if what was argued in Part II of this book is roughly correct, Bradley's approach to metaphysics is more like Plato's than the approaches of contemporary realists like Moore and Russell. Plato and the Eleatics had an intellectual bond; they agreed on what the crucial questions for philosophy were, and they looked for the most general explanatory structures. Furthermore, they saw the most fundamental issue in ethics as being to find the right place for humans in the larger scheme of things. They carried out this project in different ontological settings, but with the same orientation. They would agree that a person who has found his station in life and who understands the larger reality of which he is a part will do what are ordinarily regarded as the morally appropriate things.

As we shall see, in very broad terms both Plato and Bradley worked out what is called in this book an ideal ethics, but the contexts within which they did so are quite different. Bradley wrote in the second half of the nineteenth and the first part of the twentieth century in conscious opposition to what he took to be the two dominant ethical theories of his time: the utilitarianism of Bentham and Kant's deontic ethics. A full-scale treatment of Bradley's ethics would have to include not only its echoes of Plato, but also his acute criticisms of these rival schools, which cannot be attempted within the confines of this book. Plato, by contrast, did not have fully worked out versions of utilitarianism and deontic ethics in front of him, but rather, hedonistic versions of utilitarianism. Yet even these are interpreted in the dialogues as versions, albeit very inadequate ones, of ideal ethics. Ultimately, for Plato, the question to be raised about the hedonist is not: Does he have an adequate analysis of what we mean by "good"?, but rather, How does the human who is basically just pleasure-seeking fit into the larger structure of reality? Can such a person really find meaning and purpose in life? The Platonic discussions of ethics give us even fewer clues about how he would argue against a philosopher like Kant. His objections must be mostly a matter of reconstruction.

On the basis of this preamble and the differences drawn, I shall concentrate on three points at which similarities between Plato and Bradley can be seen as setting them apart from mainstream modern thought.

1 Like Plato, Bradley sees the human ideal as having an adequate understanding of reality and finding one's proper place within it.
2 Like Plato, Bradley sees human beings as essentially social creatures who require communal ties for the full realization of worthy human potentialities and, in particular, require communal interaction in order to find their "station" as sketched in (1). Like Plato, too, he interprets attaining the right human ideal as involving being members of the right kinds of communities, and such communities are more than mere sums of parts.
3 Like Plato, Bradley sees all virtues as forming an integrated field, without a basic dichotomy between moral and nonmoral ones.

To be sure, Bradley places less stringent intellectual demands on humans than Plato does. But he does think that a good human must find the proper place for members of humanity in reality, and, like Plato, he sees the reality of appearances as organized into wholes which make up larger wholes.[18] When we attain this state, Bradley thinks we are realizing both human potential at its best and the moral good.[19] As I have already pointed out, ultimately Bradley's idealism and Plato's theory of Forms present us with different ontologies. But, as applied to human experience and especially the ethical, there is a resemblance not only with respect to the general point already made, but also in the emphasis on harmony as a key criterion both internally within the individual and externally in the relations hips the individual has with others.

The term "self-realization" that Bradley uses occasionally can easily be misunderstood. For some people it means that we start with a conception of human psychological and physical needs, presumably determined empirically, and then describe the human good and the fulfillment of these needs. Then we try to show that this will also bring with it morally appropriate conduct. But this is neither Plato's nor Bradley's scheme. This conception is in conflict with what we called the "plasticity of human nature," a conception subscribed to by both Plato and Bradley. According to their view, the self is not fixed except in terms of broadly defined capacities. It is given determinate structure in different humans only according to their overall aims and aspirations. Furthermore, these character- and self-determining elements depend on our relations to other elements of reality: in particular, to certain possible objects of thought. Thus one should not assimilate their type of ideal ethics to the kind of self-realizationist ethics mentioned above.

There is an obvious link between points 1 and 2 above. If our overall aim should be to fit into larger structures of reality, it is not surprising that both Plato and Bradley assume that all human beings have one of the key underlying capacities required for this task: namely, being essentially social, in the sense articulated above. Given the general metaphysical view already sketched, the communities of which we are parts are wholes, and as such have a value and a station of their own, and some of our communal relations are as essential to our being humans as the more individual ones.[20] But Plato and Bradley differ on the psychological sources of this communality.

For Bradley, the psychological source of communality lies in basic natural organizations like the family.[21] In that context, at its best, we see the flourishing of love, care, concern, and respect. Furthermore, the manifestation and development of these capacities need not take place always on the conscious level. Bradley takes the complex state of being part of a well-functioning family as psychologically fundamental. He also realizes that this is a very complex state, involving many layers of feelings, attitudes, conceptions, and activities. He does not think that all this can be extended to large segments of humanity with which we are in contact. But he thinks that some layers of the complex state of being a family can be taken out of that context and extended towards all our fellow human beings. This extension of parts of familial ties is, according to Bradley, an essential part of finding our station in life.

Plato's account of the psychology of communal ties is much more intellectual. The core unit for him is not the family, but a group of intelligent beings gathered on the basis of certain shared values and engaged in the realization of these. Bradley sees not only intellectual but also emotional ties as crucial. Plato would agree, but he would concentrate on the emotions that evolve among co-workers as they jointly tackle an intellectually demanding problem. Plato is aware of the fact that such a community cannot exist on a large scale, never mind globally. But he thinks that some of these attitudes and activities of cooperation can be extended to all potential "recollectors" and thus to all humanity. Thus we see that although they start with different basic units and different cognitive and emotional complexes, both philosophers have a major "extension problem" at the heart of their moral psychologies.

Bradley thinks that having the right communal relations is part of happiness.[22] Thus, for him, happiness and the cooperative moral and social virtues do not constitute two separate categories. This leads us to the third main point of comparison: namely, the "unitarian" view of human virtues. Bradley says that for him all virtues are moral virtues, taking his notion of "moral."[23] He admits that one can distinguish social from nonsocial virtues, but this distinction does not, for him, have important moral significance. Striving for truth, for example, is for Bradley a nonsocial virtue; but it has the same moral worth as any of the social ones. Bradley echoes Plato's "unitarianism," but in a different terminology.

It is difficult to decide whether the difference between Plato and Bradley on this point is merely terminological. Plato would agree with Bradley that striving for truth is as much a virtue, constitutive of an adequate ideal, as any of the more socially oriented ones – and if anything, even more so. Furthermore, Plato recognizes the distinction between social and nonsocial virtues, just as Bradley does. The difference turns on the modern English word "moral" and whatever one might pick as the equivalent word or phrase in classical Greek. If one associates the modern English word with a theory of a special moral faculty – that is, uniquely moral beliefs, motivation, commitments – then there is a genuine difference between Plato and Bradley. For on that view, Bradley is saying that we have two different sources of motivation and attitude: the striving towards happiness and a distinctively moral source, but that we can bring the two into harmony. According to Plato, there is only one source for the virtues: insight into reality and the resulting desire to find one's proper place. Both philosophers recognized the importance of duties. What is unclear is whether either of them thought that the underlying motives have a different source from other motives underlying the striving for excellence. One can believe that there are different motivational sources even if one rejects – as I assume both Plato and Bradley did – the claim of "duty for duty's sake."

Different ways of thinking about morality and virtues are partly accounted for by differences in philosophical psychology. Bradley's psychology is voluntaristic; that is, he postulates a separate psychological element called the will, which plays a fundamental role in decision making in general and in our moral lives in particular.[24] To be sure, both Plato and Bradley would draw a distinction between the voluntary – that is, what is up to us to do or not to do – and the involuntary or nonvoluntary – that is, what is not up to us to do or not to do and yet is an action in the ordinary sense. One can draw, this distinction in different ways, however. It does not require a voluntaristic psychology. A voluntaristic psychology attempts to answer the question of what happens when we decide on something that is neither a matter of pure rationality nor a matter of our needs and desires. Of course, this already presupposes that there are situations that can best be described in those terms. Some of these situations are aspects of our religious lives, as interpreted within the Judeo-Christian tradition: for example, Abraham on Mount Moriah. Thus it is not surprising that Plato would have little, if any, interest in such cases. Bradley assumes that there are moral dilemmas in which ultimately we need to exercise will, above and beyond letting reason and our desires influence our choices. Thus he believes that goodness is ultimately a matter of having the right kind of will. For Plato, there is no need to introduce this element into psychology. Reason is the light and magnet, and the emotions and desires, if all goes well, will be attracted to the right things and structures accordingly. Within Bradley's scheme, one can explain what Abraham did on Mount Moriah; within Plato's scheme, such a thing is incomprehensible.[25]

These brief remarks suggest the value of examining a variety of ideal ethics. Perhaps in an age in which ideal ethics was one of the main schools represented by professional philosophers, one would not view the features we have seen in Bradley as distinctive Platonic echoes. But the three points sketched above do show, by contrast with modern thought, affinities in orientation. The differences should serve only to stress the fact that ideal ethics admits of a wide variety.

Some Elements in Wittgenstein's Ethical Outlook

On the surface, Wittgenstein's thought would seem to be an unpromising area for mining and finding nuggets resembling Plato's wisdom. One associates Wittgenstein with an anti-metaphysical stance and with the view that philosophy should be primarily descriptive and not produce theories about reality and knowledge. Furthermore, Wittgenstein did not write a treatise on ethics. We have to put together a picture of his ethical outlook from a large number of fragmentary remarks. Still, when one looks at the various remarks, one can see the outlines of a view that resembles Plato's in certain ways, especially when one contrasts both with mainstream trends in contemporary moral philosophy. In this brief survey, four points of similarity will be covered:

1   For Wittgenstein, ethics is not an autonomous discipline dealing solely with duties and obligations, but a view of life in general and of the meaning that we can find in our lives.
2   The meaning of life that we can discover involves finding our place in the larger scheme of things.
3   Wittgenstein's moral epistemology includes a notion of "seeing as" that resembles the outlook Plato thinks we gain once we have reached the theoretical insight that Plato values so highly.
4   Both Plato and Wittgenstein believe, albeit on the basis of different considerations, that philosophy can help humans in their daily lives and in their struggles to find meaning in life.

We shall take up these topics one by one. As an introduction to Wittgenstein's view of ethics, let us consider a quote from a lecture he gave in the academic year 1929–30.[26]

Having quoted G. E. Moore on what ethics is – a quote that represents what would have been then, and still is today, a standard academic conception – he says that he wants to use "ethics" in a wider sense.

Now instead of saying "Ethics is the inquiry into what is good", I could have said Ethics is the inquiry into what is valuable, or, into what is really important, or I could have said Ethics is the inquiry into the meaning of life, into what makes life worth living, or into the right way of living.[27]

We need to interpret the "right" of the last clause in the context of the whole series of assertions. Wittgenstein does not mean by "right" distinctly moralistic, but rather, a way of life that makes sense, embodies what is valuable, and leads to dealing with other people in appropriate ways. What ties these three conditions together is the meaning that one can find in life. Wittgenstein uses "meaning of life" in the objective sense mentioned above. We make sense of our lives by finding life's (objective) meaning.

This combination of the objective sense or importance, the (objectively) valuable, and the appropriate interpersonal relations indeed echoes the similar combination in Plato's ethics. For Plato, too, finding purpose in our lives leads to having cooperative relationships with others.

Yet there is an important difference. For Socrates and Plato, as is often noted, the unexamined life is not worth living. An implication of this is that the ethical life must be an examined life. For Wittgenstein too, the unethical life is not worth living, but this is not because it is likely to be an unexamined life. As we shall see, the kind of insight that Wittgenstein interprets as being involved in finding meaning in our lives is far less intellectual and theoretically oriented than what Plato has in mind.

According to Wittgenstein, the insight that helps us to find meaning in our lives can be experienced in certain ways that do not involve an intellectual grasp of all reality. Talking about such experiences, he says:

I believe that the best way of describing it is to say that when I have it I wonder at the existence of the world. And I am inclined to use such phrases as "how extraordinary that the world should exist." I will mention another experience straight away which I also know and which others of you might be acquainted with: it is, what one might call, the experience of feeling absolutely safe. I mean the state of mind in which one is inclined to say: "I am safe, nothing can injure me, whatever happens."[28]

Or again:

And I now describe the experience of wondering at the existence of the world by saying, it is the experience of seeing the world as a miracle.[29]

There are both Platonic and non-Platonic elements in these quotations. The feeling of safety and of being immune to injury is reminiscent of self-sufficiency, one of the Platonic marks of the right ideal. But Platonic self-sufficiency is the independence from all external factors of a human who is dedicated to a life of seeking understanding. It requires much preparation and knowledge. In this respect it differs from what Wittgenstein describes. Wittgenstein's feeling of safety can also be experienced by people who do not have a predominantly intellectual orientation. Secondly, there is the similarity between Wittgenstein's wonder at the world and Plato's wonder at harmony in the most abstract and fundamental structures. But again, Wittgenstein's wonder is not based on a thoroughgoing understanding of the relevant disciplines. His describing the world as miraculous suggests that he sees it in a light that is beyond rational explanation, even if not against it.

We can sum up the differences by turning to the dichotomy of "aristocratic" versus "democratic" world views. The aristocratic world view requires extensive preparation, which is typically intellectual. It also requires special talent; for example, above-average intelligence. The democratic world view is accessible to all humans with normal cognitive and emotional make-up. In terms of this dichotomy, Plato has an aristocratic world view, and Wittgenstein a democratic one. Wittgenstein's wonderment at the world neither requires nor excludes knowledge of chemistry, biology, physics, and philosophical theories. It requires that we view the world in terms of features that are given in common sense, but view it in a special way. We shall return to the epistemology of this later.

Given that Plato and Wittgenstein had different conceptions of what it takes to see the world in the right way, it is not surprising that they had different ideals. Of course, this description presupposes that both had versions of ideal ethics. Showing this is made more difficult by the fact, mentioned already, that Wittgenstein did not write a sustained philosophical piece on ethics – unless one takes the *Tractatus*, on a certain reading, that way.

Wittgenstein does use the word "ideal" in his ethical reflections. He wrote in 1929: "My ideal is a certain coolness. A temple providing a setting for the passions without meddling with them."[30] This by itself does not rule out the possibility that Wittgenstein's use of "ideal" and the use of this term in the phrase "ideal ethics" is mere verbal coincidence. The quote, after all, does not say anything about setting aims or any required character. Still, it does hold up to us a certain ideal character or personality structure – to be sure, more of a Stoic than a Platonic one. The "coolness" of this quote hardly sounds like the eros of the *Symposium*.

When we place this quote side by side with some of the earlier ones, we collect several ingredients of an ideal ethics. There is the stress on the meaning of life, on seeing the world in the right way, and on a certain character or personality structure. It is not clear, however, how the third is linked to the other two. There are other texts, however, which show that Wittgenstein construes the ethical life as a matter of activities, concepts, beliefs, and attitudes interwoven so as to constitute what he calls a "form of life."[31] This gives us the link between the three ingredients, though without the stress on overall aim and orientation.

Does this interpretation of Wittgenstein's outlook fit what he says about various psychological traits and happiness? Certainly his remarks on these topics show just as much aversion to both Kantian and utilitarian ethics as does Bradley's ethical thought. Still, there are also un-Platonic elements in these characterizations. For example, we find the following comment on wisdom, written in 1947: "Wisdom is grey; life, on the other hand, and religion, are full of colours."[32] This seems to be in harmony with what he wrote about happiness in 1948: "Man's greatest happiness is love."[33] But it is not clear that Wittgenstein held a consistent view on these matters throughout his life. Earlier he wrote: "To be happy is to be in agreement with the world."[34] This sounds more other-worldly than the later comments.

It seems that Wittgenstein does not have a hedonistic or simply satisfaction-based conception of either happiness or human character and its good. On the other hand, happiness, character, and finding meaning in life are not linked as closely as in Plato. Nor is there much about setting aims and overall orientation. Given Wittgenstein's views on metaphysics, one could hardly expect to find in his writings a sketch of overall orientation for humans given in metaphysical terms like in Plato or Bradley. At the same time, his conception of happiness is in harmony with an ideal of self-sufficiency; it does not depend on projects that would require favorable external circumstances over long periods of time.[35]

In summary, one can say that Wittgenstein's ethics has some but not all the ingredients of ideal ethics. Instead of being focused on the setting of aims, Wittgenstein's ethics includes a "democratic" way of finding meaning in life and having a satisfactory conception of the world from the ethical point of view, as well as at least a partial characterization of desirable human character structures. These ingredients function as constraints within which people with diverse aims – and many perhaps with only a series of short-range aims – can build up lives that are worth living.

Wittgenstein's remarks on ethics do not suggest a conception of morality as a deductive system of rules with a few basic principles. Nor is it a conception that involves simply developing a series of dispositions to act properly. At the heart of his remarks is a conception of humans seeing the world in the right way and through this finding meaning in life. This suggests as the key element in Wittgenstein's moral epistemology the notion of "seeing as"; for example, seeing the world as a miracle. If this interpretation is sound, then this epistemology is an echo of Platonic moral epistemology, in which, as we have seen, this notion plays a fundamental role – for example, seeing another human as a participant in a number of Forms. This epistemic state is analogous to what we find in interpreting objects of aesthetic appreciation. One can look at a picture twice, with no additional information in one's mind at the second look, yet see more structure, order, and arrangement of parts the second time. We find the same phenomenon in the famous example of the picture that can be seen as a duck or as a rabbit, without additional information influencing one's change of perception. That is the way, it seems, one turns from a perception of the world as an environment to be used and interacted with to its perception as wonder and a miracle. The notion applies also to more restricted moral contexts. We may see a man as a business competitor for years, and then, suddenly, we see him also as a worried father with two teenage children. We see and treat someone as a successful professional and then realize that she should also be viewed as someone's daughter or mother.

It seems, then, that Plato and Wittgenstein are closer in terms of moral epistemology than they are in terms of the respective ideals that they sketch. Still, as regards their overall philosophies, there are many important differences.[36] This, too, drives home a lesson; ideal ethics, or at least ethics with many ingredients of that approach, can emerge in widely different philosophical contexts. Wittgenstein's moral psychology is voluntaristic.[37] This may be linked to his life-long struggle with Christianity and Christian conceptions, since Christian moral psychology is voluntaristic, the will being the psychological anchor for religious faith.

To conclude, the main benefit of comparing Wittgenstein's remarks on ethics with Plato's is that it enables us to see that the denial of what we called the autonomy thesis for morality need not lead to ideal ethics as defined, but can also lead to an ethics that has many, but not all, of the ingredients of ideal ethics. Understanding this enlarges our vista of the possibilities for ethical thought.

We have also noted that both Wittgenstein and Plato thought that their respective philosophies could help people lead better lives.[38] Wittgenstein thinks that this is made possible by helping people to see the world in the right way and to reflect on that "form of life" which is the ethical. It takes more interpretation to show that, albeit in a different way, Plato, too, thought that his philosophizing could help us with concrete problems. We shall turn to this topic now.

Plato on Insight and Action

As will be shown, the conceptual structure of some dialogues helps us to see how understanding fundamental elements of reality can, according to Plato, help us to solve concrete problems of morality and excellence. Our two examples will be the *Phaedo* and the *Republic*. In both these dialogues we see two structures at work: the conceptual and the dramatic. The dramatic includes interludes, attention to the personalities of the inter-locutors, and so forth. One cannot expect complete isomorphism between the conceptual and the dramatic, but the two in fact complement each other.

The *Phaedo* starts with a concrete question: "How shall Socrates die?" This is shown to lead immediately to the question: "How should a human die?" Reason generalizes. The generalization justifies the correct answer to the concrete question. For the Platonist, however, the generalization cannot include inadequately understood notions. Thus the second question leads immediately to an examination of what it is to be a human. In the ensuing discussion of human nature, body and soul are distinguished, and there follows an examination of the notion of death as bodily decay, leaving open the question of psychic survival.

This initial consideration of human nature leads to an examination of reason, since this is the most fundamental ingredient in the human psyche. Reason, however, is specified in terms of its objects. In this way, starting with the question of how Socrates should die, we arrive at the characteriza-tion of the Forms, the objects of knowledge and the most fundamental elements of reality. Within the dome-like structure of the *Phaedo* (see figure 8.1) this is the highest level. The heart of the dialogue contains an extended discussion of the nature of the Forms, their explanatory roles and interrelations.

With an adequate conception of reality as the background, we can now return to the notion of immortality and give what seems to Plato to be an adequate proof of the imperishability of reason, or rationality. Since this proof presupposes the theory of Forms, it can be given only at this "descending" state of the dialogue.

From this point, the dialogue descends even further, to the level of individuality. Myth and speculation are presented about individual survival. Since genuine knowledge in this sphere is not attainable, only this kind of conjectural story is appropriate. Finally, we return to our original question. With Socrates and humanity placed in their proper places within the larger scheme of things, we now know how this wise human is to die. The final, concrete answer is neither theoretical insight nor conjecture, but action. The right action is the choice of the agent who understands reality and has found purpose in his life. Aristotle's view that the final conclusion of a practical syllogism is action must have had its roots in the Stagirite's pondering of the structure of the *Phaedo*. Adequate understanding brings the soul into a healthy state and hence to the right action.

The dome-like structure shows the movement from the individual to the general and from the general to the abstract. One the way down, we go through the process in reverse, but now with adequate understanding, and hence fewer stops.

Two interludes, containing summaries, objections, and side issues,

(5) Existence, nature of Forms, immortality (72e–105b) Interludes: 77a–78b, 80c–95a	(6) Forms; as explanations, their interrelations (95a–105b)
(4) Accounts of immortality (69e–72e)	(7) Final argument for immortality (105b–107b)
(3) Reflections on human nature (64c–69e)	(8) Myth, speculation on afterlife (107c–115a)
(2) How should a rational human die? (62c–64c)	(9) How Socrates dies (117–118)
(1) How should Socrates die? (57a–62b)	

Figure 8.1 The Dome-like Structure of the *Phaedo*

interrupt the most difficult part of the dialogue: namely, the exposition of the theory of the Forms. The audience needs rest between passages dealing with the heart of the Platonic conceptual revolution.

The link between the last scene and the preceding sections can be easily misunderstood. The section on speculations about individual survival is not supposed to be a "pie in the sky" message to make the individual less fearful in the face of death. It is merely a secondary addendum to the main passage that places Socrates and human nature within the proper ontological framework. As Socrates faces death, his assurance is not that of personal survival but rather the firm conviction that his goodness contributed to making this a better world. This gives Socrates the quiet contentment that comes from seeing sense and value in one's life, despite its finiteness and other limitations.

The movement from the individual to the general and then to the abstract, followed by the reverse process is also found in the structure of the *Republic* (see figure 8.2).[39] This dialogue starts out with the question of what right living ("justice") is and shows quickly that this notion cannot be captured by behavioral codes prescribing that one should pay back one's

(6) Nature of the Forms, static similes of light (Book 6, 506d–end)

(5) The right ideal articulated in light of the theory of Forms (Book 6)

(4) The Forms and their intelligibility (Book 5, 475b–end)
Interlude (449a–475b)

(3) Human nature and the right ideal (Book 4, 436a–445b)

(2) Reflection on the right ideal for individuals and institutions (Books 2–4)

(1) Right living on the level of the individual: as a code? as a drive for power? Inadequacies presented (Book 1)

(7) Nature of the Forms and education; dynamic simile (Book 7)

(8) Types of life: individual and communal; final evaluations (Books 8 and 9)

(9) Discussions of matters pertaining to the individual and sensible art and immortality (Book 10, to 614a)

(10) Mythical speculation (Book 10, 614a–end)

Figure 8.2 The Dome-like Structure of the *Republic*

debts and so on, for such dicta are at once too concrete and too rigid. It moves on to consider the building of ideals, starting with a consideration of the worst ideal: namely, that of the power-hungry individual.

After the ideal of power has been shown to be defective, the discussion moves up a level to consider the general question of the healthy human individual in the healthy society. The proper human ideal, however, cannot be spelled out without an account of human nature. Thus human nature and the right ideal are spelled out in Book 4. Since the Platonic ideal centers on increase in knowledge, its description leads to the question of what knowledge is. As we have seen, this is discussed near the end of Book 5. As in the *Phaedo*, so here, knowledge and understanding are characterized in terms of their objects – hence the move from epistemology to ontology. The highest level in the dome-like construction is found in Books 6 and 7, in which the theory of Forms is developed. Arguments are mixed with similes, since Plato is talking about basic undefinable elements and relations.

Education and freedom within the Platonic conception, can be spelled out only against the background of the theory of Forms. Education enables us to realize the human ideal, since it leads to the understanding of the Forms, and this is an essential aspect of the ideal. With that ideal in mind, we are in a position to survey and grade different types of communal and individual lives. In the end, the right kind of life is shown to be superior, even by vulgar standards of success. These discussions take place in Books 8 and 9. The dialogue then moves on to an evaluation of the plastic and descriptive arts, showing these not to be about genuine elements of reality; thus they play, at best, a secondary positive or, more likely, a negative role in the community. Finally, we descend to the level of the individual. Mythical speculation is presented about an afterlife, since genuine knowledge about individual fates is impossible.

Unlike the *Phaedo*, the *Republic* does not have a concrete situation as its focus. Hence the dialogue does not end with an action. Still, at the beginning, we encounter questions raised at the level of the individual. The question of Thrasymachus's ideal, however, is turned quickly into questions about the human ideal and human nature. Once more, we move from the level of the individual to the level of generality. In the middle core of the dialogue, we arrive at the level of the abstract and the fundamental. With this as the background, we descend once more to the level of the general, taking up the individual, speculatively, only at the end. The myth is once more in a subordinate position; it concerns that with regard to which we can only speculate, since the objects are not on a high enough level to be objects of Platonic knowledge and understanding. These structures, then, show us how understanding reality and all its realms and being able to place ourselves within this scheme enable us to find answers to such questions as how to die and how to make use of education to distinguish better and worse life-styles.

Companing Plato and Wittgenstein on the issue of how philosophy helps people in their daily struggles, Plato's way seems more difficult to reconstruct in today's world. The main reason for this is that we are less confident of being able to detect the kind of order and harmony that Plato thought he had discovered on a cosmic scale and are less sure about how one would apply such an order to human life, even if this order could be recovered in Platonic terms. It is difficult to make "operational" (as one might put it today) the Platonic move from the cosmic to the individual and the communal. Wittgenstein's way is not easy either; the will and the sensitivity required to see the world as a miracle do not fit easily into the list of capacities and abilities in terms of which people ordinarily regard themselves as successful in a technologically oriented society. There is, however, a very practical element in the thoughts of both philosophers which people in all ages should wish to incorporate in their lives as a key ingredient. This is the conception of a group of humans drawn together by shared values and aspirations, flourishing together, whether in physical proximity or separated in place, regarding both their community and their individual lives as of intrinsic value, and invoking conceptions of well-being that derive from their values and aspirations and not from conventional wisdom and contemporary fashion. To illustrate this point, we shall look briefly at a comparison of the last hours of Plato's philosophic hero, Socrates, and the last hours of Wittgenstein.

The key element in the account of Socrates' last hours, as Plato presents it, is not the calmness and serenity of Socrates, but the grounds for these, as seen by Plato. As we have seen, prior to the account of Socrates' last hours, Plato presents him as someone who has discovered the true structure of reality, his own place within that order, and thus has also achieved an understanding of himself. The dome-like structure of the dialogue, surveyed earlier, witnesses to this.

Plato's view of Socrates' death can be expressed in terms of a paradox. Socrates interprets death as a release of the soul (64c). His physical imprisonment leads to this real release. His convictions lead him to refuse the superficial release, that from prison, and he is thereby led to the genuine release. The paradox — at least on the surface — is that he refuses to be released from prison and is thereby led to a release from "prison." This paradox is resolved in the death scene. We see that the paradox is such only on the surface. The two releases are not on a par: one of them does not affect the soul in an important way; the other does. Socrates shows what it is to opt for the real release. His conviction hinges not on expectations of personal immortality but on his view that his choice is consistent with his ideals, that his has been was a well lived life, and that it has been one of intrinsic value, besides contributing to the realization of goodness.

Wittgenstein's view of his life and its end was not based on grand metaphysical structures. But it, too, included a way of viewing the whole world and finding a place within it that makes one's strivings, efforts, and interactions with others worthwhile. He, too, saw his life as realizing what is worthwhile and important. As reported, his last words were: "Tell them that I had a wonderful life."[40] This echoes the feeling one senses in the account of Socrates' last hours (*Phaedo* 117b–118a). On the surface, and by the standards of conventional wisdom, neither had a wonderful life. Socrates was misunderstood and unjustly executed. Wittgenstein, was also, by and large, misunderstood and led a rather solitary life. But at the end, they both saw their happiness realized in the values that their lives expressed.

It is interesting and comforting to note that their respective last words were addressed to friends. Socrates' friends were in his physical vicinity, whereas Wittgenstein's were scattered across two continents. But the physical differences are superficial; what counts is that both, at the end, could address friends with whom they shared ideals.[41] The two circles of people were linked not only by regard for each other as unique individuals, but by their sharing in something that was impersonal or, at least, interpersonal.

Whewell's Challenge

Let us look back at this part of the book with Whewell's challenge — quoted at the outset — in mind. The sketches of a few echoes that have been presented clearly do not meet that challenge. To meet it fully would require another book at least equal in length to this one. But Part III of this book should be seen as a prolegomenon to the meeting of the challenge. Meeting the challenge presupposes that Plato can "supply a philosophy for us," to use Whewell's words, and that it can be "expressed in our own language." Our survey of ethical and ontological themes provides some evidence that Plato can indeed supply a philosophy for us. For in some of the fields canvassed, we saw what can be described without anachronism as Platonic positions among the main alternatives facing the philosopher today. This is particularly true in the foundations of mathematics, and it could be extended to other subfields of ontology. We have also seen cases in which the current technical framework is not geared to Platonic concepts and theses, and yet real problems in our daily lives require the Platonic approach. The most obvious example is the epistemology of role modeling, which has not been worked out in professional philosophy but is much needed in various professions today.

How about the question of "expressing" Plato's philosophy in our language? Presumably the latter is the language developed by modern philosophers. This part of the book clears the ground for this enterprise, for it shows what are and what are not genuine Platonic problems, concepts, and claims. There is a danger that in the attempt to "express" Plato's thought, we will make what we take to be his views bear too much resemblance to current views and controversies. Such anachronism not only blocks our view of Plato; it also masks a cultural arrogance. To think that Plato did something right when he said something or asked something similar to what "we" say or ask is to take an absurdly optimistic view of the intellectual perambulations of our own century. Part III of this book – and indeed the whole book – is intended not only to reconstruct Plato so as to find echoes, but also to show clearly the great differences between his outlook and that of many modern philosophers. This is particularly true in ethics. In this field, only a few of the echoes we uncovered relate a modern philosopher to something uniquely Platonistic. The "echoes" here are more indicative of the difference between modern ethics and the various ethical theories of several eras in our past.

The echoes in the philosophy of mathematics help us to see how certain basic questions remain constant across the centuries. Problems in the ontology of mathematics do not center merely on the question of whether there are universals, or properties. Rather, they center on the questions: (a) In what ways is a Platonistic ontology of explanatory value to mathematics? and (b) Does the positing (or discovery?) of Platonistic interpretations of mathematical entities as a plurality of intelligible entities constituting a self-sufficient domain really answer the Eleatic challenge? It was interesting to note that Gödel and Bernays – and, in fact, Ramsey[42] too – converge on seeing (b) as a fundamental issue.

The Eleatic challenge needs to be met in all fields of ontology, not only mathematics. The most general way of phrasing it is this: Do at least some of the principles of individuation used in what are acknowledged to be genuine rational disciplines correspond to something in reality? or are they all products of instrumental human reasoning, tainted with human bias and interest? If they are only the latter, then they belong to what Parmenides described in his poem as the "world of appearance." To wrestle with this question is far more crucial to Platonism as a viable philosophy than to worry about how his thought might relate to what he would think of as secondary matters, such as the current vogue of "naturalism" and "naturalistic epistemology," neither of which has made any headway with mathematics.

The remarks on epistemology clear the way to understanding what key questions Platonism must answer. These questions do not center around what we would today call a priori knowledge, though that question would enter in a secondary way. The main issue is the contrast between epistemologies organized around the notion of information processing and those – including Plato's – that center on insight and understanding and deny that these notions can be reduced to the vocabulary we use to explain information processing.

The chapter on ethics shows how deep the differences can be between what we consider ethics and what other eras took to be ethics. As we saw, Plato's ethics is geared primarily to questions of the articulation and sustenance of ideals and, when needed, drastic reorientation from one, inadequate, ideal to another. By contrast, most modern moral philosophies are concerned with the problem of how people with widely different ideals can nevertheless recognize certain moral principles as governing their interactions and create an atmosphere that, even if it is not cooperative, is at least nonaggressive. The acceptance or rejection of the "autonomy principle" and fundamental differences in moral psychology can all be derived from this difference in overall orientation.

As we look at the world today, both kinds of ethics seem to be needed. Some might think that if we found an adequate ethics for dealing with conflicts between people with widely different ideals, then this would also help us with life among people with the same ideals. But this does not follow. Injecting, somehow, tolerance, compromise, and mutual acceptance into the lives of humans does not yield all the conceptual tools required to turn humans from one ideal to a drastically different one or to sustain interest and dedication to the same ideal over long periods of time. There are plenty of potential conflicts between people of different ideals, and one would like to see these handled in a nonviolent, nonoppressive way. But there are various global problems, such as health, environmental policy, and nuclear proliferation, that seem to call for cooperation based on shared ideals.

It would be absurd and arrogant to claim that Platonism can, at one fell swoop, solve all these problems. But the key elements of drastic reorientations of ideals are in the dialogues. Plato sees the task of the *Gorgias* as helping people to turn from a pleasure-worshipping life to a life focused on wisdom and on finding a place for the individual within larger units. He sees that of the *Republic* as turning people who are power-hungry into people who are virtue-hungry.

To meet Whewell's challenge in the field of moral philosophy involves restating ethical approaches centering on the adoption of ideals and seeing how these can also deal with the question of how people with different ideals should interact with each other. The remarks on Plato's ethics scattered throughout the book and the brief sketch of echoes in this chapter are only the first small steps we must take in order to satisfy Whewell's demands.

NOTE

1 See J. Moravcsik, *Thought and Language.*
2 See ibid.
3 H. Joseph, *Knowledge and the Good in Plato's* Republic, pp. 6, 12.
4 F. Bussell, *The School of Plato*, p. 147.
5 W. Hardie, *A Study in Plato*, p. 144.
6 See J. Annas, *An Introduction to Plato's* Republic, ch. 6, esp. p. 157.
7 J. Rawls, *A Theory of Justice*, pt 3.
8 Ibid., p. 548.
9 Ibid., p. 426.
10 Ibid., p. 440.
11 Ibid.
12 Ibid., p. 441.
13 Ibid., p. 411.
14 Ibid., p. 412.
15 Ibid.
16 Ibid.
17 Ibid., p. 454.

18 F. Bradley, *Ethical Studies*; e.g. p. 179.
19 F. Bradley's conception of the relation between self-interest and the moral underwent changes; see e.g. ibid., pp. 80, 214–50.
20 Ibid., pp. 163–74.
21 Ibid.
22 Ibid., p. 163.
23 Ibid., pp. 223, 228.
24 Ibid.; e.g. pp. 1–71 *passim*, and p. 161.
25 Montaigne and Aristotle on friendship also offer an interesting contrast between voluntaristic and nonvoluntaristic moral psychologies.
26 L. Wittgenstein, "A Lecture on Ethics."
27 Ibid., p. 5.
28 Ibid., p. 8.
29 Ibid., p. 11.
30 L. Wittgenstein, *Culture and Value*, p. 2.
31 See B. McGuinness (ed.), *Wittgenstein in Relation to his Times*, p. 111. The earlier *Tractatus* places the will at the center of ethics and puts less emphasis on the social aspects of ethics.
32 Wittgenstein, *Culture and Value*, p. 62. One wonders whether Wittgenstein had Goethe's *Faust* in mind: "Grau mein Freund sind alle Theorien, doch grün des Lebens goldner Baum."
33 Ibid., p. 77.
34 L. Wittgenstein, *Notebooks (1914–16)*, p. 75.
35 Ibid., p. 73.
36 For a good survey of Wittgenstein, see D. Pears, *Ludwig Wittgenstein*.
37 Wittgenstein, *Notebooks (1914–16)*, p. 79.
38 Wittgenstein, *Culture and Value*, p. 43.
39 Articulaton of this overall structure for this dialogue is independent of speculations about its possible multiple origins.
40 As reported in N. Malcolm, *Ludwig Wittgenstein: A Memoir*, p. 81.
41 The importance of fraternal relations and their significance for political relations is well described by G. Vlastos, *Platonic Studies*, p. 11: "The ideal society of the *Republic* is a political community held together by bonds of fraternal love."
42 F. Ramsey, "Universals" (1931), in *The Foundations of Mathematics*, pp. 112–37.

Bibliography

◆

The following is a list of works referred to or consulted during the writing of this book. There is a very good bibliography on Plato compiled by the Oxford Philosophy Faculty, available from its Merton Street library. There is also a good Plato bibliography in R. McKirahan, *Socrates and Plato: A Comprehensive Bibliography, 1958–1973*, Garland Publishing Company, New York, 1978.

Ackrill, J. L., "In Defense of Plato's Divisions," in *Ryle: A Collection of Critical Essays*, ed. G. Pitcher and O. Wood, (Doubleday, New York, 1970), pp. 373–92.

Ackrill, J. L., "Plato and the Copula," *Journal of Hellenic Studies*, 77 (1957), part 1, pp. 1–6.

Allen, R., *Plato's Parmenides*, University of Minnesota Press, Minneapolis, 1983.

Annas, J., *An Introduction to Plato's* Republic, Oxford University Press, Oxford, 1981.

Apelt, O., *Sophistes*, Meiner Verlag, Leipzig, 1914.

Austin, J., *Philosophical Papers*, Clarendon Press, Oxford, 1961.

Bealer, G., *Quality and Concept*, Oxford University Press, Oxford, 1982.

Benacerraf, P., and Putnam, H. (eds), *Philosophy of Mathematics*, Prentice-Hall, Englewood Cliffs, N. J., 1964.

Bernays, P., "On Platonism in Mathematics," trans. in Benacerraf and Putnam (eds), *Philosophy of Mathematics*, pp. 274–86.

Bernays, P., "Über den Platonismus in der Mathematik," in *Abhandlungen zur Philosophie der Mathematik* (Wissenschaftliche Buchgesellschaft, Darmstadt, 1976).

Block, N. (ed.), *Readings in Philosophy of Psychology*, vols 1 and 2, Harvard University Press, Cambridge, Mass., 1981.

Bluck, R., *Plato's* Meno, Cambridge University Press, Cambridge, 1961.

Blundell, M., *Helping Friends and Harming Enemies*, Cambridge University Press, Cambridge, 1989.

Bonitz, H., *Platonische Studien*, Berlin, 1886; Olms Verlag, Hildesheim, 1968.

Bradley, F., *Ethical Studies*, Oxford 1876; Clarendon Press, Oxford, 1927.

Burkert, W., "Konstruktion und Seinsstruktur: Praxis und Platonismus in der Griechischen Mathematik," *Abhandlungen der Branuschweigischen Wissenschaftlichen Gesellschaft*, 34 (1982), pp. 125−41.

Burnyeat, M., "Examples in Epistemology; Socrates, Theaetetus, and G. E. Moore," *Philosophy*, 52 (1977), pp. 382−4.

Burnyeat, M., "Idealism and Greek Philosophy: What Descartes Saw and Berkeley Missed," *Philosophical Review*, 91 (1982), pp. 3−40.

Burnyeat, M., "Protagoras and Self-Refutation in Later Greek Philosophy," *Philosophical Review*, 85 (1976), pp. 44−69.

Bussell, F., *The School of Plato*, Methuen, London, 1896.

Campbell, L., *Sophistes and Politicus*, ed. and annotated, Clarendon Press, Oxford, 1867.

Cherniss, H., *Aristotle's Criticism of Plato and the Academy*, Johns Hopkins University Press, Baltimore, 1944.

Cherniss, H., "The Philosophical Economy of Plato's Theory of Ideas," *American Journal of Philology*, 57 (1936), pp. 1−12; repr. in *Studies in Plato's Metaphysics*, ed. R. Allen (Routledge and Kegan Paul, London, 1965), pp. 1−12.

Cherniss, H., "The Relation of the *Timaeus* to Plato's Later Dialogues," *American Journal of Philology*, 78 (1957), pp. 225−66.

Chisholm, R., *Theory of Knowledge*, Prentice-Hall, Englewood Cliffs, N. J., 1966.

Chomsky, N., *Cartesian Linguistics*, Harper and Row, New York, 1966.

Cobb-Stevens, V., "Commentary," in *Proceedings of the Boston Area Colloquium in Ancient Philosophy*, vol. 1, ed. J. Cleary (University Press of America, Lanham, 1986), pp. 22−38.

Cohen, M., "The Logic of the *Third man*," *Philosophical Review*, 80 (1971), pp. 448−75.

Cohen, M., "Plato's Method of Division," in Moravcsik, *Patterns in Plato's Thought*, pp. 181−91.

Cooper, J., "Plato's Theory of Human Good in the *Philebus*," *Journal of Philosophy*, 74 (1977), pp. 714−30.

Cooper, J., "Plato's Theory of Human Motivation," *History of Philosophy Quarterly*, 1 (1984), pp. 3−25.

Cornford, F., *Plato and Parmenides*, Routledge and Kegan Paul, London, 1939.

Cornford, F., *Plato's Theory of Knowledge*, Routledge and Kegan Paul, London, 1934.

Crombie, I., *An Examination of Plato's Doctrines*, vols 1 and 2, Routledge and Kegan Paul, London, 1963.

Cross, R., and Woozley, A., *Plato's* Republic: *a Philosophical Commentary*, Macmillan, London, 1964.

Denyer, N., "Plato's Theory of Stuffs," *Philosophy*, 58 (1983), pp. 315–27.

Dodds, E., *Plato's* Gorgias, Oxford University Press, Oxford, 1959.

Dover, K., *Greek Popular Morality in the Time of Plato and Aristotle*, University of California Press, Berkeley, 1974.

Dover, K., *Plato:* Symposium, Cambridge University Press, Cambridge, 1980.

Dover, K., "The Portrayal of Moral Evaluation in Greek Poetry," *Journal of Hellenic Studies*, 103 (1983), pp. 35–48.

Dürr, K., "Die Moderne Darstellung der Platonischen Logik," *Museum Helveticum*, 2 (1945), pp. 166–95.

Edwards, J., *Ethics without Philosophy; Wittgenstein and the Moral Life*, University Presses of Florida, Tampa, 1982.

Farris, J., *Plato's Theory of Forms and Cantor's Theory of Sets*, University of Belfast, Belfast, 1968.

Feinberg, J., *Social Philosophy*, Prentice-Hall, Englewood Cliffs, N. J., 1973.

Finley, J., *Thucydides*, Harvard University Press, Cambridge, Mass., 1942.

Forbes, R., *Studies in Ancient Technology*, vol. 6, Brill, Leiden, 1958.

Fowler, H., *Plato's* Sophist, trans. and commentary, Loeb Classical Library, Harvard University Press, Cambridge, Mass., 1921.

Frankena, W., *Ethics*, Prentice-Hall, Englewood Cliffs, N. J., 1963.

Frede, M., "Predikation und Existenzaussage," *Hypomnemata*, 18 (Vandenhoeck & Rupprecht, Göttingen, 1967).

Frege, G., *The Foundations of Arithmetic*, trans. J. Austin, Blackwell, Oxford, 1953.

Gadamer, H., "Natural Science and Hermeneutics: The Concept of Nature in Ancient Philosophy," in *Proceedings of the Boston Area Colloquium in Ancient Philosophy*, vol. 1, ed. J. Cleary (University Press of America, Lanham, 1986), pp. 39–52.

Gallop, D., "Plato and the Alphabet," *Philosophical Review*, 72 (1963), pp. 364–76.

Gallop, D., *Plato's* Phaedo, trans. and commentary, Clarendon Press, Oxford, 1975.

Geach, P., "The THIRD MAN Again," *Philosophical Review*, 65 (1956), pp. 72–82.

Gödel, K., "Russell's Mathematical Logic," (1944), in Benacerraf and Putnam (eds), *Philosophy of Mathematics*, pp. 211–32.

Goodman, N., *Fact, Fiction, Forecast*, Harvard University Press, Cambridge, Mass., 1955.

Goodman, N., *The Structure of Appearance*, Harvard University Press, Cambridge, Mass., 1951.

Gosling, J., *Plato's* Philebus, trans. and commentary, Clarendon Press, Oxford, 1975.

Graeser, A., *Geschichte der Philosophie*, vol. 2, Beck'sche Elementarbücher, Munich, 1983.

Graeser, A., *Platons Ideenlehre*, Paul Haupt, Bern, 1975.

Grube, G., *Plato's* Republic trans., Hackett, Indianapolis, 1974.

Grube, G., *Plato's Thought*, Beacon Press, Bostom, 1st edn, 1935; repr. 1958.

Gulley, N., *Plato's Theory of Knowledge*, Methuen, London, 1962.

Hackforth, R., "False Statement in Plato's SOPHIST," *Classica Quarterly*, 39 (1945), pp. 56–8.

Hackforth, R., *Plato's Examination of Pleasure*, Cambridge University Press, Cambridge, 1958.

Hackforth, R., *Plato's* Phaedo trans. and commentary, Cambridge University Press, Cambridge, 1955.

Hahm, D., "Weight and Lightness in Aristotle and his Predecessors," in *Motion, Time, Space, and Matter*, ed. P. Machamer and R. Turnbull (Ohio University Press, Columbus, 1976), pp. 56–82.

Hailperin, D., "Platonic Eros and What Men Call Love," *Ancient Philosophy*, 5 (1985), pp. 161–204.

Hamilton, E., and Cairns, H. (eds), *Collected Dialogues of Plato*, Pantheon, New York, 1961.

Hamlyn, D., "The Communion of the Forms and the Development of Plato's Logic," *Philosophical Quarterly*, 5 (1955), pp. 289–302.

Hammond, N., and Scullard, H. (eds), *Oxford Classical Dictionary*, 2nd edn, Oxford University Press, Oxford, 1970.

Hardie, W., *A Study in Plato*, Clarendon Press, Oxford, 1936.

Heinaman, R., "Being in the *Sophist*," *Archiv für die Geshichte der Philosophie*, 65 (1983), pp. 1–17.

Irwin, T., "Aristotle's Conception of Morality," in *Proceedings of the Boston Area Colloquium in Ancient Philosophy*, vol. 1, ed. J. Cleary (University Presses of America, Lanham, 1986), pp. 115–43.

Irwin, T., *Plato's* Gorgias, trans. and commentary, Clarendon Press, Oxford, 1979.

Johnson, W., *Logic*, part 1, Cambridge University Press, Cambridge, 1921.

Joseph, H., *Knowledge and Good in Plato's* Republic, Oxford University Press, Oxford, 1948.

Kaplan, D., "Quantifying In," *Synthese*, 19 (1968), pp. 178–214.

Kostman, J., "The Ambiguity of 'Partaking' in Plato's *Sophist*," *Journal of the History of Philosophy*, 27 (1989), pp. 343–63.

Kostman, J., "False Logos and Not-Being in Plato's *Sophist*," in Moravcsik, *Patternsin Plato's Thought*, pp. 192–212.

Kraut, R., "Two Conceptions of Happiness," *Philosophical Review*, 88 (1979), pp. 167–97.

Lear, J., "Katharsis," *Phronesis*, 33 (1988), pp. 297–326.

Lee, E., "Plato on Negation and Not-Being in the *Sophist*," *Philosophical Review*, 81 (1972), pp. 267–304.

Levinson, R., *In Defense of Plato*, Harvard University Press, Cambridge, Mass., 1953.

Lewis, F., "Did Plato Discover the 'estin' of Identity?" *California Studies in Classical Antiquity*, 9 (1975), pp. 113–43.

Lewis, F., "Plato on 'Not'," *California Studies in Classical Antiquity*, 9 (1976), pp. 89–115.

Liddell, H., and Scott, R., *A Greek-English Lexicon*, Clarendon Press, Oxford, 1843.

Lodge, R., *Plato's Theory of Art*, Routledge and Kegan Paul, London, 1953.

Lynch, W., *An Approach to Plato's Metaphysics through the Parmenides*, Catholic University Press, Washington, D. C., 1959.

Lyons, J., *Structural Semantics: An Analysis of a Part of the Vocabulary of Plato*, Oxford University Press, Oxford, 1963.

Mabbott, J., "Is Plato's *Republic* Utilitarian?" *Mind*, 46 (1937); repr. in *Modern Studies in Philosophy: Plato*, vol. 2, ed. G. Vlastos (Doubleday, New York, 1971), pp. 57–65.

Malcolm, N., *Ludwig Wittgenstein or: A. Memoir*, new edn, Oxford University Press, Oxford, 1984.

Manders, K., "Logic and Conceptual Relationships in Mathematics," in *Logic Colloquium '85*, (Amsterdam, 1987), pp. 193–211.

Matthen, M., "Greek Ontology and the 'is' of Truth," *Phronesis*, 28 (1983), pp. 113–35.

Matthen, M., "Plato's Treatment of Relational Statements in the *Phaedo*," *Phronesis*, 27 (1982), pp. 94–5.

McDonald, M. (ed.), *Philosophy and Analysis*, Blackwell, Oxford, 1954.

McDowell, J., "Falsehood and Not-Being in Plato's *Sophist*," in *Language and Logos: Studies in Ancient Greek Philosophy*, ed. M. Schofied and M. Nussbaum (Cambridge University Press, Cambridge, 1982), pp. 115–34.

McGuinness, B. (ed.), *Wittgenstein in Relation to his Times*, University of Chicago Press, Chicago, 1982.

Menzel, C., "A Complete Type-Free Second-Order Logic of Properties, Relations, and Propositions," CSLI Technical Report CSLI-86-40, Standford, 1986.

Menzel, C., "Frege Numbers and the Relativity Argument," *Canadian Journal of Philosophy*, 18 (1988), pp. 87–98.

Minardi, S., "On Some Aspects of Platonic Divisions," *Mind*, 92 (1983), pp. 417–23.

Moline, J., *Plato's Theory of Understanding*, University of Wisconsin Press, Madison, 1981.

Moore, G., *Philosophical Studies*, Paul, Trench and Trubner Ltd, London, 1922.

Moravcsik, J., "The Analytic and the Non-empirical," *Journal of Philosophy*, 62 (1965), pp. 415–29.

Moravcsik, J., "The Anatomy of Plato's Divisions," in *Exegesis and Argument: Studies Presented to Gregory Vlastos*, ed. E. Lee, A. Mourelatos and R. Rorty, *Phronesis*, supplementary vol. 1 (Van Gorcum, Assen, 1973), pp. 324–48.

Moravcsik, J., "Ancient and Modern Conceptions of Health and Medicine," *Journal of Medicine and Philosophy*, 1 (1976), pp. 337–48.

Moravcsik, J., "Being and Meaning in the *Sophist*," *Acta Philosophica Fennica*, 14 (1962), pp. 23–78.

Moravcsik, J., "Communal Ties," *American Philosophical Society Proceedings and Addresses*, vol. 62 (1988), pp. 211–25.

Moravcsik, J., "Forms and Dialectic in the Second Half of the *Parmenides*," *Language and Logos: Studies in Ancient Greek Philosophy*, ed. M. Schofield and M. Nussbaum (Cambridge University Press, Cambridge, 1982), pp. 135–53.

Moravcsik, J., "Forms, Nature, and the Good in the *Philebus*," *Phronesis*, 24 (1979), pp. 81–104.

Moravcsik, J., "Heraclitean Concepts and Explanations," in *Language and Thought in Early Greek Philosophy*, ed. K. Robb (Monist Library of Philosophy, La Salle, Ill., 1983), pp. 134–52.

Moravcsik, J., "Learning as Recollection," in *Modern Studies in Philosophy: Plato*, vol. 1, ed. G. Vlastos (Doubleday, New York, 1970), pp. 53–69.

Moravcsik, J., "Linguistic Theory and the Philosophy of Language," *Foundations of Language*, 3 (1967), pp. 209–33.

Moravcsik, J., "Noetic Aspiration and Artistic Inspiration," in *Plato on Beauty, Wisdom, and the Arts*, ed. J. Moravcsik and P. Temko (Rowman and Littlefield, Totowa, 1982), pp. 29–46.

Moravcsik, J., "On What We Aim at and How We Live," in *The Greeks and the Good Life*, ed. D. Depew (Hackett, Indianapolis, 1980), pp. 198–235.

Moravcsik, J. (ed.), *Patterns in Plato's Thought*, Reidel, Dordrecht 1973.

Moravcsik, J., "Plato and Pericles on Freedom and Politics," *Canadian Journal of Philosophy*, supplementary vol. 9 (1983), pp. 1–17.

Moravcsik, J., "Plato's Ethics as Ideal Building," in *Proceedings of the Boston Area Colloquium in Ancient Philosophy*, vol. 1, ed. J. Cleary (University Presses of America, Lanham, 1986), pp. 1–21.

Moravcsik, J., "Reason and Eros in the Ascent-Passage of the *Symposium*," in *Essays in Ancient Greek Philosophy*, ed. J. Anton and G. Kustas (State University of New York Press, Albany, 1971), pp. 285–302.

Moravcsik, J., "Recollecting the Theory of Forms," in *Facets of Plato's Philosophy*, ed. W. Werkmeister, *Phronesis*, supplementary vol. 2 (Van Gorcum, Assen, 1976), pp. 1–20.

Moravcsik, J., review of P. Seligman, *Being and Not-Being*, *Canadian Journal of Philosophy*, 6 (1976), pp. 737–44.

Moravcsik, J., "The Role of Virtue in Alternatives to Kantian and Utilitarian Ethics," *Philosophia*, 20 (1990), pp. 33–48.

Moravcsik, J., "Subcategorization and Abstract Terms," *Foundations of Language*, 6 (1970), pp. 473–87.

Moravcsik, J., "The *Third Man* Argument and Plato's Theory of Forms," *Phronesis*, 8 (1963), pp. 50–62.

Moravcsik, J., *Thought and Language*, Routledge, London, 1990.

Moravcsik, J., "Understanding," *Dialectica*, 33 (1979), pp. 201–16.

Moravcsik, J., "Understanding and Knowledge in Plato's Philosophy," *Neue Hefte für Philosophie*, 15/16 (1979), pp. 53–69.

Mourelatos, A., "Heraclitus, Parmenides, and the Naive Metaphysics of Things," in *Exegesis and Argument*, ed. E. Lee, A. Mourelatos and R. Rorty, *Phronesis*, supplementary vol. 1 (Van Gorcum, Assen, 1973), pp. 16–48.

Murphy, N., *The Interpretation of Plato's* Republic, Clarendon Press, Oxford, 1951.

Nehamas, A., "Self-Predication and Plato's Theory of Forms," *American Philosophical Quarterly*, 16 (1979), pp. 93–103.

Nussbaum, M., *The Fragility of Goodness*, Cambridge University Press, Cambridge, 1986.

Owen, G., "Notes on Ryle's Plato," in *Ryle: A Collection of Critical Essays*, ed. G. Pitcher and O. Wood (Doubleday, New York, 1970), pp. 341–72.

Owen, G. E. L., "The Place of the *Timaeus* in Plato's Dialogues," *Classical Quarterly*, ns 2 (1953), pp. 79–95.

Patterson, R., *Image and Reality in Plato's Metaphysics*, Hackett, Indianapolis, 1985.

Patzig, G., *Platon, Klassiker des Philosophisches Denkens*, ed. N. Hoerster, Deutscher Taschenbuch Verlag, Berlin, 1982.

Pears, D., *Ludwig Wittgenstein*, Viking Press, New York, 1973.

Peterson, S., "The Greatest Difficulty for Plato's Theory of Forms: the Unknowability Argument of the *Parmenides*," *Archiv für die Geschichte der Philosophie*, 63 (1981), pp. 1–16.

Peterson, S., "A Reasonable Self-Predication Premise for the *Third Man* Argument," *Philosophical Review*, 82 (1973), pp. 451–70.

Popper, K., *The Open Society and its Enemies*, vol. 1, 4th rev. edn, Princeton University Press, Princeton, 1961.

Quine, W., *Methods of Logic*, Holt, Rinehart and Winston, New York, 1950.

Ramsey, F., *Foundations of Mathematics*, Routledge and Kegan Paul, London, 1950.

Rawls, J., *A Theory of Justice*, Harvard University Press, Cambridge, Mass., 1971.

Reichenbach, H., *Elements of Symbolic Logic*, Macmillan, New York, 1947.

Roberts, J., "Falsity and the Problem of Not-Being in the *Sophist*," Ph.D. dissertation, University of Pittsburgh, 1982.

Roberts, J., "The Problem of Being in the *Sophist*," *History of Philosophy Quarterly*, 3 (1986), pp. 229–43.

Romily, J. de, *Thucydides and Athenian Imperialism*, trans. P. Thody, Blackwell, Oxford, 1963.

Rosenmeyer, T., "Plato's Hypothesis and the Upward Path," *American Journal of Philology*, 81 (1960), pp. 393–407.

Ross, W., *Aristotle: Physics*, trans. and commentary, Oxford University Press, Oxford, 1936.

Ross, W., *Plato's Theory of Ideas*, Clarendon Press, Oxford, 1953.

Russell, B., *The Problems of Philosophy*, Oxford University Press, Oxford, 1912.

Ryle, G., "Plato's *Parmenides*," *Mind*, 48 (1939), pp. 129–51, 302–25.

Ryle, G., *Plato's Progress*, Cambridge University Press, Cambridge, 1966.

Ryle, G., review of J. Moravcsik, *Patterns in Plato's Thought*, *Philosophia*, 1 (1976), pp. 161–2.

Santas, G., "Plato on Love, Beauty, and the Good," in *The Greeks and the Good Life*, ed. D. Depew (Hackett, Indianapolis, 1980), pp. 33–68.

Santas, G., "Two Theories of Good in Plato's *Republic*," *Archiv für die Geschichte der Philosophie*, 67 (1985), pp. 223–45.

Sayre, K., *Plato's Analytic Method*, University of Chicago Press, Chicago, 1969.

Sayre, K., *Plato's Later Ontology: A Riddle Resolved*, Princeton University Press, Princeton, 1983.

Schleiermacher, F., *Platon: Sämtliche Werke*, vol. 3, Rowohlt, Hamburg, 1958; trans. available.

Schofield, M., "The Antinomies of Plato's *Parmenides*," *Classical Quarterly*, 27 (1977), pp. 139–58.

Sellars, W., "Vlastos and the *Third Man*," *Philosophical Review*, 64 (1955), pp. 405–38.

Sherman, N., "Commentary," in *Proceedings of the Boston Area Colloquium in Ancient Philosophy*, vol. 1, ed. J. Cleary (University Presses of America, Lanham, 1986), pp. 144–50.

Shiner, R., *Knowledge and Reality in Plato's* Philebus, Van Gorcum, Assen, 1974.

Shorey, P., *Platonism, Ancient and Modern*, University of California Press, Berkeley, 1938.

Shorey, P., *The Unity of Plato's Thought*, 1903; University of Chicago Press, Chicago, 1960.

Skemp, J., *Plato's Statesman*, trans. and commentans, Routledge and Kegan Paul, London, 1952.

Snell, B., "Die Ausdrücke für den Begriff des Wissens in der Vorplatonischen Philosophie," *Philosophische Untersucungen*, Berlin, 29 (1924).

Solmsen, F., *Intellectual Experiments of the Greek Enlightenment*, Princeton University Press, Princeton, 1975.

Sprute, J., *Die Doxa in der Platonischen Philosophie*, Vandenhoeck und Rupprecht, Göttingen, 1963.

Steinthal, H., *Geschichte der Sprachenwissenschaft*, vol. 1, Berlin, 1890; reproduced by Olms Verlag, Hildesheim, 1961.

Stenzel, J., *Plato's Method of Dialectic*, trans. T. Rosenmeyer, Clarendon Press, Oxford, 1940.

Striker, G., *Peras und Apeiron: das Problem der Formen in Platons Philebos*, Vandenhoeck and Ruppert, Göttingen, 1970.

Suter, R., *Are You Moral?*, University Press of America, New York, 1984.

Taylor, A., *Plato: The* Sophist *and the* Statesman, trans. and introduction, Thomas Nelson, Edinburgh, 1961.

Teloh, H., *The Development of Plato's Metaphysics*, Pennsylvania University Press, University Park, 1981.

Vlastos, G., "Anamnesis in the *Meno*," *Dialogue*, 4 (1965), pp. 143–67.

Vlastos, G., *Platonic Studies*, Princeton University Press, Princeton, 1973.

Vlastos, G., "The *Third Man* Argument in the *Parmenides*," *Philosophical Review*, 63 (1954), pp. 319–50.

Von Wright, G., "Wittgenstein in Relation to his Times," in *Wittgenstein in Relation to his Times*, ed. B. McGuinness (University of Chicago Press, Chicago, 1982), pp. 108–20.

Wedberg, A., *Plato's Philosophy of Mathematics*, Almquist and Wiksell, Stockholm, 1955.

Weimer, W., "Psycholinguistics and Plato's Paradoxes of the *Meno*," *American Psychologist*, 28 (1973), pp. 15–33.

Whewell, W., *Of the Platonic Theory of Ideas*, Cambridge University Press, Cambridge, 1856.

Wieland, W., *Platon und die Formen des Wissens*, Vandenhoeck and Rupprecht, Göttingen, 1982.

Wiggins, D., "Sentence, Meaning, Negation and Plato's Problem of Not-Being," in *Plato: A Collection of Critical Essays*, ed. G. Vlastos (Doubleday, New York, 1971), pp. 268–303.

Williams, B., "The Analogy of City and Soul in Plato's *Republic*," *Exegesis and Argument*, ed. E. Lee, A. Mourelatos and R. Rorty (Van Gorcum, Assen, 1973), pp. 196–206.

Wittgenstein, L., *Culture and Value*, University of Chicago Press, Chicago, 1980.

Wittgenstein, L., "A Lecture on Ethics," *Philosophical Review*, 74 (1965), pp. 3–12.

Wittgenstein, L., *Notebooks (1914–16)*, Blackwell, Oxford, 1961.

Wittgenstein, L., *Tractatus Logico-Philosophicus*, Routledge and Kegan Paul, London, 1922.

Zalta, E., *Abstract Objects*, Reidel, Dordrecht, 1983.

Index

◆